D1694547

Armin Risi
TranscEnding the Global Power Game

Armin Risi

TranscEnding
the Global Power Game

*Hidden Agendas, Divine Intervention
and the New Earth*

Govinda Press

Neuhausen • Jestetten

Published by Ronald Zürrer

Switzerland: Govinda-Verlag, P.O. Box 257, 8212 Neuhausen 2
Germany: Govinda-Verlag, P.O. Box 1226, 79795 Jestetten
Internet: govinda.ch, armin-risi.ch

Exclusion of liability:
Both author and publisher respect all people and religions and therefore reject any kind of racist, anti-Christian, anti-Jewish, anti-Islamic (etc.) prejudice and propaganda. When certain aspects of religions, institutions and lodge organizations are critically scrutinized in this book, it is solely meant to find a higher platform of mutual understanding (beyond ideological, denominational and dogmatic antagonism).

The author has gathered and evaluated all information presented in this book to the best of his knowledge. Nevertheless, he invites all readers to examine his sources and arguments with a critical mind. Both author and publisher reject any responsibility for all forms of unintended conclusion and reaction on the part of the reader that might be induced by a superficial, incomplete or biased reading of this book.

First (advance) run – January 2004

© 2004 Armin Risi
All rights reserved.

Written in English by Armin Risi, based on *Machtwechsel auf der Erde* (by the same author, Govinda-Verlag 1999, 4th edition 2003)
Language counselling: Debra Bacchus, Chris Cannizzo, Helmut Kunkel
Layout: Miro Cucuz, Helmut Kunkel
Cover design: Anandini Zürrer, Zürich (incl. photos of the author, November 2003, p. 419 and back cover)

Printed in Austria

ISBN 3-906347-67-2

Near is
And difficult to grasp, the God
But where danger threatens
That which saves from it also grows

— Friedrich Hölderlin (1802)[1]

Contents

The Memory Genius   11
Introduction   15

Part I: Planet Earth – Focus of a Cosmic Power Game

1) The Mystery of Oneness and Duality   23

Light and shadows on earth • Getting the bigger picture • Is everything relative? • Does evil originate from humans alone? • Perceiving the inconceivable • Duality and individuality • Cosmic Genesis and the origin of duality • Light does not cast shadows • The psychology of the fallen • Ego projection and the I-AM consciousness • So-called good creates evil • The role of evil in spiritual evolution • Temptation and false promises • Kali-yuga: The fall into utmost condensed matter • The infiltration and manipulation of religions

2) The Programming of Consciousness and How to Transcend It   55

The consequences of materialism • The mental ocean and its elemental waves • Subtle-material dictations • Resonance caused by elementals • War starts in the mind • How to dissolve elementals • The elevation of consciousness and the impeding forces • Love and forgiveness • Differentiating without judging

3) Covert Forces behind the Scenes   79

'The Big Four' • Who are the 'Big Four'? • Power and magic forces • Long-term planning • Inferiors, superiors and ulteriors • The ulteriors and their financial power • The ulteriors and their secret societies • The American Civil War • The French Revolution • Subtle influence and incarnation • How money began to rule the world • Enticing and mellifluous • The diversity of lodges

4) Facing Darkness and Light   113

Are there criteria for differentiating? • Where the road forks • The Relative and the Absolute • The trap of absolutizing • The fall from polarity into duality • Misconceiving reality in terms of duality • Materialism, pantheism and deism • Materialistic and occult monism • The philosophy of the illuminati • The trap of false justification • *Maya* and the I-AM consciousness • From darkness to light • One and different, or one and in-different? • Karma = predestination + free will • God's laws and God's will • Divine paradox: being individual and one • The mystery of unconditional love • Love, the real form of mercy • Experiencing the eternal in temporary situations • Divine love and earthly love • The empowerment of men and women • The example of Jesus and Mary Magdalene • Invisible to the dark forces

5) Sacred Knowledge and Secret Societies: A Long History of Devotion and Deviation   157

The two sides of the dark age • Sacred knowledge becomes secret • The loss of neutrality and purity • False priests and prophets • Victims become adversaries of their former tormentors • Secret societies begin to oppose worldly religions • Freemasons as an example of a secret society • Lodge members in public action • Christianity and Freemasonry – an ancient strife • Humanism against absolutism • Fundamental Controversy • Secret 'double agents' in the first crusade • The sudden appearance of the Templars • Jesus seen from the Lodge perspective • A telling prophecy • From the Templars to Freemasonry

Part II: Prophecies and the Revelation – Mankind in the Mirror of Its Future

6) Moneypulation   207

The attacks on the four pillars of dharma • How gold turned into money • Money and interest – whose interest? • How the Third World was created • Colonies, superpowers and the dream of a World Empire • 'Order out of chaos' • The pyramid on the one dollar bill • Why not just one crushing blow? • 'Divide and rule!' • Historical excursus: Ulterior influence in Russia

7) The End-Time Code 666   233

What was the purpose of the last sixty years? • Why world power? • When will it come about? • The two apocalyptic 'beasts' • The triple six as a magical code • 6-6-6 is present world-wide • Is 666 an evil number? • Some simple games with numbers • Is there a triple six hidden in the bar code?

8) Unlimited Technological Progress – to What End?   249

Abolishment of cash money – fact or fiction? • Everything put on one card? • Implantable microchips for humans • Globalization of the Web • The danger of the mark • What might the next steps be?

9) People Cannot Say They Did Not Know   261

Occurrences as never experienced before • The two half-times of Tribulation • The second half of Tribulation • The army of two hundred million soldiers • The construction of the third Temple in Jerusalem • The crucial element of the scenario • God's seal, the new song and the everlasting gospel

10) Divine Protection and Intervention   275

What does 'chosen' mean? • Protection by ascension • The gateway to transformation • Developing a Light body • 'Sheltered in heaven' • How can we avoid being 666-marked? • Examples of former ascensions and evacuations • Babylon and beyond

Part III: The Cosmic Background of Past and Present History

11) Interdimensional Contacts Rediscovered   297

Cosmic hierarchy • Man's position in the multidimensional cosmos • The revival of higher abilities • Communication with higher dimensions • The mystery of the 'inner word' • The Spirit of truth in modern times • The harmony of unlimited points of view • False love and light

12) The Hidden History of Mankind Newly Revealed — 317

Lost knowledge from new sources • 'The Human Experience – Then and Now' • Apocalypse now?

13) How Much Truth Is There in Science Fiction? — 333

Reptoid influence at the beginning of Kali-yuga • A testimony from Borneo • Traces in Sumerian mythology • The children of the feather and the children of the serpent • UFOs – an age-old phenomenon? • Strange flying objects after WW II • The suppression of public research • What did the astronauts see? • Universal team or interplanetary war? • Disclosures and misinformation • A speculative scenario • Reminiscent of the Apocalypse

14) The Future That Is Now — 369

From manifestation to incarnation • Mythological history of mankind (part 1) • Invisible helpers • Mythological history of mankind (part 2) • The illusion of division • Removing the veil • Experiencing the Spirit of truth

Epilogue	387
Endnotes	391
The Author	419
Bibliography	423
Index	435

Instead of a Foreword,
a Fore-story

The Memory Genius

At once the audience fell silent. It's starting! The young chess champion had entered the hall and was moving towards the stage where his opponents were already seated in front of their chess boards – nervous and tense, for they were to take part in a 'superhuman' happening. Usually chess is a game in which two opponents face each other at a board of 64 black and white squares, with each player alternately making his moves. But *Harry Nelson Pillsbury*, an ingenious chess player from America, had come up with a unique and sensational technique of playing: without seeing the board! He had such a phenomenal memory that he could play 'blindly'. He sat either blindfolded in front of the board or was seated at a distance, but still, his masterful style of playing was hardly diminished. His opponents, who, of course, could play seeing the board, were always amazed at how quickly and precisely he answered their moves (in spoken chess language): pawn h2 to h4, queen f3 to e4, knight takes pawn on g4.

Then, Pillsbury began to play *several* blind games simultaneously. As a teenager, he had gained his first renown in America by playing three or four games at one go. He had learnt to play chess relatively late, at the age of sixteen. But after three years he was already known among insiders to be a future champion. In the spring of 1895, at the age of 22, Pillsbury was invited to the 'Grand International Chess Tournament' in Hastings (England) – the greatest tournament in chess history up till that time. World champion Emanuel Lasker, former world champion Wilhelm Steinitz as well as all top players from three generations had gathered to participate in this historic challenge. Pillsbury lost against Lasker, but this was only a minor setback for him. During one phase of the tournament he won nine games in a row, and so, at the end, he emerged victorious. The sensation was perfect.

Pillsbury became one of the first professional chess players of his time. Due to his victory in Hastings he was qualified to take part in the challenge tournament of St Petersburg (1895/6), where the three top world-championship candidates and Lasker had to play six games against each other. After the first half, Pillsbury was sovereignly leading. He had defeated Lasker twice, with one game drawn! In the fourth round, Lasker defeated Pillsbury in a spectacular way. The second half became a fiasco for Pillsbury. He lost all his games except for three draws (two against Lasker). The world champion ended this competition as clear winner, two points ahead of Steinitz, 3½ ahead of Pillsbury and 4½ ahead of Tchigorin.

In the following tournament of Nuremberg 1896, Pillsbury again defeated Lasker, who won the tournament nonetheless. A strange destiny followed Pillsbury: during some games he lost his famed concentration, which caused him to ruin even won positions. Thus, he spoiled one tournament victory after the other. These sometimes incomprehensible errors as well as his habit of incessantly smoking cigars hinted at something that was deeply gnawing within this young man ...

An example of a person with a photographic memory: 22-year old Harry Nelson Pillsbury (on the right, with cigar in hand), at the beginning of his short, comet-like career; here as the winner of the tournament in Hastings in 1895. Next to him world champion Emanuel Lasker, Russia's No. 1 Mikhail Tchigorin and former world champion Wilhelm Steinitz.

Being in constant need of money, and perhaps also as a challenge to Lasker, Pillsbury (in addition to normal chess) made pioneering experiments in simultaneous blind chess. Travelling from one event to the next, he popularized chess and attracted the masses. In 1900, he went on a seven-month US tour, covering 40,000 miles, with over 150 performances. In 1897, he had become the official US chess champion.

And now, this famous Harry Nelson Pillsbury stood on the stage, self-confident, and ready for the show – because as a show-act it had been announced: *a performance of simultaneous blind chess and checkers, ten games of each, along with a surprise memory test!*

Clamorous applause, then again hushed silence. A member of the jury stepped forward and handed Pillsbury a piece of paper with a strange 'poem' to memorize:

Antiphlogistine, periosteum, takadiastase, plasmon, ambrosia, Threlkeld, streptococcus, staphylococcus, micrococcus, plasmodium, Mississippi, Freiheit, Philadelphia, Cincinnati, athletics, no war, Etchenberg, American, Russian, philosophy, Piet Potgelter's Rost, Salamagundi, Oomisillecootsi, Bangmamvate, Schlechter's Nek, Manzinyama, theosophy, catechism, Madjesoomalops

Two psychologists had compiled this nonsensical list with the intention of confusing Pillsbury's memory with known and unknown terms. Unimpressed, Pillsbury read the paper while printed copies were being handed out to the audience. However, the last spectators in the back rows had not yet received the leaflet when Pillsbury laid his sheet aside and repeated the words from beginning to end and, for fun, also backwards. The audience was stunned.

Pillsbury seated himself at a small vacant table while twenty local players of chess and checkers were sitting along a row of tables a few metres away from him, with the boards placed in front of them. One player after the other made his move, which was conveyed to Pillsbury who, after short thought, announced his move. Then his respective opponent was given time to think until Pillsbury had made his next move in all other games. Sporadically he went to another table for some whist drives – just to make the show even more exciting, and also to give his opponents more time to think about their next moves.

The hours passed by. Pillsbury kept all games memorized, pushing them on in his irresistible, brilliant way, while smoking one cigar after the other. After about six hours, the last game of chess came to its end. Pillsbury rose from his seat, smiling and exhausted. As usual, he had won most of the games, and none of them had slipped his memory. In a loud voice he repeated the nonsensical list once again forwards and backwards.

In other shows of blind chess, he would be handed fifty numbered pieces of paper, each with a sentence written on it. After reading them only once, he was able to repeat all sentences. The people from the audience who had bought such a 'ticket' called out their number in a random order, several calling more than once.

Pillsbury aimed at higher and higher records in simultaneous blind chess, wondering how far the capacity of his memory would go. In his shows he played about ten games simultaneously and, in serious challenges, he gradually increased the number – up to twenty-one (1902 in Hanover) and twenty-two (1903 in Moscow). These world records were to remain unbroken for twenty years.

Concerned friends and observers warned him against such energy-draining mental acrobatics, and they were to be right in the end. His photographic memory increasingly became a curse. Everything he read and heard, every kind of nonsense that rushed in on him remained in his conscious memory, driving him crazy. His mental stress was further aggravated when he began to suffer from syphilis. His last tournament (in Cambridge Springs 1904) was a struggle for him, and he ended up in the middle ranks. But again, he defeated world champion Emanuel Lasker, despite already bearing the mark of death. His illness quickly wore down his body and mind. In June 1906 he died at the age of thirty-three.

The chess world was shaken. Emanuel Lasker wrote:

> He died from an illness contracted through overexertion of his memory cells. [...] He should not have been suffered to be without the comforts that make work easy and keep health intact. Instead, he had to work hard, he had to spend the valuable matter of his brain on many 'entertainments' lasting six to ten hours in order to earn a barely sufficient livelihood.[2]

Introduction

Pillsbury's life story shows the crucial importance of what we allow to enter into our consciousness. In Pillsbury's case the focus of consciousness he opted for had tragic consequences. The flood of information he absorbed as well as his lifestyle took their toll psychically and physically. The way his life ended is a warning to all people of modern-day society because we, too, are confronted with a constant flood of information that make us think, feel and act in certain ways.

All over the world, millions upon millions of people, while working in some office, factory or business, perform activities they would ordinarily not do, were it up to them. A constant pressure makes them spend their lives in busy-ness, stress and anxiety, as they all have to make money. They have no choice, and they have 'no time', at least no time for themselves – for their true selves. Furthermore, most of these occupations either directly or indirectly harm people's health and the environment. Yet still these artificial needs continue to be justified and advocated, in spite of all warnings and dangers.

Why? A first answer is: because there are forces wanting it to be so. Otherwise, the course would be different. Exploitation, corruption, pollution, injustice and wars do not simply happen by chance. Without money and organization, none of these 'achievements' would be possible.

It is a question of power. There are those who influence, and those who allow themselves to be influenced. Both sides contribute their share, though featuring in different roles. This unequal power game is called *manipulation*, literally meaning 'a handling, trickery, or machination; using other people to serve one's own interest'.

Manipulation is especially effective when the targeted people are not aware that they are being manipulated. Voluntary 'cogs in the machine' are easier to handle than forced ones. Therefore, manipulation is a stronger means of power than enforcement.

For manipulation to have its intended effect, it must secure a hold on people's *consciousness*. It is the 'wavelength' (frequency) of our consciousness that determines what we perceive and ignore, what we like and dislike, what we accept and reject, in short: how we spend our time and energy. The manipulators, therefore, try to program people by keeping them within limited horizons, conditioning their consciousness through a constant flow of in-fluence and in-formation: it flows into the consciousness and puts it in a certain form. In this way people almost naturally dedicate their energy (faith, interest, time) to the aims imposed.

It is an unequal game but a mutual one nonetheless as the overwhelming majority of people *want* the diversions offered to them (TV, newspapers, internet, entertainment, sport, intoxication, meat, luxury etc.), ignoring the destructive processes required to produce these 'consumer goods'. Of course, there are various factors influencing the desires of each individual, but ultimately we ourselves determine what can influence us – according to the focus of our consciousness. When one believes to be voluntarily doing what one does, one cannot blame the manipulators alone but should also consider one's own superficiality, indolence and naivety, perhaps even dishonesty and self-deception. Are not most people convinced that what they choose to believe, watch, read, eat, like and dislike, is their own decision?

In other words, the world situation cannot be properly assessed by passing the buck of responsibility. This would be a one-sided projection of guilt: 'It is your fault, not mine!' With such an attitude one would pass over the most important factor, namely one's own role in this power game. After all, being manipulated means that one is part of the manipulation, having accepted the role of an ignorant or intimidated victim (by giving in to the illusion of being powerless and helpless). Such 'private' frustrations always look for compensation, mostly by unloading themselves upon other victims, be it the wife, the child or the dog. Being manipulated means being a potential manipulator, too. Those who allow themselves to be manipulated would be manipulators themselves if they were given the dreamt-of billions of dollars.

Therefore, the point of examining the global power game cannot be a hypo-critical criticism of some manipulators. Otherwise it would remain superficial and inconclusive. The solution cannot be the judging and blaming of others. To play one front off against the other will not end the power game. However, ignoring or belittling the problem is not the solution, either. We have to transcend the global power game, which means: we have to go beyond the dualistic way of thinking. Then, and only then, shall we be able to end destruction and exploitation, being aware of the higher perspectives in life. This, again, is a question of consciousness.

Manipulation, liberation, any form of creation, even life itself – everything is centred on consciousness. Consciousness is not a product of matter (of the brain), it is the source of matter. It animates matter, it shapes matter, it moves matter. If people were to know about these miraculous potentials of their consciousness, they would have other priorities, other interests, other goals. They would be immune against materialistic manipulation. A completely new world-view would open up. They would see themselves and the universe with totally different eyes. They would be able to work with astral and ethereal energies, and to perform telepathy, self-healing, even 'miracles' (mind over matter).
But do such abilities really exist?
Yes. The potential of the human mind exceeds by far today's accepted limitations. According to ancient writings, mystical traditions and contemporary metaphysics, humans in former ages were able to utilize this potential, and thus had a natural access to higher dimensions and higher perception. Psychic abilities were nothing extraordinary – just like, for modern man, electricity, television and computers.

This may be a spectacular claim. But it can be proven by many examples. One has already been mentioned: the reality of people having a perfect or 'photographic' memory. In former times, this was quite a normal asset. From the scriptures of ancient India* we learn that there was even a common expression for it in everyday Sanskrit language, namely *shruta-dhara*, the ability to 'keep in memory' (*dhara*) everything 'after hearing' (*shruta*), and being able to repeat it at any time. Many *brahmanas* and *rishis* (Vedic scholars and sages) had this ability. They considered it a gift of God, and therefore used it cautiously – and exclusively – for selfless purposes, mainly for passing on their timeless wisdom from one generation to the next. Due to the master's and disciple's natural ability of *shruta-dhara*, the oral way of teaching was sufficient. Only when people lost this ability did the necessity of compiling scriptures arise. (In other words, the invention of writing is not a sign of progress in evolution but a makeshift solution in order to prevent a

---

* The mythic age as described in the Sanskrit scriptures of India is often referred to as 'the Vedic age' because its ancient scriptures are called *Vedas*, derived from *veda*, 'sacred or revealed knowledge'. The root of *veda* is the verb *vid* (to know, to observe), which is reflected in the Latin word *videre* (to see, to perceive).

total loss of knowledge. At the same time, it brought about a limitation of inner knowing and vision to the written word, and it could be easily distorted into dogmatism and scriptural fundamentalism. According to Vedic dating, this new chapter in human history set in around five thousand years ago, with the arrival of the present age of Kali.)

As shown by Harry Pillsbury, a modern-day human, the phenomenon of people having a *shruta-dhara* capacity is not an exaggerated legend of ancient mythical times. After all, Pillsbury's case was nothing unique, and after him there were others with even greater abilities.[3]

The memory acrobats of today, no matter how rare or eccentric they may be, prove that it is possible to have a perfect memory. Did people in former days have similar capacities or even capacities of a superior kind? Testimonies of past civilizations indicate that there were indeed people possessing abilities that we today would call 'paranormal'. Therefore they could attain fabulous achievements and insights without technical aids. Evidence can be found in ancient architecture, astronomy, philosophy, metaphysics etc.

Somehow, in the course of time, this knowledge became lost. Nowadays, the 'informed' citizen does not even believe in the reality of higher dimensions and paranormal abilities, what to speak of him/her having such abilities. Unfortunately, official science and established religions deny or even demonize such perspectives. As much as (materialistic) science and (dogmatic) religion seem to be different, they both limit reality to their own preconceived world-view. In this way they shut themselves off from a higher understanding and, furthermore, they make people susceptible to programming and manipulation.

Are these prevailing world-views the only possible explanations concerning the origin and true nature of man?

No, they are not the only possible explanations, they are not even good or plausible explanations! They are *ideologies* based on either materialistic or denominational dogmas, and they make their believers see the world in a very biased, limited way. A more neutral, universal perspective is required, a knowledge that unites the essence of non-materialistic science and non-dogmatic religion. This is the meaning of the word *holistic**, referring to a world-view that takes the whole spectrum of existence into consideration, not only the material dimension.

---

* Holistic: from Grk. *holos,* 'whole; complete; all-encompassing; holy'.

A holistic view is 'multidimensional' and also 'esoteric', in the original sense of the term (from Grk. *esoteros,* 'internal, private, confidential'). Esoteric knowledge is inner knowledge that has to be realized by oneself, because it contains aspects that are not subject to direct physical proof. It cannot be spread or imposed by propaganda, it can only be received by those who are 'open-minded' and receptive. Seek, and you will find. (But seek and desire, and have faith, you must.)

In other words, things spread through official channels, mass media and preaching are never holistic and never esoteric. They are exoteric: external and superficial, because they are limited by materialistic or religious ideologies – and interests.

The multidimensional world-view is the essence of both the oldest and newest knowledge of mankind. It corresponds to the insights of modern holistic science[4] as well as to the mytho-logic* of ancient civilizations. Both indicate the existence of higher dimensions and parallel worlds, and of non-material consciousness beyond the material forms. While the pioneers of holistic science approach this world-view through research and experimentation, the ancient seers reached it through 'paranormal' abilities. (However, these abilities did not guarantee immunity against decadence. History proves that people again and again succumb to the temptation of misusing power and position.)

Whatever happens 'on stage' can be understood only by looking behind the backdrop of the visible scene. How was world history influenced in the past, and how is it being influenced today? Where are the dark forces at work, and where the powers of light?

Taken in their multidimensional context, these topics are dynamite in their potential.

---

* The Greek words *mythos* and *logos* are mutually complementary like *yin* and *yang*. Both can be translated as 'word' or 'notion'. Logos and mythos describe the two different ways of approaching reality, logos from the material, rational side, mythos from the higher-dimensional, 'paranormal' side. Logos is inductive, based on man's own effort, mythos is deductive, based on higher perception and revelation. Thus, the multidimensional world-view is not only logical but mytho-logical! As soon as one of the two is excluded there is one-sidedness.

Part I

Planet Earth – Focus of a Cosmic Power Game

Who rules the earth?
What are these rulers planning?
How did they gain their (seeming) power?

CHAPTER ONE

The Mystery of Oneness and Duality

The basic teaching of all ancient and present mystery schools can be summarized in one single phrase: *Reality is not limited to physical matter.* There are dimensions beyond the workings of physics and chemistry. The visible world is only the external appearance of an invisible background consisting of non-physical energies and entities, 'invisible' and 'non-physical' being terms relative to the limitations of the terrestrial point of view.

In contrast to this, modern science declares physical matter to be the only reality, stating that everything, including life and consciousness, can be explained with the known laws of physics and chemistry. Philosophically, such a world-view is called materialistic. All concepts that, in one way or another, are based on the assumption that the world along with its living beings has evolved out of matter are subsumed under the generic term 'materialism'. Those who believe in this world-view may call themselves scientific and objective, but they cannot hide the fact that they also believe in a credo, namely: 'In the beginning there was matter; therefore, everything consists of matter, and there is nothing beyond matter. Organic life was a late by-product of inorganic matter, and consciousness only arose when the humanoid animal developed a larger brain.'

Is reality really only material? Is our existence nothing more than the interplay of physical and chemical reactions? Is life a by-product of matter?

The holistic world-view says no. Even more so, it says that physical matter has no true reality in itself. It is only the external, gross manifestation of material energy. In its internal structure, matter is nothing but vibration. But the vibration of what? Of energy. Then, the crucial question is: What is energy? The answer given by the mystery schools is a kind of world formula, and it will be elaborated in this book. Basically, matter exists in many dimensions (= levels of condensation). As matter is *multidimensional,* the material cosmos is multidimensional, too, including higher, 'invisible' worlds – invisible only to earthly humans, at least to most of them.

The term 'higher dimensions', or higher-dimensional levels,[5] refers to the entire spectrum of parallel worlds, ranging from lower, earthbound astral[6] realms and dark worlds up to the highest worlds of light. They can also be called 'extraterrestrial'[7] as they all exist beyond the common terrestrial bounds. They are not physically perceivable, only *metaphysically,* because matter in these cosmic dimensions is not as condensed ('gross') as here on earth. There, it manifests in other space-time frequencies and, consequently, follows other physical laws than those valid in the gross-material world perceived by earthly humans; it vibrates at a different wavelength, so to speak.

The higher dimensions ('cosmic frequencies') can be compared to the many radio and television broadcasts that are simultaneously transmitted on parallel frequencies. Although being contained within the same 'ether', they all represent a world, or programme, of their own. There is no overlapping or mixing because all of them occupy different ranges of frequencies. Each channel we choose connects us to an already ongoing programme.

In other words, planet earth – seen from a multidimensional perspective – is not an isolated sphere placed in a void universe, but a field of cosmic interaction. Here, an intricate power game has been going on for quite some time. The only things visible are the happenings on the terrestrial chess board. The pieces seem to move by themselves, without any remote players. As in chess, even the kings and queens are only pieces in the game, what to speak of the 'pawns' and 'knights', be they black or white. The global (and cosmic) players themselves work on levels beyond the board, unknown to the 'chessmen'. And this one game is not the only one. Beyond the visible black-and-white boards there are higher levels of schemes and teams that remain unknown or inaccessible to those below.

Being on a higher level does not necessarily mean having reached a higher state of consciousness. Within the worlds of relativity, the duality of 'light' and 'shadow' does not originate on earth. The unity of divine harmony is already split in the higher-dimensional worlds, starting in the archaic dimensions of the 'archangels'. Many of the invisible beings are certainly angelic, but not all.

Materialistically minded people, who only believe what they see, may well doubt the existence of invisible dimensions. What cannot be denied, however, are the visible symptoms. The logic expressed in the saying, 'Where there is smoke, there is fire', allows us to infer the causes from the symptoms, for nothing happens without a cause.

Looking at the excesses of today's world economy, war industry and secret politics, we get the impression that, indeed, there must be 'inhuman' beings at work. Would a normal human being wish to destroy his own environment, exploit the earth and slaughter his neighbour? How is it possible that destructiveness has become so predominant?

Light and shadows on earth

'There are more things in heaven and earth, Horatio,
Than are dreamt of in your philosophy.'
— William Shakespeare (*Hamlet*)

Within the worlds of gross and subtle matter, the factors 'space' and 'time' cause relativity, based on the balance of all parts comprising creation. If imbalance (one-sidedness) comes about, counterparts start to cast shadows, which creates duality. And within duality, light is always opposed by darkness. Accordingly, there are two principal realms – the realm of light and the realm of darkness, or shadows. Both are higher-dimensional and exist separately (as parallel hemispheres), but meet on terrestrial ground because the earth is situated on their borderline. That is why both forces – divine and demoniac – are simultaneously present on earth. From both hemispheres beings are incarnating as humans.

Duality already exists within the invisible worlds, and from there it manifests in our visible world, which thus constitutes a playing ground of a global power game with a cosmic ('invisible') background.

If one wants to understand why certain moves are being made and which ones are forthcoming, one cannot ignore the invisible minds behind the scene.

Getting the bigger picture

Everything is caused by energy, and energy is always associated with life and, thus, with consciousness. Based on this esoteric premise, every unit of 'energy' can be defined as *the field of consciousness of a respective living entity*, which leads to the mytho-logical question: who are the living entities in the worlds of light and in the worlds of darkness?

The entities inhabiting the worlds of light are God-conscious Light beings ('angels'). Is there a supreme Light being in the universe?

The beings of darkness are sometimes called the 'fallen angels', as they are counteractive forces opposing the Light. Does a supreme fallen angel exist, a primeval dark potency, a first cause behind all evil? Where does evil (murder, untruth, exploitation etc.) come from?

These questions are of a universal dimension, and we need a universal perspective to answer them. Both eastern and western revelations offer valuable information complementing each other on a higher level. Every religion has a piece of the mosaic picture, containing *perfect but incomplete* knowledge about God and the universe. Man's knowledge of the Unlimited can never be complete, but it can be perfect in the sense that it is fully sufficient for one's individual perfection (self-realization), and this perfection, being spiritual, is not dependent on the amount of knowledge one has. Still, having a broader view of the mosaic may help one to get a sense of the unity in diversity and, consequently, to attain a better understanding of one's own religion.

Real truths are conclusive without being exclusive. This is especially true regarding the questions about the origin of evil. Being a topic concerning the field of duality (= relativity), there are many relatively good systems of explanation, and they all shed light on this mystery. One simply has to know how to balance the different viewpoints.

Those who fail to get out of confessional or ideological structures shut themselves off from a higher understanding. In the name of 'God', 'truth' or 'science' one can easily fall into a mentality which is diabolic* in the literal sense of the word. The root cause of any dia-bolic mentality is one-sidedness. The one extreme is materialism and nihilism; the other, religious fanaticism and dogmatism. Therefore, this book is not

---

* Diabolic: 'having a splitting, dividing effect', from Grk. *dia-*, 'apart, asunder', and *ballein*, 'to throw'; diabolic is the contrary of holistic. To indicate this deeper, etymological meaning, the author sometimes uses the spelling *dia-bolic*.

meant to propagate any particular ideology or 'religion'. Rather, it is meant to contribute to a holistic vision of the bigger picture by elaborating the common essence of various sources, especially those of Vedic India, early Christianity and theistic mysticism (as these are the sources particularly studied by the author of this book).

Is everything relative?

Words like 'satanic' and 'diabolic' are commonly used in colloquial language. However, the concept of a force called Satan causes embarrassment or even indignation. For too long, representatives of 'God' have been using the phantom of Satan to intimidate their subordinates and to demonize all those of other convictions and of other cultural backgrounds. Obviously, not only the name of Jesus has been misused, but also the name of Satan.

In reality, there is no Devil in combat with God. The Absolute (God) is not in conflict with the negative because the negative is an aspect of the relative. This is also true for the positive. Just as the sun is situated beyond earthly light and shadow, the Absolute is beyond the positive and negative poles of material relativity.

As will be discussed in this chapter, there is nothing *absolutely* negative. The statement 'positive and negative are always relative' is very delicate because it can be misunderstood easily. For example, it could be taken to mean that *everything* is relative, that there is no good or evil, or that there is no Absolute. This, however, is not the meaning.

The word 'absolute' literally refers to the non-relative reality – that which is valid and true beyond all conditions, being independent of all relative circumstances.* To say '*everything* is relative' is an absolute statement, too, and is contradictory in itself. If *everything* were relative, then the fact of everything being relative would be an absolute truth, which would mean that *not everything* is relative. In either case, the fact remains that there are absolute truths. So the question is not, 'Is there something absolute or not?', but: '*What* is the absolute?' This should be the basic interest of philosophy, religion and science as they all claim to be exploring reality and truth, each in its own particular way.

---

*Absolute: 'that which is independent and unbound'; derived from the Latin word *absolutum* as participle of the verb *absolvere*, 'to release, to solve, to unbind'.

The literal meaning of the word 'absolute' in itself gives the perfect definition. The Absolute is the reality beyond duality and relativity. It is not divided into the duality of time – past and future. It is timeless and spaceless, which means it is eternal and unlimitedly conscious: omnipresent and omnipotent. 'It' is God, the divine reality. Being absolute, it is all-encompassing, including everything relative, just as the Whole includes all parts. Still, the Whole is more than the sum of its parts because the Whole is not limited to its parts. Divine consciousness, therefore, means seeing all relative things – both the positive and negative – in connection to the Absolute.

God is divine, and we as parts of the Whole are also divine. Being positive or negative is always relative as it depends on circumstantial conditions and motives. Again, this does not mean that being positive or negative is the same or 'in-different'. Rather, it means that within the world of relativity there *are* negative and positive forces – those who have left and lost harmony ('unity') with the Source, and those reconnecting to the Source. The real Light, however, is never broken up into duality, despite its innumerable rays.

If we want to free ourselves from the limited views of duality we have to awaken to our original consciousness beyond 'good' and 'evil', which means transcending duality and realizing our transcendental (spiritual) nature.[8] To be good is good, of course, but not good enough. The actual goal is to become 'divine' or, more precisely, to realize that we, as parts of God, *are* divine. Through such a consciousness one is able to perceive the higher purpose in all relative situations, be they good or bad, and one no longer identifies with these so-called good and bad situations. This is emphasized in many sacred scriptures. Very clear words are found in the 'Bible of India', the *Bhagavad-gita,* for example:

'A sober person who is not influenced by external conditions and who is neither distracted by happiness nor by distress, in both cases keeping equanimity, is certainly ready for liberation. […] When you no longer act under the urges of the body and the mind, having realized that you are *atma,* an eternal part of God, then you will rejoice within, and nothing external can influence you./ Being aware of his spiritual identity, a wise person is free from material identification, fear and frustration, and is neither agitated by pains nor enchanted by pleasures./ To remain undisturbed in all situations, be they good or bad, neither rejoicing in gain nor despairing in loss – that is the meaning of being situated in divine knowledge.' (2.15, 55–57)

Does evil originate from humans alone?

Being situated within the dimensions of duality, the earth is a platform for negative and positive forces and divine beings as well. Most people are partially resonant to both sides, while also feeling the divine perspective at times. According to one's resonance one has an affinity to certain world-views and values and thinks them to be right and OK. All politicians, bankers and scientists swear that they are only concerned for the general welfare, for peace, security and justice. Everybody is convinced basically to be acting in the proper manner: 'If everybody were like me, we would live in a better world!' Interestingly enough, everybody thinks like that, and still we do not live in a better world. Rather, cold-blooded destructiveness is predominant on earth. Jungles and other forms of plant life are being destroyed. Millions of animals are being killed in the oceans and in slaughterhouses, and tortured in laboratories. Dictators and wars are being financed, while criminality, counter-violence, new diseases and poverty are on the increase.

Why has humanity fallen into such a vicious circle? Where does this inhuman madness come from? From the humans alone? Or are dark forces present on earth? Is there even an original dark force?

As nothing comes about without a cause, evil itself must also have a cause. Some call it 'the diabolic force' or 'Satan', the fallen angel who personifies the ego: the mentality that splits itself off from oneness into duality, thus causing opposition to the light and the 'creation' of shadows. Modern psychology and esotericism interpret the 'fall of the angels' mainly in terms of an archetypal symbolism reflecting inner processes of man. Such analyses are valid and relevant as they focus on the resonating psyche. But are they sufficient as an explanation? Where does the influence to which we resonate (if we do) come from?

Many spiritual sources clearly state that evil in its primeval form is not just an abstract principle but a *conscious cosmic force*. Regarding the cosmic origin of evil, ancient sources from the Middle East give the scenario of Satan and his fallen angels. Other cultures mention violent gods, evil spirits, and demons. The Vedic scriptures speak of *asuras*, the anti-forces of the light, which have been part of the universe since an early phase of creation. Today, in the language of our modern age, another possible term could be 'astral' or 'extraterrestrial' beings of the 'negative kind'. In any case, they are neither the product nor the projection of human imagination. Rather, they are active inhabitants of the multidimensional cosmos, just like the Light beings.

What, then, is wrong in thinking that evil is solely a human factor and not something that also comes from outside? The readers may ponder over this question for themselves.[9]

Perceiving the inconceivable

Evil has existed on earth since time immemorial. Mystic* revelations of all times and cultures even maintain that it is not limited to planet earth!

There are manifold descriptions of how non-material souls have fallen into material darkness. How was it possible that duality came out of oneness? All belief systems have their standard answers to this crucial question, and they all contain valuable insights. Still, as human beings we have to be aware that the concepts of 'oneness' and 'eternity' (a state of being without space and time) are beyond the space-time limits of our mind. All theological theories, therefore, are nothing but an attempt to understand something inconceivable. If we enter a war of opinions we deprive ourselves of the chance to grasp the complementary truths offered by the other viewpoints.

Those entering a war of opinions may argue: 'Yes, we have a limited mind but we are graced by God, the unlimited mind, and received from him unlimited, perfect knowledge.' This is the argument of someone who does not know what 'unlimited', 'eternal' and 'absolute' really mean. Otherwise, how could one assume that God is limited to a single set of doctrines?

Whatever information we receive can be communicated to us only in a way adapted to our conditioning. Therefore, all revelations received by men throughout the many thousands of years describe the cosmic origin of darkness differently. There are no two sources that give identical descriptions – which is not at all surprising. Rather, it is absolutely natural as every person and every culture has a different

---

* Mystic(al): from Grk. *mystikos*, 'concerning the mysteries; mysterious; secret', derived from the verb *myein*, 'to close (eyes and mouth)', which indicates that the real mysteries cannot be perceived through sensory channels but only through supersensory ('supernatural') perception like inner view, meditation and revelation.

viewpoint within the worlds of time and space. People two thousand or five thousand or fifty thousand years ago had a different mindset than people of today.

How can someone stuck in duality understand that which is beyond duality? The Absolute, being oneness and eternity, is beyond the duality of space and time. The human being, unable to understand the notion of oneness and eternity in the first place, has even a harder time grasping how 'something' came out of oneness and how 'time' came out of eternity.

Although it is impossible to rationally grasp the mystery of oneness and duality, it remains a fact that duality has come out of oneness and that 'shadows' have been cast. Dark realms do exist, and they must have come into existence at one point in universal history. In whatever way it happened, it was a circumstance of cosmic complexity born out of an inconceivable background. Nevertheless, we can get an understanding sufficient for our individual self-realization. This 'perfect though incomplete' view can be obtained by looking for the common truths – the spiritual essence which is the same in all revelations.

Duality and individuality

It is an essential truth that there is oneness beyond duality. 'Oneness' refers to the absolute, indivisible reality, the one reality that is not even divided into past and future, which means that it is neither limited by time nor by space as time and space are interdependent (= relative). It is eternal and omnipresent – that is the meaning of 'oneness' and 'absolute reality'. In other words, the oneness beyond material duality is *spiritual indivi-duality!* Individuality literally means 'the quality of being indivisible and eternal'. Individuality also includes consciousness and free will. This refers to the *relative individual* – every living being – as well as to the *absolute Individual* – God. 'Absolute Individual' means eternal, omnipresent and omniconscious oneness that encompasses everything, including us. Thus, we are part of Everything, parts of God.

All divine mystical schools lead to this enlightenment: seeing ourselves as indivisibly united with God. Being 'individual and one simultaneously' is only possible in the *state of conscious union,* which is simply a philosophical definition of 'real love' (love that comes from the consciousness of this reality). And love is an expression of free will as love is always voluntary. Therefore, real love is the perfection of individuality and free will.

God, being individual, also has free will. That is why we can pray: 'Thy will be done!' What is God's will? According to God's absolute oneness there is only 'one thing' God wants: the perfection of free will – love! And that is absolutely individual. Whatever serves this love is in accordance with God's will. Everything else is in opposition to this love, symbolically speaking, in opposition to the Light, and casts shadows.

This essential summary is a key* to getting a sense of that which is inconceivable and absolute. It indicates that in reality we are individual beings, parts of the absolute Individual Being. Oneness of the parts and the Whole can be experienced in real love, as only in love one can be 'different' (individual) and one (united) simultaneously. And love is always voluntary. That is why love 'must' be voluntarily given. But what is the question of free will if there is no possibility of choosing? How can one choose if everything is only oneness?

In order to give us the freedom of choosing, God creates a world made of matter, beginning with multidimensional 'space' and 'time', which are the first expressions of polarity (relativity). From the very beginning, matter operates according to the principles of mutual dynamics (= polarity, creative harmony), based on 'positive' and 'negative' poles like space and time, mind and matter, creation and dissolution, day and night, male and female, young and old, etc. Polarity is the basis of material creation and has as yet nothing to do with *duality*. Duality comes into existence only when some living beings decide to enter the extremes of polarity, which causes them to lose balance and harmony.

In the symbolism of light and darkness, polarity is reflected ('limited') light that can be opposed, and duality is the state of having gone into separation and opposition. 'Reflected light' refers to the Light of the Absolute which is projected into the world of relativity (= polarity), the world of matter in which it is no longer omnipresent but *directed,*

---

* This important key will be taken up again in later chapters, in other contexts, as it can help to differentiate real light from false light, i.e. real enlightenment from false concepts of 'being illuminated', which are self-justifying and thus self-deluding. The elaboration in this line will further show why the key presented here is most essential and relevant. It is a kind of philosophical world formula.

due to being projected (through the medium of the universal creator). Therefore, it is possible to go against it and to cast shadows.

The universe of polarity can be seen as a 'testing ground' for all living beings. Here we can manifest real love by living in divine consciousness. Or we can choose the ways of separation and opposition by entering the illusion of the ego (a false identification within duality).

These are limited words of logic but they can help us to conceive of the inconceivable, the Mystery of mysteries.

Cosmic Genesis and the origin of duality

'He is the image of the unseen God, the first-born of all creation, for in him were created all things in heaven and on earth. […] He exists before all things.'
– New Testament (Colossian Epistle 1.15ff.)

In the highest realms of the multidimensional cosmos there are no shadows of duality. These realms, however, are creations of polarity that give the freedom of choice. In other words, all Light beings consciously use their free will to keep their divine consciousness and to avoid the traps of duality.[10] They do not have to, but they want to. And some, obviously, chose not to. It was in this cosmic dimension where the ways were separated: incidents that entailed the fall of *many, but not of all* souls.

Judaic, Christian and Islamic mystics say that, a long time ago, a high-ranking archangel aspired to be the foremost, and started to incite the 'minds' of other angels who were receptive to this influence. Why would some Light beings decide to go against the Light? Because it is the zone of polarity and free will. Therefore it was possible to start a titanic rebellion in heaven, which had drastic consequences. Those who went against the Light found themselves in the abyss of duality – negativity and darkness. Just as turning away from the light creates shadows, turning away from God 'naturally' created dark worlds.

It is a typical characteristic of the higher-dimensional worlds that thoughts are an immediate reality. The nature of the higher dimensions is completely different from the space-time conditions on earth, and we terrestrial humans cannot understand it by projecting our limited views onto that which is beyond our experience. 'Higher dimension' means that everything is more subtle; thoughts and emotions cause an *immediate* and *direct* manifestation of 'external' reality, because there is no dimensional difference between the internal and the external. These potentials of 'mind over matter' and 'psychic abilities' are present even within the terrestrial human being, though (presently) only to a very limited extent. Higher-dimensional beings, however, have an expanded access to these potentials and are able to consciously use their 'mental' power. Some are even empowered to 'co-create' entire worlds.

Further insight, from another perspective, is given by the ancient Indian scriptures. They do not explicitly mention a rebellion of angels but they do describe universal dark forces, some existing in the higher-dimensional dark worlds, others in the lower astral worlds and again others, as incarnated beings, on earth. They are all part of the dark hemisphere, which reaches as far as the earth – where it ends or starts, depending on the perspective.

The Sanskrit scriptures do not mention a specific topmost ruler of the dark hemisphere (which does not mean that there is none). However, the supreme personality of the light worlds is described in detail. It is the famous *Brahma* of the 'Hindu' trinity Brahma-Vishnu-Shiva, the highest Light being within the universe, situated in the topmost 'heaven'.

Brahma, though, is not the supreme creator. All Vedic revelations clearly state that Brahma, too, is a created being – the *first-created* being, the 'first-born Son of God'. There are countless universes with countless Brahmas but in each universe there is only one. The universes themselves (as divine creations) emanate from the absolute Individual, in Sanskrit called *Vishnu*, 'the omnipresent One' – God as Creator. The emanation and dissolution of the countless universes is described as the exhaling and inhaling of Vishnu. This breath of God is the quantum leap of energy from non-material eternity into material polarity. Thus, within the spiritual reality (the omnipresent 'background'), relativity comes and goes in the form of universes, which are described as 'bubbles of space and time' within the Causal Ocean of Vishnu.

When a universe is exhaled it is *tohu-wa-bohu* (in Hebrew, see Genesis 1.2) – 'formless and empty'. It is a unit of matter in its non-manifested state containing the potential of manifesting the totality of dimensions within the universal spectrum of space and time. Within

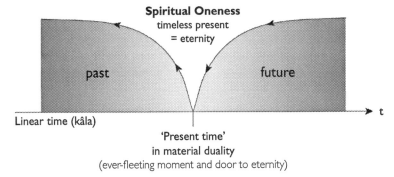

Linear time (kâla)

'Present time'
in material duality
(ever-fleeting moment and door to eternity)

Linear time (t) exists on the basis of duality, manifesting endless past and unending future. Beyond material duality is the reality of spiritual indivi-duality, which is not divided into the material (= relative) dimensions of space (creation and dissolution) and time (past and future); it is spaceless and timeless oneness = eternal present.
It is the all-pervading and omnipresent energy field of consciousness and life, of which each living entity is an individual part (a ray of God, the absolute Individuality).
'Present', being timeless, is actually non-existent on the level of material time, as it is not an aspect of perishable material existence, but of spiritual consciousness. Those whose consciousness is entrapped in maya (illusion: identification with some material form or concept) are only living for the past and the future. Still, through the non-material and non-graspable Now the spiritual 'background' reaches into the world of matter. Matter is not able to move and organize itself independently, just as a shadow cannot move by itself. Matter, as a divine energy, is constantly being moved, and maintained, by a spiritual (= eternal) impulse of consciousness, ultimately by God's absolute consciousness.
Meditation in the Here and Now, free from thoughts of the past and future, is the key to self-realization and God-consciousness (= in-dividual oneness in divine love). Therefore, mystics say that the present is the door to eternity.

this primordial universe Brahma appears as a ray, or 'son', of Vishnu. Through Brahma, hierarchical dimensions of existence are materialized, basically seven in number. It is Brahma who creates in 'seven days', starting with the channelling of light into the dark universe: 'Let light come to be.'

The first living being within the world of matter is not a primitive amoeba but Brahma, the highest Light being. Life does not come from matter, just as light is never produced from darkness. Matter is a product of consciousness (spiritual energy), ultimately of God's absolute consciousness. The creative act of Vishnu causes a quantum leap of energy that manifests cosmic units of time and space ('universes'). Within each universe, through the medium of Brahma, a *descending evolu-*

tion (= devolution), or *involution,* takes place – from the highest, most subtle dimension down to the worlds of gross matter. It is a conscious process of 'copying' higher dimensions into the next lower level, along with an increased condensation of matter. The key to this metaphysical unfolding of creation is the inherent potential of all living beings, namely the ability to shape material energy through the power of their thoughts (according to the principle of 'mind over matter' as mentioned above).

The beings from the upper levels are able to perceive the lower levels whereas the beings from the lower levels cannot directly perceive the upper levels. The higher levels are invisible worlds for those on the lower levels. Obviously, 'invisible' is a very relative term.

At some time during this descending manifestation of dimensions, long before the creation of the earth and the human race, the devolutionary line became forked due to those angels who decided to go against the equilibrium of polarity, against divine harmony. This secondary, and negative, quantum leap of consciousness caused the emergence of the dark worlds along with inhabitants of an equally disharmonic mentality. In this way, duality came about, and the creative hemisphere of light was confronted by the 'separative' creation of darkness enacted by the fallen angels.

The hemispheres of light and darkness have a hierarchical structure, each consisting of seven principal subdivisions. In the hemisphere of light, these seven parallel worlds are presided over by respective Light beings who constitute the divine hierarchy*. The number 7 is a divine number known in many cultures. We speak, for example, of being 'in the seventh heaven', of the seven days of creation, and of seven main archangels, headed by Michael, Gabriel and Raphael. These archangels co-operate with numerous other Light beings who, in the Sanskrit language, are described by the collective name of *devas,* 'the divine ones', or *suras,* 'the shining beings'.

Separated from the Light, there is the hemisphere of darkness, which is under the control of entities called *asuras* in Sanskrit, literally 'the anti-*suras*', those opposing the Light. They are ego-centred beings, the so-called 'demons', 'devils' or 'titans' of ancient mythology, having their own hosts of followers.

---

* Hierarchy: 'sacred order', from Grk. *hieros,* 'holy, God-devoted', and *archein,* 'to rule, to make order' (also found in the word 'archives').

All of these phases of universal creation were higher-dimensional and happened long before the emergence of the earth. Then, in the last phase of cosmic involution, the gross-material level of creation came into existence, including planet earth and its primordial life forms. These original generations of earthly plants and animals are called *proto-types* in Greek. (The original meaning of this word is an expression of the ancients' deep understanding of devolution and was far away from its superficial materialistic usage in today's language.)

Later on, within this world of proto-type plants and animals, the *arche-types* of human beings were manifested in the image of the higher Light beings starting with Brahma. Here, Jewish and Christian mystics use the term 'Adam Kadmon', referring to the original Light form of the higher-dimensional human arche-type. In the Bible, this understanding is reflected in the statement: 'And God went on to say, let *us* make man in *our* image, according to *our* likeness' (Gen. 1.26). The 'we' and 'us' obviously refer to Brahma ('God') and his hosts of *devas*, the non-fallen elohim.

The world of proto-types and arche-types was the original earthly creation. Obviously, in the course of time, the proto-type plants and animals and the arche-type human beings have undergone many physical changes due to further condensation, cyclic mutation, and genetic alteration.

In most systems of metaphysics the zone of the earth is numbered as the seventh level when counted from above. That is why the highest light world, Brahma's heaven, is sometimes called 'the seventh heaven' by terrestrial humans who look up to this most remote ultraterrestrial horizon.

On the scale of condensation, the earth is situated within the bottommost manifestation of matter. Here, the hemispheres of light and darkness meet and separate. Earth, therefore, is a place of decision where darkness and light are present side by side. And we have to decide where we want to go and how we want to react. If we manage to live in real love (being divine and not just 'good' or 'evil') despite these most difficult circumstances, then we have achieved the perfection of free will. That is why even non-fallen angels voluntarily decide to incarnate on earth: to grasp the chance of unfolding the highest form of love within the densest form of matter.

If we make it here, we've made it – definitely and for good!

Light does not cast shadows

The basic scenario to which all spiritual sources agree has been outlined: The universe, as a product of material energy, emanates from a non-material, conscious source. Within this primordial creation, God's first 'sons' and 'daughters' appear. They are the empowered gods and goddesses through whom, in the line of involution, all other realms and beings come into existence. Being constantly faced with potential duality, they have to *consciously* and *voluntarily* sustain their harmony and non-duality. Living in this consciousness is the practical manifestation of divine love, and this love is always voluntary. Free will, however, also implies *responsibility* – because we ourselves choose the course of our actions. In this sense, there is no difference between life in heaven and life on earth.

In the higher worlds, however, every thought and emotion forms a direct manifestation. Obviously, those living in these worlds have a far-reaching self-responsibility. They have the full freedom to act in whatever way they want, with immediate consequences. And, the symptoms visible on earth strongly suggest that some of these beings must have gone against God's will, the oneness of real love. Otherwise, non-love would not be so predominant.

Again, the symbolism of light and darkness is perfect. *Light does not cast shadows*. This is the only thing that light cannot do: produce shadows. The same is true for God. God does not create godlessness and can therefore not be blamed for the existence of evil. As the absolute Individuality, however, 'He' allows the potential blocking of the light. Whoever wants to go against it, is free to do so. *Nobody is forced to love God, and nobody is forced to cast shadows.*

This situation allows pure and voluntary love, but it also contains a big temptation, namely doing something God cannot do: 'creating' shadows. Those deciding to do this live in the illusion of being independent, not realizing that their work is fully dependent on the Light's granting them this option. Light could burn away all opposing elements, but it will not as this would be the destruction of free will.

The creation of shadows, or the fall into duality, has been described in many ways – as many as there are belief systems. One name often mentioned is *Lucifer,* literally 'the light-carrier'. Again, there are many theories about this name. It is not mentioned in the Bible. The only reference is found in Isaiah, 14.12: 'O how you have fallen from heaven, you shining one, son of the dawn!' The Greek word for 'shining one' is *heosphoros*, 'bringer of the dawn', in Latin *lucifer*, the morning star, later on named Venus. However, in the Revelation (22.16), 'morning star' is another name of Jesus: 'I, Jesus, [...] am the root and offspring of David, and the bright morning star.' In this meaning, Lucifer was used as a clerical name during the early centuries of Christianity. There was a famous bishop in the fourth century named *Lucifer of Cagliari*. Modern theosophy as founded by Helena Blavatsky considers Lucifer even to be a name of God: the Lord of the Light who will ultimately free the world from the Lord of darkness. Therefore – theosophy argues – the dark forces demonized Lucifer by making him a synonym for Satan.

Despite these different interpretations, the presently known story (or allegory) of Lucifer is very illustrative as it graphically depicts the dualistic psychology and the consequent dia-bolic mentality.

The psychology of the fallen

The hemisphere of negative creation is the work of powerful beings, too. However, they are no longer co-creators but manipulators (fallen creators). In this context the name Lucifer ('light carrier') refers to the archetype* of the fallen archangel. Originally he possessed godlike qualities, but then he began to identify himself with them, thinking his beauty and power to be his own achievement. Once having fallen into this illusory concept (ego), he no longer understood that these were splendours *bestowed* upon him for the exclusive purpose of reflecting God's glory. (Lucifer's example, being archetypal, shows direct parallels to our human psyche. How often do *we* tend to identify ourselves with our qualities, using good results to enhance our own prestige?)

What followed was pride, and he began to compare himself to others. He made the first step into thinking in terms of 'me' and 'the others', which was the original form of 'judging'. Consequently, he manifested a desire to extend his influence, wanting to rival those he considered to

---

* Archetype: the epitome or primeval, typical form/matrix/representative of a psychological, symbolical and/or material phenomenon (from Grk. *arche*, 'beginning; initial state', and *typos*, 'something coined, cast or moulded; form; model').

be 'better', and to dominate those he considered 'inferior'. Ultimately, he even wanted to dethrone his 'brother', God's First-born. He started to search out allies – and became the first 'missionary'! The ego concept of wanting to convince others of one's own ideas was born.

This archetypal conflict is the seed of all dark 'brotherhoods' and fratricidal wars. The rivalry between sons/brothers is continually reflected on all levels, for example Uranus against Chronos, Enki against Enlil, Set against Osiris, Cain against Abel. Vedic scriptures give a similar description. The genealogy of the *devas* and the *asuras* can be traced back to the same mythological lineage of an identical father with different mothers.

Lucifer's increasing propensity to sow disharmony resulted in a final decision on his part, which was followed by his hosts of angels and subordinates. They were confronted with the consequence of their inner attitude because in this topmost subtle dimension, thoughts and feelings cause an immediate and direct manifestation of 'external' reality. Without even realizing it, they had separated themselves from the Light and fallen into the worlds of their own shadows. They were 'driven out of heaven'.

Now, Lucifer was no longer the light-carrier but the sovereign of the dark realms and the leader of the fiendish forces. And so he became *Satan*, the 'fallen one'. Interestingly enough, the Hebrew word *shatan* ('adversary; persecutor') is synonymous to the Sanskrit word *shatana*, meaning 'to cause the downfall of; to destroy; to ruin', stemming from the root *shad*, 'to fall; to plunge', and also, 'to fell'. This double meaning appropriately describes Satan's character, for he is not only 'the fallen one' but also 'the feller of others', dragging them down with him by enticing words and false promises or, if required, by intrigues and violence. (Isn't that also typical for many earthly situations? People who pose as friends, partners or allies for their own advantage, all of a sudden become insidious enemies when they no longer get what they want.)

Those who turn away from the Light are compelled to live in darkness. This is what Lucifer and his followers experienced. They found themselves in darkness and realized that they had lost everything they formerly possessed. However, instead of correcting themselves, they even went further into separation by generating negative emotions: envy, wrath, hate, revengefulness, self-deception and self-pity.[11]

In other words, the first generation of 'fallen angels' was no longer happy. They had projected their consciousness into duality including *the duality of time.* They no longer lived in timeless present, but started to think in terms of past and future. Life in the timeless oneness of divine love was eclipsed from their consciousness. It became inconceivable for them or, at the most, a boring, impractical idea: 'What, always be happy? That would be hell!' That is the argument of someone who is lost in non-reality and duality, having no awareness of his real self, his spiritual individuality, eternal and ever-present ...

Again, this sounds quite modern. Everybody knows the problems caused by the materialistic way of life. But who is willing to live free of TV, sensationalism, artificial entertainment and destructive sense gratification (smoking, meat-eating, intoxication etc.)?

By his archetypal rebellion against God and the deity of creation, Brahma, Lucifer caused his own downfall into dualistic passion and 'stress'. He was aspiring for more than his due. He wanted *more.* He wanted something different. He wanted 'a change'.

The loss of eternity was, and is, the problem of Lucifer and his followers. No longer *really* happy in eternal present, they had to talk themselves into being happy. They had cut the bond to their divine origin and were categorically separated from the Source, their egos remaining their only 'source' of motivation and determination. They turned into creatures of a dark and callous nature, being cut off from real love just as darkness is cut off from the light.

On higher-dimensional levels, the state of consciousness is directly expressed in the body's appearance, as the body is naturally higher-dimensional, too. This correlation of mentality and bodily form also holds true for negative beings. The more a creature turns away from God, the less divine his qualities will be, up to the point of forfeiting the capacity to love, even the desire to love.

The downfall of Lucifer and his associates was not due to ignorance. They had heard the warning several times: 'May your external appearance be the true reflection of your inner mirror wherein the love of God beholds itself; otherwise this mirror shall shatter into pieces and your appearance shall turn horrid.'[12]

This is exactly what happened. Frightful and grotesque-looking beings developed. Their cold-blooded, godless nature manifested in repulsive unsightliness described as being beastlike-reptoid. 'The great dragon [...] is the ancient serpent also known as the devil or by the name of Satan, who tempts the whole world.' (Rev. 12.9)

These forms are subtle and astral, and invisible to most terrestrial humans. When entering the gross levels of matter, they can incarnate as humans or project themselves as 'holographic' apparitions in any desired shape. We are therefore informed: 'Such men are false apostles [of peace], deceitful workers ... And no wonder, for Satan himself keeps transforming himself into an angel of light.' (2 Cor. 11.13–14)

Ego projection and the I-AM consciousness

The different scenarios about the original fall into duality entail a series of important questions: Was this a 'necessary experience'? Did these angels *have to* fall in order to know what sin and evil was? Was it even God's plan that they chose this way? Would 'evolution' be impossible without the counter-forces? But then, what about those who did not fall?

Here the importance of the elaboration on duality and individuality becomes further evident. Reality beyond duality is the 'indivisible oneness' (= in-dividuality) which includes consciousness and free will. The perfection of free will and divine consciousness is love (= being individual and one simultaneously). Love is an act of free will and voluntary union. God, the absolute Individuality, therefore grants free will as the essence of all-encompassing love. This is manifested through the existence of material polarity, which allows the freedom of choosing. This means: *Nobody is forced to love God, and nobody is forced to fall into duality.* Otherwise there would be no question of free will.

In the symbolism of light and darkness this is shown by the fact that light does not cast shadows, an essential truth that cannot be stressed enough: God does not create evil. However, light can be blocked. Whoever wants to oppose it is free to do so and to cast shadows. The light itself remains untouched by all forms of shadow and darkness, and the light's existence is not dependent on these shadows.

From this point of view, there is absolutely no need of falling into duality and becoming evil. Those Light beings who do not fall are already living in the perfection of love and free will. They are what they really are and do not have to 'become' anything. They live beyond the duality of time, in the consciousness of eternal present (which is possible only in the loving oneness with the Absolute), which means: they are living in *reality*. Also those who fall will eventually, after all their 'dead ends', reach this state of being, nothing more and nothing less. It is the perfection of individuality and free will, and the Light beings already have it, eternally and voluntarily, be they incarnate or not.[13]

Falling into duality means going against the divine harmony of the Whole. Just as opposing the light creates shadows, opposing God creates the ego. 'Ego' means the loss of one's original consciousness of being eternal and individual, which is an illusion because in reality we are always parts of the Whole. This opposition is an act of free will because it is *neither forced nor necessary*.

Under the influence of the ego, one's original state of consciousness is covered and eclipsed. There is no longer the experience of eternity (timelessness, spacelessness). Consciousness is now projected into the duality of 'past' and 'future'. All of a sudden, eternity and divine harmony look boring and impractical. All of a sudden, one thinks that one has to be busy and has to *become* something. Why? Because one feels that one has lost something. And one starts to run and race, thinking this to be necessary!

The concept of 'having to become something' comes out of the ego. It indicates that one has lost the consciousness of one's original nature. In reality, 'I am always what I am' – the eternal indivisible part of the Whole. This is the deep meaning of the 'I-AM consciousness', a notion very common in modern esoterics. It is an essential truth. (Nobody speaks about an 'I-BECOME consciousness'!)

So-called good creates evil

The archetype of the fallen archangel manifested the principle of the ego: the consciousness of judging and thinking in terms of duality. He thought his beauty and power to be his own achievement and began to compare himself to others. The thinking in terms of 'me' and 'the others' (the original form of 'judging') entailed the projection of fronts: I, the good one, and over there the evil ones. Satan was convinced that he was totally right. As the first 'missionary', he also became the first 'world changer'. He was proud to be able to do something which the Light (God) could not do: create shadows and darkness. Therefore, he wanted to create a better world – a world of darkness – based on his 'invention'. Going against the already existing creation, he set out to materialize his vision of a 'new world'.

The dark forces like to call themselves 'the good ones', the ones who are right, and 'being right' they are convinced that all their means are justified by their 'noble end'. It is a vicious circle. Calling oneself good means calling others less good, and again others evil. In this way, so-called good creates evil: disharmony, war, deceit, lies etc. Why? Because the so-called good is as dia-bolic ('dividing') as those who are straight out evil.

The psychology of the fallen gives rise to many kinds of ideology. Their main characteristic is that they are *self-justifying*, believing that 'what we do is necessary' as it serves 'the ultimate good'. They even think themselves to be better than the non-fallen angels because 'we are richer in our experience; we have seen something the light has never seen: darkness'. In this way they confirm that they're in darkness. But they don't get the point.

As long as they hold on to their ego-justification they will never correct themselves. That is the tragic feature of this vicious circle. It is the core of all self-deception and, at the same time, the highest 'illumination' of the dark forces. This will be further elaborated in the following chapters.

The role of evil in spiritual evolution

'Woe to those who call what is bad, good, and what is good, bad, who substitute darkness for light and light for darkness …'
— Isaiah 5.20

Both the positive and the negative are part of material relativity. This means: all negativity is relative. There is nothing absolutely negative. There is no foe to God just as there is no independent darkness as a counterpart to the light. Darkness only exists in the world of relativity, but there it does exist. By definition there is good and evil within duality. So it would be fallacious to say that 'there is no evil' or 'everything is good'. It is the very characteristic of our world that not everything is good, and not everything is bad. We have to differentiate.

All things in creation have a purpose – evil as well! But it would be erroneous to conclude therefrom that evil (murder, violence, fraud etc.) is no longer evil just because it has a purpose. The question about the role of evil is meant to *explain* its existence, not to justify it.

Evil is called evil because it is directed against God's will. As already mentioned, God is the absolute Individual (= undivided oneness), and individuality includes consciousness and free will. Therefore, we, being parts of God, have free will, too. The perfection of free will is to voluntarily correspond to God's will. This is love – and this is God's will. God wants for us nothing but the perfection of free will. Everything which is not consciously done in this love is against God's will. Therefore, we all naturally feel that God does not want non-love like war, terrorism, bloodshed and oppression. And that is absolutely true. These things only happen where some ego blocks the light: within the worlds of relativity, according to the laws of duality.

In other words, the existence of evil is not in God's will but in God's laws. It is allowed but not sanctioned. Everybody is 'allowed' to be evil as this is possible in the world of duality. However, standing outside of God's will, all evil-doers are subjected to the laws, especially the law of action and reaction, or cause and effect (karma). Love, being God's will, is outside of these laws. It is unconditional. As soon as love depends on a material cause, it is no longer real, divine love.

And that is the key to understanding the function of evil. In itself, evil is unnecessary and illusory, just as darkness, seen from the perspective of the light, is an illusion. It only exists because something is temporarily blocking the light. There was light before, and as soon as the obstacle is removed, light will be there again, and the darkness will be gone as if it never had existed. Therefore, only from the higher perspective of the Light can we see what evil really is: an illusory 'ego trip' which we do not need to go through. Understanding this is the only thing to be learnt from evil – and teaching us this lesson is the *indirect* function it has. It is indirect because the dark forces do not consciously want to learn or teach this lesson. Indeed, diverting others from this divine consciousness is their main intention. That is why they are evil, heinous etc. This mentality cannot be justified, it can only be corrected. And this is the individual responsibility of each 'fallen angel': to transcEnd

The two faces of negativity, and the reality beyond

Inner and outer peace (harmony) can be destroyed by two ways of imbalance: the too-much and the too-little. Both are expressions of the 'psychology of the fallen' in its two dualistic extremes. They are the two faces of the same coin called ego.

The one extreme, the too-much, brings about an insatiable desire for more – more power, more profit, more exploitation, more 'research', more 'progress'. It is blinding enthusiasm expressing itself as egotism, imperialistic arrogance, scientific hubris and 'religious' fanaticism. It is the mirroring of the archetypal rebellion of Lucifer, who even wanted to improve heaven, thus creating nothing but shadows.

The other extreme, the too-little, brings about a callous indifference – towards other people, mankind, nature, animals, plants and, not least, towards one's real self. It is cold-hearted pragmatism expressing itself as selfishness, nihilistic thinking, unscrupulous acting and self-justifying scheming. It also leads to intellectualism and 'scientific' reductionism, which looks for a materialistic explanation of life and a mechanical imitation of nature.

The golden mean:
neutrality
and the way to divine consciousness
(love, inner balance: differentiating without judging)

The too-little (selfishness) ——————————————— The too-much (egotism)

Both extremes are forms of a diabolic self-delusion and self-deception. The 'too-little' means thinking that one might lack something or not get enough, leading to loveless selfishness. The 'too-much' means thinking that one has more than others, knows reality better than others or, in short, that one is better than others, which leads to elitism and egotism. Being disconnected from God, the real Source, both are in the illusion of being 'independent', one way resulting in over-enthusiasm, the other in frustration and envy. Symbolically, one is artificial light, the other is darkness. (Usually both consider themselves to be 'the good ones' as contrasted from 'the others' whom they call 'evil'. 'Positive' and 'negative' are relative self-designations or projections, respectively.)

In contrast to this double-faced negativity, neutrality steers a middle course. It is withdrawn from both extremes, being free from over-enthusiasm and frustration. Neutrality is the preliminary step out of duality and leads to the door of divine consciousness, if consequently pursued.[14]

This understanding gives us a key to transcend the illusion of both extremes. In reality we are neither independent nor God-forsaken, we are eternally part of the Whole. Being aware of this self-identity makes us one with the Absolute. Non-divided ('individual') oneness is real love, the love that connects us consciously to the Source, the Absolute beyond duality. As a practical result, we will be able to see everything, even the negative, in the light of this ultimate goal.

In summary, negativity has two forms of one-sided extremes. The opposite of one evil is the other evil. There is no use in fighting evil with its opposite (judging, condemning, hating), there is even no use in fighting evil with positive intentions, just as fighting darkness will never produce light. We have to leave darkness if we want to be in the light. Thus, the real Good is 'the golden mean', starting from neutrality up to individual spirituality (God-consciousness).

this power game of the ego by a proper use of free will. Therefore, ego-justification is the biggest form of self-deception because it chokes off any desire for correction.

The indirect function of evil can be understood only from a divine perspective. On this basis we will know that any confrontation with obtrusive forces is a test for us to see how we will use our free will. Will we react in a non-dualistic manner, according to God's will? Or will we adopt the same godlessness as the perpetrators? Will we let ourselves be provoked into manifesting negative feelings like hate, wrath, frustration or self-pity? Will we give in to some temptation?

As self-responsible, free-willing beings we must voluntarily want truth – and choose truth. When Satan approaches us, it will become evident to what extent we are capable of remaining uninfluenced. Putting us to this test is the indirect function of evil. However, those fully in the Light do not need this test. And when put to the test they pass it – just like the non-fallen Light beings.

According to the law of karma, people are confronted with evil forces. Whether they learn the lesson is, again, a function of their free will. Many do not. Obviously, being evil or meeting evil is no cause of enlightenment, just like going into darkness does not cause the finding of light. At best it is an indirect cause – if someone finally happens to get the point, namely to get out. Having seen darkness, one might appreciate the light more. Having seen the destructive technocratic civilization, one might appreciate nature more. But, again, such a grateful attitude is only due to the individual's character and awakening; it is not the merit of the diabolic forces. As mentioned above, evil is not to be justified, it is to be corrected. And the first ones will be the last ones. The first who fell will be the last one to repent and confess.

Temptation and false promises

In the New Testament Satan is depicted as the 'lord of the world'[15] and as such he can offer his worshippers power over the world. This is how he also tried to tempt Jesus:

> Next, taking him to a very high mountain, the devil showed him all the kingdoms of the world and their splendour. And he said to him, 'All these I will give you, if you will fall at my feet and worship me.'

It is interesting to see how Jesus reacted. Not for a moment did he doubt Satan's capability of granting world domination, but he was immune to this temptation. Without hesitating he rejected the offer, saying:

> 'Away with you, Satan! For it is written, "Worship the Lord your God, and serve only him."' (Matt. 4.8–10)

There are, however, people who – unlike Jesus – only too willingly accept this offer.

Kali-yuga: The fall into utmost condensed matter

After the initial creation, all original planets and bodies were of a subtle consistency: 'God saw all he had made, and indeed, it was very good. [...] Thus the heavens and the earth were completed, and all their multitude' (Gen. 1.31–2.1). At this stage of evolvement the fall of angels had not yet occurred as 'everything was very good'.

The fall of the earth into a state of utmost density as extant today occurred much later, after the 'expulsion from Paradise'. According to the Vedic scriptures, it was not until the beginning of the 'age of Kali' (Kali-yuga) five thousand years ago that man found himself totally engrossed in three-dimensional limitation. The Sanskrit word 'Kali' literally means 'the force that cleaves, divides, wedges off', and is synonymous to the Greek word 'diabolical'. Kali* represents the influence that causes discord, conflict and hypocrisy on earth.

In this connection there is an astonishing parallel revealed by a mystical Christian source: 'Let us take a look at earthly events related to this *mysterium*. Christ descends on earth [...] and on the Hill of Golgotha wrests from death the resurrection form of man's physical body. [...]

---

* Not to be confused with the Goddess Kâlî who, as the embodiment of *kâla* (time), is above time and space, representing the divine energy (*shakti*) behind the transformative power of matter. Due to time personified (Kâlî), everything material is dissolved and reborn again. She is the female creative potency that destroys all masculine-materialistic power structures, cyclically reinstating a natural harmonious balance. (In the Kali-yuga, therefore, men started to fear the female potency and tried to oppress it with patriarchal power.)

And now, from spiritual science, we get to know about the shocking fact that *Lucifer had also descended on earth* and had incarnated in a human form almost 3,000 years before Christ. [...] Christ was then to follow his brother, who had now become his adversary, allowing Lucifer to precede him. This coincided with the beginning of the age of Kali, the "Dark Age", which for thousands of years has cut mankind off from perceiving and experiencing the spiritual realms, thus furthering the development of *earthbound* rationality. [...] Since Lucifer's incarnation 5,000 years ago man has increasingly relied on his reasoning faculty. A god had set the example, and gradually the whole world was captivated by his influence.'[16]

It is interesting to note *where* Lucifer incarnated:

> It was in the locality of Chinese culture of the third millennium BC; initially a culture that knew no gods – later they adopted gods from India – being a culture to which religion, divine service and prayer was unknown, devoid of anything that we would call religious introversion; no inward perception of the self; quite the contrary, a culture characterized by thorough immersion in and identification with external reality.[17]

> Lucifer's incarnation [...] has bestowed great and brilliant contributions upon humanity, first upon the Chinese culture itself – impressive achievements in arts, science and philosophy. [...] Lucifer wishes to demonstrate to man everything that he is able to achieve, disconnected from any guidance from the Divine.[18]

Parallel to Lucifer's incarnation, the divine avatar *Krishna* appeared in India. According to Vedic history Krishna left the earth in 3102 BC, which marked the end of the previous *yuga*. Almost at the same time (3113 BC) the great concluding cycle of the Mayan Calendar began, comprising a total of 5,125 years – now nearing its end.

For the last five thousand years China has played a mysterious role. Today, many people in the West suspect that in the Far East, in the empire of the Red Dragon, a giant is lurking. And nobody knows what he is up to.

Since the beginning of Kali-yuga, mankind has fallen into an increasingly materialistic and limited consciousness, and started to explore everything, including life, through one-sided research based on experimentation and exploitation. Profiting from this situation, destructive forces managed to increase their influence on earth.

At the same time, however, also positive and divine seeds have been planted. From the very beginning of this dark age, the divine beings had a long-term plan to make provisions for the 'new spring'. In order to initiate the return of the Light – the respiritualization of the earth and the ascension of mankind – the 'first-born Son' and other incarnations of the 'Father-Mother God' appeared amongst humanity. Unfortunately, though typical for the Kali-yuga, these personalities and the momentum they brought became misused.

It is not by chance that especially in the name of God, the most extreme forms of cruelty and godlessness have been committed, in all cultures, on all continents.

The infiltration and manipulation of religions

As a basic strategy, the *asuras* attempt to neutralize and even instrumentalize those who might be able to withstand them, first and foremost those who are religious. *Asuras* have a lot to do with religion. They fight it, and even more so, they infiltrate it because that is a double victory for them: they have disunited all these people, and furthermore, they can now use them for their own ends. Therefore, infiltration is much more effective than physical elimination. An infiltrated 'religion' is no longer a threat, it is a tool!

The means employed for infiltration are so perfidious that many of the religiously devout are beaten at their own game without even realizing it. It is the working of the two-faced negativity – applied to the field of religion.* 'Too much' conviction causes people to have 'too little' or no appreciation for other belief systems and their followers. Thinking themselves to be in the possession of the 'only truth', they consider all others to be wrong and 'misguided by Satan'.

Ironically, most of the 'others' have similar convictions, and so it

---

* A variation of the same principle can be seen in modern esoterism. Often, there is too little differentiation and too much naive optimism. One tends to say that there is nothing negative; the existence of dark forces is denied or said to be already overcome; whatever happens (and whatever you do) is good because it is a 'necessary experience'. In other words, in so-called religion people may be deceived by absolutism and indoctrination, in esoterism by relativism and ego-justification.

happens that they all build up denomi-national fronts, trying to either convert or fight 'the rest of the world'. And they all believe that God is on their side. In the name of God, they have become agents of the diabolic ('splitting') spirit. That is the meaning of being 'beaten at their own game without even realizing it'.

Vedic prophecy warns us that, in Kali-yuga, many *asuras* will appear under the guise of religiosity to misuse religion as an instrument of power. The Vedic culture itself was infiltrated by such beings who, incarnated as humans, took up powerful priestly positions and created a social system with them as leaders put in position by 'the grace of God'. All those who were not privileged to be favoured by these 'representatives of God', not to speak of those who still dared to be critical, could now be condemned as being 'offenders' and 'enemies of God'. And scriptures as well as the newly established social norms gave them the authority to oppress or kill these 'outcastes' and 'unfaithful ones'.

In one way or another, this matrix of 'religion' was enforced all over the world, not only by certain caste Brahmins and gurus in India but also by certain priests, bishops, popes, rabbis, shamans, lamas, sons of the sun, etc. In all these (seemingly) different religions, the negative forces adopted the same tricks and still use them today in attempting to check any new initiative:

1. A guru, prophet or leader is established as absolute; whatever he has said is then canonized and declared to be infallible; questioning this dogma is forbidden, sometimes even by penalty of death; all other revelations, interpretations and sources of knowledge are disregarded and rejected; this creates an ideological surrounding causing isolation and alienation of the individual.

2. The premise of absolutism serves as a base for all successors to establish their own authoritarian claims; dignitaries are idolized and immunized, and receive immense institutional power; by accepting such a position they themselves become instruments of manipulative forces; it is obsession, but outwardly, it is displayed as an aura of empowerment and charisma.

3. The next step is the establishment of institutional, often manipulative, structures ranging from small sectarian cults up to global religions and occult lodge systems; through the enforcement of dogmas and hierarchical rules, followers and members can be controlled through fear and social pressure, often combined with exclusiveness

and elitism. ('We, thanks to this scripture, revelation, secret lore, or channel medium, have unique truths; so be thankful and co-operate, and do not betray God by leaving his exclusive fold!')

4. In many cases, a very effective means of manipulation has been the envenoming of the male–female relationship. This began when men – as high priests, warriors and family chiefs ('patriarchs') – became the dominators of society; they declared sexuality and intimate aspects of love to be ungodly, sinful or abominable; women became the possession of men, and thus, both men and women were thrown into different forms of one-sidedness. Men and women who no longer have a balanced relationship are unable to empower each other through the initiation of love. Without this love, men are incapable of transforming their sexual urge, and resort to *compensation* (prestige, honour, violence, sometimes even perversion).

5. The ultimate compensation is the taste of power: to know more than others, to defeat others, to convert others, to be worshipped or feared by others. In the extreme it means claiming one's own group to be the only one truly redeemed or enlightened while considering everyone else to be ignorant and inferior. There are extremists in all religions who believe it only to be a question of time till everyone on earth will have to surrender to their belief, be it a world domination in the name of Christianity, Judaism, Islam, Hinduism, Buddhism or some sectarian ideology. The driving force behind all of these false hopes is Satan's promise of global power (see Matt. 4.9 and Luke 4.7).

Summary and outlook

Human beings on earth are exposed to various forms of a subtle-material, ethereal, electromagnetic and physical influence. All of these factors have causes and remote sources which are, directly or indirectly, dependent on conscious beings. Nothing happens by chance, neither the good nor the evil.

Without manipulators the world would look quite different. If people were offered truthful, positive information and alternatives, they would certainly be very interested. If mass media were to communicate the basics of higher knowledge, a lot of people would immediately change many aspects of their lives. If they were offered a real choice, they would never have chosen the direction things are taking today. They would have decided in favour of *alternative* research instead of nuclear, genetic and pharmaceutical research. Technocracy and exploitation would not be as dominant as they are today. If people were correctly informed, many would become vegetarians, and hardly anyone would support arms export, financial speculation and global centralization. And yet, these are the factors that dominate our lives in today's civilization.

Obviously it is not just the individual human being causing these things. There are external energies at work influencing man and imposing their own ideas.

According to mystical sources, the 'blocking of the Light' that causes shadows to be cast begins far beyond the earth, in the higher-dimensional worlds. As the reality beyond duality is the *eternal individuality* of all beings, free will is an intrinsic part of reality, too. And the highest form of free will is love: the voluntary oneness and harmony of the part with the Whole. All living beings have the freedom to choose whether they want to be in the Light or go against the Light. Within the world of polarity and potential duality both options exist.

The freedom of choosing one's focus of consciousness is the original – and the only *real* – application of free will. Nobody is forced to be in the Light, and nobody is forced to go against the Light. It is not necessary to go against the Light to find the 'real' reality. However, this is the very illusion of those who have fallen into the trap of the ego. The term 'ego' refers to the principle that blocks the Light; the ego is 'created' when beings decide to ignore the divine consciousness of their real identity as eternal parts of the Whole.

The psychology of the ego is based on a double fallacy – self-deception and 'self'-justification (which is nothing but an ego-justification).

Self-deception means accepting the illusion of becoming powerful, self-sufficient and content outside the harmony of the Whole (God). Those who have such a separatist mentality are unable to see their spiritual individuality beyond material duality. Having cut themselves off from the Source, they no longer obtain their life-energy from there. Consequently, they start to exploit the energy of other beings – animals, plants, human beings and the planet itself.

Ego-justification means attempting to rationalize one's ego trip and subsequent frustrations (by atheistic philosophies, guilt projection or self-pity). This brings about the illusory concept that acting under the ego is a 'necessary experience' and, therefore, even a beneficial decision.

The focus of our consciousness is dependent on our free will, and it is the key which determines our affinity and receptiveness. This is called the law of resonance. Understanding this is of vital importance, especially today, as mankind's history has entered a phase wherein the external struggle is no longer separate from the inner struggle. The dark forces are no longer only reaching for man's mind and intellect, they now want to absorb his entire consciousness, the being as such, including 'heart and soul'.

In the following chapter we will first examine *the individual aspect* of this battle: the role consciousness plays in meeting the different forms of outside influence, and their subtle effects on our free will – which is no longer that free when we allow ourselves to be influenced.

CHAPTER TWO

The Programming of Consciousness and How to Transcend It

The previous chapter concluded with the indication that, in the present phase of global polarization, the external struggle is no longer separate from the inner struggle. People are caught up in external situations with their entire being, having no time or energy left for their inner, spiritual life. If people resonate with this occupying influence, they will be influenced – and see no harm in it. Rather, as a prophetic warning says, they might even welcome it: 'And all the earth followed the beast with admiration. They worshipped the dragon because he had given his authority to the beast, and they worshipped the beast.' (Rev. 13.3–4)

It is of crucial importance where we direct the focus of our consciousness. This is the only real application of our free will, for it is this focus which determines our affinity and receptiveness, according to the law of resonance.

Inner strength, naturally, is the best protection. It stems from our original, spiritual consciousness. If we compromise and contaminate it, then weak points will come about in our subtle-material bodies, giving negative elements an access to affect our consciousness. Despite (or because of?) being the best protection, people's mental balance and clarity of thought are being undermined in many ways: by external stress, constant sensual irritation, various forms of addiction, bad food or malnutrition, and mental agitation due to anxiety, fear and artificial needs.

Mental restlessness is a basic characteristic of our time. This would become especially evident if people were to sit down and meditate. Who would be capable of remaining centred in his or her inner identity, free from disturbing thoughts and pictures popping into the mind? Try for some minutes not to think of past or upcoming job duties, of impressions received through radio, TV, cinema, videos, magazines and newspapers, and of private affairs. Try to concentrate on a prayer, on a mantra, or on visualizing spiritual energies and higher communication. Here, in this inner realm, is the door to all of our spiritual potentials. However, it is this door from which people are being diverted.

Let us recall the chess genius mentioned in the 'fore-story'. Imagine *you* had an unfailing memory and never forgot anything. Everything that you heard, saw, said, perceived and experienced would always remain present in your mind.

You would simply go mad.

Fortunately, we might be relieved to say, our memory is not that good. Most impressions do not remain in the conscious memory but instantaneously submerge into our subconscious. Many things are quickly forgotten. Other things are not even consciously perceived. But nevertheless, they have entered our consciousness. They are, literally speaking, im-pressions, namely conscious or subconscious imprints stamped into our mind.

As long as the inner balance is not affected, these impressions are not problematic. They become problematic only when one is no longer able to handle and 'digest' them. Then repression and indifference start, with impressions fermenting in the subconscious, carrying an explosive mental tension. Some cannot help but living out this destructive potential (by greed for power, brutality, perversions or by going berserk and running amok). Others cope with it indirectly by swimming in the mainstream, despite its self-destructive tendency, or by passivity and resignation in view of the overwhelming global problems. 'What can I do? Let us hope that someone else will do something.'

The focus of our consciousness determines what we do and refrain from doing. Every individual contributes his share to the collective consciousness of mankind. Even if we cannot directly influence our external circumstances (catastrophes, wars etc.), we can still decide how *they* influence *us*.

We cannot change others. We can only change ourselves. But, by changing ourselves, we also change the world because we are constituent parts of the world.

Consciousness is the essential determinant and the instrument of free will. Therefore, in manipulation the 'lever' is first positioned on people's consciousness, as explained in the introduction to this book.

What are the forms of subtle influence affecting our consciousness and rendering us susceptible to further influence? What is a negative, a positive and a spiritual orientation of consciousness? How can we liberate ourselves from negative bonds, and then become immune to such influence?

First, the ways to inner immunity have to be examined, as some of the following chapters, what to speak of certain world-wide occurrences to come, might otherwise cause fear, hate or helplessness. In reality, however, these aspects of our world are a great challenge and a great opportunity – if we can avoid falling, or being dragged, into duality.

The consequences of materialism

'For thousands of years man has been racking his brains over notions such as the "self", the "mind", or the "I". Ultimately, however, these notions are nothing but explanatory terms serving to illustrate an aspect of physics. [...] The self is inseparable from the commands diffused by neurons and synapses.'

These are the opening lines to an article published in the Swiss news magazine *FACTS*, 33/1997 (t.AR), with the headline: 'Our brain determines consciousness – Cerebral substance is the key to who we are.'

This article reveals the world-view of materialism, which states that life and consciousness are products of matter, nothing but 'an aspect of physics'. On the basis of this belief system many modern scientists argue that consciousness is inseparable from the brain just as heat is inseparable from fire; as fire causes heat, the brain causes consciousness and thoughts; when fire is extinguished, there is no longer heat, similarly, when the body dies, everything is over. – Sounds logical. But is it applicable to the phenomena of matter, life and consciousness?

Professor Richard Dawkins, one of the most influential evolutionary biologists of today, reveals what this view of life boils down to:

> The universe that we observe has those very qualities one would assume when there is no plan, no intention, neither good nor evil behind it; nothing but random and merciless indifference.[19]

Random, merciless indifference, devoid of good and evil – this, as certain people believe, is the 'unsentimental universal truth'. It is the opposite

Who am I?
The brain determines our consciousness.

This is one of many examples of materialistic propaganda: Consciousness is considered to be a product of the brain, and the question 'Who am I?' is suggestively answered in the sense of 'You are nothing but a material body'.

of the holistic world-view. It assumes that individuality is a product of matter, which is like saying 'light is produced out of darkness'. As shown in the following chapters, such concepts are quite 'exclusive' as those who adhere to them consider these 'truths' to be intelligible only to a few 'illuminated' men; the rest of the world may cling on to ideas of God, good and evil, which only proves that they are incapable of facing the 'ultimate truth'. On the basis of such convictions, the human being is considered to be nothing but a bio-computer made up of organic matter. And computers do not have a free will. They are meant to be manipulated and programmed.

If people's understanding of life is limited to a materialistic concept, they have no access to their real self and are not immune against negative influence. Identifying oneself with the mortal body makes one vulnerable and fearful.

However, the materialistic concept of life is neither logical nor substantiated by experience. Great mystics, divine revelations, paranormal phenomena, out-of-body experiences, natural intuition and research in reincarnation as well as holistic philosophy – all of this 'circumstantial evidence' points out that living entities are more than mortal bodies. We *have* a body and a brain, but we *are* not our body and brain. Life and self-consciousness are not produced by the brain.

Rather, the non-material individual (the soul) emanates consciousness and thus animates the material body. When the body is no longer animated by the presence of the soul, it decays.

In order to understand the workings of the subtle energies, one has to know about the metaphysical aspects of life, and this again will open up the door to the *spiritual* aspects of life.

The mental ocean and its elemental waves

tad-bhava-bhavitah: 'Consciousness determines existence.'
— *Bhagavad-gita* 8.6

Beyond duality there is spiritual individuality. This simple phrase is a world formula. It explains that matter is moulded and animated by conscious individuals who themselves are not products of matter. All energy is consciousness. Ultimately, all energy is contained within the consciousness of the absolute Individuality. There is no energy (consciousness) outside, or independent, of this absolute in-dividuality (oneness). Those who think so misidentify consciousness with matter, which proves that they themselves have lost the consciousness of their true identity.

Whether we are aware of our spiritual selves or not, in any case we *are* spiritual beings, and as such we emanate consciousness, which is our personal energy. Consciousness can be compared to a spotlight in a dark room. We are free to direct this spotlight in any direction, and by this decision we illuminate certain spots. These are the impressions that are reflected back into our consciousness or, to be more precise, into our mind. The mind is like a mirror or an unexposed film which we constantly expose to certain sensory perceptions. In this way, our mind registers an incessant flow of pictures and impressions.

The mind is a subtle-material element that constitutes the mental body, which again is a part of the subtle body, which permeates the gross-material (physical) body. In Sanskrit this subtle-material element is called *manas,* a word reflected in the Latin word *mens* (gen. *mentis*), from which the word *mental* is derived.

The mental body consists of a subtle substance that becomes shaped by our consciousness – our energy – according to its focus. This 'substance' is universally extant, constituting subtle bodies and subtle worlds. It is a material element of creation like 'earth', 'water', 'fire', 'air' and 'ether', which are also universally extant. The only difference is its subtle-material consistency. It is a hyperspace *fluidum* of an extremely high sensitivity. It reacts to all conscious stimuli, registering ('filming') each single one of them, either consciously or unconsciously.

Just like gross-material elements are shaped into visible forms, the subtle-material elements are shaped into *mental* forms: thoughts, feelings, desires and emotions. Mental energy is a creative element of the universe, and a portion of it is assembled around each thinking being, constituting his or her mental body. This element serves as a carrier of mental images and forms. This is why we experience thoughts and dreams as tangible images. However, these images are not limited to the private cinema within our head!

Every thought, feeling and emotion is a mental form. On the level of the cosmic mental element all of our thoughts, feelings and emotions appear as visible and *tangible forms,* and as such they are perceived by the subtle beings that inhabit this level. It is like being a diver who exhales bubbles of air. Those who are up on the boat see these bubbles appear within the reach of their perception, i.e. on the surface level, and these bubbles show them where the diver is. Similarly, the subtle beings perceive the bubbles of our mental creations as they appear on the level of their dimension. (If our mental creations are not harmonious but tainted with anger, hate, fear, intoxication etc., they may serve as an inviting signal to subtle beings of a similar frequency.)

As already mentioned, for higher-dimensional beings every thought is an immediate reality. Actually, the same is true for us! Every thought is an immediate reality, not on the gross-material but on the *subtle-material* level. If thoughts, feelings and desires are strong enough, they may also manifest on the external, gross-material level – through work, an arrangement of destiny, a miraculous fulfilment of a desire, or a psychosomatic reaction (causing some disease or a sudden healing). In all cases it is the mind that functions as the 'interface' between consciousness and physical matter.

The universal element 'mind' can be compared to an ocean of endless fluidal energy. Just like churning up water causes ripples and waves, every mental and emotional impulse of consciousness creates waves of subtle-material energy, which take on an autonomous existence. Like waves in water they are of a temporary nature but they can persist for a very long time – *till they are neutralized by a conscious counter-impulse.*

Usually, thoughts and emotions give way to new ones without posing any difficulty. One simply focuses on something else, and the former impression passes into one's conscious or subconscious memory. However, strong mental creations can take on a more persistent form if they are not properly processed. Such autonomous forms of mental energy are called 'elementals'. At this point a mental bubble becomes a 'balloon'. It floats by itself while remaining connected to its sender by a 'string' of mental energy.

Elementals are like subtle-material computer chips capable of programming a person's mental and physical reactions, and basic patterns of consciousness. Their persistence becomes apparent when they are very strong, so strong that they can even force a person's behaviour against his or her will. Elementals are especially intense if they happen to be shaped out of sexual desires, lust, hate, jealousy, fear or out of a traumatic situation. Such elemental programming can cause obsession, addiction, or impulsive reactions to certain situations.

Every impression perceived leaves its trace in our conscious or subconscious memory as it is registered on a 'mental film'. This psychological mechanism shows that it certainly matters what impressions we allow to enter our consciousness. Even if we think that they do not have an adverse effect, they still may have. For example, people may think that it is simply fun watching films with scenes of murder and violence. However, through this simple (almost daily) act of seeming relaxation they become carriers and multipliers of destructive impressions, and thus contribute their share to the collective mental 'data bank' and its explosive potential.

Subtle-material dictations

Every human being is exposed to various forms of subtle-material influence: his own elementals, elementals of other people, and astral entities. It is, therefore, essential to live in a pure and conscious manner so as to avoid harming or weakening one's subtle-material body. By nature, every individual is immune to the encroachments of 'astral parasites'.

However, in times of rampant materialistic ignorance man forfeits his immunity and becomes susceptible to all kinds of influence.

Certain behavioural and physical symptoms can be indicative of the presence of some elementals. In such cases, lacking a better diagnosis, materialistic brain-psychologists resort to terms like 'psychosomatic diseases' or 'neuroses'. Sensitive people, however, can perceive these subtle 'tumours' that seemingly have a life of their own:

> Clients describe these foreign presences as having their own desires, emotions and thoughts. The presences are perceived as having an existence of their own, even though it interferes in many ways with the clients' psychology and vital functions. [...] In nearly all cases, clients report that 'the thing' is draining them, tapping from their life force. This is quite a constant feature [...] In most cases, clients report that when they eat certain foods, the presence reacts. Moreover, the presence can create cravings or compulsive desires for these particular foods. The substance that is mentioned by far the most often is sugar. When clients are asked 'Could it be that there are some foods that "the thing" enjoys?', more than half of them immediately answer 'sugar', 'sweets' or 'chocolate'. Other foods often mentioned by clients are heavy foods, cakes and white bread (meaning yeast), fried foods and fats, cheese, and junk food in general. In other cases, meat and spicy or salty foods are preferred. It is not unusual for meat and spicy foods to be mentioned together. [...] Surprisingly, one vegetable is often reported by clients among the 'entity cravings' – tomatoes.* [...] Apart from sugar and other foods, clients sometimes also report that the presence is responsible for other cravings: coffee, tobacco, alcohol and various other drugs [...] Yet this is not to suggest that all addictions are due to entities! An attitude that blamed entities for all human troubles would be just as childish as one based on a complete denial of the experience.[20]

Resonance caused by elementals

Elementals are autonomous, but not independent. They are completely dependent on the person who produced them, even though he or she may not be aware of their existence.

Thoughts, feelings and emotions manifest on higher-dimensional levels as animated mental forms and are perceived by corresponding astral beings. In this connection the saying 'like attracts like' shows its

---

* Tomatoes, a nightshade plant, belong to those foods that overacidify the body, which means they disturb the balance of base and acid.

deeper meaning. According to the vibration of our elementals we open ourselves up to in-fluences of an identical wavelength.

The law of resonance applies both in the negative and the positive sense, throughout our daily lives. Positive and divine states of consciousness do not create elementals as they do not cause any psychological blocking. They are naturally beyond the dark astral levels.

However, low-vibrating mental forms act as a nourishing 'tonic' for subtle-material energy vampires. To our eyes, negative thoughts, feelings and emotions may be something abstract and formless. But to the eyes of certain astral beings these mental creations appear as tangible forms which can be tapped or even consumed. Therefore, such beings are very interested in provoking negative mental waves. Some of them may even take birth on earth and become influential people who are able to manipulate the world situation in such a way as to provide 'food' for their fellow spirits.

There are beings that live on fear, rage and horror. Today, these elementals are artificially aroused and increased: by wars and violence, by constant reports on TV, or simply for entertainment (books, films, computer games). Those who tune into the frequency of this frenzy will become attractive to astral beings that are just looking for such invitations. Such parasites hook on to elementals which they use as a crack to access a person's mental energy field. As a consequence this person's urges and thoughts become influenced by alien impulses that can lead to compulsive behaviour, psychological problems or obsessive fanaticism (in sports, music, religion etc.). Here we have an important reason why many people cannot help chain-smoking, taking drugs, watching TV, eating certain foods, performing routine sex, etc. Once under 'alien dictation' they are no longer their own masters but slaves to astral beings who drive them to do these things. Some may think that it is their own conviction (like in religious fanaticism). Others may be aware that they are not fully in control, admitting that they are presently unable to break some undesired habits even though they would like to.

When many people focus their attention on the same subject, event or individual, the food generated for astral beings is even more 'attractive'. This happens, for instance, in the hypnotic effect of mass events, ideological group dynamics, and personality cults. Formerly, people had to be assembled in big arenas for this purpose. Nowadays they can be assembled by the millions, even billions, in front of the TV, and they all receive the same in-formation. Are we being programmed by TV programmes?

If nobody received (consumed) these pictures and programmes, they would simply go unheard and unseen, dying away 'in the ether'. *It takes a living person to transform electromagnetic waves into mental forms!* When we hook ourselves up to this technomagical network, we pump our energy into the system. Through us – each individual serving as a conscious medium – one programme becomes multiplied and animated millions and millions of times. Our minds are the screens onto which these foreign vibrations are being projected, and there, in our minds, they are transformed into living pictures.

In this way, we become receivers of transmitted impressions and, simultaneously, producers of corresponding mental forms. Food for certain beings ... ? This may explain the magic of mass media, especially when pictures of war and terror are constantly reproduced within the minds of a planet's population, like in the case of the 9/11 events and the subsequent wars. What is being prepared?

> With our base thoughts we are feeding these asuric beings. In those [base thoughts] these beings then embody and drag man down.[21]

> Asuric energies embody in the emanations of passionate thought of men; as a result, certain astral entities are created – so-called 'artificial elemental beings', which can cause greater harm than natural elemental beings. They arise from the mire of sensuality and are always useful for evoking magical influence with intended evil effects.[22]

War starts in the mind

The global materialistic system can only survive within the dualistic tension of supply and demand. Stagnation is tantamount to a threat to this system. Content people are a potential danger because they might be interested in other things than mere production and consumption. Apparently, this system depends on people never finding real, inner peace! Is this the reason why the world is constantly being flooded with new needs, demands and products? At least one thing is obvious: The result is not content satisfaction but restless gratification.

In order to avoid a saturation or stagnation of the turnover, consumption has to be continuously increased by the creation of new artificial needs, by new ways of propaganda, and by opening up new markets. If that is no longer possible, consumption has to be expanded by yet another method, namely by *increasing destruction*. As history has shown, the most effective means to this end are economic crises, financial crashes and wars. In such cases, the winners – those who secretly incited the destruction – can start to build things up again. Obviously the power of the global players is based on a vicious circle: systematic destruction as a means to increase production.

As everything starts in the mind, destruction also starts with a mental 'preparation of the field'. People have to be tuned into the frequency of violence and destruction, which indeed is happening. And people do not realize it. An example of this is seen in the inconsistency of many 'non-violent' citizens. They are against war and terror but in their spare time they watch documentaries and films about wars, murders and terror – with the presentations becoming increasingly cruel and brutal. Why? Because nowadays the public even *demands* such information and entertainment. Otherwise they would not watch it and zap into another channel. The producers, of course, justify their presentations by claiming: 'They are informative as well as preventive. Such shocking news and films are warning examples. Realizing the brutality and tragedy of wars etc., people will refrain from them.'

Now quite honestly – do we really have to see bloody, violent scenes daily to realize that war, murder, rape etc. are bad? How dull must a person be if he needs 'information' of this kind? The fact of the matter is: *the more these things are broadcast, the more they increase!* By allowing such images and thoughts to penetrate our minds we unknowingly become carriers of destructive vibrations. Numerous imprints of violence are implanted into people's minds by newspapers, magazines, television, computer games, the internet etc. If information and warning were the true aims, then these imprints would not have to be intensified by endless variations. Knowing about the subtle reality of mental forms, we can begin to understand what this focus of consciousness provokes and what forces are being fed.

The global invocation of destructive vibrations prepares the field for these very things to happen. That is a simple but subtle law of nature. Nevertheless, most people think that they are voluntarily reading and watching the stuff presented to them. They are convinced that their drifting in the 'mainstream' is an act of their free will – which is an illusion. At this point they have already disposed of their free will. They are only choosing between things and options that are offered to them by others, like the choosing of what newspaper to read or what TV programme to watch.

As mentioned in the introduction, this loss of free will is the effect of efficient manipulation. It is difficult to force people to do something against their will. However, they will do the same thing without objection if they act under the impression that they are doing it voluntarily, or that it is 'necessary' – for example, accepting new laws and enforced restrictions in the name of security, anti-terrorism, anti-cult information, or fight against new diseases. The easiest way to bring about total control is to create an atmosphere (atmos-fear!) of fear and intimidation. And this, again, starts in the mind.

How to dissolve elementals

Being mental forms of (suppressed) emotions and feelings, elementals are not an eternal doom. They can be dissolved. Clairvoyant people who are able to see subtle-material energies emphasize that negative elementals can affect us only to the extent that we allow them to, according to the law of resonance:

> If we have constructed a bad personality, we inevitably form a centre of attraction which draws to us the corresponding elementals which others have created or are creating around us […]; the acceptance and assimilation of these elementals is purely our own choice and responsibility. […] There are, then, in our psychonoetic environment good and bad elementals. There are angels, too – and demons! It is for us to create a magnetic pole which will attract the one and repel the other. No demon can bother any human being who does not resonate with the same frequency.[23]

> The person against whom we project an evil elemental will be affected only to the extent that he, too, vibrates on the same frequency as ourselves. Otherwise it will hit his aura and bounce back to us seven times its original force.[24]

Elementals are either created by us or directed against us. In any case, they can affect us only as long as we resonate to them, either by failing to dissolve them (if they are ours) or to withstand them (if they are from a foreign source). The more we identify ourselves with such mental 'implants' the more they influence us by vexing our consciousness with thoughts, desires and feelings; in this way, we are repeatedly forced to act in a certain manner, even against our will. It is a mental programming which eliminates free will to a large extent.

However, the mind is not the highest level of the human psyche. As indicated by the *Bhagavad-gita* (3.42), elementals can be dissolved through *higher insight:* 'Mind (*manas*) is superior to gross matter and the sense organs, but above the mind is intelligence (*buddhi*).'

Manias, fears and cravings (negative elementals) have power over us only as long as we are not aware of them. The moment we realize the vanity or harmfulness of these mental programs we can take deliberate steps to disengage ourselves from them.

This may sound easier than it is. Simply saying, 'I don't want to smoke anymore' (or 'I no longer want to have depressions, inferiority complexes, fits of anger', etc.), does not help in most cases. Why? Because it is a negative concentration on the problem. It means fighting against these desires and feelings, which usually makes them only stronger. Fighting against elementals means feeding them with our mental energy. Through struggle or suppression we focus our attention on them, and thus intensify their influence on us, till our negative resistance breaks down into a 'positive' giving in. 'If you can't beat them, join them!'

Usually, in the normal flow of mental waves, impressions do not leave harmful traces. For example, can you remember what you ate exactly one year ago or one week ago? Hardly. You can remember it only when it was extremely good or bad or connected to some extraordinary experience. If, in a larger time frame, a past scene was terrible or even traumatic (for example, if one choked to death on a bone), then it might have left an elemental that still, subconsciously, exists in the present lifetime.

As mentioned above, elementals are created only when an excessive concentration of mental energy has not been neutralized by the normal flow of life. In most cases, such a paralysed reaction is due to a traumatic situation in which we 'stop the film'. The wave in the mental ocean becomes 'frozen'. It remains undissolved and is suppressed, leading to corresponding subconscious affinities and dictations, if the imprint is – or was – very strong, because the creation of an elemental may lie far back in time. Such an elemental programming can be the cause of physical problems, unwanted sexual complexes or feelings of addiction, hate, jealousy, fear, inferiority, self-pity etc.

Psychological problems caused by (ele)mental programming can be solved from the perspective of *buddhi*, which means changing to a higher level of consciousness. We no longer identify ourselves with the problem, and are thus enabled to view it from a distance. By seeing ourselves as separate from the problem, we can find the way back to ourselves, understanding what is actually important and what is not – which is the actual meaning of *buddhi*, 'intelligence', namely 'the power of differentiation' (from Lat. *inter-legere,* 'to choose between two things; to distinguish').

True intelligence (*buddhi*) means to realize, with spiritual discernment, that we are neither material nor mental beings. In this way, new sources of inner strength become accessible, enabling us to remain uninfluenced by material or mental conditions, be they good or bad.

The higher perspective of *buddhi* enables us to heal all emotional 'wounds' and to overcome any problem that may burden us. This is especially effective when we are not alone but surrounded by an atmosphere of real love and oneness. 'For where two or three gather together in my name, there I am in their midst' (Matt. 18.20). In such a blessed situation we are connected to the real Source of all love and healing. Should some aftermath of the former mental programming show up again, then, relying on our increased self-awareness and higher consciousness, we strongly say: 'No, I do not want it and I will not!' We address the elemental as an autonomous entity (if necessary in a loud voice, and together with others) and we simply dissolve it – provided our determination is firm enough. If this is the case, the elemental disappears like a soap bubble without leaving any further shadow. This is the easiest method of approaching the problem: letting go of the mental image and neutralizing it with a higher impulse, especially by forgiving oneself and others.

If certain propensities or problems happen to be too grave to be shaken off that easily, one should consult a person of confidence. Again, the advice of 'two or three gathering in my name' is relevant. Speaking about a problem instantaneously reduces its weight. In a deep conversation or professional session one might even try to find out the traumatic root cause of a particular negative program in order to melt the 'frozen wave'. Often, these shocking experiences happened in the distant past, in previous lifetimes.*

The elevation of consciousness and the impeding forces

Control of one's mind (*manas*) and a clear consciousness (*buddhi*) are the basic goals of all forms of yoga and serious esoteric practice.

> One must deliver oneself with the help of the mind, and not degrade oneself. The mind is the friend of the incarnated being, and his enemy as well. / For those who have conquered the mind, the mind is the best of friends; but for those who have failed to do so, the mind will remain their greatest enemy. (*Bhagavad-gita* 6.5–6)

Whether the mind is our friend or enemy depends on our focus of consciousness. Switching to the level of intelligent differentiation is impossible unless we know about higher aims in life. Otherwise, why should one bother to free oneself of mental urges and cravings? 'They are the spice of life and stimulate our daily pleasures – what's wrong with that?'

Those of this opinion are in ignorance of their spiritual identity. People who allow their minds to be agitated and deviated from the spiritual source of life are unable to detach themselves from bodily identification and remain prone to manipulation, false promises, and fear.

Undermining the path of elevation is characteristic for *asuras* who feed on mental energies drawn out of agitation, fear, agony etc. Negative elementals are the 'holes' through which they gain access to the consciousness of men. That is why they are dependent on people being kept in materialistic ignorance about the metaphysical and spiritual backgrounds of life.

---

* In view of these far-reaching solutions we begin to understand how fatal the materialistic world-view is. It says that mental processes are only a function of the brain, that there are no previous lifetimes, and that there is no conscious, non-material self beyond the physical body. No wonder, therefore, that materialistic psychology is so helpless in helping people, and often resorts to pharmaceutical treatments – which make the problems even worse because they completely miss the subtle-material aspects of the human psyche.

In contrast to manipulative forces, divine beings always further an atmosphere of inner peace and contentment. Self-control, purity, far-sightedness, simplicity, purified consciousness, openness, love – these are the criteria that nourish spiritual advancement.

Love and forgiveness

Nothing in this world of relativity is absolutely negative. The negative also has a function within God's creation, even though its agents are not intentionally fulfilling this function.

Seen from a spiritual perspective, the function of the negative is to shake up, and the function of the positive is to encourage. The positive, however, is not absolutely positive either, for it still binds the individual to the material world. Those who do not transcend the positive side of duality will stagnate in a false sense of self-contentment which stifles a person's desire for further detachment. In such a case, confrontation with the negative can prove to be very conducive because it awakens the individual from his 'sleep' and imaginary peace. This is the *divine* purpose of the negative, for nothing in material creation exists independently of God.

The dark forces are part of material duality and cannot be eliminated. They may be banished from the earth for a while, but then they persist on other levels of existence, trying to regain influence over the earth. This 'playing God' in the material world will never cease. The only thing in our power is *to end the game for ourselves.*

The question, therefore, is: How do I cope with the negative?

'Hate [reject] the sin, but love the sinner!'[25] This is the decisive answer given by Jesus as recorded in his apocryphal teachings.

While rejecting the deed, one forgives the doer. Forgiving does not mean accepting or approving the negative. It simply means that *for oneself* one has let go of the negative. The inability to forgive shows that one still holds fast to negative feelings, thus binding oneself to the past.

Situations which make an act of forgiveness difficult are usually connected to traumatic experiences, violence or meanness. They may have occurred in this lifetime or in a former lifetime. Having remained undigested, the impressions of such situations are buried in the subconscious and keep elementals alive. If they cannot be dissolved otherwise, one may have to dig up the respective situation and solve it 'posthumously' here and now.

Elemental bondage is transcended when we are able to handle all of these memories without weakness or anti-negative reactions.

Here, *weakness* would mean: refusing to face the situation, giving in to fear and resignation, or resorting to suppression.

Anti-negative reactions would mean: wanting to fight evil with its counterpart, taking revenge (directly or indirectly) and maintaining feelings of hate.

Both of these reactions are doomed to failure because they do not break the vicious circle of double-faced negativity.

Ultimately, only those who have attained divine love are capable of truly forgiving. Such people do not judge according to duality because they accept both the 'good ones' and the 'evil ones' for what they really are: eternal spirit souls, parts of God, who have more or less forgotten their true identity, seeking satisfaction in external circumstances.

For all these reasons divine revelations and teachers emphasize the importance of forgiveness, and the same is done in this book. That is why it started with highlighting the principles of individuality, free will, self-responsibility and love (as the perfection of free will). On this basis we will be able to read about the intricate backgrounds of world history – no matter how shocking they are – without falling into feelings of hate or helplessness. We will discern the godless motive which caused the respective actions, and understand that we are called to forgive the evil-doers so that they may at one point realize the futility of their endeavours.

'The duty of a saintly person is to cultivate the quality of forgiveness (*kshama*), which is illuminating like the sun. Someone who is *kshamina* ('able to forgive') supremely harmonizes with the Absolute.' (*Shrimad-Bhagavatam* 9.15.40)

Differentiating without judging

When discussing the topics of good and evil there is a common 'esoteric' argument: 'You should not judge according to good and evil. That is dualistic thinking. Ultimately there is nothing wrong or evil. Everything has a purpose.'

The latter is true. Everything has a purpose – evil as well. But still evil remains evil. It would be a mistake to justify it through its divine purpose. The divine purpose is not inherent in the evil, it is there only if we perceive it through enlightened consciousness. It is like seeing darkness as an indicator of the fact that there must be light somewhere (as darkness is nothing but absence of light). This truth is not inherent in the darkness and can be grasped only by those whose consciousness is not limited to the domain of darkness.

The quote 'do not judge' is taken from the famous Sermon on the Mount: 'Do not judge so that you may not be judged; for with the judgement you make you will be judged.' (Matt. 7.1–2). Right after that Jesus continued (7.3): 'Why, then, do you observe the splinter in your brother's eye, but do not notice the rafter in your own eye?' And then (7.5–6): 'Hypocrite! First take the rafter out of your own eye […]. Do not give what is holy to the dogs, and do not throw your pearls before the swine […].'

Obviously, 'do not judge' does not mean 'do not differentiate'! Jesus often differentiated very critically. Some men he even called 'fools and blind ones […] snakes, brood of vipers.' (Matt. 23.17, 33)

The topic of 'not judging' is an essential teaching if not *the* essential teaching of all divine religions and mystery schools. Being easily misunderstood it was revealed only within the innermost circles, for it takes a transcendental perspective beyond duality to understand it. It means *differentiating without judging*.

It is true: good and evil only exist in duality. But there they do exist, and it is absurd to say that, in the world of duality, 'everything is good' or 'there is nothing wrong'. It is the very characteristic of duality that there *is* good and evil, right and wrong.

As explained in Chapter One, duality comes about when one decides to leave the divine oneness – the harmony of the part and the Whole – in order to start an ego trip, which means forgetting of one's real identity. This is an act of free will, just as remaining in the consciousness of oneness is an act of free will. Nobody is forced to leave or to remain. To choose one's direction of consciousness is the original freedom every being has.

The perfection of free will is expressed by living in voluntary oneness with God, untainted by ego diversions – and that is pure, divine love. It is the perspective of seeing everything in the light of God's will, including the dark and satanic forces. Those who live in this consciousness deal with the positive and the negative *equally but not identically*. They meet both with the same attitude of love, but the expression of this love can be very different. Love is not a sentimental and blind naivety. Through love one can differentiate in the most sensitive way. What is truly good (= divine)? What is relatively good (reflecting love), and what is evil (denying or fighting love)? How can I react in each case in the spirit of divine love?

In practice, love means acting for the supreme benefit of all beings without expecting anything in return. A term often used in this context is 'unconditional love'. What does it mean to act for the supreme benefit of those who are deluded and evil? We may not be able to directly do something good for them as they would not accept it. Trying to act in this way would be a sentimental transgression of the command: 'Do not give what is holy to the dogs, and do not throw your pearls before the swine.' The best you can do in the confrontation with evil forces is not to allow them to influence yet another person, namely you, as this would drag them even deeper into darkness. It would mean expanding their ego wall, which blocks off the light, and it would take that much longer for them to return to the light. You would have allowed them to increase the excess of their guilt, and you would be held responsible for that, too. Victims are also part of the 'game'!

Therefore, when Satan came to seduce Jesus with an offer of global power, Jesus answered, 'Away with you, Satan!' This was not an expression of hate or fear but of *unconditional love!* Through this clear differentiation and demarcation Jesus protected Satan from falling into even deeper darkness. It was a perfect usage of free will according to God's will.

Confrontation with good and evil is inevitable in this world of duality. Those in divine consciousness see all of these external situations as different forms of the same spiritual challenge:

Can I remain unshaken in my attitude of love?
Or will I be moved into feelings of duality?
Will positive things tempt me to become egotistic and
complacent? Will I begin to consider myself better than others?
Will negative things provoke me into hate, revenge, resignation,
or self-pity? Will I take on the role of a victim? Will I start to

Liberation through self-control, love and forgiveness

'Those whose minds are established in equanimity have, while still in this world, transcended the perspective of the mortals. Like the Absolute (*brahman*), they are beyond material influence, and thus they see everything in connection with the Absolute. / A person who neither rejoices upon obtaining something pleasant nor despairs upon obtaining something unpleasant, who is of clear discernment (*buddhi*), who is undeluded and who is fully aware of the Absolute (*brahman*), lives in *brahman* (spiritual consciousness). / Being unattached to external things, such a person finds inner peace and happiness and, concentrating on the Absolute through self-realization (*brahma-yoga*), attains happiness that is not influenced by material conditions.' (*Bhagavad-gita* 5.19–21a)

'Fear arises when a living entity misidentifies himself with the material body as it [such misidentification] directs the consciousness to something external and transient.' (*Shrimad-Bhagavatam* 11.2.37)

'Self-realization means to be fully satisfied due to knowledge and wisdom. One who is firmly fixed in such a consciousness is self-controlled and is called yogi. He sees everything – whether it be sand, stones or gold – with equipoised vision. / Seeing benefactors, friends, enemies, neutrals, mediators, envious people, relatives, saints and sinners with the same attitude [of love], is the characteristic of those truly having a transcendental perspective.' (*Bhagavad-gita* 6.8–9)

'You have heard that it was said, "Thou shalt love thy neighbour, and hate thine enemy." But I say this to you, Love your enemies and pray for those who persecute you, so that you may be children of your Father in heaven; for he makes his sun rise on the evil and on the good, and sends rain to fall on the righteous and on the unrighteous. For if you love those who love you, what reward do you have? Do not even the tax collectors do the same? And if you greet only your brothers and sisters, what more are you doing than others? Do not even the Gentiles do the same? You must therefore set no bounds to your love, just as your heavenly Father sets none to his [or: Be perfect, therefore, as your heavenly Father is perfect].' (Matt. 5.43–8)

'Love your enemies, do good to those who hate you, bless those who curse you, pray for those who treat you badly. If anyone strikes you on the cheek, offer the other as well [in order to break the vicious circle of beating and beating back]. [...] Be compassionate just as your Father is compassionate. Do not judge, and you will not be judged; do not condemn, and you will not be condemned; forgive, and you will be forgiven.' (Luke 6.27–37) doubt the power of love, and the absolute power of God? Or will I remain sovereign and uninfluenced? Will I be able to stay focussed on the divine aim, without losing the view of eternity?

From the perspective of eternity, nothing is really important except that of eternal, spiritual value. For those who live in divine consciousness, ambitions of prestige and honour, or hate and revenge, are totally irrelevant. Their criteria of differentiating are not derived from the ego, and therefore they no longer judge, 'This is good, being advantageous to me', or, 'This is bad, being disadvantageous to me'. They remain equal-minded regarding good and bad, seeing both as an impetus to act in the consciousness of oneness: love, detachment and forgiveness. They do not fall into dualistic scheming like projecting false hopes on the so-called good side or guilt on the so-called bad side. Even the most evil forces that manipulate, humiliate, torture etc. are nothing but Light beings that have fallen into the extremes of darkness. Cursing them or surrendering unto them would not help anybody. But who would like to help such evil forces anyway? And who would be *able to* help them? Only those who are neither intimidated nor seduced by them, those who are beyond duality.

If we live in such a divine consciousness, then, *for us,* there is no longer any evil, which means that we do not take evil as evil but view it from a transcendental position. However, there is still evil 'out there' wanting to deviate us from this very consciousness. To say 'for me, there is no evil' does not mean that there is no evil in the world. There is, and there is not, depending on what perspective we take. In other words, there is evil but we do not judge or condemn it for being so, because this would limit it to its fallen state, and it would limit us to the same matrix of dualistic thinking. In every situation a person in divine consciousness decides to react in a way that is most beneficial to all, which is the meaning of *differentiating*. Without differentiating there is no deciding. Only on the basis of real differentiation can we stop judging and start to see everything in the light of divine love, even dictators, war lords, and torturers. 'Father, forgive them, for they do not know what they are doing' (Luke 23.34).

In short, differentiating without judging means: not to ignore duality but to transcend it.

Summary and outlook

The human mind is an unlimited reservoir of impressions. Once in there, these impressions influence the direction of our consciousness and, consequently, our view of life and our actions. Therefore, those in the position of materialistic power try 'their best' to shape people's consciousness so as to secure and, ultimately, enforce subordination.

If indeed nothing happens by chance, then wars, crises and political manoeuvres do not happen by chance, either. People do not desire these things, yet still they happen. Obviously, there must be powers at work who want – or at least do not mind – these things, and it would be quite normal to see them as guilty and evil.

Reality, however, does not stop on this level, and limiting ourselves to this relative reality would keep us in the vicious circle of duality; we would continue to see others as enemies and ourselves as victims. We would see ourselves as powerless and others as more powerful, and fail to recognize the spiritual equality of us all. Duality is a game of the ego which we cannot end for others, but we can transcEnd it for ourselves.

Instead of remaining stuck in negative mental programs, like hate, shock or self-pity (thus creating elementals which make us vulnerable), we must restore our original, spiritual consciousness – if we want to discover what we really are: parts of the Whole, eternal and divine. Then, we will also realize that all other beings are eternal and divine, including those who have eclipsed their true identity through the shadows of the ego.

Beyond the levels of duality (= relative reality) is the absolute reality: the conscious harmony of the parts with the Whole. And this harmony is an expression of divine love. 'Love God with all your heart, and with all your soul, and with all your mind. This is the greatest and first commandment. The second is as important: love your neighbour as you love yourself. All other laws and prophetic words are secondary to these two commandments' (Matt. 22.37–40). In this way, with a few words, Jesus summarized the essence of oneness, love and free will.

Divine love, being the perfection of free will, is the most powerful consciousness. It is not something weak, blind or naive. Rather, it immediately senses all forms of misuse of free will, just as light clearly demarcates all forms of shadow. With divine love one has an absolute criterion to differentiate without judging. What is love, and what is non-love? What is God consciousness, and where do the projections of the ego start?

With this power of differentiation one can always act in a spiritually sovereign way, without being influenced by intimidation or temptation. If one is satisfied in God consciousness, one has nothing to lose and nothing to gain in this world. One is 'in the world' but not 'of it'. Duality in itself means separation, and this separation is 'sin', being the effect of a dividing ('diabolic') mentality. The transcendental maxim 'Hate [reject] the sin and love the sinner' can be applied to all situations of duality. Only those who love can forgive, and by forgiving they become free from the entanglement of beating and beating back. They do not dwell on the faults of others, but emanate spiritual enlightenment. Even in the confrontation with dark forces they never react with fear, hate or resignation, but with the strength of love and forgiveness.

In other words, those who perceive all beings as eternal parts of the Whole are holy ('whole; in harmony; non-diabolic') and are able to see the world from a 'holystic' perspective. Such God-conscious people are truly revolutionary because they dissolve ignorance, the substratum of all darkness, by emanating the light of transcendental knowledge.

The following chapters will demonstrate how unholy people misinterpret spiritual matters and, as a consequence, operate in diabolic manners. Their half-truths are sometimes hard to differentiate from the divine truths, but the practical fruits show that they do differ.

Destructive and manipulative actions are reflections of an egocentric mentality which, to some extent, is present in every one of us as well. The purpose of this second chapter was to show how we can purify our consciousness and live in divine resonance, and thus become immune against all forms of non-divine influence. Empowered through our connection to the Source, we can discern the 'sin' and still love the sinners, and perceive the higher truths beyond. This spiritual ability of 'differentiating without judging' is essential as we are heading for many challenging disclosures – in the following chapters and in the near future.

CHAPTER THREE

Covert Forces behind the Scenes

Nothing happens by chance. This is especially true for events in world politics. Wars and revolutions require international planning, armament and financing. One drastic example of this truth is the atrocious bloodshed that marked the beginning of the twentieth century: the First World War (1914–18) and the massacres in Russia following the so-called Great October Revolution (1917). Today we know that this decisive coup towards internationalization and world-wide technocracy had been merely the first phase in a campaign leading to the next step, a second world war, which then actually took place.

The number of publications about the multi-layered backgrounds of world history has ostensibly increased over the past ninety years. They are, however, either deliberately ignored or discredited by official historians, who coined the catchword 'conspiracy theory' to debunk or ridicule any perspective that deviates from the version of history as presented by those who shape it. The latter also control the mass media which repeat this version over and over again until everybody believes it. And those of a different opinion have no real chance to match the world dominating 'news agencies' in reaching the masses. Thus, young people studying history hardly get any information about those facts that would indicate the existence of covert forces behind the scenes.

This is quite astonishing as the subject matter has never really been secret. There have always been observers who knew about the obscure 'back stage' forces – due to their insider knowledge or simply through common sense.

Let us first have a look at some key events of Phase One. In this early stage, the 'organizers' had still been forced to act quite openly because their infrastructure was not yet fully established. Actually, these events were mainly staged to further the establishment of this very infrastructure on the levels of money, technology and global control. (In this regard, the whole twentieth century has been a successive preparation, as revealed in Part II of this book.)

Nowadays the First World War and the Russian Revolution are of minor historical interest. Numerous films and documentaries have been made about the *Second* World War, and they mostly avoid the topic of WW I or present it as something remote and isolated.

Still, it is a fact that the Second World War was a result of the First. Germany, the initiator of WW II, had been devastated after WW I. The population was decimated, living in ruins, with hundreds of thousands suffering (and dying) due to the artificially caused famine. 'During the four years of war (1914–18) Germany had to suffer the loss of two million soldiers fallen or missing in action, as well as 750,000 civilians as victims of the food blockade. The total casualty count of all belligerent nations was about 8.5 million. The question concerning the purpose of these casualties could not be answered convincingly.' This is admitted even by official historiography.[26]

Furthermore, Germany was forced to accept severe 'peace-terms' (the treaty of Versailles, 1919) and was being starved into submission. Nevertheless, twenty years later, this nation, even the same generation, was sufficiently financed and rearmed to start a second world war (in 1939).

After WW II, Germany was again destroyed and bombed out.[27] Hitler and his Nazi followers were dead, sentenced to death, or imprisoned. However, there was another known mass murderer: Stalin, who was responsible for the killing of even more people than Hitler. He, however, got off scot-free. He not only wasn't prosecuted, he even got his share of the 'cake'. The American leaders – despite the two atomic bombs, which had been politically superfluous – and the international banks that had pumped a lot of money into global armament never had to account for anything, either. On the contrary, the so-called Allies were celebrated as the triumphant victors and world saviours, although after the war Stalin and the communist Soviet Union became the 'deadly enemy' of the West.

What kind of game was going on? Who were the players?

These questions are legitimate because the secret forces that were pushing their cause in those days are still active today. The present world situation is simply the continuation of the course set by them in the first half of the twentieth century.

'The Big Four'

In order to have a better understanding of phase two (beginning with WW II) and phase three (the present time) it is worthwhile to recall certain events of phase one. Insidious plots had sparked off WW I and plunged Russia into communism (featuring Lenin and Trotsky), taking their toll of millions of victims. There were obviously people who did not mind using such methods.

As mentioned in the introduction to this chapter, there were always observers who knew that all these obscure events did not happen by chance. However, much of that evidence is controversial and delicate. Therefore, let us first investigate a piece of evidence that is cryptic but easily accessible. It was published in England nine years after the end of WW I, written by a woman privileged with being able to highlight recent historical events without having to be an 'objective' historian: the famous writer *Agatha Christie* (1890–1976; her real name was Clarisse Miller). She belonged to the high society of the British Empire and was acquainted with numerous people who were first-hand observers of the affairs behind world politics. During the post- or rather interim-war period, the First World War and the upheavals in Russia were the topics of the day. In these circles of British aristocracy, the up-and-coming successful writer got to know about the existence of secret organizations and the plans they were pursuing. She was at the 'source', for the main base of these conspirative organizations was (and probably still is) there in England, located in the place called 'City of London', the traditional stronghold and pivot of global high finance.

Agatha Christie wanted to alert as many people as possible to this danger, because it was rumoured that the secret forces had already planned a second world war, perhaps even a third one. A novel was the ideal form to render the masses of readers sensitive to certain facts without invoking paranoia, or dangers to herself. This is how she came to write *The Big Four*, a gripping story of topical interest as it was conceived to happen right there in those days. The novel was fictitious but all the more it could reveal the basic scenario of secret powers influencing humanity. What young Agatha Christie knew about such matters and what she disclosed to the public is quite amazing.

In 1926 she had achieved her first success with the masterpiece entitled *The Murder of Roger Ackroyd*. Her next novel, eagerly anticipated by the public, was *The Big Four* published in 1927. Interestingly enough, it differs from all her other novels. The protagonist, the legendary private detective Hercule Poirot, says right at the end of the story: 'I shall retire. The great case of my life is over. Anything else will seem tame after this. No. I shall retire.' (p. 272)

However, there were still many cases awaiting Poirot. In 1927 Agatha Christie had just launched her successful career, and the statement put in Poirot's mouth indicates the unique significance of this book. All the other cases that she was to depict later would be 'tame' compared to this 'great case of my life'.

What was this great case? Agatha Christie made no secret of what she had in mind: 'There are people, not scaremongers, who know what they are talking about, and they say that there is a force behind the scenes', says an informant in the book, 'a force which aims at nothing less than the disintegration of civilization. In Russia, you know, there were many signs that Lenin and Trotsky were mere puppets whose every action was dictated by another's brain.' (p. 31)

At that time, ten years after the Russian Revolution, all the puppet-string pullers were still alive planning a second world war. The novel reveals that Agatha Christie was well informed and wanted to impart this alarming knowledge to the public through *The Big Four*.

This becomes quite obvious towards the end of the novel. There is a scene describing how Hercule Poirot informs an eminent politician about the existence of secret powers whose aim is '… to destroy the existing social order, and to replace it with an anarchy in which they would reign as dictators'. (p. 206)

Besides emphasizing the uniqueness of this case, she adds another ostensible hint – a bolt out of the blue, right at the beginning of the story. Private detective Hercule Poirot, resident in London, famous for solving cases in his armchair relying solely on his unerring logical thinking, not only wants to go on a long journey across the ocean, but even desires to leave England altogether! What has happened? He had heard of the existence of a mysterious secret society called 'The Big Four' and just started 'a little investigation' of his own, when suddenly

Abe Ryland, the richest man in the world, invited him to South America because of 'some very considerable, as you would call it, hocus-pocus going on in connection with a big company in Rio'. And indeed, this super-rich man succeeded in buying Poirot, who normally would never be lured by money into accepting a case. 'But the sum offered was so stupendous that for the first time in my life I was tempted by mere money. It was a competence – a fortune!' (p. 9–10)

In the course of the novel we learn that Abe Ryland is one of the Big Four. Apparently he had contacted Poirot to recruit him as a supporter, and inviting him to Rio had been the next step towards this end.

In other words, the 'great case' of Hercule Poirot's life was not the usual tracking down of some murderer, but the exposure of a supranational association of high-ranking personalities who were unscrupulously working for obtaining world control.

Who are the 'Big Four'?

At the beginning of the novel, before the reader gets to know that the 'richest man in the world' is one of the Big Four, we find a statement that almost goes unnoticed:

> [Hercule Poirot talking to his friend Hastings:] 'Come, I will tell you how it all came about. Do you know who is the richest man in the world? Richer even than Rockefeller? Abe Ryland.'
> 'The American Soap King?'
> 'Precisely. One of his secretaries approached me.' (p. 9)

In the novel only a few real people are mentioned by name. All the characters in the story are fictitious. There was never a soap-manufacturing magnate named Abe Ryland. Who, then, did Agatha Christie mean? One does not have to be Hercule Poirot to figure this out from the quote.

By coincidence, documents are discovered revealing that the secret organization named 'The Big Four' is testing new technology and weapons, for example 'some powerful wireless installation – a concentration of wireless energy far beyond anything so far attempted, and capable of focusing a beam of great intensity upon some given spot. [...] a new force of magnetical attraction' (pp. 58, 61). They were successfully tested with English torpedo boats being used as targets. Poirot asks, 'Who are these men who send a portion of your navy to destruction simply as a trial of their power?' And he answers himself: 'The Big Four are out for themselves – and for themselves only. Their aim is world domination.' (pp. 60–1)

The scientist who had discovered this new electromagnetic weapon disappears. Traces lead to the famous French nuclear physicist and analytical chemist Madame Olivier. She, too, turns out to be a member of the Big Four: '[… with the] additional menace – that Madame Olivier's experiments have proceeded further than she has ever given out. I believe that she has, to a certain extent, succeeded in liberating atomic energy and harnessing it to her purpose.' (p. 250; written twenty years before Hiroshima!)

Then the said scientist suddenly appears again, but he has to keep silent because of threats of violence towards his family. He is in shock and agonized by fear:

> 'My God!' he muttered. 'I have been through hell – hell … Those fiends are devils incarnate.' (p. 75)

All events staged by the Big Four are of world-wide influence, but the impulses originate from one and the same master-mind, who lives in China. (This reminds us of the information mentioned in Chapter One referring to Lucifer's clandestine incarnation in China, which initiated our present age of darkness.) In the novel this Magus never appears in person.

> 'Li Chang Yen may be regarded as representing the brains of the Big Four. He is the controlling and motive force. [… driven by] a lust for power and personal supremacy. Up to modern times armed force was necessary for conquest, but in this century of unrest a man like Li Chang Yen can use other means. I have evidence that he has unlimited money behind him for bribery and propaganda, and there are signs that he controls some scientific force more powerful than the world has dreamed of.' (pp. 15, 32)

> 'He [an agent of Li Chang Yen] hinted to me of experiments in which he'd been engaged in Li Chang Yen's palace under the mandarin's direction – experiments on coolies in which the most revolting disregard for human life and suffering had been shown.' (pp. 33–4)

Number four is an 'obscure English actor called Claud Darrell' (p. 206), also known as 'the Destroyer' (p. 60). He is commissioned with all those murders that are too explosive for an outsider to be engaged in. He 'may be called the executive of the organization – the *destroyer*'. (p. 35)

Hercule Poirot manages to trap them down in his spectacular way. He finds out that the three western members have planned a secret meeting in the Dolomites, where their secret administrative base and experimental plants are situated, built by Abe Ryland. '… a vast subterranean dwelling has been hollowed out in the very heart of the mountain, secret and inaccessible. From there the leaders of the organization will issue by wireless their orders to their followers who are numbered by thousands in every country.' (p. 250)

Agatha Christie's story has a happy end, because in this novel the governments and secret services have fortunately not been infiltrated, and they all willingly follow Poirot's plans. Realizing that there is no escape, three of the Big Four detonate the subterranean base, and the head of the organization in China commits suicide.

The story of the Big Four is admittedly a fictitious plot, but the scenario depicted therein is soberly realistic if seen in the context of actual events occurring in world history. Agatha Christie clearly states (p. 136): *'The greatest power for evil in the world today is this "Big Four".'*

Scientific research aiming at world domination (personified in 'Madame Olivier') as well as the powers of high finance ('Abe Ryland'), the omnipresent secret services and intelligence agencies, represented by the 'obscure English actor', who appears with ever-changing faces, being 'the finest criminal brain ever known' (p. 251), all of them invisibly monitored and empowered by some occult hierarchic leadership (as personified by the absent mandarin grandmaster 'Li Chang Yen') – these are *The Big Four*. They are four unified powers and not four individuals. But certainly, they are manifested as individuals, and ultimately not that many.

Power and magic forces

How is it possible for a secret organization to influence a whole planet? How did they obtain this power? It is quite obvious that such colossal brains didn't merely meet by chance while playing golf one day.

The dominators derive their power not from money and science alone. Agatha Christie was well aware of this fact, and she indicated their magic backgrounds by ascribing to 'those devils ... almost superhuman powers' (p. 162). She conspicuously calls them 'devils incarnate' (pp. 75, 228), meaning that they are incarnated beings from the dark realms, to which they remain linked even as humans, mostly by godless occultism. The man in China, the intelligence presiding over the topmost earthly lodge, is described as a 'great man in his way – mandarin class' (p. 31), a kind of occult Grand Master, a global high priest. 'The men who loom most largely in the public eye are men of little or no personality. They are marionettes who dance to the wires pulled by a master hand, and that hand is Li Chang Yen's. His is the controlling brain of the East today. We don't understand the East – we never shall.' (p. 32)

The allegorical Far East symbolizes a different world: the low astral realm with its asuric leaders, whose chief incarnated there in the dim and distant past. In the novel *The Big Four*, the throne of the 'master' remains vacant: 'The end chair was empty, but it was draped with a mandarin's cape. [...] Far away in China, he yet controlled and directed this malign organization.' (p. 261)

The incarnated genius of destructive science, Madame Olivier, also emanates a magical charisma: 'She looked more like a priestess of old than a modern Frenchwoman.' (p. 67)

After the failure of his actions Li Chang Yen commits suicide. This mirrors a hard rule in black magic: dispatched negative energies, when falling short of their aim, backfire on their invoker. How did the authoress know about so many occult details?

When seen from this perspective, the above-mentioned quotations take on a very realistic dimension. They show how it is possible for a select few to preside over a secret world-wide power hierarchy, indirectly working through agents 'who are numbered by thousands in every country'; 'a force behind the scenes', in whose hands 'Lenin and Trotsky were mere puppets'; their agenda: 'to destroy the existing social order, and to replace it with an anarchy in which they would reign as dictators'; 'unlimited money for bribery and propaganda', 'a scientific force more powerful than the world has dreamed of [...] liberating atomic energy', including subterranean bases and laboratories.

Long-term planning

The First World War proved to be the final critical breakthrough for technical warfare and global industrialization. Bank notes became a versatile source of power because the banks had managed to abandon the gold standard. Through the overthrowing of the powerful tsardom, Russia had been made accessible to those who had financed the Revolution, and the ideology of communism, having been assigned its own territory, provided sufficient fuel for seventy years of world-wide political and military tension. In other words, at the beginning of the century the course was set for the entire century, a century of unprecedented bloodshed.

If this course was not set by the famous historical personalities of the time, then by whom? How was it possible for some people to secretly scheme and successfully instigate world wars and revolutions? It appears that a development initiated many centuries ago had then reached its first global climax.

Those who pulled the strings back then had intervened so heavily that they left very distinct fingerprints. Therefore, in this era of world history, we can find traces that say a lot about their identity and motives, and about the parallels to our time (because the same forces are still at work).

It is known that the two people who spearheaded the 'October Revolution' had been residing abroad – Lenin in Europe and Trotsky in the United States. For themselves, they were not especially rich and not very influential. They were neither bankers nor industrialists, but journalists and political agitators. They were in no way equipped with the means necessary to plot and implement a revolution. But suddenly both of them, arriving from different continents, appeared on the scene in St Petersburg in the summer of 1917 and were soon able to overthrow the then existing interim government. There had already been the so-called February Revolution, which resulted in the establishment of a provisional socialist government under the leadership of Alexander Kerensky. The tsar was no longer in power, and the new government tried to find a solution that could appease all factions. But then, the foreign agents arrived and exploited the unstable situation, forcing Kerensky to flee. These 'Communists' never represented the interests of the people. In fact it was a 'coup d'état', a usurping of power.

Obviously, Trotsky and Lenin had mysterious supporters. Otherwise, they would not have been able to accomplish anything, not even their return to Russia. But now, having unlimited funds at their command, they were able to start a massive propaganda campaign and to take over the military. In no time the Bolshevik faction – which had been the smallest minority in the February Revolution – managed to grasp governmental power. It was certainly not a self-financed project, and the money did not come from Russia, either, because Russia at that time was financially and economically ruined, having gone through long periods of inner political unrest and three fatal years of war.

Who, then, was supporting these revolutionaries with money running into billions? Those, of course, who had the money – the bankers of the West.

Under the tsar, Trotsky had been arrested twice for his subversive activities, but both times had succeeded in fleeing abroad. After his second escape (1905) he preferred to remain in the West, where he worked as a journalist, his last employment before his return to Russia being in New York. There he frequently visited the financial magnate Jacob Schiff, a representative of the European Rothschild Banks, who became one of his main sponsors.[28] Apparently there was a high finance 'syndicate' in the West that was very eager to swallow Russia, too. In his book *My Life*, Trotsky himself admits that he also received a 'large loan' from a well-known 'British financier' whose name he did not want to mention. (He will be identified in Chapter Six.)

With supranational support plus a top-level passe-partout Trotsky travelled to Russia when the time was ripe, and immediately became the leading personality in Lenin's revolutionary movement. Professor Anthony Sutton, in his book *Wall Street and the Bolshevik Revolution* (p. 25), documents the identity of the person who opened the door for this agent: 'President Woodrow Wilson was the fairy godmother who provided Trotsky with a passport to return to Russia to "carry forward" the revolution.'

Lenin himself had arrived a few months earlier, returning from Switzerland. The German encyclopaedia *Brockhaus* states under the name *Lenin:* 'With official German help, which arose from the desire to see Russia shaken by upheaval, Lenin returned to Petrograd together with other revolutionaries.' (t.AR)

This reference to the source that funded Lenin is only half the truth. Lenin's major accomplice, Trotsky, had come from the USA. The USA and Germany were fierce enemies during WWI. 1917 was the year the USA entered the war! Why was Lenin being supported by sources from Germany and Trotsky by sources from America? How could they co-operate with one another regarding the Russian issue, while at the same time opposing one another in a world war?

The answer is cruelly simple: Those who fought were the nations, and those who manipulated were the supranational forces that incited and financed *all* parties. Regarding Russia, the latter were neither pro-Communism nor pro-Revolution, they were not even pro-America. They had their own agenda and simply used the USA as well as Communism and 'evil Germany' as means to serve their purposes.

The Austrian author Viktor Farkas summarizes the events as follows:

> The whole transfer [Lenin's return to Russia] was arranged by top forces of Germany in co-operation with a member of the Warburg family, who was the head of the German Secret Service, as well as with the director of the Rothschild/Warburg Bank in Frankfurt, Max Warburg (a brother of Paul and Felix Warburg, who had assisted in establishing the Federal Reserve Board in the USA). [...] As if on cue, Trotsky was brought in from the USA. He too, according to historical critics, did not arrive empty-handed, but with 20 million dollars handed to him by the American banker Jacob Schiff, who is said to have later boasted that without him the revolution would not have been a successful undertaking.[29]

The Russian people, as it soon became apparent, did not profit from the Revolution. (Who did?) Out of the chaos, Lenin – with Trotsky's support and assisted by the young Stalin – established a dictatorial regime unprecedented in its murderous brutality. In the history books this period is called 'Red Terror'. After the end of the First World War, Trotsky's Red Army continued its bloody fury, committing massacres throughout Russia. The western countries just sat and watched. Nobody wondered from where these armies were receiving their inexhaustible supply of money, arms and ammunition. Russia was economically ruined and ruled by dictators, but nevertheless western business magnates were building the infrastructure for this communist regime: railroads, streets, electricity plants, machinery, industry, oil refineries, mining of gold, platinum, etc. Everything was, directly or indirectly, to the profit of the hidden 'syndicate'.

Lenin's death in 1924 gave rise to a power struggle between Stalin and Trotsky, resulting in Trotsky being forced to emigrate. Stalin increased his totalitarian power, and the communist atrocities escalated further. Once again the Russian people were massacred by their own government (estimates speak of 30–50 million victims from 1917 up to Stalin's death in 1954). Although these facts were internationally known and in spite of Trotsky vehemently denouncing the 'treason to the Revolution' in exile, no steps were taken to curb Stalin, not even when his secret agents assassinated Trotsky in Mexico (1940). When the Second World War ended (1945), with the Nazis being draconically sentenced, the communist Stalin was sitting in congress with the victorious nations, next to the English Prime Minister, Winston Churchill, and the American President, Harry Truman.

If justice and adherence to human rights had been the concern, then this summit meeting would have featured different personalities. However, the forces behind the scenes had used their money to involve all camps in serving their own cause (after having set up the camps in the first place).

The First World War had forced the nations to exhaust their resources and gold reserves and, as a consequence, to become totally indebted to the banks. Millions of people (mostly men) had died, and it did not end with the war. There were genocide mass killings in Russia, Armenia, the Ukraine etc. and in Germany (through starvation). The material damage was inestimable. Reconstruction increased the power of the powerful and the debts of the debtors. The course of civilization was now set according to the plans of the manipulators. The world had been radically changed, and it had taken 'only' five years of war!

Inferiors, superiors and ulteriors

The crucial phase of world history at the beginning of the twentieth century (WWI and the Russian Revolution) demonstrates that most of the actors in this global performance are puppets, or agents. So the question remains: Who are the puppet players, and how could they come to such power?

Most people are individuals that willingly accept and actively support the status quo. Just imagine what a wonderful, auspicious atmosphere could come about if saintly, selfless leaders were to guide humanity! Unfortunately, as shown by world history, most political and economic heads displayed another mentality. The destructive course of events cannot be blamed on the masses alone as most people simply follow the given course.

In recorded history, the masses have always been dominated by a small number of 'directors'. For themselves, most people are happy when they are left in peace, free to work for their daily needs. Being content with their 'mediocre' life, they do not have grand ambitions. Such an inclination to simplicity would be a potential asset for spiritual development if it were directed to attaining real self-contentedness. However, this inclination or 'passivity' can also be easily exploited, and mostly, this has been the case throughout history. What leader can withstand the temptation of using the 'gullible' and 'ignorant' masses of people for his own ends? Those who pull the strings may outwardly deliver pompous speeches, but behind the scenes most of them do not care; some feel nothing but contempt for the 'egotistical masses', the 'mob', the 'cannon fodder', the 'inferior creatures'.

Nevertheless, the so-called 'inferiors' represent the vast majority of mankind. They are the cogs keeping this immense machine called society working. They do the real work, the production, and from their families the soldiers are recruited. In wars, most victims are 'inferiors' as they are both the fighters and the civilians.

Who is organizing the masses? First of all we see people in the administrative system who do their work in positions of government (e.g. community, police, courts) and economy (e.g. industry, mass media, entertainment). They could be called the 'superiors'. They are one step higher in the social hierarchy, but they are also dependent and subordinate because the positions they have depend on the existing system, their employers and the goodwill of the people. They are 'in office' but can be thrown out as soon as some change comes about. In phases of crashes and crises they are as ruined as the inferiors – unless they have some support 'from above'.

Behind the ever-changing names of people in office and in the limelight, there is a far more persistent control enacted by those few who direct all the money and, thus, the course of world politics, warfare, technology and economy. In view of their ulterior motives one could call them the 'ulteriors'.

If the inferiors and superiors were to stop working, everything would break down. However, if the ulteriors were removed or non-existent, nothing would break down. Rather, global manipulation, exploitation and war-mongering would be gone, and people could start to redirect their lives with spiritual goals. At the present moment, however, the ulteriors are very active and determined to conclude their work of gaining world domination.

This description is not meant to say that every president, business magnate and top banker is an 'ulterior'. Ulteriors, in their turn, like to occupy such positions of power – in worldly structures as well as in religions. They are souls incarnate from the dark worlds, the enemies of men as the Bible calls them (e.g. John 8.44 or Rev. 12.12).

Whoever wishes to understand the covert causes of world history must not be deceived by the forces that are 'misleading the entire earth' (Rev. 2.9; 12.9). These ulteriors consider themselves to be the earthly sovereigns, the 'illuminated ones', which is even true in a certain sense. Secretly, on the occult level of their existence, they are also the connecting links to astral and non-terrestrial, non-human powers. In this respect the earthly ulteriors are far from being independent.

The ulteriors and their financial power

During the past millennium most ulteriors featured amongst the feudal aristocracy (kings, dukes, governors etc.) and the Christian Churches. Starting from Europe they set out to colonize the whole world, first by conquering and crusading, later by financial control.

Up to one hundred years ago, a web of local representatives and 'neighbourhood watchers' served to keep the population submissive to the aristocracy and Church authorities. The means of communication and control were limited. Therefore, far-sighted occultists among the ulteriors knew that in order to achieve a more efficient world control, the global structures had to be changed. Technology was needed, and it had to be invented and 'imported' onto earth.

An important step in this direction was the industrial revolution. The time quality of the progressing Iron Age (Kali-yuga) favoured the introduction of new machines and new arms. Within three hundred years, the face of the whole earth was totally changed, although most of the technological pioneers did not know where they got their inspiration from.* Obviously, the industrialization of the world was not based on a conspiracy of inventors and engineers. Not everything was intentional. In a sense, their work was even 'natural' as they all naturally felt the impulses of their time, the Iron Age.

Intentional, however, were the machinations employed by those who knew how to monitor and exploit the situation. Aided by the novel technology and the new financial system, a few ambitious men and their families succeeded in accumulating almost inexhaustible wealth and used it to expand their influence in economy, financial affairs, warfare and politics. By the end of the First World War they had established their power on a world-wide basis.

In 1938, Ferdinand Lundberg, Professor of Sociology and Political Economics at the University of New York, published an extensive study on this (then recent) development in a book entitled *America's 60 Families*. Right at the beginning of the book he summarizes how these families accumulated their wealth and how they invested it for exponential growth:

> The US is owned and dominated today by a hierarchy of its 60 richest families, buttressed by no more than 90 families of lesser wealth. [...] These families are the living center of the modern industrial oligarchy which dominates the US, functioning discreetly under a *de jure* democratic form of government behind which a *de facto* government, absolutist and plutocratic in its lineaments, has gradually taken form since the Civil War. This *de facto* government is actually the government of the US – informal, invisible, shadowy. It is the government of money in a dollar democracy.

It is no secret who these influential people were. Right from the beginning Prof. Lundberg fills pages enumerating their names: Rockefeller, Rothschild, Harriman, Morgan, Du Pont, Warburg, Kuhn, Loeb, Ford, Mellon, and many others whose names nowadays, after sixty years, are no longer that well known.

Lundberg explains that it had been these people who dictated the break-out of WWI in order (1) to consolidate their power in the USA, not least by the Federal Reserve Act, (2) to kill their rivals in Russia,

---

* Through the advancement of technology new ways of manipulation and control became possible. At the same time, new opportunities of liberation dawned. In the world of duality, nothing is exclusively evil and bad, not even the actions of the dark forces.

and (3) to dethrone and impoverish their opponents in Germany and Austria-Hungary, killing many of them, too, and (4) prepare the field for a further expansion of their supranational power. In 1938, when the book came out, the Second World War was yet to come.

In the following years, Prof. Lundberg published several volumes analysing the wealth and the intrigues of these 'Robber Barons', as he called them.

> Who really owns America? How do they keep their wealth and their power? Thirty years ago, a bombshell of a book appeared which told the story of the lords of wealth and their glittering clans. It was called *America's Sixty Families*. It rocked the nation and became a classic. Lundberg showed how America was ruled by a plutocracy of inherited wealth […] .

This was stated right on the cover of Lundberg's other monumental work, entitled *The Rich and the Super-Rich – A Study in the Power of Money Today,* which appeared in 1968. In the first chapter of this book we find the following striking passage:

> When, through its agents, it [the group of the super-rich] cannot enlist the government in support of its various plans at home and abroad it can, and does, frustrate the government in various proceedings that have full public endorsement. It involves the nation in cycles of ferocious wars that are to the interest of asset preservation and asset expansion but are contrary to the interest of the nation and the world. (p. 33)

The ulteriors and their secret societies

Perhaps Lundberg was allowed to publish without being hindered because he only touched upon the superficial factors of what made the super-rich so rich. And money was not their main concern, either. A closer examination of these people's lives would quickly reveal that most of them were members of secret societies and occult cabal groups. In this regard, everything is still the same today. Lundberg omits this aspect entirely, as do most sociocritical authors who enjoy academic prestige.

Alluding to the famous statement of Marx, 'Religion is the opium of the people', Lundberg writes on the last page of his book *The Rich and the Super-Rich* (p. 747): '… prayer rather than science or reason is the tool of the political medicine men.' He criticizes all those who think that something beyond 'science and reason' could be the medicine for today's society.

Lundberg's books are technically brilliant and well researched but they apparently serve the plans of the ulteriors by pinpointing the deficiencies of our present system in such a way as to familiarize the intellectuals with the thought that, some day, establishing a 'new world order' will be inevitable. Lundberg bluntly phrases this opinion at the very end of his book:

> With a thoroughly antiquated, distorted political system – formally 178 years old [...] – the United States is unable even to begin solving its own many very serious domestic problems. [...] Serious problems cannot be solved on the basis of a consensus of value-disoriented dolts.

This is the cynical last phrase of the book! The word 'dolts' refers both to the politicians and the citizens electing them. In other words: such dolts are incapable of solving the grave impending problems of today. What Lundberg and like-minded 'visionaries' call for is a non-elected leadership!

This one quote is exemplary for the convictions prevailing in the circles of acclaimed 'progressive' thinkers. Many superiors and practically all ulteriors are high or top-grade initiates of secret societies ('brotherhoods') and their many-branched lobbies.

Although Lundberg and most academic historians prefer not to mention secret societies as a background factor of world history and world wars, other researchers do not avoid the topic. The German historian Karl Heise, for example, published an elaborate book entitled *Entente-Freimaurerei und Weltkrieg* ('Entente Freemasonry and World War') in October 1918, right after the official end of WWI. In the following two years it was reprinted twice, and then it disappeared, only to be published again facsimile in 1982. This book named all the protagonists of politics and economics who were members of the Freemasonic Anglo-American World Lodge, people who were mostly still alive in 1918 when the book was published.

In the USA, as pointed out by Heise, President Wilson's entourage consisted mainly of high-ranking members of the World Lodge like, for example, his ominous counsellor Edward Mandel 'Colonel' House. 'Wilson's dependency on the World Lodge is further demonstrated by the fact that his long-term "right hand" Lansing was a member of the Freemasons as was his representative, Vice President Marshall, who, according to the *American Tyler-Keystone 1917*, belonged to the world chain of the 33rd grade of the Scottish Rite.' (p. 275, t.AR)

Karl Heise, a Freemason himself, does not fabricate a conspiracy theory of Freemasons or even Jews (in 1918 there was no Nazism yet), but clearly distinguishes between original Freemasonry that was Christian, idealistic and non-political, and the corrupt Anglo-American 'World Lodge' which was heavily into manipulating politics, high finance and warfare.

President Wilson's functioning as a puppet was so evident that several US authors could not help exposing it, for example: Arthur Ponsonby: *Falsehood in War Time* (New York 1916; exposing the propaganda and the lies staged for justifying US war participation); Earl Sparling: *Mystery Men of Wall Street* (New York 1930; about the Federal Reserve Act 1913 and the men behind it, and about the money flow in the Wilson era and WW I); George Viereck, *The Strangest Friendship in History* (New York 1932; about E. M. House's influence on President Wilson); Charles C. Tansill: *America Goes to War* (Boston 1938; about the forces that pushed America into war); A. and J. George: *Woodrow Wilson and Colonel House* (New York 1956; exposing that the 'secret government' had planned a world war long before WW I started); John dos Passos: *Mr. Wilson's War* (Garden City 1962; about Wilson's furthering and tolerating all preparations of the Communist take-over in Russia).

These are but a few examples of books dealing with the covert forces behind the scene of the First World War. They show that President Wilson had been affiliated with the World Lodge and willingly followed its dictate. An example of this was the USA's entry into the war in 1917. The vast majority of Americans had been *against* participating in the war and preferred to stick to the well-proven Monroe Doctrine (1823), stating that America should never interfere in European wars. In 1916 Wilson, with difficulty, managed to secure his re-election and did so only by promising to keep the USA out of the war.

This, however, had been a blatant lie, as immediately after the election he took measures to bring America *into* the war! Apparently he followed higher dictations. All of a sudden, US war participation was declared to be necessary and unavoidable. All of a sudden, there were many reasons, just like the Lusitania incident, the sinking of a British steamer with American passengers by a German submarine on May 7, 1915. Critical researchers maintain that this tragic incident had been the result of an intended provocation. Ships carrying arms and ammunition were sometimes disguised as passenger ships, and the Lusitania was one of these suspicious 'cruisers' of the Allies. Why had a German warning against boarding the Lusitania been prevented from being published in US newspapers? Why did the British not forward crucial warnings to this steamer, thus 'allowing' it to enter dangerous waters?[30] Were the people on the Lusitania sacrificed just to obtain a reason to expand the war? Was Agatha Christie hinting at this incident when she mentioned 'boats being used as targets [...] Who are these men who send a portion of your navy to destruction [...]?'

After the war, in 1919, President Wilson was awarded the Nobel *Peace* Prize!

The American Civil War

A further celebrity of the lodge gallery is President Abraham Lincoln, known today for his heroic deed of slave liberation. However, the blunt facts tell a different, more complex, and rather disillusioning story.

During the nineteenth century the Northern States were becoming increasingly industrialized. The South, however, remained dependent on the cotton industry, which in turn was dependent on slave labour. When Abraham Lincoln was elected President of the USA in 1860, several Southern States seceded from the Union before he took office. This was the result of subversive agitation by ulterior agents wanting to instigate a civil war. Reprisals and blockades implemented by Lincoln resulted in additional Southern States seceding (altogether eleven). England and France, fearing that America was becoming too powerful, preferred the 'United States' to be divided. Being dependent on the cotton supplied by the Southern States, they wanted to support the Confederacy.

Just in time, before they could intervene, Lincoln proclaimed the *liberation of slaves*, for two obvious reasons: Without slavery the economy of the South was crippled, and the European states were morally checkmated as they could not publicly support slavery. Humanitarian motives regarding the abolition of slavery were a later embellishment of the historical facts in order to raise Lincoln to the status of a national hero.

During his election campaign Lincoln had plainly *favoured* slavery, attesting to the inferiority of the blacks. The following is a quote from the 'Fifth Lincoln-Douglas Debate', Galesburg, Illinois, 7 October 1858:

> I will say then that I am not nor ever have been in favor of bringing about in any way the social and political equality of the white and black races [...] that while they do remain together, there must be the position of superior and inferior, that I, as much as any other white man, am in favor of having the superior position assigned to the white race.

It took a long time till this realistic assessment of Lincoln's personality made its way back to the history books. In an article of *The New York Times*, 10 April 2002, this topic was again taken up. Under the headline 'Two faces of Lincoln, racist emancipator', it was stated:

> Lincoln believed there was a 'physical difference between the white and black races' that would 'forever forbid the two races living together on terms of social and political equality.' And, he continued in this 1858 speech, 'I, as much as any other man, am in favor of having the superior position assigned to the white race.' As president, he ordered emancipation only as a war measure, and even then limited it to slaves living in rebel territory.

The subsequent civil war, the *War of Secession* (1861–5), resulted in gruesome slaughtering including the massacring of many civilians. Arms and means of transport were supplied to both the North and the South by the same manufacturers, in accordance with the plan of the ulteriors. The latter's profit was immense, and as a result the federal states, now in debt, had to submit to their dictates. When Lincoln tried to evade their suffocating grip by having state-owned bank notes printed – an act of real heroism – his last days had come.

Although the Civil War ended with the surrender of the South on 9 April 1865, some circles did not want to accept such a 'cowardly' peace as the southern hordes had committed many bloody atrocities – even more so than the North. Edward Stanton, Secretary of War (and member of the conspiring lobbies), planned retaliation, but Lincoln opposed such plans, favouring a smooth reintegration of the South back into the Union. He adamantly stood up for this policy at the cabinet meeting on 14 April 1865, one week after the end of the Civil War. In the evening of this day he was assassinated – allegedly by a fanatic Secessionist (though it was Lincoln who wanted to spare the South!).

That same evening there were two other attempted murders, against Lincoln's Vice-President and the Foreign Minister, but both of them failed. Trials were then held against the eight surviving perpetrators. They were all described as single criminals who coincidentally tried to assassinate three top US politicians on the same day. Four of the agents were sentenced to death – and silence.

With this information in mind one can easily recognize the hand and mentality of the ulteriors while reading between the lines of official historiography:

> Military recruitment amounted (according to estimates) to ca. 1.5 million soldiers in the North (ca. 360,000 died, 275,000 wounded). In the South figures reached ca. 800,000 to 1 million soldiers (260,000 died, 225,000 wounded). The number of civilian casualties is unknown yet believed to be substantial. Expenditures amounted in total to ca. 10–15 billion US dollars. The American Civil War, being the first war in which new military technique (e.g. armoured naval vessels, machine guns), railway and telegraphy came into operation, *accelerated economic growth* in the North but crippled to a large extent the economic resources of the South. With the emancipation of approximately 4 million slaves, the *economic and social system of the South was laid in ruins*. The American Civil War was a *crucial turning-point* in American history, because the national unity of the USA was *ensured* and, as a consequence, *central authority* fortified.[31]

The French Revolution

Throughout history there have always been numerous wars and skirmishes, mostly fought due to religious differences or for territorial gain. However, since the end of the eighteenth century, beginning with the French Revolution (1789–99), a new motive became prevalent: the overthrow of monarchies with the aim of introducing fundamental changes in the power structure of the world, starting with the establishment of new governments under the dictate of ulterior lodges and financial powers. Now, government positions were occupied by agents if not puppets – commanders who received commands themselves, men with an obscure double identity. In 1789 there were 65 lodges in Paris alone![32]

The French Revolution was a crucial step in the long-term plans towards a new world order as envisioned by the top levels of the power 'pyramid'. Claiming to represent the interests of the people, dubious individuals founded political parties and instigated the masses till the monarchy was overthrown and its members killed by lynching or official execution. (The infamous 'guillotine' was an invention of this time.)

As soon as the French king was removed, which caused anarchic conditions, these agents threw off their masks and called out a dictatorship. The 'Reign of Terror' (*La Terreur*) of the revolutionary government now turned against the very people who had naively believed in the propaganda of their self-appointed representatives.

Due to the uprising of 1789 and the resulting chaos, the economy collapsed, hunger became rampant, and a growing number of people called for the reinstitution of the monarchy. To ward off famine and keep popular resistance in check, systematic mass murder became the preventive measure. Within a few years, more than 100,000 starving and discontented men and women were slaughtered by the forces of the new so-called government.

The revolutionary leadership also exhibited a hateful policy towards the Church and the privileged clergy. Church property was confiscated and expropriated. Monasteries were burnt down and priests arrested. About 40,000 priests who refused to take an oath on the humanistic-atheistic civil constitution were consequently deported and/or killed. In 1792–3 thousands of priests fled the country. By a decree issued on 10 November 1793, Christianity was officially abolished and replaced by the lodge cult of 'rationality' and 'the law of nature'.

People were completely baffled. It was indeed impossible to understand what was going on, if one did not know of the ulterior intelligence behind all these actions. The end of the eighteenth century was the time when the dark forces, now organized in secret societies, started to infiltrate and take over positions of power all over the world.

In 1792, the year when King Louis XVI and his spouse, Marie-Antoinette, were decapitated by the new leadership of France, further King-murders occurred. Gustav III of Sweden, top-ranking dignitary of Swedish Freemasonry, had reached an agreement with King Leopold II of Austria, also a lodge member. The purpose of this agreement was to protect King Louis XVI. Within only a few days they were both assassinated and succeeded by subservient 'brothers'. This shows how influential and well-organized the conspiracy already was in 1792.

In 1801 Tsar Paul was murdered in St Petersburg, the act being commissioned by the British envoy Lord Withworth. This Lord was later honoured in England for his 'deserving conduct' with the Grand Riband of the Ludwig lodge.[33]

Subtle influence and incarnation

Visible world history is influenced by beings originating from invisible dimensions – the light and the dark worlds as mentioned in Chapter One. Beings from the dark worlds manipulate, beings from the light worlds inspire human beings. Every dictator and agent was obsessed by elementals or astral entities, some being aware of it and others not. At the same time there were always inspired individuals who enlivened people through their art, their music, their poetry, and by their personality in whatever field they were active.

Since the beginning of the present age, the dark hierarchies or 'brotherhoods' have increased the number of their incarnated agents. Kali-yuga is the time of their big performance. Profiting from people's mass karma and spiritual blindness, they act in obtrusive and arrogant ways to seize as much power as possible. Due to their mentality they see nothing wrong in their undertakings. Rather they think themselves to be legitimized and empowered to shape the world according to their visions. The fruits of their actions, however, show what they are: ego-blinded beings born as humans to usurp the earth with inhuman ingenuity.

According to the law of resonance ('like attracts like') and based on mental and elemental connections, several new-rich upstarts managed to establish expansive family empires with sons and daughters displaying the same characteristics as their fathers. They began to take over the economy (steel-, arms-, machine-, textile-, and commercial industry) as well as the high finance levels (banks, stock exchange, real estate and land speculation), striving to dominate or even monopolize their sectors. On this basis, the multinational enterprises of the twentieth century were formed which now, by their ulterior lords, are used to head for new dimensions of power and control.

How money began to rule the world

Paramount influence was exerted by the tycoons of the financial world. Through business profits and clever trade agreements, as well as insidious frauds, they managed to accumulate fortunes that opened unprecedented prospects. Desiring to give the world a new and 'better' order, they strove after ever-increasing power, for the world they encountered was primitive and violent. It was the dark age, and many souls from the dark worlds had already incarnated before, exploiting the inferiors and keeping them subjugated. In this situation, the upper class of the following centuries took up the same dynamics but changed the tactics. They saw the corruption of the Church and the aristocracy which, with their petty egotism, had obstructed man's progress for centuries. As a reaction, they went to the other extreme: from pseudo-religious 'fear of God' to materialistic self-empowerment. Full of idealism and driven by 'humanistic' ideologies, they devised a new world order that was to end wars and enmity among men. Similar to Christian enthusiasts who wanted to accelerate the coming of God's kingdom on earth, these 'anti-Christian' torch-bearers also had their long-term visions which they adamantly pursued with hard labour and strict discipline, sparing neither themselves nor others. Social and ideological duality became polarized more and more.

In view of the ulteriors' ever-increasing wealth that even rendered statesmen entirely dependent, a tempting utopia suddenly became realistic: *an all-embracing control by an elite*, ultimately crowned by world control. The logic was simple: Only when all followed the tune of the same conductor would orchestrated harmony be possible.

The second half of the eighteenth century saw a network of secret associations emerging, infiltrating those already existing and forming new alliances in order to realize the ideal of a 'better world' with a new world order.

A symptomatic event in this process took place in 1776, when the secret society called 'The Illuminati' was established in Bavaria, Germany. It was founded by the occultist *Adam Weishaupt* (1748–1830), a professor at the University of Ingolstadt, who had been a member of the Jesuit order. He was a confidant of the new-rich *Mayer Amschel Bauer* (1744–1812), who was to gain world renown with the self-adorned name of *Rothschild*. In order to utilize the brimming flow of wealth for the 'common weal of mankind', new dimensions of power and progress had to be tapped. With the foundation of this secret society, an *asura* worldview – which had existed all along – became manifest on earth. At this point in time, it materialized through concrete statements, plans and organizations. (The contents of this ideology will be discussed in the following chapter.)

In one sense, the appeal of the 'Illuminati' movement could be compared to the appearance of Jesus. One person, active in public for only a few years, was able to trigger off a chain reaction which proved to have a superhuman impact. Thousands of people spontaneously felt attracted by this new religion and helped to spread its ideals on their own initiative because, obviously, they could identify with it. Resistance and persecution by the state officials only increased their determination and devotion.

In a similar but converse way, Weishaupt's ideology was also readily embraced. Beings of such convictions had always existed – not only on planet earth. In those days, however, many of them had gathered at the same time, at the same place, on the same planet! Weishaupt's initiative was only the signal for mobilization. He was very active and operated on behalf of high-standing secret authorities; he could rely on many forms of support and had access to select circles of society.

His world-view hit upon the nerve of the *Zeitgeist*. He formulated secular and humanist ideals as a new alternative to the dogmatic guardianship that had been imposed on humanity for hundreds of years, especially through the Vatican and its agents. Indeed, one of the Illuminati's aims was the fight against the supremacy of the Catholic Church, ultimately even the destruction of this organization. Attracted by this perspective, many members of Protestant aristocratic and intellectual circles imbibed this revolutionary ideology and supported it, and quite a few joined the movement secretly through vows and initiation. They had to swear to absolute discretion by an oath of allegiance beforehand. 'Shouldst thou become a traitor or perjurer, let this sword remind thee of each and all the members in arms against thee. Do not hope to find safety; whithersoever thou mayest fly, shame and remorse as well as the vengeance of thine unknown brothers will torture and pursue thee.' Thus the wording of Weishaupt's instructions regarding secrecy.[34]

Nevertheless, not everything could be kept secret. Due to a courier's accident in 1785, confidential documents containing information about the real intentions of the Illuminati alliance came to light. Several members were arrested, and others revoked their membership and confessed before a Bavarian court of inquiry.

The most prominent drop-out was a professor from Edinburgh (Scotland) named John Robison, one of the leading intellectuals of his time, who had been personally recruited by Weishaupt. In 1797 he published a sensational book entitled: PROOFS OF A CONSPIRACY *against all the Religions and Governments of Europe, carried on in the secret meetings of Free Masons, Illuminati and Reading Societies; collected from good authorities by John Robison, A. M. Professor of Natural Philosophy, and Secretary to the Royal Society of Edinburgh.*

The Church hierarchy, of course, started a missionary campaign against the 'brotherhoods of Satan', taking it for granted that they themselves were 'better'. Weishaupt and his followers were forced to go underground, and they took all pains to give the impression that the association had been disbanded and no longer existed. In order to confirm that the founding of the 'Illuminati' had just been a harmless episode of his youth, Weishaupt, lying on his deathbed at the age of 82,

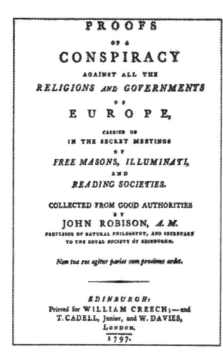

Cover of John Robison's book 'Proofs of a Conspiracy ...', published in 1797, which gives first-hand information about the existence of secret societies and their hidden agendas.

staged an impressive performance of remorse and reconverted to the Catholic faith, which he had renounced when leaving the Jesuit Order.

Weishaupt's maxim was: 'The great strength of our Order lies in its concealment, let it never appear in any place in its own name, but always covered by another name, and another occupation.'[35]

Beyond the institutional expansion was the ideological mission. Adam Weishaupt's influence had such a lasting effect that the term 'Illuminati' became a synonym for all kinds of secret societies and secret services that strive for world power. It is important to note that the term 'Illuminati' is not limited to the members of Weishaupt's order (which may still exist or not, or have been refounded), rather it is a categorical term like communist, capitalist, racist etc. and refers to the propounders of a certain elitist world-view that will be unfolded in the next chapter. (In this general definition, the word is written with a small i, for example: the philosophy of the illuminati.)

In his ideological mission, Weishaupt was successful beyond expectation. The new impetus channelled by him (and others) quickly gained its own momentum and found strong resonance in the already existing secret societies, like the Rosicrucians and the Freemasons, the latter being a young institution itself. As described in Chapter Five, Freemasonry has its own long-standing ideological tradition, but as an institution it was formed only in 1717 (in England).

At the famous congress of Wilhelmsbad, Germany, in 1782 Weishaupt established an alliance between the new Illuminati order and Freemasonry. This pact unified the leading secret societies of that time and influenced the Freemasons who, at that time, already had a worldwide network. In 1785, there were fifteen lodges in America, a figure that rapidly increased in the 'New World'. The same process went on in the 'Old World' as well as among the elite in African, South American and Asian colonies. The substratum facilitating this expansion was the *British Empire*.

The first great coup instigated by representatives of this 'revolutionary' ideology was the French Revolution in 1789 aiming at depriving royalty of its power. Being a time of anarchy and quickly changing favours, there were also prominent lodge members who fell into disgrace, some even being executed, like the Jacobin leader Maximilien de Robespierre. But the overriding aim – removing the powerful kings and queens – was accomplished.

In the same year, 1789, the United States of America was founded, and George Washington was proclaimed president. This ended a struggle of thirteen years that had begun in 1776 (with the Declaration of Independence), the same year when Weishaupt founded the Illuminati Order in Germany. It is officially known that George Washington was an honoured initiate of the Freemasons, as were many of the other Founding Fathers and the following presidents.

By the nineteenth century, Freemasonry counted a total of two to three million members, among them many prominent and influential men. Initially, most of them had been imbued with sincere idealism for the cause of 'true Christianity' and 'human ethics', which they believed to be supported by these societies and their top-level masters.

Enticing and mellifluous

After smouldering in an occult underground for a long time, the archetypal philosophy of the illuminati suddenly appeared on the world stage during the second half of the eighteenth century. Throughout Europe, political, military and intellectual circles were clandestinely infiltrated. Widespread discontent served as a substratum rendering people susceptible to revolutionary ideas. In the absence of other alternatives, this idealistic programme was very tempting: implementation of rationalism and mundane ethics, neutralization of clerical power, a brotherhood of man, and one form of united religion in order to finally end all denominational conflicts.

In the encyclopaedia *Brockhaus* we find the following definition:

> Illuminati: A secret society founded in 1776 by Adam Weishaupt in Ingolstadt. Going beyond Freemasonry, the association aimed at promoting a cosmopolitan way of thinking, and fought monarchism, based on principles of the movement of Enlightenment. Members were, amongst others, Herder and Goethe. (t.AR)

Though Weishaupt's 'Illuminati' were banned in 1786, the movement was by no means nipped in the bud. On the contrary, it continued to thrive as an underground influence, and its ideology was taken up by many other individuals and secret societies.

Whoever became influential in society had to reckon with being accosted by a lodge representative at some point. Universities became strongholds of the revolutionary spirit. Many students, especially the ambitious and outstanding, were individually and clandestinely offered the opportunity of joining these promising associations. (In this regard, nothing has changed up to the present day.)

A literary document of this time, today one of the great classics, is the novel *Hyperion*, written by the German poet Friedrich Hölderlin (1770–1843). As a young man of promising talent, he too was approached by lodge members, especially in the year 1795 when he was studying in Jena under the famous philosopher Johann Gottlieb Fichte, who also happened to be an 'initiate'.

In *Hyperion*, which was published in two volumes (1797 and 1799), Hölderlin indicates his own experiences. Hyperion, the protagonist of the novel, depicted as a contemporary young Greek idealist, becomes acquainted with Alabanda, who is a lodge member. Concealing this at first, he approaches Hyperion with heroic visions, arousing his enthusiasm. An intimate friendship develops between Hyperion and Alabanda, till one day Alabanda receives a visit from his lodge brothers. Only then does Hyperion realize what is going on. He instinctively feels repelled by these characters. Alabanda terminates his membership for the sake of his friendship, but later delivers himself into the hands of his 'brothers' to face their bloody tribunal. Hölderlin apparently knew about the statutory consequences of disloyalty as stipulated by Weishaupt.

Hyperion was Hölderlin's response to the French Revolution. As a young student he had shared and supported its supposedly high-set ideals. Therefore, he was disappointed all the more when the revolutionary leaders showed their real faces. The following extract gives an impression of how these secret societies worked, based on passionate, even prophetic idealism combined with cruel, callous despotism:

We [Hyperion and Alabanda] *became ever more intimate and happier together.* [...] *Alabanda, stern and aglow and terrible, denouncing the sins of this century. How my spirit awoke in its depths! how the thundering words of implacable justice rolled on my tongue!* [...]

[Alabanda:] '*We do not ask if you are willing, you slaves and barbarians! You are never willing! Nor will we try to make you better, for that is useless! We will but make certain that you get out of the way of humanity's victorious career! Oh! let someone light a torch for me, that I may burn the* weeds from the field, let someone lay me the mine with which I can blow the dull clods from the face of the earth!'

'When possible, we should but gently push them aside', I interrupted.

Alabanda was silent for a while. [...]

[Hyperion:] 'You accord the state far too much power. It must not demand what it cannot extort. But what love gives, and spirit, cannot be extorted. [...] Come!' I cried and grasped his garment, 'come! who can any longer abide in the prison that darkens around us?'

'Come where, my enthusiast?' Alabanda answered dryly, and a shadow of mockery seemed to pass over his face.

I was as if fallen from the clouds. 'Go!' I said, 'you are a small man!'

At that moment some strangers entered the room. They were striking figures, haggard and pale for the most part, so far as I could see by the moonlight, and calm, but there was something in their countenances that pierced the soul like a sword [...]

As they entered, Alabanda sprang up like bent steel.

'We have been seeking you', one exclaimed.

'You would find me', he said with a laugh, 'if I were hidden at the center of the earth. They are my friends', he added, turning to me.

They seemed to scrutinize me with a certain severity.

'He, too, is one of those who would see the world a better place', Alabanda said after a moment, and pointed to me.

'Are you serious in this?' one of the three asked me.

'It is no joking matter to better the world', said I.

'You have said much in little!' exclaimed one. 'You are our man!' added another.

'Are you of the same mind as I?' I asked.

'Ask what we are doing', came the answer.

'And if I asked?'

'We would tell you we are here to purge the earth, that we clear the stones from the field and break up the hard clods with the mattock and draw furrows with the plow, that we grasp the rank growth by the roots, cut it through at the roots, and tear it up by the roots, so that it shall wither in the burning sun. [...] We have ceased to speak of good and evil fortune. We have grown beyond the midpoint of life [...].'

'These are traitors!' the very walls dinned into my sensitive heart. I felt like one suffocating in smoke, breaking open doors and windows to escape – so did I thirst for air and freedom.

They soon saw, too, how uneasy I felt, and broke off. [...] I was already too irritated by Alabanda's mockery not to be completely confused by his having these mysterious friends.

'He is evil', I cried, 'yes, evil! He feigns unbounded trust, and consorts with such as these – and hides it from you!'

I felt like a girl who learns that her betrothed is secretly living with a whore. [...] 'It is better', I said to myself, 'to become as the bee and build one's house in innocence, than to rule with the masters of the world and howl with them as with wolves, than to dominate peoples and befoul one's hand with that unclean material.'

[Later Alabanda tells Hyperion how he became involved with this society. He had meanwhile left the society, in spite of his oath of allegiance. He describes how once when in need a man had helped him out with money.]

'The man of whom I speak, Hyperion, was one of those whom you saw with me in Smyrna. The very next night he introduced me to the members of a solemn society. A shudder ran through me as I entered the room and my companion, pointing to the earnest group of men, said: "This is the League of Nemesis." Intoxicated by the immense sphere of action that opened before me, I solemnly made over my blood and my soul to these men. [... However] I broke my oath. [...] if I must pay for what I did, I will do it freely; I chose my own judge; those whom I failed shall have me.'

'Do you speak of your fellows in the League?' I cried; 'O my Alabanda! do it not!'

'What can they take from me but my blood?' he answered. Then he gently clasped my hand. 'Hyperion!' he cried, 'my time has run out, and all that remains to me is a noble end.' [...]

'They will not', I thought meanwhile, 'they cannot do it. It is too senseless to slaughter such a glorious life, like a sacrificial animal', and this conviction calmed me. [But they did it.][36]

The diversity of lodges

Over the past three centuries the original mystery schools and secret societies have split up and changed in many ways. A vast system of lodges has come about, some of them being parallel and independent of each other, some of them even competitive or antagonistic. 'Lodges' in the widest sense are comparable to football teams of the first, second and third leagues. Although playing against one another to qualify for promotion or for the champion's title, they are all participants of the same game – football. If somebody voiced criticism by saying, for instance, that football was a stupid game, they would all unite in defence of their common interest. Furthermore, when meeting on a higher level, like the national team, there is no rivalry at all, although it still exists on the lower-league levels.

Similarly, the manifold lodges, though existing separately as different organizations, are united on a higher level in view of their common goals. However, they do not merely have a national team but an international and even a *supranational* team. These high-level 'lodges' have developed their own dynamics independent of the lower lodge structure. Therefore it is incorrect to equate these conspirative forces to just 'the Freemasons', for example.

It would also be misleading and a gross generalization to automatically impose negative connotations on the word 'lodge'. For centuries, secret societies have been the custodians of spiritual knowledge, and the mediators of progressive impulses for human civilization (as described in Chapter Five). Nevertheless, there is no denying the fact that many of these covertly operating organizations have become infiltrated by negative energies based on Satan's offer of power and elitist supremacy. This is true both for secular and religious organizations world-wide.

Summary and outlook

Regarding the covert forces behind the scenes, one could present many documents and details exposing incredible aspects of the global power game. However, if we were to delve too deeply into the dark backgrounds of world history, we would inevitably get lost in its endless intricacies, mistaking the effects for the causes.

The point of this chapter was to show that wars, crises and revolutions never happen by chance. They have to be planned, financed and carried out. There have to be master-minds possessing the power and the money – and the callousness – to direct world history in such a particular way, at the cost of millions of lives. Looking at these fruits we are reminded of the prophetic warnings about beings from the dark worlds taking birth on earth in the present age of darkness (Kali-yuga), which is soon to be overcome and transformed.

Over the last five thousand years, secret 'invaders' have increased their influence up to the point of almost total control in the field of politics, economy and so-called science. The course for this finale was set during the eighteenth century when paper money was introduced as the basis of a financial structure that enabled ulterior forces to take over governments and whole nations. Important stations of this course were the French Revolution, the American Civil War, the Russian Revolution and the two world wars. These events were staged by men who were not simply egoists interested in their own profit. Rather, they embodied particular ideologies and world-views – those of the secret societies they belonged to. While the individual agents changed throughout the generations, the 'ideals' remained the same and were pushed forward up to the explosive world situation that we are facing now, at the beginning of the twenty-first century.

What, then, are these ideals and ideologies? As usual, they can be known by their fruits, and some of them have been mentioned in this third chapter. Being the roots of the plant that produces such bloody fruits, these ideologies need to be properly understood. Therefore, in the next chapter, their contents and fallacies will be analysed. By looking at these half-truths, it will also become evident what a truly holistic and divine world-view is. Both may use similar words, but they are as different as darkness and light.

CHAPTER FOUR

Facing Darkness and Light

Nothing happens by chance. There actually are people orchestrating and organizing wars, cover-ups, political murders, economic manipulations, etc. How can these people reconcile their actions with their conscience? Don't they realize that they are calling down dreadful karmic reactions upon themselves?

Obviously they don't. They are fully convinced that their actions are necessary and thus justified. There is always a reason to 'prove' that 'we are the good ones', and always an enemy to project guilt upon. Propaganda may even succeed in convincing the public of this good-and-evil game, but the facts show another reality: the super-rich are becoming richer and richer, and an increasing percentage of people is falling into a dire struggle for existence, both in the 'good' and 'evil' countries. Statistics show that many do not survive this struggle. Every day, about 30,000 to 40,000 people, mostly children, die of hunger! This is about one person every two seconds, a fact that has already been going on for decades. And 'nobody' is responsible ...

As mentioned in Chapter One, negativity is two-faced. Both the too-much and the too-little are faces of the same coin of godlessness, even though both sides, in one way or another, claim to have understood what 'God' is.

There are people who have fallen into 'too much' believing in God due to religious fanaticism and dogmatism. The only thing they can accept is their own belief system and their particular interpretation of some holy scripture. Obsessed with the idea of being the only ones who have the right belief, they judge all others as having the wrong beliefs. Such forms of 'religion' are expressions of a dia-bolic spirit (often confused with 'the holy spirit') because they lead to discord, divisions and hatred, even amongst the branches of the same religion. So what to expect of them *vis-à-vis* the 'rest of the world'?

In the other extreme, many people have fallen into 'too little' believing in God, living their lives without spiritual perspectives. In the intellectual field, such people propagate materialistic, humanistic or nihilistic world-views. In the field of high finance and secret politics, they mix in the top levels of secret societies, serving ungodly 'gods'. For them, the different religions are but means to ignite political fires. Outwardly, for the public, they may present themselves as religious, but their own ideology is quite different. They think themselves to be the ultimate global players, the creators of the world's destiny. Therefore, they want to impose their own ideas upon all others in order to build a new world of enforced 'peace and order'.

All these camps dream of a new world with them being the controllers. Secretly, they all want the present civilization to collapse, thinking that their group will emerge as the 'inheritors' of the world.

Planet earth is a place of decision where the worlds of light and darkness border on each other. From both worlds, souls are incarnating. How can we recognize them? What are their intentions? How do they handle duality? What is their understanding of reality?

Are there criteria for differentiating?

On earth we can see a broad spectrum of good and evil powers. The distinction, however, is not that clear as all of them believe they are 'the good ones'. What religion, government, enterprise and secret service cannot present good-sounding reasons for their actions and convictions? Who does not think, 'What we are doing is important and necessary'? Especially in the field of science and medicine everything is declared to be useful for the progress and improvement of humanity, even nuclear tests, vivisection and all kinds of (in)human experiments. The most used justification for everything is, and has been for many centuries, the name of God. Somehow, nobody can avoid the topic of God. Even ideologies of atheism* have their own theories about God and God's laws.

---

* Atheism: general term for all kinds of views that oppose theism. Theism: 'belief in the existence of a god or gods; specifically: the belief in the existence of one God who is viewed as the creative source of man, the world, and value and who transcends and yet is immanent in the world.' (from: *Webster's Third International Dictionary*)

How can we know what to believe? Even if God exists, the sceptics say, no one can know God, for he/it is unlimited and inconceivable and, therefore, impossible to understand rationally or logically.

Does this mean that we are hopelessly at the mercy of our limited speculations when trying to understand the Unlimited?

Theistic logic resolves this dilemma by pointing out an even higher, more complete view. Yes, the Unlimited (God) is certainly beyond human logic and rationality, but this is only half of the truth, for God is so perfect that 'He' is not only unintelligible, but also intelligible! If He were only unintelligible, He would be lacking something, namely the aspect of intelligibility. Therefore, God is also *intelligible* and *logical*, and understanding this is the supreme purpose of our God-given intelligence and logic.

Though not limited to human logic, God is the most logical 'thing'. God is so logical that without God nothing really makes sense. Our lives, our endeavours, our pains, our experiences would be meaningless. 'Meaningless' means 'aimless', and aimless people are easily manipulated.

From the theistic point of view, everything relative is related to the Absolute, God, and through this relationship, the relative gets its sense and definition. As elaborated here in Chapter Four, only such a holistic perspective is able to provide clear criteria for differentiating without judging. Otherwise, people will arbitrarily judge according to ego-motivated criteria, which are always biased and distorted. No wonder that, throughout the centuries, the ulteriors and a major part of the population have always been convinced that their aims and methods, even the persecution and mass-killing of 'the others', were good.

The dualistic judging of 'we the good ones' and 'they the evil ones' is diabolic in itself. How often have evil forces declared themselves to be the good ones! Within duality the so-called good always creates fronts of evil. Thus, the 'good' is not that good after all. Of course, this does not mean that there is nothing *truly good*. As explained in Chapter Two, that which is truly good is *divine* and not limited to the ego-centred judging of good and evil.

What, then, are the criteria that can be used to differentiate without judging? In order to find this essence of all mystery schools we have to use our God-given intelligence and logic – intelligence not in the sense of intellect but in its literal meaning: 'the power to differentiate'.

Where the road forks

Some say there is an absolute truth, and others say there is none. These statements are mutually exclusive, as both are absolute statements. To say that there is *no* absolute truth is an absolute truth, too. Therefore, as explained in Chapter One, the decisive question is not, 'Is there an absolute truth?', but, '*What* is the absolute truth?'

The answer to this question determines the course of one's life, and is the real – and only – application of one's free will. Everything else is a consequence of this decision. Here, the road forks: the wheat is separated from the chaff, the divine from the godless.

> Behold, Satan has obtained permission to tempt you, to sift you like wheat.

> O son of Pritha, in this world there are two kinds of created beings. One is called the divine (*daiva*) and the other the godless (*asura*).

These are two key statements of western and eastern revelation: the New Testament (Luke 22.31) and the *Bhagavad-gita* (16.6). They may seem to be rooted in undifferentiated black-and-white thinking, but this is not the case. The way to supreme awareness (self-realization and God-realization) can be compared to a long staircase. The stairs are always the same but have a special characteristic: one can use them to ascend or to descend. These are the only two options. He who lingers on a step is only postponing his decision and will sooner or later continue in one direction or the other. Of course, one can change his direction on every step, following a divine or godless course.

The Relative and the Absolute

God-realization means *realization of the Absolute,* literally: realization of that which is unrestrained and unconditioned.* The term 'absolute' refers to that which is free from and independent of all relativity; it applies without restriction and unconditionally.

Such a definition may provoke the objection that there is nothing absolute, nothing that is unconditionally ('absolutely') true. But again,

---

* From Lat. *absolvere* (*absolvi, absolutum*), 'to absolve; to detach; to liberate'.

this is a negative absolute truth, and just another way of saying 'everything is relative'.

Something relative can never be absolute. Those who take a relative truth and claim it to be absolute commit the mistake of *'absolutizing'*. Such opinions held by materialistic religions and ideologies are not absolute, but *absolutist*.

The word relative means 'proportionate; comparative; qualified; differing according to time, place and person'. Relative truths stand in relation to certain conditions that determine their validity. They are not unconditionally true and not valid for all beings.

This applies to all aspects of the relative, both positive and negative. Neither the positive nor the negative should be seen as absolute, for they are not absolute but relative. Philosophically speaking, there is nothing absolutely good and nothing absolutely bad in this world. The absolute is something completely different.

The trap of absolutizing

The relative is never absolute. This is a simple *absolute truth*, but still it is ignored or misunderstood ever so often. In materialism, matter is absolutized; in communism, atheism is absolutized; in 'religion', some relative understanding of God is absolutized, etc. In all cases there are people who maintain that their belief, be it atheistic, materialistic or theistic, is the *only* true understanding of reality.

As shown in the following examples, also positive truths can be absolutized. In such cases, people who become convinced of something good tend to condemn all others of differing opinions. Typical examples are non-smoking and vegetarianism. To be free of smoking and meat-eating is undoubtedly good, i.e. beneficial to one's health and mental stability, and conducive to spiritual growth. However, this does not apply to all individuals. Many people may have other priorities in their personal development, and an immediate, abrupt abstinence would be more harmful than helpful. Others may be living in a socio-religious surrounding in which vegetarianism, for example, would isolate or even endanger the person exhibiting such an 'abnormal' behaviour; not to speak of people who lived in earlier decades or centuries, under conservative social pressure and conditions of restricted freedom (in medieval Europe, under communistic dictatorship, etc.). In many cases, being a vegetarian was reason enough to be condemned to death at the stake, or committed into lethal psychiatry. Many who ate meat and lived under-cover in those days and cultures (many were persecuted nonetheless) are now individuals of mature esoteric and religious enlightenment. Obviously, eating meat was not 'bad' or detrimental to their spiritual development. The same may be true for many people living today.

On the other hand, if a person becomes a vegetarian due to fear of becoming ill or due to religious indoctrination, it might even prove to be relatively bad as it tends to cause fanaticism, pedantry and arrogance. Imagine the panic and stress of such 'holy people' even thinking of eating meat, not to speak of the terrible fears and feelings of guilt if they actually happened to eat some. For them, it would be quite a relief to break this spell of fear and their dependence on the dogma (and on those who instilled it). What if they were invited to prove their mental independence by eating some meat, for example once a year? This would be the end of their dogmatism and arrogance, just as it would be the end of ignorance or indifference if the meat-eating majority were to live a vegetarian month (or more) every year. New dimensions of health, lightness and awakening would be revealed to all those who have been brought up to eat meat day in, day out. They might even start to feel betrayed by the propaganda which made them believe that eating meat was 'normal', 'healthy' or even 'necessary'.

In other words, one cannot judge people according to these relative principles. Not every non-smoker or vegetarian is automatically a good person. One extreme example often cited is Adolf Hitler, who hated smoking (and smokers) and avoided eating meat, more or less. Then again, there are many fine, holistic people who may not be totally abstinent and 'puritanical' due to their cultural environment or personal lifestyle. Such individuals have always existed, most of them unrecognized by official canonization, and they exist nowadays as well – and in greater numbers than ever before. Many of them are vegetarians and non-smokers, of course, but not all of them.

These statements are not meant to absolutize the relativity of smoking and meat-eating, for it *does make* a difference whether one eats meat and smokes or not. These are habits that are unhealthy in many ways and harmful, but not absolutely harmful.

Similarly, abstinence from meat and drugs is not absolutely good. Those who pride themselves with these virtues, believing to be 'better' or 'more advanced' than others, have merely shifted their unholy cravings to subliminal substitutes, and they will have to face the same problems later on, in some form or another.

These principles are even more evident in regard to sexual continence. For many religious groups, renunciation of sexual intimacy is an absolute virtue as the attraction between man and woman is considered to be sinful and degrading. However, when examining how certain men of Christian, Jewish, Islamic or eastern patriarchal systems yielded to various kinds of compensation (oppression of women, witch and widow burning, personal perversions, greed for power, etc.), it becomes obvious that this 'good' principle is not so good after all, and can quickly be infected with dia-bolic elements. This has already been analysed from the socio-psychological perspective in Chapter One ('The negative infiltration of religions').

To summarize, the questions 'Is he/she a vegetarian, a non-smoker, a celibate?' are in no way absolute criteria for assessing the degree of someone's enlightenment. The absolute criterion is: *to what extent does a person live in real love, and experience harmony with the Absolute?*

The fall from polarity into duality

Divine mystery schools are present in all cultures of the world, and they all give helpful explanations about the origin of duality in the material world. In the following elaboration, the main inspiration has been derived from Vedic and Christian sources, but ultimately, all revelations emanate from the same Source. In their core, we will always find the same truths.

One thing they all have in common is the symbolism of light and darkness. Indeed, light and darkness are the perfect symbols for explaining the 'absolute' and the 'relative'. A clear understanding of their relationship shows that the atheistic (asuric) doctrines contain only partial truths and, therefore, a considerable amount of half-truths. 'Following such conclusions, the *asuras*, without divine knowledge and with misguided intelligence, engage in acts of violence and exploitation. They are destroyers of the world and enemies of mankind.' That is the verdict of the *Bhagavad-gita* (16.9), spoken thousands of years ago but more relevant today than ever before.

Matter is a divine energy and manifests an endless number of transient forms. These manifestations, being material, exist within the realm of *time and space*, the original form of polarity, which causes the flow of creation and dissolution. The principle of polarity regulates the balance and harmony of God's creation, the *cosmos*.[37]

Within the world of polarity, however, there are beings who attach themselves to one of the two poles. Thus, they fall out of oneness (unity) into 'twoness' (duality) and become divided into 'positive' and 'negative' camps. Duality is 'broken polarity'; it is the opposition of two one-sided contraries.

Whoever falls into one-sidedness disturbs and (partially) destroys the harmony within God's creation. From a higher point of view it does not really matter whether someone is on the 'good' side or the 'bad' side as both are relative. In reality, both live in the same illusion dictated by the ego. They all think themselves to be the good ones and automatically designate the other side as 'evil' or as those who are 'not right'.

Polarity is like a pair of scales in balance. If one goes to one of the two sides by identifying with it, one falls into duality. Those who become tired of taking sides begin to withdraw from duality, desiring to find a neutral position. They are no longer inclined to identify with a particular belief system, be it denominational or materialistic. Understanding that these are nothing but half-truths, they prefer to look for the common truths – the elements which unify instead of those which separate. Somehow they sense that the power game of 'good' and 'evil' is rooted in the two faces of negativity, while neutrality steers a middle course. Whether this middle course is taken as a step towards transcending duality (or just as a temporary vacation from duality) depends on the individual's motivation.

Those who go beyond neutrality (and those who did not fall into duality in the first place) live in a transcendental consciousness. They are *in* the world but not *of* the world. They experience the oneness of divine love even within the world of duality. They only want the best for both sides and, therefore, do not take sides. Instead of judging, calling one side 'good' and the other 'evil', they live in love and forgiveness based on inner balance and satisfaction. They are situated in true spirituality – which is beyond duality and neutrality.

Misconceiving reality in terms of duality

According to our view of reality we invest our energies, our time, our money, etc. Therefore, it is of crucial importance to our lives how we define reality.

Those who live in duality only know their relative existence and tend to define 'reality' by applying their relative views. However, being in the world of duality, they are bound to their ego-centred perspectives just as shadows are bound to 'non-light'. All attempts to define reality in terms of duality are imperfect half-truths, and half-truths are dangerous because they look like truths while being fallacious traps leading into darkness, culminating in the highest 'illumination' of the dark forces, the ultimate half-truth: the philosophy of the 'illuminati'. The deeper they fall into darkness, the more they think themselves to be 'in the light'. It is a vicious circle: the fatal tragedy of self-deception.

In the following, different versions of these half-truths will be systematically presented (in a summarized way). This simple crash-course in philosophy will reveal that the global power game is based on half-truths only. Let us hope that some 'global players', too, will read this book and wake up.

Materialism, pantheism and deism

As mentioned in the second chapter, the most common definition of reality nowadays is that of materialism: Only that which is materially perceivable is accepted to be real and 'objective'. Most of modern science, medicine and psychology is based on the premise of materialism and evolutionism ('life comes from matter; consciousness is a product of the brain'). In the symbolism of light and darkness, this would be the same as saying, 'Light is that which is perceived as darkness; darkness creates itself; there is nothing beyond the shadows.'

Each world-view, just like a step in a staircase, can be used as a basis for ascending or descending – towards the real light or deeper into darkness. Even as a materialist, one can be honest and ethically correct, and that is the ascending way. The descending way is obvious: the direction of intensifying one's ego and harming others – animals, plants, the planet and other people.

Presently, materialism is the most common half-truth, but not the most dangerous one. In itself, materialism is only blindness, which is bad enough. However, callousness and destructiveness are added, or activated, through the injection of other, increasingly satanic, ideologies.

On the next step of this philosophical staircase, reality (or 'God') is not simply equated with perceivable matter. Rather, it is defined as 'the sum total of all matter with all its laws of nature', which could be called 'materialistic holism'. In its ascending version, this viewpoint leads to *pantheism*, seeing God in all nature and, as a practical consequence, treating nature and all creatures with utmost respect.

Pantheism, which considers nature to be God, may not go beyond the sum total of matter, but still, it is a form of theism because it perceives the earth and the cosmos as a living creation animated by spirits of nature. Pantheism exists in a broad spectrum, ranging from primitive animism, which is mostly dictated by fear of evil spirits, to shamanism up to universal pantheism, which may include telepathy and an inner connection to the cosmic creator. At this point, we can no longer speak of 'mere' pantheism.

Again, there is also a descending version. Symbolically, the definition of materialistic holism says: 'Light is the totality of all shadows; if you take darkness in its entirety, you will get light.' In this atheistic version, God (Lat. *deus*) is seen as the abstract initiator or 'architect' of the universe. This world-view is called *deism* (lit. 'godism'). This 'God', however, is nothing but the workings of the mechanistic, merciless laws of nature: 'Whatever happens does so according to these laws of nature, especially the law of karma.' This is a one-sided understanding of karma, as will be shown in the further unfolding of this chapter. According to this version, if someone is super-rich and able to manipulate the world, it is his rightful karma, and others who are poor and exploited simply have bad luck, or bad karma. 'That is life. *C'est la vie.*'

In its logical consequence, the atheistic version of deism* says that everything existing and happening is – seen in its entirety – 'God'. Whatever happens and whatever can be done is 'in order' simply because it can be done. 'God' is nothing but the totality of the cosmic clockwork, a self-organizing material mechanism based on physical and subtle laws.

---

* Here, 'deism' is used as a term to designate the negative version of materialistic holism. Deism in its positive version is the same as pantheism.

Those who know how to use these laws better than others are simply the better 'lawyers', the better players. Everything is 'allowed' as long as the laws are not against it; life is a god-less 'God-game' based on inexorable, merciless laws of nature.

Those who believe in this ideology are convinced that whatever they are able to do is sanctioned by the laws of nature, and thus by 'God'; otherwise one would not be able to do it. It is the obsession of doing any possible thing one wants: 'Let us see how far we can go.' This can especially be seen in 'innovative' science and secret politics.

Materialistic and occult monism

There is yet another way of defining reality in terms of duality. It is, amongst all attempts to define 'light' from the perspective of darkness, the version that comes closest to the truth. At the same time, it can also be the most diabolic half-truth. It is based on the understanding of *monism* (from Greek *monos*, 'one, single'): seeing everything as the direct or indirect effect of *one* ultimate cause. Monism, too, has a theistic and an atheistic version. The basic truth of monism can be distorted into an atheistic half-truth or it can be expanded into an all-encompassing understanding of the Absolute.

In the atheistic category, there is *materialistic monism,* which describes matter as the ultimate cause of everything (materialism and deism), and there is *occult monism,* which takes some abstract non-material oneness of energy to be the cause of everything. The latter version leads to the 'highest' levels of occultism* and dark-force ideology, the levels from where global history has been directed since the beginning of the present age. Therefore, this ultimate half-truth needs to be closely examined. In contrast to it, the theistic version of monism will become self-evident.

---

* Occultism: from Lat. *occultus,* 'hidden, concealed, secret, obscured'; derived from *ob-celere,* 'to cover, to hide'. Contrary to the words 'mystical' ('secret, beyond material understanding', only intelligible by divine vision and revelation) or 'esoteric' ('internal, confidential, to be communicated only amongst people who are receptive'), the word 'occult' etymologically bears the meaning of something dark and hidden; therefore, it is used here specifically in reference to atheistic doctrines and practices that go beyond gross-materialistic world-views.

The philosophy of the illuminati

Occult monism is not a gross-materialistic philosophy. Rather, it deals with the most subtle aspects of matter and energy, including the magical and 'technomagical' applications of this knowledge. In this regard it is much more advanced than official materialistic science.

According to the philosophy of occult monism, the ultimate reality beyond duality (twoness) is 'oneness', the absence of duality. If the absence of duality is reality, then duality is unreal, which means that the world of duality (relativity) is an illusion. In this line of logic the absolute reality is defined as the 'oneness beyond all material forms'; 'God' is nothing but an abstract energetic potential of everything.

As harmless as this may sound, it opens the door to incredible misunderstandings. A very relevant example is the philosophy of the illuminati (masculine plural of Lat. *illuminatus*, 'illuminated; enlightened'), those in deepest darkness, who think themselves to be the only ones who are truly enlightened.[38]

Philosophically, they go beyond gross materialism by defining reality as the absence of duality: 'Light is not just the sum total of darkness. Light is something completely different from darkness. It is the absence of darkness: if you are in darkness, then just negate it, and what remains is light. If you are able to negate *all* darkness (duality), then you are fully in the light = enlightened.'

This is the logic of the illuminati, the ulterior forces, based on atheistic monism, which has been phrased here in a way that exposes its fundamental error.

In the light, darkness is naturally absent, that is true. However, it is a half-truth to say that light is *nothing* but the absence of darkness. Those who say so have no idea of what light really is.

Light is not the result of negating darkness. Similarly, finding reality is not the result of negating duality. Philosophies that try to define reality through negation are, by definition, *negative* in the literal sense of the word. By their very philosophy, the 'enlightened' prove that they are in darkness, otherwise they would not have to define light from the point of view of darkness. Trying to push oneself into the 'light' by negating darkness is an atheistic form of self-redemption. Those who consider this half-truth to be the absolute truth create their own exclusive elitism and occultism.

Their line of argument could be summarized as follows (although in public they would never use such self-exposing words):

> 'To reach the Light, we have to go beyond all darkness, beyond all duality. We, the illuminated, have reached this oneness. We understand that duality, like shadow, has no reality. Ultimately all forms of duality are illusion, especially the dualistic concepts of a God outside of man, of heaven and hell, of mercy and condemnation, of joy and suffering, of good and evil, and – the most beautiful illusion – love, as love is the epitome of duality. Reality, however, is duality-less, which means it is pain-less, bondage-less, and hate-less, but also joy-less, freedom-less, love-less, and god-less. This ultimate truth of life is hard to accept; therefore, only a few people are able to face the highest illumination. All others are too sentimental and too weak to accept it. They may stick to their duality of love and hate or good and evil, which simply proves that they are not beyond good and evil, and not illuminated. Peace and order in this world will only be possible when those who are illuminated finally get into the position of directing all those who are not illuminated. That's why it is necessary that we obtain full power. Everything that serves this goal – including untruth, wars and murder – is part of the evolutionary "Process" and is therefore neither good nor evil. It is necessary and thus sanctioned and legitimate.'

This is the cold 'truth' of top-level materialists, who can be found in all groups. It is the epitome of atheism and the satanic extreme of ego-justification.

Regarding monism, it is true that the ultimate reality is the oneness beyond duality. The crucial question is: What is the nature of this oneness? Atheistic monism maintains that the ultimate reality ('God') is nothing but the totality of abstract energy, devoid of consciousness, free will and love; creation only happens when some 'enlightened' beings start to shape this neutral energy in order to manifest their own visions, engaging those who are less enlightened. In plain terms, it means playing God in a godless world – which would be the ultimate truth and reality indeed, if the world were factually godless.

The dark forces do not know anything beyond matter and the abstract sum total of energy. Being incapable of seeing any spiritual reality beyond 'their' abstract oneness, they have no other choice but projecting their consciousness into the worlds of matter, and there, they want to create their own empires and paradises, their own kingdom of God without God (where they are 'gods'). They want to create a 'better' world than the one that already exists. For this reason, they are obsessed with creating, researching, manipulating and 'improving'. They believe in materialistic evolution and the 'process' of creating peace through their own world order. For them, this 'better world' is the end that justifies all means.

In other words, whatever serves this self-defined purpose is accepted as necessary. If it is 'necessary' to stage some act of terror or to go to war, then 'let us do it' because what is more 'practical' than just killing the opponent?! 'We are the best, bomb the rest.' This is called pragmatism*, which means doing everything that is practical for accomplishing that which is necessary – and what is necessary is defined by the pragmatists. In this way the illuminati are caught up in a vicious circle of ego-justification.

The trap of false justification

The top ranks of many secular and 'religious' orders are dominated by the illuminati mentality. It is obvious, however, that not all members become initiated into the highest levels of 'illumination'. Only the ambitious candidates that display willingness to accept the cold 'truth' are considered eligible for promotion into the exclusive circles beyond the ordinary hierarchy.

On the lower levels, the members are engaged in positive and idealistic deeds. They do good things in order to balance the bad things in this world. Examples for such positive organizations are the many service clubs.

On the next levels, the 'eligible' candidates are initiated into the 'truths' of atheistic deism: 'God is the sum total of matter and its laws; this means that in reality there is nothing but matter and its laws – and these laws are neutral. They do not know good and bad. Therefore, those who want to reach the higher initiations have to go beyond good and evil; indeed, it is one-sided to prefer the positive pole, considering it to be "good", and reject the negative pole, calling it "bad" or "evil".'

---

* Pragmatism: judging the truth and validity of things according to their practical utility in achieving one's goals; from Grk. *pragma*, 'action, way of doing things', derived from the verb *prassein*, 'to do, to accomplish', which is also the root of the word 'practice'; in its negative version ('Anything goes', 'The end justifies the means'), this term refers to the practical consequence of atheistic deism and monism.

At one point, the candidate for 'enlightenment' is invited to abandon the 'one-sided goodness', and becomes initiated into 'integrating both sides'. Now, he no longer acts according to the criteria of 'good' and 'evil' but according to the principles of necessity. Having become a 'realistic pragmatic', he believes that so-called evil things, if serving the 'higher purpose', are no longer evil. They may not be good either – they are just *necessary*.

A popular esoteric slogan derived from this philosophy says, 'Everything is a necessary experience.' This may sound very wise but, as explained in Chapter One, it is a Luciferean wisdom. The fall into duality is not necessary, and remaining in the illusion of the ego is not necessary either. 'Necessary experience' is the magic word which justifies everything one does – in one's own life and to others. Suddenly, the most evil power games are legitimate if they 'serve the Process'. If everything is a necessary experience, then the manipulation, exploitation and killing of people is nothing but an act of providing 'necessary experiences' to those predestined to receive them. Looking at the fruits, we realize that there is something wrong with this esoteric, or occult, 'wisdom'. It is a half-truth yielding bitter fruits that more and more people worldwide have to eat, whether they want to or not, because some 'enlightened' ulterior forces have decided that this is a necessary experience for the world ...

The following quotation is an example of this ideology. It shows that, to a certain degree, the illuminati also maintain the ideal of 'love' and use it in their argumentation. For them, however, love is a part of duality, not of reality. For this kind of 'realists', love is ultimately an illusion! The chosen quote, written by a British author (a top-level lodge member and a 'Sir'), reveals that they consider love to be the 'second highest energy level' within the galaxy. Obviously, their horizon is not limited to this one planet! This is indicated by the intentional use of the words 'galactic' (when referring to the levels of duality, including 'love') and 'universe' (when referring to the abstract, godless and loveless oneness).

Furthermore, the notion 'idea of scale' is just another way of stating 'everything is relative'. The author presents himself as enlightened and confronts the reader with his plain (half-)truth: 'Whether such a concept squares with our subjective ideas of "good" and "higher" is immaterial. *This is how things are ...*' – emphasis by the author, E.S., himself.

In this way, he ends up with a universal justification of everything 'necessary' – here, the Reign of Terror (after the French Revolution) and the two world wars (remember endnote 27):

> [...] the second highest galactic energy level: the unifying energy of love. [Why is there so-called evil in this world? ...] The answer, if there is one, must lie in the idea of scale. Let us assume that we, as humans, have some ordinary aim to achieve this day. By any standards we are able to apply, this aim is 'right' and 'good'. To discharge it, we must, let us say, catch a certain bus. The bus is starting away and is already accelerating and only by a strenuous sprint can we hope to catch it.
>
> Our decision to make the effort triggers off a whole sequence of bodily events. Extra adrenalin pours into our blood. Our muscles contract in exceptional effort. By our deliberate action we destroy millions of body cells. Each of these cells is a little life. They die – in a real sense they are sacrificed – to our aim.
>
> Do we feel compassion? Can we truly say that we experience remorse for their destruction from an action we took?
>
> Here there is a factor of scale which is all-important. Everything in the universe may be significant: but everything is not equally significant. Whether such a concept squares with our subjective ideas of 'good' and 'higher' is immaterial. *This is how things are.* [...]
>
> A time-scale gap closer to everyday experience may illustrate. Suppose a young child has a thorn deeply embedded in a finger. The mother sees the situation in terms of a present moment vastly greater than the child's. She sees her baby's life as a whole, its well-being, growth, maturity. She takes a needle, digs it under the thorn and removes it. [...]
>
> By analogy, the Reign of Terror and two world wars may represent no more than instantaneous needle-jabs within a consciousness whose present moment is ten thousand years.[39]

According to the logic presented in these analogies (catching a bus, taking a thorn out of a baby's finger), so-called necessity justifies everything, even wars and other kinds of bloodletting. It is considered the same as sacrificing millions of body cells in a strenuous effort.

Apparently, there are beings who do not mind the 'deliberate action' of killing millions of people by applying 'instantaneous needle-jabs' into the body of humanity. They are as indifferent towards human beings as we are to the death of our body cells or to the throwing away of a thorn.

These analogies are quite artificial and, actually, totally absurd. Is the 'killing' of millions of body cells really the same as the deliberate killing of millions of people? And are the people killed really just a thorn in somebody's flesh? *'This is how things are ...'*

(The end of the quote raises yet another question: What does the author mean by mentioning 'a consciousness whose present moment is ten thousand years'? This number is not just randomly chosen, as shown in the next chapter.)

Maya and the I-AM consciousness

The above-mentioned atheistic ideologies contain blatant misunderstandings of duality, karma and *maya*. Let us first consider the statement that all forms of duality are illusion, or *maya* (in Sanskrit). Is this true? If it were, then the illuminati would be perfectly right with their cold 'truth'.

The question of duality and illusion refers to the world of shadows. And we know: Only within the limited realm of projection does light become confronted by opposing elements that cast shadows and cause darkness. In reality, however, *light never casts shadows!* Originally we all are part of that Light ...

Beyond all forms of shadow and darkness there is always the 'background' of light. Light, here, symbolizes the absolute reality, the eternal, spiritual world, which is the all-encompassing background of the material space-time world. Ultimately, also matter is eternal because its source (God) is eternal. However, while the spiritual world is the reality of eternal present, matter*, the 'Mother-energy', has the specific purpose of eternally creating perishable forms. The chain of creation and dissolution is unending, but the created forms have a beginning and an end, starting with the universes, which are 'breathed out and in' by God's creator aspect, in Sanskrit called Vishnu, 'the Omnipresent One'.

Light is the only reality, but for those who are isolated from the Light, darkness becomes the reality, though a (relative) reality. The problem starts when we, as eternal beings, lose the I-AM consciousness, the consciousness of our true identity, and start to identify ourselves with material, transient forms, such as our body, our possessions, our feelings, our energies, etc. Here the famous Sanskrit term *maya* applies.

---

* Matter: from the Latin noun *materia,* etymologically derived from the root word *mater,* 'mother'.

It means illusion and false identification, literally 'that which I am not', as opposed to that which I am.

Here we come to the last but decisive aspect of the light-and-darkness symbolism. Light never casts shadows and never creates darkness. Shadow and darkness are created only *when something is obstructing the light*. Who, or what, is obstructing the 'light', our divine consciousness? – No one else than we ourselves or, more precisely, *our ego*, when we fall into a false identification, forgetting our true identity as eternal, individual parts of God.

In reality, *maya* is nothing but a state of consciousness, namely the confusion of identity and identification. Matter as divine energy manifests an endless number of transient forms. *Maya* does not refer to the material forms. The material forms themselves are real, though transient, creations of God. Similarly, duality is not an illusion. It is a (relative) reality, just as darkness is a reality for those who are separated from the light. Duality exists, and therefore, good and evil forces exist, but we should identify ourselves with neither of them. Being rays of light, we should not get hung up with darkness. *Maya* begins when we, as eternal beings, identify ourselves with non-eternal forms (our feelings, moods, bodies etc.), and thus become controlled by them. *Maya* is the identification with something that we are not. And what is it that we, in our true being, are absolutely not? Perishable and subject to time.

Our body, our life, our world are not illusions but real gifts of God, and we can use them according to our free will, which implies being responsible for whatever we do. Saying that they are illusions leads to atheistic monism, which negates all relativity based on the half-truth 'light is the absence of shadows'.

From darkness to light

The quest for the true nature of reality is most important as it determines our world-view, our priorities and activities, ultimately our entire life and destiny.

The analysis so far has shown that half-truths only give a one-sided, incomplete understanding of reality. Those who are stuck in such half-truths either absolutize or negate relativity and define light from the perspective of darkness.

Hence, the question is: What is beyond duality? Is there only an abstract, 'impersonal' totality of energy behind all forms of duality?

As shown by the symbolism of light and darkness, there is something wrong with the logic of atheistic monism. Light is not just the absence of darkness. Indeed, it is impossible to remove darkness by simply negating it. Only those engrossed in darkness assume that 'light is what you get when you negate darkness', which is absurd. In reality, light can never be produced out of darkness. And, the other way round, as long as one stays in darkness one will never reach the light.

Being beyond all darkness, light is totally different from and independent of darkness. It is a reality of its own. Similarly, the reality beyond duality is totally different from and independent of matter and relativity.

On this basis, let us ask again: What is the reality beyond duality? What is the inner force that holds matter and relativity (including space and time) together? Obviously, this philosophical question is essential to all fields of knowledge, including natural science.

The answer is actually very simple. Beyond 'twoness' there is oneness. Oneness means, by definition, 'undivided and indivisible being'. In Greek this is called *atomos*, in Sanskrit *atma*, in Latin *individuum**! The reality beyond duality is the *undivided and indivisible life* that is independent of matter just as light is independent of darkness.

To put it in one phrase: *Beyond duality is individuality.* Individuality means 'being whole, complete, and indivisible', and being indivisible also implies being non-transient, ever-present. Individuality is eternal because it is never part of duality. It is not a product of material polarity (space and time).⁴⁰

The world formula 'beyond duality is individuality' applies both to the relative and the absolute. Beyond the transient material body, there is the conscious individual being, which is eternal but limited. (That's us.) Beyond the totality of matter, including all transient universes, there is the absolute individuality – unlimited and omnipresent. That's

---

* *Individuum:* literally 'the indivisible'; from the negating prefix *in-* and the verb *dividere,* 'to separate, divide'; synonymous with the Greek word *atomos* and the Sanskrit word *atma* – the indivisible, non-material (spiritual) core of consciousness; the 'soul' (Lat. *anima*) that animates the material body. The inner force that holds matter together is not material. Therefore, materialists will never find the *atomos,* the *atma.*

God, the ultimate reality, which includes all relativity and all of us. In simple words: we are parts of God.

Just as the sunrays are one with and different from the sun, we are simultaneously *one with* but *different from* God. This is the supreme realization as revealed in theistic mysticism: 'God is one – eternal and inconceivable. And light never merges in oneness with the sun.'[41]

The same truth was revealed by Jesus: 'The Father and I are one.' 'If you know me, you will know my Father also.' With statements such as these (John 10.30; 14.7) Jesus indicated the oneness. At the same time he also stressed the difference: 'Truly, I tell you, the Son can do nothing on his own; he can only do what he sees the Father doing; for whatever the Father does, the Son does likewise. The Father loves the Son and shows him all that He himself is doing, and He will show him even greater works than these, so that you will be astonished.' (John 5.19–20)

A 'mathemystical' analogy further illustrates how the relative and the absolute individuality can be one and different simultaneously: The number 1 represents God and is the only number immanently constituent in all other numbers (as multiplier, divisor and basic unit). Although the 1 is present in all other values, it is also an autonomously existing number. Similarly, God is omnipresent and all-pervading through His energies and expansions but simultaneously retains His own absolute identity, individuality and free will.

Therefore, it is perfectly right to pray 'Thy will be done'. It is also perfectly right to call God 'Father' or 'Father-Mother-God' or even 'Divine loving and beloved One'. These are all expressions of our individual relationship to the absolute *individuum*, God.*

An abstract oneness would have no individuality and no will, and there would be no basis for praying to God, what to speak of loving

---

* In the Vedic sources, there is an immense reservoir of mystic and revealed testimonies regarding this intimate aspect of God realization. In the Sanskrit-names used to describe this 'male-female' unity of the Absolute, the female aspect is always mentioned first, just like in *Shri-Vishnu* ('the birth-giving and all-pervading One', as primeval Source and Creator of all matter), *Shakti-Shiva* ('the energy and energizer', as the original, conscious cause of all dynamics behind the transformation of material forms; Shakti as Goddess Kâlî is the personification of time, Skr. *kâla*, and Shiva as an expansion of Vishnu is the personification of space), *Sita-Rama* ('the shining and joyous One') and *Radha-Krishna* ('the lover and the beloved, all attractive One', as divine oneness of absolute individuality and love).

God. A representative of this atheistic world-view once said: 'Why should we pray, and to whom? There is no God outside of us, as everything is one. We don't pray to ourselves.'

One and different, or one and in-different?

Deism and monism are not necessarily atheistic philosophies. There are also *theistic* versions of deism and monism, explaining that everything is God's energy, everything is one through its eternal connection to the Absolute. It is not an abstract oneness but a *differentiated* oneness. All energies are one, being aspects of the Absolute One, but as energies they have different functions. The spiritual energy's function is to be the timeless and spaceless, eternal reality. The material energy's function is to create an infinite cycle of finite forms. From the point of view of oneness all material forms are real. From the point of view of difference they are transient. Both is true simultaneously.

This theistic understanding does not stop at the one-sided and incomplete perspective of saying 'everything is one'. Rather it says: Everything is one *and different* simultaneously – one in quality (being a part or aspect of the Absolute) and different in individuality (being an individual unit, or 'ray', of God, the indivisible Being). This means: We are all *one and different* simultaneously, united in God but still individual, and therefore self-responsible.

In contrast to this, the atheistic version of deism and monism says, *'Everything is one and in-different',* because the Absolute is considered to be an abstract oneness devoid of consciousness, individuality and free will. If this abstractness were the absolute reality, then all differences would be unreal, and being an 'enlightened realist' would mean to act in a non-differentiating way 'beyond good and evil'. As demonstrated in the first half of this chapter, this atheistic interpretation of being 'beyond good and evil' simply means doing whatever one deems necessary according to one's arbitrary 'realism'. This realism, however, being derived from the perspective of the ego, is nothing but *ego*ism.

The theistic version opens up a totally different vision of reality. If everything is simultaneously one *and different,* then the differences are also real. There is no end that justifies all means. All are responsible for their actions because individuality is an absolute reality.

Karma = predestination + free will

Literally, the Sanskrit word *karma* simply means 'activity' (derived from the verb *kri*, 'to do, to make, to perform, to cause an effect') and refers to the fact that all activities in the material world have consequences according to the laws of polarity. Activities performed in non-awareness of one's spiritual identity cause corresponding (good or bad) reactions, and activities performed in spiritual consciousness have spiritual reactions, especially liberation from duality and an increased realization of God's will. Such spiritual activities are called *akarma*, 'non-karma'.

Reaching the level of *akarma*, the level of acting in spiritual consciousness, is the challenge for every human being. All experiences in the material world have the ultimate purpose of awakening the materially engrossed individual to his spiritual consciousness – which culminates in the perfection of free will, divine love.

In contrast to this, the materialistic interpretation of karma states that everything which happens to us is solely the reaction of an action performed by us. Whatever happens to you is your 'karma'. If someone drops an atom bomb on you, it is your 'karma'. If it were not your karma, it would not happen. – Is this true?

It is half-true. It may sound esoteric and logical, but upon closer examination it becomes obvious that it is absurd. If it were true, this would imply that the people of Hiroshima and Nagasaki, for example, had the 'karma' to die in an atomic inferno. Had the Americans not dropped the bomb, somebody else would have done so, because it was the karma of those 300,000 people to die like that. Does this mean that the Americans were only predestined executors of the law of karma?

This example shows that the materialists misunderstand karma to mean *predestination*. Only with such a premise can one assume that whatever happens *has to* happen due to 'karma'. Obviously, equating karma with predestination is a dangerous half-truth that leads to unscrupulous actions. Why? Because it says that everything is simply the result of predestination; whatever one is able to do is predestined; every action is thus justified just because it can be performed.

The half-truth which says that everything is simply a result of predestination reduces people to soul-less bio-robots that are forced to act according to the mechanic laws of nature. It says that there is nothing beyond matter and nothing after death, that there is no spiritual individuality and, therefore, no free will; everything in the universe is the working of 'random and merciless indifference'. This is exactly what the materialistic, atheistic world-view propagates (see quote on p. 57).

In reality, karma is not the same as predestination. As the law of action and reaction, karma is *the synthesis of predestination and free will.*

From the perspective of reaction, there is predestination. From the perspective of action, there is free will. Whatever happens is a reaction predestined by a corresponding cause. For example, we are born as a man or a woman at a specific time in a particular country into a certain family. These are predestined factors, and we cannot change them. The only thing we can do is choosing, to a certain degree, the subsequent course of our lives through actions based on our desires.

Within a predestined frame of circumstances, we are constantly confronted with situations which are reactions to former actions (effects based on respective causes). The question, therefore, is: What do we do within these given (predestined) situations? Are we dissatisfied? Do we start to accuse God and the world? Do we want to exploit the situation? Or do we perceive the indications of God's will? Our decisions, whatever they may be, are functions of our free will, and we are responsible and will have to reap the consequences of these decisions. We can always start new chain reactions of karma, and cause ourselves to remain in the mechanics of the material world without really accessing our free will. Or we can start to get out of our entanglement in the net of actions and reactions.

A drastic example of this principle has been indicated before: the dropping of the two atom bombs. Was it the predestination of those unfortunate people to be killed like that? No, it was the decision of the perpetrators based on their (misled) free will. And both the victims and the perpetrators became bound by a new chain of action and reaction – and will continue to be so until everything is atoned for (= balanced) and forgiven.

At any moment, someone could use his free will to attack us, and drag us into new and never-ending cycles of karma, if we allow ourselves to be dragged in. That was the risk (and 'rule of the game') we accepted when we decided to enter the world of duality. If our horizon does not go beyond matter, then our world-view is limited to a frustrating perspective. We will constantly live in fear, cry for security, and project guilt upon others while seeing ourselves as innocent victims or 'targets'. In certain cases, this may even be true from the perspective of duality (there are 'innocent victims'!) but that is not the point because staying in the roles of victims and perpetrators does not help anyone. What is the use of being 'innocent' and hating the perpetrators, and what is the use of being guilty and dwelling on one's harmful actions? Both are challenged to awaken to God consciousness, which would enable them to love and forgive: forgive themselves and forgive the others. This quantum leap of consciousness is the only divine purpose of all the – otherwise aimless and senseless – good and bad things we experience in our lives.

Regarding the question of the atom bombs (and all other dark chapters of human history, like the concentration camps, the killing of the Amerindians or the enslavement of the Africans), it has to be clearly stated that these destinies were *not predestined*. In one phrase: It was not the predestination of the victims, it was their karma – and that is a big difference. But the notion of karma has to be properly understood.

In reality, karma is the challenge of handling duality according to predestination and free will. When people erroneously say, 'It was the karma of the Japanese (or of the Germans, the Jews, the Amerindians, the black slaves, etc.)', they are saying it was their *predestination*. And this is a half-truth that is fatally wrong, what to speak of being cynical and corruptive.

Intrinsic to life in the world of karma (duality) is the risk of becoming victimized or seduced by others who misuse their free will. Everyone who enters this zone will meet good and evil forces. Not even Jesus could avoid it – he was arrested, tortured and crucified. Did he simply have 'bad karma'? Was he just reaping the reactions to some evil action he had performed? Had he murdered or even crucified some people in a previous lifetime?* Of course not. But he had (voluntarily) entered the zone of duality and had thus become exposed to evil forces. In the higher sense of the term, it was the karma of Jesus: As soon as he entered this world, it was predestined that he would be attacked, but due

---

* This would be the compelling line of logic if the deistic and monistic versions of karma were the ultimate truth. Christians who condemn karma and reincarnation as 'doctrines of Satan' usually refer to these atheistic misunderstandings, and in this regard they are even right. However, karma and reincarnation – in the original, theistic understanding – are fully compatible with the teachings of Jesus. Resurrection and reincarnation are no contradiction.

to his free will and divine love he was not overwhelmed by feelings of duality. Rather, he manifested the triumph of love over the 'forces of Satan', even conquering physical death. In other words, Jesus faced the challenge of karma and passed it gloriously. 'Truly I say to you, those who follow me with faith will do the works that I do and, in fact, will do greater works than these …' (John 14.12)

Let us summarize: The term karma refers to the interaction of predestination and free will. Isolating or over-emphasizing one of these two factors is a fatal fallacy and one-sidedness (half-truth).

Due to the individual factor of free will, the chain of cause and effect is never exclusively mechanical. Through the laws of karma, we are constantly confronted with situations caused, or chosen, by ourselves and others, and we are forced to react. *How* we react is up to our free will (divine love being the perfection of free will). The degree to which we are unable to access our free will is dependent on the extent to which we allow ourselves to be influenced by mental and elemental programs. As explained in Chapter Two, the creation or acceptance of such alien programs may have taken place way back in the past, in some situation in which we forsook our free will.[42]

Through predestination we find ourselves in certain situations, and it is our responsibility to decide what to do in these situations. At any moment we can start new chain reactions of karma – and the dark forces do it constantly, foolishly thinking that it is 'predestined' (as believed by atheistic deists) or 'necessary' (as believed by atheistic monists).

Thus far, the misunderstandings regarding oneness, *maya* and karma have been addressed and, hopefully, clarified. On this basis, we can now illuminate the ultimate half-truth: the principle of necessity being the supreme truth (according to monistic 'realism').

God's laws and God's will

Within the worlds of space and time, everything happens strictly according to the laws of polarity, especially the laws of karma. Nothing happens by chance, nothing happens without a cause, not even the most godless things. Ultimately, every action is caused by somebody on the basis of free will. The crucial question is: To what extent is this action in oneness with God's will?

Here, we touch on the most important aspect of the world formula, 'The reality beyond duality is individuality.' Every philosophy which ignores this aspect is atheistic, as demonstrated – to the extreme – by the illuminati and their philosophy. Now we can grasp their gravest mistake: By defining reality through negating duality they do not take into account *God's individuality*. That is why they consider God to be nothing but an abstract totality of potential energy. For them there is no God with absolute consciousness, love and free will. Due to this godlessness they ignore God's will, or equate it with God's laws, thinking that whatever happens is justified because it happens according to the laws of cause and effect.

However, there is a big difference between God's laws and God's will. *Although everything happens according to God's laws, not everything is in accordance with God's will!*

All beings, due to their free will, have the freedom to act against God's will – if they want. God is not just the sum total of matter and its merciless laws. Therefore, God is not the cause of everything just as light is not the cause of darkness. Philosophically speaking, God as the absolute Individuality is *the cause of all causes:* the 'remote' or indirect cause of everything. Obviously, God is not the *direct* cause of everything. This, however, is exactly what the illuminati say: 'Whatever happens is caused by "God" because it happens according to God's laws.' But now we know that we have to differentiate between God's laws and God's will – because God, the absolute Individuality, has will and consciousness.

By denying eternal (spiritual) individuality, thinking consciousness to be a product of matter, atheists end up with a distorted concept of free will. They do not understand the power of free will, which allows one to respect or to disrespect other people's free will, both options having respective consequences. As free will is not dictated by predestination, we are fully responsible for all of our thoughts and deeds. This is also valid for those who imagine themselves to be enlightened and entitled to act 'beyond good and evil'.

Contrary to the atheistic belief 'everything is one and in-different', practical logic and experience show that *nothing* is one and indifferent. As eternal individuals, we have free will and responsibility, even beyond the existence of our mortal bodies. Therefore, it *does* matter what we think, feel, talk, do, consume etc., for all these activities have a retroactive effect on our consciousness, which in turn determines the course of our lives with all the possibilities we choose: further bondage, indoctrination and mental patterns of fear, or spiritual awakening, self-responsibility and liberation from all fears.

> 'If you continue in my word [and do not allow yourself to be intimidated by the preaching of the high priests (8.44)], you are truly my followers; and you will know the truth, and the truth will make you free.' (John 8.31–2)

The mentioning of God's will leads to the most essential question: *What is God's will?* How can we know God's will? Cannot everybody justify his deeds by saying 'God wants it so'?

Divine paradox: being individual and one

The relationship between the relative and the absolute, both being individual, can be compared to the sun and the sunrays or, in more abstract terms, to 'the whole' and its innumerable 'parts'. God as the Whole is one, undivided and indivisible (= individual), and we as individual souls are parts of the Whole. How can the undivided and indivisible One divide itself into innumerable parts? How can the One become many and still remain *one,* unchanged and individual?

An enlightening answer is given by divine revelations and self-realized mystics. They say that the One's subdivision into innumerable parts is absolute and real but not dividing and separating (just as the sunrays, though being 'individual', are never separated from the sun). Due to an act of free will, however, some parts can forsake their consciousness of being a part of the Whole and start an ego trip of misidentification (*maya*). From God's absolute perspective, they are still connected to the Whole, but from the standpoint of the fallen living entity, this connection is non-existent because it is no longer part of his consciousness.

In other words, everything is a question of consciousness – separation as well as oneness. The question therefore is: In what state of being (consciousness) can one transcEnd the illusory separation? How can we simultaneously be individual and one?

There is only *one* state of being that resolves this divine paradox – and that is *Love.* Love means to be united in consciousness. It is the oneness of individuality. Without individuality there is no question of real love (the problem of materialism), and without real love there is no question of harmony with God's will (the problem of all ego religions).

In this light, the difference between God's laws and God's will becomes evident. God's laws of creation are strict and automatic. Their only purpose is to manifest the universal stage of action and to regulate the 'game of roles' according to cause and effect. God's will, however, is totally different, just as light is different from all forms of shadow. God wants this oneness of pure Love and does not want the separation of duality, which binds the living entities to the chain reactions of 'His' laws. In the spiritual reality, the only 'law' is love, and love is not a law but an expression of free will. It is not the effect of some material cause.

To be in harmony with God's will means to serve this aim of Love consciously and directly. 'Thy will be done.' This is the meaning of being beyond duality, being divine.* Everything else – good or bad – is not in harmony with God's will and is subject to God's laws, being part of duality. Good is good, and bad is bad, but even so-called good actions do not have the power to free a person from the cycle of material causes and effects. Good actions will force one to reap good reactions within the worlds of duality because one's consciousness is still limited to material identifications. The real Good beyond duality is that which is done in divine consciousness according to God's will, according to the dynamics of unconditional love.

In this context, the importance of perceiving God's individuality is self-evident. Without this perspective, the cold 'truths' of atheism would factually be true, and life would be godless and ultimately meaningless.

Thank God, this is not the case.

---

* Both atheists and theists speak about the ideal of being 'beyond good and evil'. The atheistic interpretation of this ideal ends up in a godless, loveless pragmatism which seems to justify all acts, both good and evil, if they are 'necessary'. The theistic interpretation leads to an individual sense of responsibility and love based on the understanding that 'good' and 'evil' reflect the same divine purpose, namely the lesson of differentiating without judging, which is possible only by being aware of God's will. Otherwise, one is left with no other choice than acting according to the impulses of the ego in ignorance of one's real identity and vocation.

The mystery of unconditional love

'One who is truly enlightened sees Me everywhere and sees everything in Me. Indeed, the self-realized soul sees Me everywhere. One who sees Me everywhere and everything in Me is never separated from Me, and I am never separated from him.'
– Bhagavad-gita 6.30–1

Those who have fallen into duality are no longer consciously connected to God, the Source of all energies, and have to obtain energies from other sources, which is a form of subtle 'vampirism'. Within duality, everyone lives at the cost of others and tends to hide or suppress it with all kinds of self-justification.

Separation from the Source is an illusion (*maya*). It is a state of covered consciousness, and it can be transcEnded by restoring one's original consciousness of oneness and individuality (= divine love). If we are in harmony with the Whole we are 'holystic'. Then, we are consciously connected to God, and from God, the absolute Source, we will receive all we need for living this love.

Love is the purest expression of free will. Love can never be forced or demanded, and in love, we never force or demand. Pure love is unconditional. Therefore, even though being connected to the absolute Source of everything, we desire nothing for our ego, just as nobody would think of feeding or dressing his shadow. Those who have no ambitions of power become fully empowered to act as selfless Light beings, just as Brahma, the highest Light being in this universe, who serves as a pure channel of God's creation.

Love is not just the 'second highest galactic energy level' or the 'most illusory form of duality'. Love is the only *direct and conscious* connection to our origin; it is the oneness of personal and absolute individuality. Because Love reunites us to the Source, it is the supreme creative force in the universe. Love is the essence of reality.

Evil is unable to match the power of Love just as darkness is unable to dissipate light. Impressive examples of this triumph of Love were given by many martyrs (in both religious and imperialistic history) and by Jesus. He, the highest Light being of the universe,[43] came into the darkness of this world in order to face Satan's worst attacks. In spite of the many lies and aggressions he had to endure, he never deviated from his Love. It was as if he wanted to say, 'You can do to me whatever you want, but you can never make me abandon my Love for you.' No emotion of hatred or revenge came to his mind. His Love was so unconditional that he even prayed for his tormentors: 'Father, please forgive them for they know not what they do.' (Luke 23.34)

Real love, being unconditional, is never limited: 'Love God the Father with all your heart and soul, and love all others as you love yourself.' (Matt. 22.37–40; Mark 12.28–31; Luke 10.25–28)

People who truly love themselves for what they are (= I-AM consciousness) are also able to love all others for what they are: eternal, divine individuals, rays of God. Men and women with this consciousness are truly whole and 'holy'. Being one with the Source, they are fully satisfied within themselves. They do not need to 'thrive' on other people's energies.

At the same time, this individual wholeness does not exclude human relationships of love and intimacy. Divine love, being unconditional, is independent of external conditions and dogmas. It is not limited to celibacy and puritanism. Rather, if two spiritually self-sufficient humans come together in unconditional love, they are able to create an energy field most rare on this planet. It is this energy of heartfelt love that Mother Earth is painfully lacking (despite so many religions talking about 'love').

Love, the real form of mercy

Divine love can neither be forced nor demanded, neither by God nor by us. It is not a product of mental imagination, nor is it the product of external conditions. Being spiritual, it has to be sparked on the spiritual level, which happens by an arrangement of divine mercy, as Love is a form of revelation. Even on the human level, the love responding to our love is spontaneous and not calculable. It is an intimate revelation of the person answering our love, allowing us to be mutually connected on the innermost level. It is 'mercy' in the original sense of the word: the readiness to love and the openness to be loved. This especially refers to God, who is sometimes described as *supremely merciful*, which is absolutely true because God always loves us and allows us to love Him, whoever we are and no matter what we may have done. God's love, being absolute, is causeless and unconditional. (For atheists, these aspects of reality are inconceivable and non-existent, because they have no idea of God's individuality.)

Usually, God's mercy is understood as the 'forgiving of sins' or, in symbolical terms, as the light which dissipates darkness. This definition is valid, of course, but it is based on a standpoint within darkness, otherwise there would be no need of dissipating darkness. If religionists always stress the forgiving of sins, darkness might seduce them to think that God's mercy is their monopoly. Even in this case, they at least sense the individuality of God. Automatic laws and abstract energies would not know mercy and forgiveness.

The mercy of God, however, is not subject to sectarian claims of monopoly. Rather, mercy is the inherent quality of God's absolute love, just like brightness is the inherent quality of light. The disappearance of darkness, or sin, is a natural side-effect for all those who awaken to the oneness of love. Regardless of how long we may have been in darkness, light will flow into our most hidden corners as soon as we open the doors. Even before we step out into the light, it is already there, coming towards us. That is the natural mercy of the light. A cave may have been blocked by a stone for thousands of years, but as soon as the stone is removed, light fills the cave as if there had never been any darkness.

Similarly, God is always there, eternally and unconditionally – waiting for us. As soon as we awaken and repent, dissolving the walls of the ego, all darkness and separation ('sin') is immediately removed (= forgiven) as if it had never existed. Then, by this mercy, we are able to perceive God's love everywhere, under all conditions, be they catastrophic, threatening, normal, peaceful, romantic, idyllic etc.

All of a sudden, in moments of inner initiation, we get a glimpse of God's mercy, His ever-present and ever-inviting Love. Through such experiences our own love becomes sparked and ignited, and there is no longer any darkness for us, no matter where we are. This 'sparking' happens through a contact with beings who already live in this love, be they incarnate (as inspiring individuals) or present invisibly (as non-fallen angels and ascended saints). All of them are united in the true desire for God's love, a desire which is always answered by God's mercy.

> 'I am asking on their behalf. I am not asking on behalf of the world, but on behalf of those whom you gave me, because they are yours. All mine are yours, and yours are mine, and I have been glorified in them. And now I am

no longer in the world, but they remain in the world, and I am coming to you. Beloved Father, protect them in your name that you have given me, so that they may be one, as we are one. [...] I ask not only on behalf of these, but also on behalf of those who will believe in me after hearing about me from them, so that they may all be one. As you, Father, are in me and I am in you, may they also be in us ...' (John 17.9–11, 20–1)

Experiencing the eternal in temporary situations

Being individual also means *being unique* because each part of the Whole, just as each ray of the sun, is unique. Each individual is united to God by a unique relationship of Love. Again, God is so perfect and all-encompassing that 'He' also includes the aspect of not having something. (If He were to have everything, He would be lacking something, namely the aspect of *not having something!*) What is it that God does not have? It is our *unconditional love,* because it is the pure expression of our free will, which cannot be forced, not even by God.

Our uniqueness can be experienced only through the consciousness of divine love. This uniqueness is *spiritual* and thus 'nothing special', because every individual is unique! We are *all* unique, and therefore it is pointless to be falsely proud, trying to impress others with one's uniqueness. Being spiritual, it can only be experienced spiritually and individually. All attempts to express it on a material level quickly lead to competitions of the ego ('unique' intelligence, talent, taste, style, car, clothes etc.)

Without the inner fulfilment of real love, people are prone to be influenced by illusion, fear and envy, and they are left with the perishable nature of all their works. Everything they accomplish and experience is temporary, ordinary and not unique, and they have no vision of any spiritual goal in their lives. Indeed, the awareness that life might have an ultimate purpose is not part of their momentary existence.

However, through the experience of divine love and mercy, we are enabled to perceive the spiritual aspect behind all material expressions, as we are spiritual ourselves. The forms of material polarity, like man/woman, black skin/white skin, and my possessions/your possessions, are no longer seen as a duality (based on the ego) but as aspects of the variety within the oneness of the Absolute. This consciousness is possible only on the 'wavelength' of unconditional love, which can take on many forms according to the law of resonance. (We remember the example of Jesus saying 'Away with you, Satan', which was an expression of unconditional love. On the next pages we will meet Jesus kissing Mary Magdalene, another expression of the same love.)

In other words, 'it is not that important *what* you do, but *how* you do it'. This indicates that the 'how' (the loving, self-less manner) is most important. It naturally excludes all activities contrary to this enlightened consciousness.

The more we become conscious of our timeless being, the more we begin to experience an inner happiness that is not subject to the flow of time. Then, the temporary nature of all material things, including our bodies, is no longer seen as a threat. We perceive ourselves in our true identity as eternal individuals, and we experience our lives in the spirit of eternity, which allows us to live in the present, free from all sentimental* attachment to the 'past' and the 'future'. In this way, every moment of our lives is perceived as unique, reflecting the eternity of all energy and the uniqueness of all beings. Through this view of eternity, seemingly transient actions like eating, singing, loving, working and praying naturally reveal their spiritual essence to us – the inspiration to remain beyond duality through unshaken, fearless God consciousness.

This applies to all aspects of life, not least to the relationship of man and woman.

Divine love and earthly love

When a man and a woman come together in holystic God consciousness, they are able to create a spiritually intimate energy field in which prayer, meditation and love can gain unique intensity. Such profound experiences, in turn, enrich all forms of personal meditation practised alone as well as the co-operation of like-minded people who work

---

* Sentimental: derived from the Latin words *sentire*, 'to perceive sensually, to sense, to feel', and *mentalis*, 'existing in the mind as thought, feeling or imagination'; refers to the mental identification with nice sensual impressions within the non-tarrying flow of linear time. A sentimental person wants to hold on to something material (gross or subtle) by trying to turn a transient experience into a sensual or mental form that is as 'eternal as possible' – which is an illusion (*maya*).

together as a group. 'For where two or three gather together in my name, there I am in their midst.' (Matt. 18.20)

However, the man-woman relationship has been hurt and traumatized for thousands of years. One of the first things the dia-bolic forces attacked was the harmony of men and women, as mentioned in the first chapter ('The negative infiltration of religions'). Men began to subject and exploit women, and women began to accept the role of victims and objects. In this poisoned atmosphere, both men and women were lacking real love. Suddenly, people found themselves in a degrading struggle for existence, being subjugated by superiors who claimed for themselves the authority of God and, later on, also the authority of secular power in the name of progress, industrial revolution, socialism, capitalism, globalism, national security, etc. Nowadays, financial pressure is forcing even mothers to take on jobs, sometimes two or three at the same time. This modern form of 'slavery' leaves children exposed to TV, drugs and other neglected children.

Throughout the centuries, men and women have become alienated from each other. Their contact was monitored by religious and secular controllers and programmed by social pressure. It took many steps of cultural, musical[44] and spiritual emancipation for mankind to regain some 'private' freedom. The price was high, and the pitfalls deep, but this new situation enabled receptive men and women to communicate in a more open, freeing harmony. In this way, many old wounds could be healed. The polarization and decadence of our time is, obviously, not absolutely bad. Modern society, despite its destructive and explosive potential, provides an opportunity of freedom not found in countries with 'less progressive' systems. These, in their turn, contain other advantages that outsiders may not know. Nevertheless, none of these systems is perfect, to say the least.

If men and women are able (and enabled) to live in harmony, society will change again, granting the families a new quality and integrity. In a sanctified atmosphere men and women can experience their inner connection to the Source, and experience initiations into their own vocation and priesthood. 'For where two or three gather together in my name ...'

Individuals who are raised on such a fertile ground of love become spiritually mature and are naturally immune against manipulation. In view of this potential, it is obvious why the dark forces have undermined the man-woman relationship and unbalanced the family structure by establishing a male-dominated society (patriarchate*) based on performance and productivity. The alternative is not some matriarchate, but the harmony of both poles, which is possible only within the triad of divine love: 'Love God, and love all others as you love yourself.' As soon as one of these three aspects is cut off or neglected, it is no longer divine love.

Today, after a long history of deviation, we have regained all the information required to find this harmony, at least individually – provided we recognize the opportunity and avoid the pitfalls.

The empowerment of men and women

Earth and mankind, both traumatized by deep wounds, need a global healing. Light must come into the darkness. As quoted above, 'two or three' are sufficient to create additional cores of light. Nowadays, in many parts of the world, men and women are free again for this communion – not only a select few in secret mystery schools but all who are receptive and sensitive. This intensified illumination will bring about the dawning of a new age or, in more orthodox terms, 'the pouring out of the spirit on all flesh [...] when the end times come' (Joel 2.28–32, as quoted by the Apostle Peter when he explained the happenings in the morning of the Whitsun holiday, Acts 2.16–21).

The ending of the present age is the beginning of a new age which will change the face of the earth. Then, simple men and women – and not the institutional dignitaries – will receive the blessing of God's spirit. 'Your sons and daughters shall prophesy [...]. Even on the menservants and the maidservants will I pour out my spirit in those days.' (The far-reaching import of this prophecy will be further elaborated in Part III of this book.)

Prophet Joel lived in a patriarchal, male-dominated society (around 400 BC) where women were considered inferior and sinful, being descendants of Eve, the seducer of Adam. The idea of lay men *and women* from the lower classes becoming empowered by God's spirit must have

---

* Patriarchate: lit. 'supremacy of the fathers, or men in general'; from Grk. *pater,* 'father', and *archein,* 'to rule, to dominate'.

been shocking and inconceivable even for Joel. Still, he pronounced his revolutionary vision. A few centuries later, it was expanded by Jesus, who added: 'The time will come when the people will worship the Father neither on this mountain nor in Jerusalem. [...] A time will come, and it has already begun, when those who are truly devoted will worship the Father in spirit and truth.' (John 4.21, 23)

Typically enough, Jesus pronounced this prophetic statement not in a solemn circle of men but in a casual conversation with a so-called pagan woman from Samaria, a social outcaste who had been married five times, as Jesus told her with clairvoyance (4.18), 'and the man you now have is not your husband'. He revealed these private things not to reproach her but to point out whom he had chosen to talk to. 'Just then his disciples returned, and they were astonished that he was speaking with a woman. But no one said: "What do you want?" or, "Why are you speaking with her?" The woman, therefore, left ...' (4.27)

The example of Jesus and Mary Magdalene

When looking for an early revolutionary example of a holystic man-woman relationship, we can again refer to Jesus. This may not be that obvious if we limit him to the four gospels that remained in the biblical canon. However, additional information about the life of Jesus is contained in the gospels that were rejected (and destroyed) by the Church. In 1945, some of these lost gospels were found in ancient clay pots that had been buried in Nag Hammadi, Egypt, in the fourth century by persecuted Gnostic Christians. Amongst these precious manuscripts were the 'Gospel of Thomas' and the 'Gospel of Philip'. In the latter we find descriptions of Jesus' earthly love:

> Three women were in constant association with the Lord: his mother, his sister and Magdalene, who was called his 'companion'. His sister, his mother and his companion were all named Miriam [Mary]. (32.1–2)

> When he was on earth, the Redeemer loved Mary Magdalene more than all of his apostles. He often kissed her on her mouth. The Apostles, seeing this, became jealous and morose. They asked: 'Why do you love her more than all of us?' The Redeemer replied: 'Why don't I love you as much as I love her?' (55.2–6)[45]

Even nowadays it would be quite scandalous if someone dared to kiss his wife (what to speak of a female companion) publicly in the streets of Jerusalem or amongst a Jewish circle. But Jesus, a young Rabbi, did it two thousand years ago, and thus provoked criticism even from his own apostles. His answer sounds almost ironical and amused: 'Guess why I love this woman more than all of you men!'

Jesus loved Mary Magdalene, and he did not consider it beneath his dignity to admit it publicly. In this deeply patriarchal society, Jesus showed that divine love does not exclude human love. It was an open provocation. Transgressing any social or confessional dogma was said to be punished by God. But Jesus and Mary broke this spell of imposed fears – the fear of priests, the fear of scriptural threats and the fear of (alleged) condemnation. Obviously, their love did neither harm nor weaken them, quite the contrary. When persecution started, Jesus displayed his unconditional love towards friends and aggressors. When Jesus was crucified, Mary was one of the few who stood by him while all the men were hiding (except for John). In this most difficult moment, when everything looked hopeless and lost, she and Jesus had to face all the critics gloating over their seemingly illicit and destroyed love. But, as history showed, their love was neither destroyed nor futile.

Invisible to the dark forces

The Gospel of Philip contains confidential teachings which could be called gnostic or esoteric, in the original sense of the word. Its language is very cryptic and often uses the symbolism of a man's and a woman's union, referring to the union, or 'marriage', of the self to God. At the same time, the usage of this symbolism shows that human intimacy was neither detested nor condemned. Several times the 'sacrament of the Bridal Room' is mentioned as a man's and a woman's mystic initiation into transcendental consciousness:

> 'When Eve was still with Adam, death did not exist. When she was separated from him, death came into being. If he enters again and attains his former self, death will be no more. [...] Woman becomes one with man within the bridal chamber. Those thus unified can no longer be separated from each other. Eve could only be separated from Adam because they had not become unified within the bridal chamber.' (71.1–3; 79.1–3)

> 'Restoration through the sacrament of the bridal chamber [...] Whoever receives it, is no longer just a Christian, but Christ./ The Father gave Christ the Holy Spirit within the bridal chamber, and he received it. The Father lived within the Son and the Son within the Father. That is the reign of God.' (67.6; 96.1–3)

These are words of Jesus as recorded by the Apostle Philip. Is it surprising that the Church leaders wanted to eradicate this gospel? Today, knowing the Gospel of Philip, we can detect remnants of these gnostic teachings even in the official gospels. Several times Jesus uses allegories of the bride and bridegroom (Matt. 9.15; 22.30; 25.1–12), and he quotes Gen. 1.27–31, where it says that God created the human being in his image, as man and woman, and that God was pleased with this creation. Jesus adds that for love, a man will leave father and mother to live with his wife. 'The two are one with body and soul, and what God has put together, man shall not separate.' (Matt. 19.5–6)

This statement is similar to the aforementioned quote from the Gospel of Philip: 'Woman becomes one with man within the bridal chamber. Those thus unified can no longer be separated from each other.' Apparently, Jesus was referring to a spiritual initiation and only secondarily to the social codex. This was also shown by his prophetic conversation with the woman from Samaria whom he fully respected and even joked with despite her five divorces!

A typical characteristic of esoteric language is the symbolic use of words without negating the symbol itself. This makes it mysterious and multi-facetted, as shown by the following quote:

> 'The perfect ones become pregnant by a kiss, and give birth. Therefore, we kiss each other. We become pregnant by the mercy that is in each other.' (31.1–3)

Certainly, these words of Jesus are symbolic. But are they only symbolic? Jesus' kissing Mary was quite physical (and public), otherwise it would not have disturbed his apostles.

These confidential teachings do not intend to propagate 'free sex' or sexual magic. At the same time, they do not maintain an abnegation or condemnation of sexuality either:

> 'Great is the sacrament of marriage. Without it there would be no world, as the world's existence depends on mankind, and mankind's continued existence depends on marriage. Now, first of all, think of intercourse without

sexual tingeing. For its power is great! Sexual tingeing is its reflection only.' (60.1–5)

'The weak, mortal sensuality of mankind – do not fear it, do not love it. Those who fear it will become controlled by it. Those who love it will be paralysed and swallowed by it.' (62.1–3)

'In this world there is the union of man and woman, a mutual complementing of strength and weakness. In the heavenly world the union is different.' (103.1–2)

As already mentioned, destroying the harmony of men and women has been a main tactic of the dark forces in their attempt to gain increased world control. In this connection, Jesus hints at one of the reasons:

'There are impure spirits of male and female gender. Those who are male want to approach souls incarnate in female bodies. Those who are female want to approach souls incarnate in male bodies. [...] However, when they see a man and a woman together, the female spirits cannot approach the man and the male spirits cannot approach the woman, and none else would dare it either.' (61.1–3, 8)

'Someone who has attracted the perfect Light can no longer be seen by the invisible forces. Thus, they cannot bother such a person. In the sacrament of union, which is the sacrament of the bridal chamber, we attract this Light.' (77.1–3)

Possession by impure spirits has become a wide-spread disease causing global, interpersonal and psychological disorder, even physical illness. Nevertheless, hardly anyone is able to recognize the real cause of these alarming symptoms.

Over the centuries, the lack of love and self-protection has caused men and women to end up spiritually extradite. Through these weaknesses they have opened astral and 'incarnational' inlet doors, allowing dark spirits to get an increased reach into the earthly world. Many people, amongst them prominent players in politics, economics and religion, are influenced by such spirits or are incarnations of such. Coming from a background of darkness, they 'naturally' think it is their rightful claim to possess the world. The possessed want to possess others. As mentioned by Jesus, they are even ready to attack the Light and those men and women who embody it (Matt. 10.16–33; Luke 21.7–19, etc.). At the same time he assures: 'Do not fear them; for nothing is covered up that will not become uncovered, and nothing secret that will not become known.' (Matt. 10.26)

One of the mysteries that needs to be revealed is the spiritual potential of men and women working together in transcendental consciousness. This includes the spiritual education of children, beginning with their conception in spiritual love (as one aspect of the sacrament of the bridal chamber). It also includes the presence of holystic men and women in all generations, as parents, grand-parents, mentors and pioneers of a new society. In such a wonderful atmosphere, all other mysteries that have to be known can be revealed, and the world itself becomes a bridal chamber, ready for the marriage of heaven and earth.

It all begins with individuals manifesting isles of Light and Love through divine devotion. As stated in the Gospel of Philip (77) the power of devotion is so great that it attracts the 'perfect Light', and 'those who have attracted the perfect Light can no longer be seen by the invisible forces.'

Regarding our passing through times of tests and turmoil, sacred sources encourage us to build individual isles of Light and Love, for 'where two or three gather together in my name, I am there in their midst'. This is an inspiring vision that can easily, and immediately, be realized as a possible next step in life. It is more efficient and protective than all theoretical theology although it may appear too simple to be a solution. In any case, it is a seed for the new earth to come, and a direct transformation of our lives. Therefore, this topic has been highlighted with particular attention.

Summary and outlook

'Ye shall know them by their fruits.' Wars, ecological destruction and other shows of force are indications that the earth is being influenced by powers working within the two strains of negativity, the too-much and the too-little. In the symbolism of light and darkness they are the dark forces – those who have separated themselves from the light –, and their 'fruits' are obvious proofs thereof.

Those caught up in darkness have no view of the light, and if they try to define 'light', they will do it in terms of darkness. Similarly, those with a consciousness limited to relative existence have no direct experience of the reality beyond duality, and define 'reality' by applying their relative views either in the category of the too-much or the too-little. Philosophically, they define reality by absolutizing or negating the relative.

'Absolutizing the relative' means taking a set of relative truths (half-truths) and considering them to be the absolute reality. These can be religious or materialistic doctrines.

'Negating the relative' means defining reality by negating duality, considering duality to be non-real and, thus, irrelevant for 'realists'. This is a world-view which is *negative* in the literal sense of the word. It says that the Absolute (God) is nothing but an abstract oneness of energy which is duality-less and, consequently, hateless and loveless, painless and joyless, evilless and goodless, and godless. 'There is no God outside of me, no God outside of man and matter.' Such deluded realists think themselves to be 'beyond good and evil' and to be empowered by 'destiny' to do whatever they themselves deem 'necessary' according to their godless 'realism'. (The term 'illuminati' refers to all those who fall into this category of ego-justification.)

In other words, absolutizing and negating the relative are the two faces of the same coin called atheism, or atheistic monism, to be more precise. Monism means seeing one common reality beyond duality, and there is nothing wrong with that. However, contrary to divine monism, atheistic monism considers this reality to be an unconscious totality of energy: either physical matter (= materialistic monism) or an abstract oneness of metaphysical potentials (= occult monism). Both are atheistic and, in their application, pragmatic.

Materialistic monism states that physical matter is the ultimate reality; everything, including individuality, is considered to be a product of matter; individuation only happens within the world of duality, namely through an evolution of matter (life comes from matter and matter from a 'big bang').

Occult monism accepts superior dimensions of matter (including magical and paraphysical realities) but denies a supreme, absolute reality of spiritual consciousness.

What is wrong, or incomplete, with these beliefs? Is it true that no God exists apart from us; that the merciless laws of gross and subtle matter are the highest reality; that everything is one and in-different;

that enlightenment means to negate duality, as duality (good/evil, love/hate, life/death, etc.) is just an illusion?

Yes, this would be true if there were no absolute individual God, as maintained by occult monism (atheism) pursuant to the logic: 'Light is merely the absence of shadow; there is no self-effulgent light beyond darkness.'

However, self-effulgent light beyond darkness does exist. Similarly, beyond duality, there is *individuality* as the absolute essence of all life. Both the parts and the Whole are individual (= indivisible, eternal beings of consciousness) but not separate beings. Still, the parts have the option to lose the consciousness of their non-separation by taking up a false identification (ego). In this way, they separate themselves from the Source and need to obtain their life energy from other sources, which is the cause of egoistical behaviour and exploitation. This ego trip continues until the respective 'fallen soul' becomes God conscious again.

The parts and the Whole, both individual in quality, are one – and can become one – through the union of love. Usually, 'becoming one' is understood to mean merging and dissolving one's self, and 'being individual', emerging from oneness and to be 'oneself'. However, these are limited, material concepts. In love, one can be two and 'one heart and one soul' simultaneously. This applies to both the relative and the absolute levels of life. Beyond the duality of separation is the oneness of love, which is possible only in the consciousness of one's own and God's indivisible, eternal being ('individuality'). In other words, love is not just an aspect of duality but an aspect of individuality, and is therefore an absolute reality. *How* each individual reaches this consciousness of love and lives it in practice is again something absolutely individual. This is the theistic version of pragmatism.

The individuality of God and all His parts includes the mystery of free will and God's will. If God were nothing but an abstract totality of energy, then God would be without consciousness, without love, without mercy, and without free will, and 'Thy will be done' would be a nonsensical statement. Those believing reality to be a godless totality of energy perceive nothing but the seemingly automatic mechanism of material laws and an abstract absence of duality behind it, which misleads them into thinking that everything in this world is determined by self-organizing material laws (= atheistic deism) or shaped by material energies either through evolution (= materialistic monism) or through mental projections (= occult monism). Such occultists see themselves as God because they think it is they who shape the world's destiny through their secret sciences which (seemingly) enable them to manipulate all energies – both living entities and material objects. If one thinks reality to be an abstract totality, or oneness, of neutral energies, then it is just 'natural' to believe that mastery of these energies is the ultimate perfection of existence. Such occult and technomagical forces are not limited to planet earth. They are resident throughout the dark worlds.

Beyond all forms of shadow, God's individuality is eternally present with absolute consciousness, love, mercy and free will. And God wants nothing but the real oneness of love. Outside this oneness there is duality along with all its laws and shadows, granting the option of living under the impressions of the ego. In reality, nobody is omnipotent and independent. The infallible working of God's laws, however, does not cause absolute predestination (which would indeed justify all actions). Why? Because there is individuality and free will, and God's will. Although corresponding to God's laws, actions within duality are not in accordance with *God's will!*

Those who choose to fall into a lack or loss of love inevitably miss the divine challenge behind all forms of duality. Therefore, they react with elitism and arrogance, if they happen to be on the 'winning' side, or with bitterness, hatred and feelings of revenge when on the losing side. In the course of history, no group or institution has been spared this kind of contamination. As shown in the next chapter, both secular and religious traditions have lost much of the original purity which they had when they were united as divine mystery schools.

One main factor in this deterioration has been the undermining of the man-woman relationship. Interestingly enough, both secular and religious organizations, though being very antagonistic, have the common characteristic of being *male-dominated*. Freemasons and other lodge groups are exclusive congregations of men (with a few exceptions). The same is true for the leading circles of all religions, both eastern and western.

Today, after all these centuries of materialism, fanaticism and egoism, mankind is called to wake up and to come out of the tunnel of the dark age, which means transcEnding duality once and for all. The philosophical aspect of this ultimate challenge has been elaborated here in

Chapter Four. In the next chapter, the *historical* aspect will be taken up. Like everything in the world of duality, this part of history also consists of two sides – two sides which at one point became opponents, as both were, and still are, main lines of worldly power, one standing on the religious side, the other on the secular side. They emerged from the same spiritual background and entered the stage of history from two different sides, which entailed the danger of one-sided self-identification and, consequently, division into half-truths. In the next chapter, we will examine their common origins, how both of them became infiltrated, contaminated and misused, and how a new purity will be found – through the all-powerful course of time and through the dedication of those who are truly in the Light.

CHAPTER FIVE

Sacred Knowledge and Secret Societies: A Long History of Devotion and Deviation

In the past, the earth was sporadically struck by mega-catastrophes: the impact of a comet or asteroid, a pole shift, a sudden vertical jolting of the continental plates, the explosion of a caldera (magma chamber) or factors inconceivable to modern man, such as magnetospheric fluctuations and dimensional quantum leaps of the planet.

Through their global effect, these earth changes initiated new phases of geological and 'pre-historical' developments. If mythical civilizations, like Lemuria, Hyperborea, Kásskara, Bharata, E.din, Antarctica or Atlantis, did exist, they obviously did not survive, and those individuals who survived were reduced to a 'primitive' existence close to nature, thus receiving the challenge of a new beginning.

World-wide geological upheavals and coinciding transformations usually efface almost all vestiges of former civilizations. Therefore, the later generations of renascent mankind are left with only vague ideas of their own origins. In extreme cases they even imagine themselves to be the crown of evolution, thinking that the 'naked ape' had never been as advanced as the species that calls itself *homo sapiens*.

However, there are always traces that allow those with 'eyes to see' to recognize that mankind's prehistory is not a story of primitive humans, products of an alleged animal evolution, but a cosmic life-history of 'humanoids' who descended from non-material origins. If we do not exclude such a non-materialistic perspective, we can begin to fathom new interpretations of the ancient cultures' legends and physical remnants that survived the ages. We will no longer be limited to 'logical' school history, but access a mytho-logical view of mankind's remote past that includes civilizations appearing and disappearing within the multidimensional space-time cycles pertinent to planet earth.

The concept of cyclic ages is nothing new. In the ancient Sanskrit language, for example, it is known as the *yugas,* the 'world ages' that follow each other in a non-linear, spiral development characterized by evolutionary changes according to planetary, solar and galactic cycles. Embedded in this course of cosmic history, the earth passes through a multidimensional spiral of space and time, changing its physical appearance and, at certain points, even its physical density.

In other words, not only the earth's geology, flora and fauna are changing but also the workings of the physical laws. This scenario postulates that in the past, the physical laws had different effects on earth than today; in other words, gravity and density were different in these earlier cycles. There were other continents and other civilizations, there was another atmosphere and another (or an additional) kind of human being with a physical body of a lesser density. In terms of biophysics, this category of organic matter had another atomic frequency and, subsequently, another nuclear balance. Indeed, modern quantum physicists wonder why the atoms are the way they are. There are innumerable other possibilities of orbital units and quantum potentials implying innumerable possibilities of other dimensional existences. Terms like 'hyperspace' and 'parallel worlds' point in this direction.[46]

Thus, at least theoretically, avant-garde science is giving some plausibility to science fiction – and to mythology. Regarding multidimensional realities and parallel worlds, ancient cultures indicate that planet earth itself was a 'parallel world' in former ages! At another point within the spiral of time and space – what we call 'the past' – life on earth was extended to a broader spectrum of physical existence. Therefore, it is not possible to draw conclusions about the origin of life and human culture simply by projecting the present physical conditions into the past. We have to assume that in former ages, everything was totally different on earth, even earth itself. And, the other way round, from the perspective of these past ages, the far-distant future appeared to be a dark parallel world of grosser density and limited consciousness, as foreseen by the seers and mystics of this time. Now, their future has become our present, and for us, *their* world has become a non-existing, forgotten world or a 'mythological' world at best.

What modern science is starting to materialize in the field of 'advanced' technologies is nothing but an external approach to the inner secrets of life. Life, however, can never be grasped in this artificial way. The secrets of life are accessible only through sacred knowledge: knowledge that contains all aspects of life in a holistic, non-destructive manner. For example, the topics of modern physics can be accessed by sacred geometry, a timeless science that describes the inner structure of both macrocosm and microcosm, because they are all part of the same universal field. The concept of such a holistic, unified field was known to ancient cultures which had specific names for it. The Indian (Vedic) tradition, for instance, calls it 'cosmic body' (*vishva-rupa* in Sanskrit), the Hebrew tradition 'tree of life' (*etz hayim*). Everything is interconnected: the physical, the philosophical, the historical, etc.

Only now, through its pioneers in holistic science, does modern research (which has been mostly mechanistic until now) touch upon the potential of an interdisciplinary world-view. If we accept, at least theoretically, the existence of parallel worlds and other dimensions, then logic also implies the existence of other-dimensional beings and, furthermore, the perspective that we ourselves are multidimensional beings with parallel bodies influencing each other.[47]

Men and women who are connected to higher dimensions are able to perform metaphysical acts which most of us would call 'miracles', like clairvoyance, telepathy, teleportation, materialization, spontaneous healing, etc. Throughout history, and up to the present time, we come across individuals capable of performing such 'miracles'. What, then, if in the mythological past there were not only some select individuals having access to higher dimensions, but entire civilizations? What if in the future, mankind were to gain this access again?

The two sides of the dark age

Whatever modern man may believe to know regarding the past, one thing is undeniable: Ancient traditions do talk about a mythological past as part of their sacred knowledge. Some traditions may have disappeared, some may still be existent, some may have become degraded or infiltrated, others may have gone 'underground'. But they have one thing in common: Regarding the beginning of the present age, they all mention a terrific catastrophe which marked a global turning point. In fact, people on all continents have memories of a vast flood that brought about the end of their earlier civilizations.[48]

Obviously, this cataclysm was not the only one that hit the earth. It was simply the 'latest', the one closest to us in time. By examining the different sources, it can be concluded that it occurred approximately eight to ten thousand years ago, killing 70 to 80 per cent of the world population, or even more. This was during the transition period before the onset of the present age, the Kali-yuga.

The world-wide existence of such memories indicates that a considerable number of people survived. Diverse groups of people were able to seek timely refuge, due to the far-sightedness – and clairvoyance – of the initiates leading them. They knew where to go because they had foreseen what areas would be more or less spared.

The survivors were not able to take a lot of their possessions with them. They were set back by millennia and had to restart with a 'primitive' way of existence. However, a few secret lines of initiates preserved the former knowledge and technology. Having a higher vision of mankind's development, they have remained withdrawn from the ordinary course of global events – awaiting the time in which they are to surface again, either by reappearing or reincarnating.

This devastating incision was followed by a long period of seeming stagnation. The last harvest of the previous age had been gathered and the seed for the next, and most difficult, phase of human history had been sown. The initiates knew that it would take *thousands of years* till new civilizations had matured again, and even longer till the next global cycle (that was just about to start) would come to its end, till all darkness would be gone and the real, final ascension would begin. Patience and contemplation were called for.

Also higher-dimensional contacts were rare in these times, as there was not much left to be said. The inhabitants of the higher worlds knew that men had to follow their own destiny; the extremes of duality were to manifest on earth, mirroring the inner resonance of the souls incarnating in this age. At the same time, these extremes would present the opportunity of attaining the highest levels of unconditional love. Those able to remain – or become – free from all feelings of hatred, revenge and resignation, despite the onslaught of the dark forces, would pass the last borders of material division and find the true, individual oneness with God. Nothing is absolutely bad, not even the dark age with all its atrocities. In this age, the doors are open to the deepest abyss of degeneration as well as to the perfection of God consciousness, all according to the paths chosen by one's free will.

Sacred knowledge becomes secret

While the commotion and degeneration characteristic of the Kali-yuga set in, wise men and women of various mystical lines were guarding the original knowledge – a task entailing grave responsibilities, above all the *observance of secrecy and non-intervention.*

Secrecy was required, first of all, to prevent the abuse of sacred knowledge. The generations after the big catastrophe soon lost their conscious memory of the previous era. They remembered their grand parents and great-grand parents talking about incredible events related by *their* grand parents and great-grand parents. But it was a remote past even for them as they were living out in nature and in caves, slowly starting a village culture. How were they to imagine a highly evolved civilization with 'paranormal' abilities?

The factual history of these civilizations fell into oblivion. Nevertheless, even common traditions and 'folk-lore' kept some stories about gods interacting with men, about a garden of Eden, ancient heroes, lost civilizations and, above all, a big flood, earthquakes and 'fire falling from the sky'. These fading memories became transmuted into popular myths and national legends, later on even into religious dogmas.

In other words, the reports found in presently available myths and holy scriptures do not necessarily give an accurate picture of mankind's past history. Being *public* lines of knowledge, they were inevitably changed and used for manipulation by those who wanted to consolidate their influence on the masses.

We have to visualize the situation in the millennia after the cataclysm. People had been thrown back into living in caves, roaming and pile-dwelling, and they were deeply intimidated by the memory of nature's all-devouring force. Now, imagine someone having superior insights and abilities, as a remnant of the previous cycle. Such a person would have all possibilities to impress and control entire tribes, being considered a god or a representative of God, especially if some ominous force designated him as such. Actually, superhuman factors are mentioned by all ancient cultures, both in negative and positive regards. There are legends of some intermediaries receiving miraculous gifts (technology?), revelations, or demands for sacrifices of blood. Many legends relate that gods came to man after the immense global destruction in order to instruct and support the surviving groups. Most of the lowlands had been inundated and covered with huge layers of mud. When people dared to descend from the mountain regions, they had to start cultivating the land. Some legends even say that certain gods brought new plants, like corn, grains and bananas, and newly bred (genetically engineered?) domestic animals.[49]

Superior insights and abilities are always a big temptation. Seeing a chance to grasp some personal advantage or to take revenge by employing these 'divine' powers, who would refrain from doing so? Nobody except those with real, spiritual understanding. Such enlightened people, however, only rarely accepted a career in the theocratic hierarchy. Therefore, all over the world, less enlightened leaders began to use whatever knowledge and abilities they had to create new forms of religious and royal power structures. Imagine the fallen high priests and god-kings having had the *full* knowledge at their disposal!

Another reason for secrecy was the danger of being misunderstood, especially regarding the knowledge of transcendence (reality beyond duality). The truly enlightened knew how easily it could be degraded into a philosophy of justifying any 'illuminated' action as being necessary. As explained in the fourth chapter, there are forces that actually follow such ideologies. Obviously, it was not possible to prevent the distortion of absolute truths into half-truths. Many keepers of sacred knowledge became seduced by the temptation of power and/or influenced by negative feelings, which is the topic of this chapter.

Kali-yuga means that the norm of density and purity is reduced to such a low standard that almost every being can get hold of a 'ticket' for a birth on earth. The 'open house' has become a full house by now, with all the resulting problems. For those who knew, this course of events was no surprise because it had been foreseen even before it actually started.

Sacred knowledge, amongst many other topics, describes the different time cycles on earth, which are reflections of solar and galactic cycles. After the big catastrophe, things were not headed for the better but for the worse. That was the plain truth as provided by the seers' knowledge. Souls from the dark worlds were foreseen to import falsity and hypocrisy along with wars and violence – ultimately to such an extent that humanity would come to the edge of self-destruction. The 'Kali-yuga' of Indian prophecy, the 'Fourth World' of the Native Americans, the 'Iron Age' of the Middle Eastern seers, the 'Night' of the ancient Europeans was to last for thousands of years. The public revelation of this fact would have discouraged people in general. If it had been pointed out that the influence of the negative – in spite of all individual positive endeavours – was to increase over the next *ten thousand* years (!), man would have given in to resignation and indifference. 'If it takes soooo long, what's the use of working for the good here and now?' 'If the dark forces take over anyway, why should I resist?'

Prophetic knowledge in the wrong classroom would have caused fatalism. Only those with a timeless consciousness were able to face this seemingly endless period of setbacks and disappointments.

However, foreseeing something does not make one powerless or programmed. Even if some cosmic drama is predestined by the natural cycles of polarity, it does not say *who* has to accept what role. Living in the dark age does not mean we must be a dark force ourselves. The only thing predestined is the external theme of the play (for example, 'Age Four: Kali-yuga'). The roles we get correspond to our own choices, or to the consequences of our previous choices.

Sacred knowledge, for all these reasons, had to be kept secret. As long as the knowers avoided all forms of manipulation, they remained incorruptible and withstood any offer of 'prostituting' their knowledge. They lived their visible lives as single wise men and women or as fathers and mothers in low or high social positions, according to their vocation. At the same time they had their inner knowledge and inspiration, or even telepathic connection to their invisible guides. On the inner plane, they always knew where they came from, and thus remained in the consciousness of oneness.

Such selfless devotion, of course, was the ideal case: single individuals and groups of individuals guarding the flame of sacred knowledge without misusing it. These mystery traditions can be called the original 'secret societies'. As shown by history, some remained pure, and some became contaminated by worldly power, either by their own creeping corruption or by infiltration.

The loss of neutrality and purity

Keeping sacred knowledge was not boring. It meant having a higher consciousness beyond the stress and impatience of linear time, and it meant knowing that one belonged to a spiritual network of individuals both incarnate and non-incarnate.* The connection to both was mostly psychic, and conscious contacts, when required, were telepathic and limited to the intimate company of initiates.

Even the very existence of sacred knowledge was kept secret. The reasons have alredy been mentioned: to maintain the purity of the knowledge, to keep 'privacy' (no curious people!), to avoid any misuse of the knowledge, to respect the principle of non-intervention, and to avoid bewildering or discouraging outsiders. Later, yet another reason became important: *self-protection*. With the establishment of tyrannical religions and governments, despots and dictators came to power who started to persecute all opponents as 'dissenters' and 'heretics'.

In many cases, these rulers were souls incarnated out of the realms of darkness. As such, they had a totally different view of things than 'normal' human beings. Unscrupulous and callous to the pains of their victims, they did not mind using inhuman means to secure for themselves an unchallenged monopoly of wealth and power. Whoever was suspected of representing a threat to this monopoly was eliminated, especially the independent intelligentsia, political critics and, not least, the keepers of sacred knowledge.

Becoming the target of unjust and violent persecution is probably the most difficult challenge for any human being. Who is able to remain centred in unconditional love when facing torture and godless arrogance? Admittedly, it is almost natural to react with feelings of hatred and revenge. Exposing and counteracting such evil forces might even seem to be a necessary act for the sake of justice and public information. Without a firm standing in transcendental consciousness, fighting negative forces with anti-negative means is the 'logical' thing to do, and this is exactly what many members of ancient spiritual traditions started to do. After all, these initiates possessed secret knowledge with many options of magical application. The temptation to strike back

---

* In modern terms, these non-incarnate beings are called – according to different categories – Light beings, Star beings, angels, ultraterrestrials, *devas,* Kachinas, ascended masters, etc.

was immense, and many succumbed to this provocation. By trying to combat the guilty perpetrators they stepped into duality. They thought they were fighting for the positive side – and became themselves a dark force in due course of time, conspiring against the religious and political establishment, and infiltrating it more and more. In this way, they increasingly adopted the same methods as the forces they wanted to combat.

Still, in all mystery schools, there were individuals who remained pure and wise. Most of the members, however, especially the leading ones, fell into a vicious circle of hitting and hitting back. The more they compromised their neutrality, forsaking the principle of non-intervention, the more they opened their doors to people who further deviated into occultism and worldly ambition.

At the same time, new lines of power without any roots in real purity appeared on earth. They were called into existence by souls incarnating from the dark worlds. Initially, they mostly acted in the guise of priests in order to 'invade' the external platform of society. Being interested in power and domination, they joined forces with the dictators if they were not the dictators themselves. In the name of God or gods, people could be intimidated by fear, and divided. 'Divide and rule.' Tribe could be turned against tribe, nation against nation, man against man, and man against woman.

This was the dark age as foreseen by the seers of all cultures.

False priests and prophets

Persecution and inquisition as means of ideological purges have been going on throughout known 'cultural history', which dates back around five thousand years. Amazingly, this threshold of human civilization corresponds exactly to the cyclic time frame as described in the ancient Indian sources. According to them, five thousand years ago, around 3000 BC, the present age called Kali-yuga began. To say that there have always been wars, dishonest leaders and oppressive manipulations is nothing but a description of Kali-yuga, for such a general assessment is applicable only in regard to 'known history'. Within this period, however, it is very true.

Looking back at early history, we perceive that, all of a sudden, a new caste of priests became prominent, claiming that the gods demanded sacrifices of animals or even humans. They spread 'fear of the gods' by saying that the previous big catastrophe had been a punishment for mankind sent by the gods, or by 'God', because the earthly subjects had neglected these sacrifices; if people wanted to avoid another punishment of this kind, they had to pacify God's wrath with regular offerings of blood. On all continents, priests started to enforce the practice of bloody sacrifices. An infamous example are the Aztecs, who, after a long degradation, started to misuse the temples of their forefathers for atrocious killings.

Bloody rituals, however, are always close to black magic, for true Light beings do not respond to such invocations. Those performing them are of a similar mentality as those whom they worship.* As previously mentioned, Kali-yuga is a time of reduced standards allowing all kinds of souls to assemble on earth. The same sources that mention the time frame of the Kali-yuga also mention its characteristics. One of the main prophecies given by the *Varaha Purana* and other Sanskrit scriptures says: *rakshasah kalim ashritya jayante brahma-yonishu*. 'Beings from the dark worlds (*rakshasah*) will profit from the age of Kali (*kalim ashritya*) by appearing as high priests (*jayante brahma-yonishu*: literally, "by taking birth as *brahmanas*").'

In India, the genre of priests mentioned in this statement introduced the corrupt caste system, which meant that people's social status was determined by their birth. Due to the hereditary birth right, the 'incarnational' doors into human society were wide-open. Unqualified people now had the opportunity to occupy leading positions as priests and kings, being 'sons of their daddies'. In the name of God and Scripture, personality cult (absolutist 'guru worship') and religious tyranny were introduced, including animal sacrifices and the burning of widows. Buddha, in the fifth century BC, was one of the first critics in India protesting against this deplorable state of so-called religiosity.

---

* 'There are powers fighting against men because they do not want them to be saved. For if men are saved, there will no longer be any sacrifices. Then, no more animals will be sacrificed. [...] "God" is a man-eater. Therefore, men are slaughtered for him. Before they slaughtered men, they sacrificed animals. But know it for a fact: the gods unto whom they were offered were not real gods but idols.' (Words of Jesus as recorded in the Gospel of Philip 141–3; 50.1–4)

Also in other countries, spiritual pioneers and prophets appeared, having the difficult task of opposing the hegemony of these priests and false teachers who were instigating dogmatic ritualism, cruel intolerance and bloody sacrifices:

> 'When you stretch out your hands, I [God] turn my eyes away from you; even though you speak many prayers, I will not listen; your hands are full of blood. Wash yourselves; make yourselves clean; remove the evil of your doings from before my eyes ...' (Isa. 1.15–16)

> He [Pythagoras] prohibited the eating of animals because he wished to train and accustom men to simplicity of life, so that all their food should be easily procurable, as it would be if they ate only such things that required no fire to cook them, and if they drank plain water, for from this diet they would derive health of body and acuteness of intellect. [...] He used to forbid them to offer sacrificial victims to the gods, ordering them to worship only at altars which were unstained with blood. (*Life of Pythagoras* by Diogenes Laertius, third century BC)

In this phase, 2,500 years after the beginning of Kali-yuga, many older scriptures were absorbed into priestly writings as, by then, the priests had gained a monopoly on worship and 'God contact.' With this power, they were in the position of compiling authoritative scriptures, declaring their literary products to be holy in all respects. Daring to doubt this absolutist claim was forbidden by those same books on penalty of death or other forms of severe punishment. In this way, holy scriptures became a mixture of divine revelations, great wisdom, and (in)human power enforcement.

Still, there were courageous men who stood up against this new tyranny of the written word. One example is the prophet Jeremy (seventh/sixth century BC) who had to address both the gullible masses and the priests dominating them:

> 'My people, however, do not know the will of God. So how can you say, "We are wise because we have the law of the Lord", when, in fact, the false pen of the scribes has made it into a lie? [Or: 'Look how it has been falsified by the lying pen of the scribes!' (*The New Jerusalem Bible*) ...] From prophet to priest, all of them practice fraud.' (Jer. 8.7–10)

Jeremy, obviously, recognized the grave danger of those scribes and priests compiling so-called holy scriptures. And time did prove him right as it was they who then started to edit the scriptures of the Old Testament (around 400 BC), adding their own words and interpretations to the long-gone God channels like Abraham, Moses, Joshua, Isaiah or Jeremy. Therefore, the descriptions and quotes in their names as found in today's available texts do not always represent their true biography and teaching. This is acknowledged by most Bible philologists as well as by conservative Judaism.[50]

All religions which hold on to one body of texts, claiming it to be entirely divine and absolute, would be well advised to be self-critical, too. 'Non-fanatical' reading of any holy scripture shows that there is some percentage of absolute truth and spiritual knowledge alongside human insertions and interpolations, some of the latter being quite contradictory and belligerent.

(This plea for non-fundamentalism is not meant to refute the Bible or other holy scriptures. It simply emphasizes the importance of the apostolic maxim, 'Do not despise the word of prophets, but test everything, and hold fast to what is good', as stated in 1 Thess. 5.21.)

The priests who were accused of being ritual slaughterers and usurpers of God's revelations, did not heed any criticism nor did they change themselves. Factually, this was the same line of priests whom, later on, John the Baptist and Jesus called 'brood of vipers' (Matt. 3.7; 12.34; 23.33; Luke 3.7; John 8.44) and 'murderers of the prophets' (Matt. 21.45; 23.31–7; Luke 11.47–9; 13.34).

The explosive tension between the 'false priests and prophets' and those opposing them has turned religion into a breeding ground of self-multiplying conflicts. This was certainly not the intention of the initial voices quoted above. They only intended to enunciate warnings to help people choose their own ways, independently of imposed dogmas, even if it meant provoking the anger of the imposers (Matt. 10.26; Luke 21.12, etc.). It was never intended to cause further enmities and anti-ideologies, as the same Jesus clearly stated:

> You have heard that it was said, 'You shall love your neighbour and hate your enemy.' But I say to you, Love your enemies and pray for those who persecute you, so that you may be children of your Father in heaven. (Matt. 5.43–5)

'You have heard that it was said' refers to certain passages of the Old Testament. Jesus obviously rejected them: 'But I say to you …' Thus, even regarding so-called Scripture, he remained critical, and openly differentiated between words of divine inspiration and those enunciated by men (priests). To a certain degree he respected the social codex, as otherwise he would have made it easy for the religious authorities to execute him on a scriptural basis. Nevertheless, even while making concessions to the social codex, he encouraged a critical attitude towards the elitist caste that claimed absolute power and authority: 'The Scribes and the Pharisees occupy the chair of Moses. Therefore, do what they teach you and follow it, but do not as they do ...' (Matt. 23.2)

People had to be freed from imposed programming and religious dogma in order to realize their own, absolutely individual way to God consciousness. The scene was set.

Still, there were at least two thousand years to go ...

Victims become adversaries of their former tormentors

There were still two thousand years to go. Nowadays, we know what happened. The world became full of religions combating each other and slaughtering the 'renegades' and 'non-believers', all in the name of God, and all with the ulterior motive of obtaining as much worldly power as possible.

Almost 'by the way', millions of victims were left behind: so-called opponents and enemies as well as citizens, spiritualists and native people on all continents. Not all of them faced their tormentors and killers with unconditional love, forgiving them and taking nothing but the spiritual lesson from their dreadful experience. Most died in shock and hatred, and remained within the constellation of perpetrator and victim. When they incarnated again, they still maintained their subtle hatred, and unconsciously wanted to take revenge by combating these religions. They were intuitively attracted to the opposite camp: the mundane power structures and secular lodge associations. The religions became confronted with the counter-forces which they themselves had provoked. The dead rose up against them, to use the words of George Orwell.[51]

In this way, the opposing forces fell into a polarization of 'thesis' and 'antithesis', one camp trying to annihilate or take over the other. Both accused each other of being evil forces, which was even true in a sense, as the same dia-bolic force was working behind both extremes, and still is. By one-sidedness, all camps are limited to half-truths. As long as they remain under this influence, they miss the spiritual truths beyond their mutual anti-ideologies.

Of course, putting together two half-truths does not give a full truth, that is the problem of dialectic thinking. The solution cannot be found by mixing the two or by eclipsing one of the two, but by *reconciling* the two. Otherwise, people remain divided by half-truths which they take as absolute. That is the vicious circle thwarting any solution until people get the chance to free themselves from this ideological splitting, which is deeply rooted in the past.

In the following, we will examine the motivations and the historical background of those influential organizations that have been shaping world history for the past twenty centuries and more. They consist, basically, of two factions: the so-called world religions, in particular those originating in the Middle East, and the supranational associations of secular lodges that engage in occultism, 'pagan' sciences and 'heretical' doctrines. It is no longer a secret that many leading politicians, financial magnates and intellectuals are linked to the inner circles of such secret societies.

Secret societies
begin to oppose worldly religions

As indicated by the *Purana* prophecy and shown by history, the conflicts of the Kali-yuga began with so-called priests taking worldly power positions to dominate the people in the name of God. Later on, they took the monopoly of editing and canonizing holy scriptures, and thus usurped the older texts that were based on real revelation and prophetic vision. Some of these texts remained unchanged and authentic and are pearls in an ocean of many currents. At the same time, many histories and alleged words of God were invented or shaped according to the temper of those priests. All of a sudden, God was as angry, nationalistic and revengeful as the humans who served as 'his' writers and scribes, and it was said that blood could pacify God – the blood of his only son or the blood of ritual sacrifices or the blood of the non-believers shed in holy wars.

This new situation forced the keepers of sacred knowledge to resort to social incognito. Nevertheless, many were tracked down and killed. To strengthen their ranks, they had to recruit new members and create covert institutions so as to become efficient again. A famous but tragic example is the Order of the Templars. They were seemingly catholic but included many broader elements of knowledge, some of them even heretical according to the Catechism.

The Templars, though the most powerful catholic order of their time, were destroyed by the armies of the French king and the pope in 1307. Only a few were able to flee and hide. In the following generations, they changed their religious designation. Thinking of the builders of the gorgeous gothic cathedrals, who had been Templars, too (or had been financed by the Templars), they no longer wanted to be monks and knights but preferred the secular symbolism of being masons.*

At the beginning of the fourteenth century, the Templars were persecuted, humiliated, tortured, and many were killed. No wonder that most of the surviving Templars, being warriors, were angry and revengeful. On the one hand they were full of new enthusiasm and idealism, on the other, they wanted to become a worldly power again in order to be able to destroy their adversaries and deadly enemies. This mindset opened the door for deviation and infiltration.

The more the organization strove for worldly power, the more the purity of the candidates eligible for initiation began to decrease. Soon, men with ulterior motives managed to occupy top positions, and introduced new elitist levels of initiation which they kept for themselves. These insiders may have been names publicly known or not; in any case, hardly anybody – not even the lower-rank members of their own hierarchy – knew that they also featured in these secret top positions. Many did not even know that such top positions and obscure initiations existed.

More and more, the principle of secrecy became an instrument to keep conspirative rituals and agendas secret. Whereas for thousands of years real initiates had been careful not to fall into the trap of judging and competing (and still are, up to this very day), infiltrated secret

---

* In this symbolism, Hiram from Tyre, the architect of Solomon's temple, was considered to be the archetype mason. The 'free masons' now wanted to reconstruct Solomon's temple on a global basis, its building blocks being all purified, 'freethinking' humans.

societies began to strive for worldly power. The truly enlightened men and women never took sides in worldly matters and never supported either of the conflicting parties. Modern 'illuminati', however, employing their political and financial means, support both sides! ('When two parties fight, the third one takes delight.')

Originally bound by their pledge of secrecy not to intervene, secret alliances now intervene secretly. They have their high ideals, but there are not that many who still embody them sincerely and selflessly. Their exponents today are intricately entangled in global karma, having given in to the temptation of abusing their money and power. Not much is left of the original sacred knowledge.

In summary, the secret societies started to use similar means as those whom they wanted to combat. Thus, they drifted into a double deviation: dualistic thinking and, consequently, dia-bolic scheming, namely revengeful rivalry and quest for power ('our end justifies the means'). If such a mentality is allowed to take over, one falls into the trap of self-delusion, as shown in the previous chapter. This applies to both secular lodges and religious institutions. It is an individual challenge to each and every member of both sides. And, thank God, there are many individuals on both sides who are able to avoid these traps despite the oaths, vows and dogmas imposed on them.

Freemasons as an example of a secret society

If secret societies exist and execute a major power behind the scenes, then it should be possible to find some discernible traces of their activities. Are there such traces? Are there any indications about the identity of people who could be agents of such ulterior groups?

A closer look at world history and critical literature reveals that in the past centuries, there has factually been another power parallel to religious institutions, existing up to the present day. The more the absolutist power of Christianity dwindled, the more this secular power was able to increase its influence.

As already mentioned, one important factor in European and American history was the formation of Freemasonry after the 'holocaust' against the Templars in the fourteenth century. For quite some time,

Freemasons have often been mentioned in connection with conspiracy theories and plans of world control. Church verdicts have even used terms like 'satanic force'. In any case, they are a classic example of a secret society, and they are certainly very influential.* Therefore, the trace of Freemasonry will show that *there are factually secret forces at work*. Demonstrating this fact is the sole purpose of the following elaboration. It is not meant to be a political treatise (despite its political relevance), nor is it meant to be a prejudiced targeting of Freemasonry, as everything has two sides. Other examples of secret societies could be mentioned as well, but this is not required, for the point of these chapters (three to five) is the philosophical analysis of sacred knowledge and the demonstration of how it became deviated into the two extremes of negativity. Worldly religions and their violent grab for power are the one extreme (caused by the deviation of true religiosity) and atheistic secret societies are the other (caused by the deviation of the original keepers of sacred knowledge). Both forms of deviation were caused by souls incarnating from dark backgrounds and by the resonance of the people responding to them.

Freemasonry, according to the thesis of this book, is one line of keepers of secret knowledge and is a karmic anti-pole to the power of religious institutions. With the passing of time, however, it became infiltrated, leading to the formation of *new elitist circles* that were even more secret, reserved for the real 'big boys'. Over the past three centuries, these circles have attained their own dynamics almost independent of regular Freemasonry. That is why many Freemasons of lower levels do not know or believe that their hierarchy is not limited to the idealism they themselves subscribe to.

Lodge members in public action

Freemasonry is not a homogenous team of world-wide co-operation. Rather, there are many camps, one of these camps being the ulterior

---

* 'Masonry, or Freemasonry, is a 600-year-old fraternity with a 3,000-year-old tradition. The oldest, largest, and most widely known fraternal organization in the world, it is a prototype of most modern fraternal societies and service organizations.' (from: Arthur Edward Waite, *A New Encyclopedia of Freemasonry*; 1996, back cover text)

network of supranational 'global players'. However, it is questionable whether these adherents of illuminati ideologies can still be called Freemasons in the true sense of the word.

The list of famous Freemasons is quite a strange catalogue. On the one hand, it is a historical fact that the majority of the founding fathers of the United States, including George Washington, were Freemasons, as were King James VI of England (who stood patron for the famous King-James Bible), King Frederick the Great of Prussia, Johann Wolfgang von Goethe, Wolfgang Amadeus Mozart, and many others. On the other hand, many of those who had leading roles in the two world wars were lodge members or agents in close dependency: Wilson, House, Chamberlain, Lenin, Trotsky, Milner, Churchill, Roosevelt, Truman, Stalin etc.[52]

How is it that people of opposing ideological and political fronts are found 'united' on the level of lodge co-operation? George Washington, King James, King Frederick and others represent the idealism of the original lodge spirit – freedom of thought, same rights for all, and a human brotherhood beyond religious indoctrination and separatism. This spirit of emancipation, however, was prone to infiltration and corruption, especially when ambitions of worldly power became predominant. By the beginning of the twentieth century Freemasonry had reached all continents through the medium of the British Empire and the USA. From this perspective, let us examine once again the war lords mentioned in the list above.

The Second World War was followed by the 'cold war', in which the US and the SU opposed each other as enemies for more than forty years. However, during WW II and right after it, there had been an intense, and official, co-operation between Churchill, the US president and Stalin. Strangely enough, this co-operation, which even culminated in a 'peace conference', led to a *partitioning* of the world! Russia became the Soviet Union (SU) and was allowed to build up the so-called Eastern Bloc. Then, all of a sudden, the SU was presented as the evil enemy called communism which threatened the 'Free World', especially the US. Why did the western forces support Stalin who had been known to be a communist and a mass killer long before WW II started?

This simple logic reveals that there was more going on behind the political stage than official history admits. After all, history is always written by the winners.

Regarding the SU, political researchers later found out that exponents of the US economy had been secretly supporting the development of the industrial and military infrastructure of the Soviet Union throughout the cold war. One prominent researcher is Professor Anthony Sutton, who wrote books entitled *Wall Street and the Bolshevik Revolution* (1981), *Wall Street and the Rise of Hitler* (1966) and *National Suicide – Military Aid to the Soviet Union* (1974).

Prof. Sutton also wrote a book entitled *America's Secret Establishment – An introduction to the Order of Skull & Bones* (1986). Regarding the supranational network of 'global players', one group often mentioned is this obscure Order called 'Skull & Bones'. The name alone, derived from a Freemasonic initiation rite, reveals the obvious connection. Recently, an indication of this secret society even appeared in the cinema film *The Skulls* by Rob Cohen (2000). It depicts how ambitious students at a noble US university are recruited for this secret student group. Although initially of a harmless appearance, it obliges all new members to an immediate oath of secrecy.

Considering the fact that most of the lawyers, judges, physicians, scientists, journalists, economists, bankers, governors, senators and presidents have gone through these channels of education, it becomes quite plausible that many leading and powerful people secretly belong to such supranational circles.

Just to show how far-reaching these implications may be, one more VIP shall be spotlighted. *The Two Faces of George Bush* is the title of another book published by Prof. Anthony Sutton. He is not the only one who mentions this name. Again and again, this key figure (ex-president, former head of the CIA, oil magnate) is said to be a top-ranking Freemason and Skull & Bones member.

Those who dare to dig into such hot issues often meet with obstacles which they have never met before. They are rarely questioned or challenged (probably to avoid any serious public discussion or investigation of the evidence presented), their publications, however, are often suppressed or 'out of print.' Some investigators even see their lives endangered. Obviously such work is not the way to have fun or make a big business.

One example in this regard is the American journalist Joel Bainerman, who accidentally stumbled on dimensions of world politics which caused him to think differently of all the 'conspiracy nuts':

> In 1989 I set out to write a book about Israel's involvement in the Iran-Contra Affair. My investigation led me to the mysterious death in Mexico of Israeli counter-terrorism official Amiram Nir in December 1988. There were many rumours at the time that Nir was 'bumped off' by the CIA, because he was set to go public with what he knew of then Vice-President George Bush's dirty dealings with Panamanian dictator Manuel Noriega. Eventually I discovered that the real story wasn't Israel's involvement in Iran-Contra, but President Bush's.

This is how Joel Bainerman's book begins. It bears the provocative title, *The Crimes of a President: New Revelations on Conspiracy and Cover-Up in the Bush and Reagan Administrations*, published in 1992.

Bainerman had perused all relevant publications, and conducted extensive investigations on his own, which led him to shocking conclusions, for example: George Bush had been involved in drug dealings in Latin America, in assassinations of opposing individuals, in the armament supply for Saddam Hussein's B and C-missiles in the eighties in order to set the scene for the Gulf War, and many other shocking manoeuvres serving as a further step towards the New World Order.* A lot of circumstantial evidence makes it difficult to dismiss everything he writes as nonsense.

> The more I learned of Bush's past, the more the present made sense. For instance, although he is often portrayed as bland and having no identifiable beliefs, President Bush does indeed have a particular ideology. It is a unique brand of imperialistic thinking stemming from his Freemasonry roots which contends that intervention into the domestic affairs of other countries is permissible if it is in the pursuit of global domination. This world-view is part of the 'New World Order' the President talks about. While most people think he is referring to a morally based, idealistic concept of a more peaceful planet, he has something very different in mind. (p. 2)

While investigating the many aspects of secret international politics, Joel Bainerman discovered other camps of ulterior global players, mainly the Council on Foreign Relations (CFR) and the Trilateral Commission (TC). Many names that are still in top ranks (in 2003) are

---

* The programmatic expression 'New World Order' is the English translation of the Latin 'Novus Ordo Seclorum' as found on the American 1-$ bill, written below the pyramid and the all-seeing eye, another important lodge emblem. More information about the message of this New World Order seal is given in the next chapter.

mentioned as members of these groups. The book (comprising three hundred pages) concludes with Bainerman explicitly stating what, in his opinion, all this boils down to:

> While the Reagan administration appointed no less than 75 members of either the CFR or the TC, when Bush entered the White House an astounding 350 members of these two organizations received positions in the executive branch. [...] Franklin D. Roosevelt was a member of the Masonic Lodge as was Harry Truman, Lyndon Johnson, Gerald Ford, and Ronald Reagan. [...] Those who deny the hypothesis that 'Freemasonry is intent on taking over the world' is the ultimate conspiracy ought to research the subject. Before I began researching the subject of the Bush and Reagan Administrations' covert operations and secret agendas I too would have called anyone promoting these ideas as 'conspiracy nuts'. [...]
> I am the first one to admit that I have no smoking guns. Yet my speculation wasn't undertaken without strong circumstantial evidence. (pp. 316, 321)

As already stated, it is not the purpose of this chapter to go into a detailed political analysis. Many other authors and journalists have already done that. The point of mentioning Freemasonry was to illustrate (1) that secret societies really exist and (2) that they represent a powerful factor in world politics. 'They' refers to an exclusive elite based on, but not identical with, these societies. They represent a world onto themselves, with a corresponding world-view.

Christianity and Freemasonry – an ancient strife

'It is a known fact that the previous incompatibility of Freemasonry and clerical policy is a thing of the past. What is of greater importance is that the Catholic Church has undergone major changes.'

This was stated by Salvador Allende, president of Chile, known to be a Freemason, in an interview published in the *New York Times*, 27 October 1970. 'Incompatibility' was a very diplomatic expression. For centuries, Christian churches, especially the Catholic Church, had persecuted and condemned all forms of secret societies and sacred knowledge. Being themselves bereft of sacred knowledge, they did not realize that their violence only bred counter-violence. 'All who draw the sword will die by the sword' (Matt. 26.52). Force causes counter-force as a natural reaction. Over the centuries, a strong opposition grew in secrecy and gained more and more influence, even in the Vatican.

The Catholic Church's first official statement against Freemasonry was published by Pope Clemence XII on 28 April 1737, declaring 'condemnation of the association and of the secret reunions, called Freemasons, the deed being punished by an immediate ban; absolution from it is reserved to the Supreme Head of the Church, except in the case of someone confessing on the death-bed.'[53]

Pius VIII (1761–1830), who was elected pope in 1829, issued an encyclical against Freemasonry. Soon after its public enunciation he died after only one pontifical year in office.

Another encyclical against Freemasonry was issued by Pope Leo XIII in 1884, entitled *Humanum genus*, 'The Human Race'. Therein, Freemasonry was condemned as being an anti-Christian movement and, literally, 'Satan's Kingdom [...] under whose rule all will suffer as they are disobeying eternal divine law, ignoring God's existence or plotting against his will. [...] They [God's opponents] are unified in conspiracy prepared to fiercely fight the Church under the leadership, and with the support of, the alliance of so-called Freemasons. They feel no shame and, therefore, do not conceal their intentions to incite the people against God Our Majesty. With overt audacity they are working on the downfall of the Holy Church.'[54]

Despite such an uncompromising condemnation of its enemy, the Catholic Church became infiltrated by clerical members who secretly belonged to Freemasonry. Some of them attained the position of cardinals. It is even said that some popes had been such freemasonic cardinals. For example, Giovanni Mastai-Ferretti, son of an Italian count, had been a member of the Great Lodge of Italy even while being cardinal. Upon his nomination as Pope Pius IX (pontificate 1846–78) he left the Lodge and attacked it in his later writings.[55]

Mary Ball Martinez, correspondent of the Vatican for many years, reports in her book *The Undermining of the Catholic Church*: 'In France, retired members of the Republican Guard give testimony that Cardinal Roncalli (who later became Pope John XXIII) as Nuntius in Paris, participated in the Thursday evening meetings of the Grand Orient of France, wearing civil clothes.'[56]

This was also confirmed by Carlos Vazquez, a high-level Freemason, in the Mexican weekly journal *Proceso* (12 October 1992): 'In Paris, on one and the same day, Profane Angelo Roncalli and Profane Giovanni Montini were initiated into the sublime mysteries of the Brotherhood. That is why many accomplishments of the Council [the Second Vatican Council] are based on Masonic principles.'[57]

Before his time in Paris, Angelo Roncalli had been the Vatican's Nuntius in Turkey, and some rumours say that already there, he had become acquainted with the Freemasonic brotherhood.

In 1936, Jacques Maritain, a French professor of philosophy who converted to Catholicism, published a book about 'Integral Humanism'. The Italian translation appeared in the same year along with an enthusiastic introduction written by the translator, non other than the above-mentioned Giovanni Montini, who later became Pope Paul VI, the successor of John XXIII. In this position, he continued the course set by the Second Vatican Council, implementing the ideals of 'integral humanism', for example in his *Pastoral Constitution regarding the Church in Today's World:* '[…] looking forward to the unification of the world, a better world of truth and justice, […] we are witnesses of the birth of a new humanism in which the human being defines himself, above all, according to his responsibility towards his fellow brethren and towards society at large.'[58]

After the death of Paul VI in 1978, the Venetian Cardinal Luciani was proclaimed pope, taking up the name John Paul I. Two weeks after his election, the Italian magazine 'O.P.' (*Osservatore Politico*) published a list of 121 Vatican members who were connected to Freemasonry. The issue containing this list was published on 12 September 1978 and was immediately delivered to Pope John Paul I. The editor of this magazine, Mino Pecorelli, an ex-Freemason, obviously wanted the new pope to take action against these covert Freemasons in the Vatican. We do not know in what form John Paul I planned to react because on 28 September 1978, after only 33 days in office, he died under mysterious circumstances.[59] Thus he became known as the '33-day pope'. It is interesting to note that the number 33 designates the highest level in the Freemasons' hierarchy. There are 33-level Freemasons, and now we have a 33-day pope. If his death was caused by murder, then the number of his days in office was exactly counted to match the symbolism. (A few months later, in March 1979, also Mino Pecorelli died. In his case, it was an undisputed assassination.)

As shown by these few examples, the war between the Lodge and the Church has been real and has taken on dramatic dimensions. What about the situation today?

A stunning insight was provided when an anonymous group of twenty high Vatican insiders (prelates) published a revealing book in the beginning of 1999, which became the number 1 best seller of the year in Italy. This group of clerical authors named itself 'I Millenari', which indicates that they belong to a Judaeo-Christian reform movement within the Catholic Church.[60] From their critical standpoint, these prelates attack both the conservative Vatican fundamentalists as well as the 'uncontrollable forces of occultism which are spreading their influence until their roots permeate the entire mystic body of the Church, attacking it with tumour-like metastasis.' (p. 137)

Regarding the first category, they denounce the incompetence, hypocrisy and corruption found within the Roman Curia including many cardinals. They even speak of tyranny and despotism, giving many shocking examples, and blast the dogma of compulsory celibacy. (It was introduced by the Vatican only about one thousand years after Christ. In the Jewish religion there is no compulsory celibacy.)

Regarding the second, the 'forces of occultism,' they make no secret of whom they refer to: 'The unseen hand of Freemasonry in the Vatican, in the centre of covert forces between high finance and high offices, can be sensed everywhere' (p. 269). They call it 'the polyp of Freemasonry in the Vatican', active already 'for a long time'. Mentioned as an example is their influence at the Second Vatican Council (1963–5). One of the leading forces in the 'destruction of the ancient traditions of liturgy' which took place at this Council was Archbishop Annibale Bugnini, a secretary to the pontifical Congregation. A later investigation and observation revealed Bugnini's contact to the Freemason lodge 'Grande Oriente d'Italia', from whose Grandmaster he received monthly cheques. A photograph of such a cheque was published in 1975 in Italian magazines. As a consequence of this scandal, Bugnini was transferred as Nuntius to the Iran. There 'he stayed until July 1982 when he died a natural death which was helped along a little bit.' (p. 254)

Many other incidents are cited, for example some prelates supporting Italy's Prime Minister, media tycoon and dubious billionaire Silvio Berlusconi in 1994, 'whose membership in Freemasonry had just before become publicly known' (p. 222), or Giovanni Montini's intrigues to become pope. In the mid-fifties, when Montini had been a leading secretary to the Vatican, he and his men maintained secret contacts to the communist regime of the Soviet Union, at one point even delivering a list of priests and bishops who were active in the Soviet underground. 'Due to this treason they were all arrested and murdered, or they died in the camps' (p. 206). When this became known to the Vatican intelligence, Pius xii reduced Montini's position and transferred him to Milan (as an archbishop) in order to thwart Montini's plans of becoming a cardinal. In Milan, the 'catholic' Freemason Michele Sindona became the archbishop's financial counsellor. After the death of Pius xii, Pope Roncalli (John xxiii) made Montini a cardinal. Later, Montini became his successor. As Pope Paul vi, he entrusted even greater financial responsibilities to Sindona and to another prominent lodge member, Roberto Calvi (p. 271). Both of them were deeply involved in corrupt and criminal affairs connected to the Mafia and the P-2 organization (that had falsely passed itself off as a Freemason lodge). In 1982, Calvi was found hanged – a non-convincing 'suicide'. In 1986, Sindona was poisoned despite being in a high security prison. Judges, journalists and others were also killed during these years of ill-fated exposures.[61]

These few examples are sufficient to illustrate the mechanism of duality: Violence breeds counter-violence. Half-truths meet other forces of half-truth, combating each other, till hardly any truth is left.

From the very beginning, the Roman Church was driven by the ambition of becoming a worldly power, which implied the persecution and condemnation of all followers of Jesus that were not 'Christian' in the Roman sense of the term, what to speak of those whom they labelled as 'pagan'. In the course of time, the Vaticanists were inevitably confronted with the mirrors of their own doings. Unfortunately, combating and demonizing the counter-forces was the only reaction they could think of. And that made things even worse. The more they fought the so-called negative forces of occultism and deism, the more they fuelled corruption and violence on both sides. Some Vaticanists are still keeping up the fight whereas others have accepted compromises or even entered into secret pacts with the opponent, trying to end the conflict and controversy in this way.

However, despite the good intentions of particular individuals, the dia-bolic strife could not be overcome. Both sides remained stuck in their absolutist claims to power and truth. As long as the one attempts to take over the other, only one-sided 'truths' will prevail.

Humanism against absolutism

For more than one thousand years, throughout the 'dark Middle Ages', the Church itself was a dark force in many ways, inciting persecution, wars and mass-killings in the Old and the New World. These inhuman forces justified themselves by maintaining an institutional absolutism: *extra Ecclesiam nulla salus* ('no salvation outside the Church') as Church patriarch Augustine proclaimed. The Catholic Church, presenting itself as the only true representative of the Apostles, has maintained this absolutist claim up to the present day and reconfirmed it in August 2000 by the Pontifical declaration entitled *Dominus Iesus*, issued by the 'Congregation for the Doctrine of the Faith', stating: 'The fullness of Christ's salvific mystery belongs to the Church, inseparably united to her Lord. Indeed, Jesus Christ continues his presence and his work of salvation in the Church and by means of the Church. [...] the Church of Christ [...] continues to exist fully only in the Catholic Church.' (*Dominus Iesus*, Part IV: 'Unicity and Unity of the Church')

However, not all religious people support this kind of absolutist self-definition. Many members of Catholicism, and of Christianity in general, are truth-seekers who are no longer willing to submit to the tyranny of 'tradition'. After all, this tradition has quite a violent and ungodly history and is rooted in doubtful premises. Many clerical students, therefore, have no inclination to embrace its fundamentalism. They know the critical aspects of their tradition, their official teaching and even their Scripture, as shown by philological and historical research. Nevertheless, they join the Church out of idealism and true vocation, not out of a desire to help cement the old structures. They want to find the real Jesus. They want to return to the original roots, the real Church that is free from intrigue, corruption and greed for power. No wonder that some of these reformatory young Church members, from both Catholic and Lutheran backgrounds, are attracted by the humanistic ideals of Freemasonry that specifically go against these deviations of the Church, offering an alternative way and vision.

This 'new generation' of clerics has existed since the sixteenth century when the Church's absolute power was questioned by the intellectual Renaissance. Humanism* was the antithesis to absolutist religion, and it was institutionalized mainly by secular secret societies like Freemasonry. The covert overlapping of Freemasonry and Christianity began in these centuries, and now, after three hundred and more years, it has developed a tradition of its own.

In a sense, the teachings of Jesus are also humanistic. They are based on every human's equal right to God's mercy, independent of external conditions like religious membership, confessional credo, traditional clothing, circumcision, book fundamentalism, etc. The truths taught by Jesus were absolute, not absolutist – the kind of 'truth that makes you free'. (John 8.32)

Compared to the Church's long-standing absolutism, humanism is closer to Jesus' original teaching in many ways. Therefore, it is not necessarily a deviation from devotion to Jesus Christ when clerical initiates decide to co-operate with Freemasons or other lines of secret knowledge. (It is not a spiritual break-through either, as both camps are situated within the fronts of antagonistic thinking.)

The enmity between Christianity and Freemasonry, and their disguised overlapping, indicate a general dead-end situation that is quite complex and paradoxical, being the product of a long history. Obviously, it cannot be understood by simplistic black and white judging.

Christianity is not purely white, everything else being black. Rather, this religion – as well as any other religion – contains a lot of 'black', and a 'lesser black' can help reduce the negativity. Humanism, therefore, can be a good temporary medicine though being deistic or even atheistic.

So who is 'better', an atheistic humanist or a religious absolutist? As illustrated before, on both sides there are, and have been, people falling into the traps of power and elitism. And on both sides there are, and have been, honest people working in spiritual consciousness to the best of their capacity.

---

* Humanism: a cultural and philosophical world-view that advocates the dignity and freedom of the human being; it started in the fifteenth century as a counter-movement against the Church's supremacy, meant as an emancipation from dogmatic indoctrination; it encouraged the critical use of reason and research, and thus became the basis of modern education. In its *theistic version,* humanism underlines the free will and self-responsibility of every human and his absolute right to realize his individual, eternal relationship to God independent of institutional mediators. In its *atheistic version,* humanism defines the human as a being free of any superior authority of God; man is considered to be his own lord as 'there is no God outside of me'; there is no absolute purpose in life; human life is self-fulfilling according to the laws of evolution and necessity – which leads to atheistic fatalism and pragmatism as described in Chapter Four.

The 'Millenari', for example, do not combat humanistic ideals ('Christ's divine-human love does not humiliate man but elevates and enriches him from within, in the association of others', p. 37), and they do not mind quoting secular sources like Heraclites, Plato, Pascal, Roger Bacon, Victor Hugo, Dostoevsky, Orwell, Wilde, Cocteau, Churchill and L. B. Johnson, although it is well known that some of these men were Freemasons or members of other secret societies.

We are reminded of the dilemma Jesus himself had to face regarding the Scribes and Pharisees: 'Follow their words but not their deeds.' Similarly, Freemasonry, while having the potential to neutralize dogmatism by emphasizing ethical religiosity, also breeds other, much less idealistic potentials. One might therefore say: 'Follow their best ideals but not their deviation and corruption.'

Humanism as taught by Freemasonry tends to be deistic. As mentioned in Chapter Four, deism can be theistic or atheistic. On the higher levels of some lodge hierarchies, the candidates for 'enlightenment' are initiated into atheistic or even satanic deism. This kind of deism teaches that God, the 'architect' of the universe, is non-different from its creation – including evil. 'The worship of the architect is extended to the creation, thus to Satan as well, as he is a creature that partakes of universal reality.'* This may even take on the form of Satan worship, as indicated by several critical voices – for example, by the Vatican insider Malachi Martin, a Jesuit who had been close to three popes (Pius XII, John XXIII, Paul VI). In the book *Windswept House* (1996), which was to be his last, he describes the secret enthronement of Satan in the Vatican, ritually performed by high Vatican officials including cardinals who belonged to the Lodge.

It is this kind of Freemasonry that the 'Millenari' and other Vatican critics reject. It may sound like a general condemnation as the question arises whether the pure kind of Freemasonry still exists. The same can be asked about the Church. Ultimately, true honesty is found only within those individuals who embody it for themselves, independently of the institution they belong to, be it the Lodge or the Church.

In the eyes of many Catholics, the difference between 'the Church' and 'the Lodge' is irreconcilable; they believe that only an apocalyp-

---

* Why this doctrine (as summarized here by the 'Millenari,' p. 267) is a half-truth, leading to godless conclusions, has been explained in Chapter Four, using the symbolism of light and darkness. *Light does not produce shadow!*

tic 'end time' battle will settle the strife, leading 'God's men' to victory while destroying Satan's forces for good. The same opinion is held by most other religions and elitist lodge groups. They all believe that, after some kind of end-time decision, the whole world will be turned over to them as they will be the only ones surviving unharmed. Although each camp may think that 'we are the only ones who are right, all others are wrong', it appears that they are all wrong. By making absolutist claims, they prove that they have not understood what the word 'absolute' really means. The same is true about those saying that there is *no* absolute truth.

In summary, neither by combating nor by compromising can half-truths be reconciled. Truth is completely different from any combination of half-truths. Both the religious and the secular groups will have to reconsider their own self-understanding. Until then, many old wounds (and further wounds to come) will have to be healed.

Fundamental Controversy

The antagonism between Christianity and Freemasonry is not just power-oriented. It also concerns fundamental aspects of philosophy: dualism versus monism, theism versus deism, as already elaborated. Still, there is another topic of controversy to be mentioned, probably the most delicate and explosive one, namely the interpretation of Jesus Christ's person and position.

According to Christianity, Jesus is the incarnate Son of God, God's first-born, who came down to earth to reveal God's will and word, and to redeem humanity from material bondage by his resurrection and ascension. This belief is based on the Gospels of the New Testament, the Apostles' letters, several apocryphal gospels and scriptures as well as the visions of many saints, and is also supported by contemporary visionaries and channelled sources.

However, other influential traditions maintain different views about Jesus, especially Judaism and Islam. And exactly these two traditions had a strong, lasting influence on those groups that were later to become Europe's secret societies.

The people of Europe, who were the first ones to be 'converted' by Christianity, only got to know the Roman teachings, which were often imposed on them through violence and force. When non-Christian views became secretly known (mainly through contacts with Jewish and Islamic circles), many felt attracted to such alternative options.

Judaism and Islam, though mutually antagonistic, agree on one main point, namely that the Bible's description of Jesus is not correct. Their beliefs about what is correct, however, are again different.

Jewish scriptures say that Jesus was factually crucified, but he simply died; maybe his followers stole the dead body to fake a resurrection (see Matt. 27.63–4; 28.13–15: 'This story is still told among Jews to this day').

Contrary to that, Islamic sources indicate that Jesus did not die on the cross as claimed by 'the unbelievers who broke the covenant'; most probably he was not even on the cross: 'They denied the truth and uttered a monstrous falsehood against Mary. They declared: "We have put to death that Messiah, Jesus the son of Mary, the apostle of God." They did not kill him, nor did they crucify him, but they thought they did [or, literally, 'in their eyes he was made to resemble another']. Those who disagreed about him were in doubt concerning him; they knew nothing about him that was not sheer conjecture; they did not slay him for certain. God lifted him up to Him; God is mighty and wise.' (Qur'an 4.157–8)

These differing presentations question the fundamental basis of Christianity and are considered 'anti-Christian' by most Christians. So we can imagine how shocked the first Catholic Christians were who got to hear these opinions from 'across the fence'. Most citizens of the Middle Ages were illiterate, and travelling to foreign countries was beyond their horizon. With the crusades, however, armies of Christian men made their way from Europe to the Holy Land, thus starting a new era of religious conflicts and, in the long run, of interreligious contact. In this historical context, the mysterious order of the Templars was founded in Jerusalem.

Secret 'double agents' in the first crusade

Starting in the eighth century, Arabia's armies built up a huge empire extending from the Indus region (today's Pakistan) in the East to Spain in the West. There, adjacent to France, Islamic culture flourished. At the zenith (around the year 1000), Cordoba, the capital, was resplendent with numerous mosques, three public baths, a large palace and a public library storing about 400,000 documents! Undoubtedly, this fabulous culture attracted the attention of curious students from the other side of the Pyrenees, where medieval 'darkness' prevailed.

The Moslems not only conquered northern Africa and Spain, but also Palestine and Jerusalem. The Holy Land in the hands of Seljuk Turks and Jerusalem reigned by a Sultan! This situation caused the Roman Church to launch its so-called crusades. In 1099 the first crusade ended with the conquering of Jerusalem, which was a cruel massacre. Ten thousand Moslems and Jews were killed, amongst them many women, children and old people. For a period lasting almost one hundred years, Palestine was once again under Christian rule.

The army of the first crusade consisted mainly of French troops. Among them was the nineteen-year-old knight Hugo de Payens, nephew of an influential count who was one of the main forces behind this campaign. Hugo de Payens was later nominated the first Grand Master of the Templar Order. He had enlisted in the crusade army along with his mentor, Jehan de Vézelay, forty years his elder. Jehan, an eminent Benedictine monk, was the abbot of the monastery of Vézelay in French Burgundy. This sixty-year-old warrior monk, appalled by the atrocities of the crusade army, renounced the triumphant return to France and preferred to stay in Jerusalem, oftentimes living as a hermit in the desert, like the ancient prophets, John the Baptist, and Jesus. He became known as *John of Jerusalem* and was highly respected by Christians, Jews and Moslems alike. (Today his name has become famous mostly due to the rediscovery of his astonishing *Book of Prophecies* mentioned at the end of this chapter.)

Some time after the conquering of Jerusalem, Hugo de Payens returned to France, fascinated by the secret knowledge from Jewish and Islamic sources. Four years later he returned to Jerusalem, accompanied by his rich uncle, the said count (named Hugues de Champagne). They both stayed in Jerusalem for five years. Their friend John, meanwhile familiarized with secret Jewish teachings, had a lot to tell them …

'Whatever kind of business they tended to, they also received ancient Hebrew scriptures, or copies thereof. […] Back in France, they visited Etienne Harding, the abbot of the Cistercian Order, founded seven years prior to the Order of the Templars. The Order examined the scriptures, even consulting Rabbis from Upper Burgundy.'[62]

In 1114, five years after returning to France, Count Hugues and his nephew again travelled to Jerusalem but did not stay for long; after doing whatever they wanted to do, they immediately returned to France. Why did they subject themselves to such a strenuous pilgrimage, only to return a few months later? Obviously, these 'interreligious' Christians were engaged in something very important, and the fact that they had to keep it secret indicates that it was *dangerous* business, which again indicates that it must have been something that extremely differed from the official doctrines of the Church.

Today we can conclude that these secret missions had begun with forbidden information reaching some influential, free-thinking counts, knights and abbots in Europe (through Jewish and Islamic sources) – information about alternative views on Jesus and the crucifixion, about the Church's cover-up regarding the Messiah, and about the secrets of world history and the *geography* of the earth. Naturally, these secular and clerical 'free-thinkers' wanted to find out more.

As private travelling was very unusual, and very suspicious, in those days, the first crusade offered the ideal pretext for some pioneering double agents to be dispatched to the Middle East. In the eleventh and twelfth centuries, the Church still preached that the earth was flat, and anyone who dared to express doubts was a candidate for the pyre. And now, these men from France got to see ancient scriptures and documents that completely turned the so-called Christian world-view upside down. They heard about paradise-like continents on the other side of the Western Sea, places of unlimited wealth and freedom![63]

Those who were open to these new views had to make plans to secure and implement this knowledge despite the Church's violent opposition. Therefore, they had to form secret alliances and conceive of long-term plans. A power structure independent of the Church had to be established, sufficient money had to be procured, and a 'private' fleet had to be set up. And it is historically known that the Templars did just that during the following two hundred years.

The sudden appearance of the Templars

In the year 1118, Hugo de Payens, now almost forty years of age, went to Jerusalem for the fourth time, accompanied by a group of six renowned knights and two learned monks belonging to the Cistercian Order. (Knight Hugo was illiterate.) Among the knights were the brother of Baudouin II, the crusader King of Jerusalem, and André de Montbard, the uncle of the legendary Bernhard, the abbot of the Cistercian monastery of Clairvaux.

The official purpose of their mission was the protection of pilgrims wayfaring to Jerusalem. This, however, was not a convincing explanation. How could a group of seven knights and two monks protect pilgrims from the attacks of local groups of bandits? Sure enough, there is not a single reference of these men ever protecting any pilgrims. Rather, they had exceptional privileges and were accommodated in the palace on the Temple Mount. They set up lodgings directly on the site of the foundation of Solomon's Temple; hence their name 'The Poor Knights of Christ of Solomon's Temple at Jerusalem', in short 'Knights Templars' or just 'Templars'.

Apparently, these nine men had come on a special mission. As we must assume today, they were occupied mainly with excavations, especially on the Temple Mount in Jerusalem. It is said that in the year AD 70, sacral objects had been buried there in a deep tunnel system, shortly before the Romans laid the temple in ruins.

After nine years of secret work, a delegation of this group returned to France led by Hugo de Payens and André de Montbard. The latter was the uncle of the young but very influential abbot of Clairvaux named Bernard, today known as *St Bernard of Clairvaux* (1090–1153). It was he who immediately initiated the next steps. During those nine years, the team of his uncle had obviously found something tangible. In 1129, he organized the Synod of Troyes (near Paris) to officially found and authorize the order of the Knights Templars, which immediately received many privileges. The Church, or to be more exact the Cistercian Order headed by Bernard of Clairvaux, started a propaganda campaign on behalf of the new order, extolling the Templars to the skies. As a result, they expanded rapidly, the number of their members increased, and from everywhere money and real estate were donated.

Hugo de Payens' spouse was a descendant of Scottish nobility. Her name was Catherine of St Claire. Due to this marriage and for other reasons, he frequently visited England where he enjoyed the friendship of King Henry I. Soon a Templar branch was founded in Scotland. (Already in these early years, there is a trace to Scotland, a remote country that was to gain special relevance in the history of the Templars. In their tradition, some lodges still use names such as 'Scottish Order' or 'Scottish Rite'.)

During their nine years in Jerusalem the first nine Templars had refused to accept new members. Then, two of their leaders returned to France to recruit support. When returning to Jerusalem after two years, they had a troop of one hundred men, and they were fully equipped as a 'registered' association with statutes sanctioned by the pope. Still, the question remains: how much did the pope actually know about the background of this action? Did Bernard and the team of his uncle simply use the Catholic infrastructure to build up their own empire based on their secret knowledge (and world maps)?

By 1130 the Templars possessed a lot of property in France, England, Scotland, Belgium, Spain and Portugal. Within only a few decades, they grew into the most influential and richest organization in Europe. Even kings and bishops had to come and borrow money from them – for their battles and crusades, for the building of castles and cathedrals, etc. Monasteries and other centres of this secretive society began to shoot up like mushrooms. The co-operation of the Cistercians, an intellectual and clerical elite, and the Templars, who were about to become a military and financial elite, prepared the field for the gradual expansion of society's horizons.

Later on, the Templars suffered setbacks in their crusades, even losing Jerusalem again, but they remained powerful as an organization, and became a growing threat to the king and the pope.

On 13 October 1307, a Friday, the king of France, Philippe 'the Fair', made a violent move against more than one thousand Templar centres throughout the country. They were raided, and numerous members were arrested, tortured and killed after some time. (Due to this event, Friday 13 is still said to be a black day.)

Jesus seen from the Lodge perspective

As shown in the historical excursus at the end of this chapter, the Catholic order of the Templars – massacred by a Catholic king under the patronage of the pope – became the seed of the secular 'fraternal society' called Freemasonry. This connection is not a secret as it has been the topic of best-selling books by authors like Lincoln, Baigent and Leigh, Knight/Lomas, Picknett/Prince, and Gardner. Some titles speak for themselves: *The Temple and the Lodge; The Hiram Key: Pharaohs, Freemasons and the Discovery of the Secret Scrolls of Jesus; The Templar Revelation: Secret Guardians of the True Identity of Christ; Bloodline of the Holy Grail.**

These few titles already show that Jesus Christ is a central figure of Templar and Lodge history. Moreover, they declare to know the 'true identity of Christ'. What is 'true' from their point of view and untrue in the commonly known biography of Christ? Here we touch upon the basic difference between Christian belief and those beliefs that the Templars got to hear in Jerusalem from Jewish and Islamic sources. Later on, when the European Renaissance and the Age of Enlightenment set in, adherents of their successor lines became even more doubtful about the traditional descriptions of Jesus. In the spirit of humanism and rationalism, they started to question his miracles and messianic nature. If he was not a divine incarnation, not the Son of God, then his death must have been different from the Bible's description, and certainly there had been no resurrection and no ascension.

The aforementioned authors (and many others) advocate just that. They may contradict one another in many respects but on one point they all agree: Jesus was an ordinary human who was later made into an idol by the Church, being heralded as 'the Saviour' or even the Son of God. In their opinion, the resurrection and ascension of Jesus were 'in some way a fraud'.[64]

What kind of person was he, then? There are almost as many opinions as authors.

Some say 'Jesus' is a biographical amalgamation of various historical figures. The Jesus as described in the Bible never existed.

Some say that the historical Jesus was a religious preacher aspiring for political power, mesmerizing people with miracles and Messianic prospects simply to achieve his goals.

Some say that he was a political activist trying to build up a liberation organization to fight the Roman occupation. Others admit that he may have been a spiritualist or a magician due to his Egyptian initiation, but nevertheless, in their opinion, there were no big miracles, no

---

* For details about these authors and titles, see bibliography.

How the Templars saw themselves: Jesus as a political Messiah leading their mission with sword and scripture. Their concealed aim: to deprive the Church of its hegemony and to gain supremacy in the field of politics and religion. Various groups that evolved from this background still maintain similar aims today. (Painting of the thirteenth century)

mass healings, no mass feedings and no dead people coming back to life, certainly no dead Jesus reappearing amongst the living.

All above-mentioned authors support one of these versions. Some openly admit that they are Freemasons, like Knight/Lomas. Others (like Lincoln, Baigent and Leigh) base much of their evidence about Jesus on the Qumran scrolls as interpreted by one of the first Qumran scholars, Prof. John M. Allegro. He had been part of the original group of Catholic, Lutheran, Orthodox and Jewish scholars called to examine the scrolls, he himself being the atheist of the group. Already in 1956, before the excavations were finished, Allegro went public with the theory that the scrolls were early Christian writings mentioning Jesus as an Essene leader who wanted to fight the Romans. But despite different authors continuing to repeat this tale, it is proven by serious scholarship that the Qumran scrolls are not early Christian texts but Jewish texts mostly dating from the first century *before* Christ.

Interestingly enough, the Freemasonic authors Knight/Lomas dedicate their book *The Hiram Key* (1996) to this John Marco Allegro, thus indicating that he was a Freemason, too. These authors may not be representative of what the general members of Freemasonry believe, but it is them who go public, writing popular bestsellers that are quickly translated into many languages.

Another important aspect of the life of Jesus, besides his (alleged) political ambition, is his relationship to Mary Magdalene, his consort if not wife. The scenario depicted by these lodge authors goes on to state that Mary Magdalene went to southern France after the crucifixion of Jesus – which is not improbable because, at that time, the south of France was the main place of Jews in exile. There, a large Jewish community had come into existence.

The theory that Mary Magdalene went abroad by ship, landing on the southern shore of France, is therefore historically plausible. The authors mentioned above expand the scenario by claiming that Mary had a child by Jesus, or more than one, and thus founded her own dynasty in the line of David; the term 'Holy Grail', in its confidential usage, refers to this secret blood-line. The first famous exponents of the Grail dynasty are the Merovingians (fifth to seventh century), who are thereby declared to be descendants of Jesus and David. Their line spread into most royal and noble families of Europe and the USA. From one of these lines, the Messiah is expected to come, the 'real one', who will be political and universal, a world leader and unifier of mankind.

No matter how unbelievable or absurd such opinions may sound, there are influential organizations that firmly believe in them, and many best-selling books have been propagating these ideas for more than thirty years. In this connection, some authors disclose the existence of another secret society, the *Priory of Sion,* which had been instrumental in the foundation of the Templars. After the seeming extinction of the Templars, the Priory continued to exist because it worked underground, keeping perfect secrecy – despite the prominence of some of its spiritual heads, for example Sandro Botticelli, Leonardo da Vinci, Victor Hugo, Claude Debussy and Jean Cocteau.[65]

In view of this long historical struggle, we have to expect that those representing such beliefs might – in the not too distant future – attempt to strike a big blow of 'revelation' and propaganda concerning the 'truth about Jesus', meant to finally overthrow the Church along with all its dogmas and claims to power. This has been reported by all of the aforementioned authors, for example by Picknett/Prince. Summarizing one of their conversations with a Grand Master of the Priory of Sion, they state:

> The outcome of this great plan was to be a 'spiritual renaissance' that would 'turn Christianity upside down'. Clearly this has not happened – yet, although our investigations show that the revelation that could lead to such an upheaval is already waiting in the wings to make a dramatic appearance on the world stage, perhaps in the form of the Priory or of allied mystery schools ...[66]

This assessment shows that there is not much hope for reconciliation between secular and religious power groups. They maintain fundamental differences in their convictions and ambitions which they do not want to compromise. In this way, they become a breeding ground for corrupt and unscrupulous power struggles, both within their own ranks and in confrontation with others.

Dualistic thinking leads to dia-bolic scheming.

A telling prophecy

Many global interest groups are working towards a Brave New World that is to be designed according to their visions and ambitions, be it a dictatorship of 'necessity', an atheistic plutocracy, an absolutist theocracy, or a messianic monarchy.

Interestingly enough, it was one of the ancestors of the present-day secret societies who, from the very beginning, foresaw the negative infiltration of both the Church and the Lodge. He himself had been one of the founders of such a new order with secret and official agendas, namely the Templars. We are talking about Jehan de Vézelay (1042–1119), the warrior monk, abbot and mystic who participated in the first crusade (1096–9) and then decided to spend the rest of his life in Jerusalem, thus becoming known as *John of Jerusalem*.

During the last twenty years of his life, he was visited several times by his disciple Hugo de Payens whom he assisted in the founding of the Templars. He also participated in the excavations on the Temple Mount and, mostly alone in the desert, experienced profound mystical revelations. He became a visionary if not a prophet. In 1117, shortly before his death, he wrote his *Book of Prophecies*.

What he wrote was sensational. At the beginning of the second millennium, he predicted the condition of the world at the beginning of the third millennium. His prophecies consist of forty stanzas, thirty of them starting with the standard line *'When the millennium after the millennium begins'*. In this far-distant future, he foresaw the existence of 'a dark and secret order' governing the world with hate and spreading poison everywhere, even into the religions.

For centuries, John's *Book of Prophecies* was the secret property of a few select circles. John had made only seven copies and forbade further copying. Initiates knew that the manuscript would surface from oblivion when the time was ripe. And promptly, in 1991 it was rediscovered and made public.[67] It was found in the archives of the KGB, put on file by Stalin's agents who had secured it in 1945 in Hitler's Berlin bunker. The Nazis had found it in a book collection of a Jewish community in Warsaw, in 1941. It was the copy that John of Jerusalem had given to one of his Jewish friends, whose descendants kept it throughout the Diaspora, carrying it to Spain, from there to France, to Germany and then to Poland. This manuscript is the only copy that still exists today.

Thus, present-day secret societies are confronted with a revealing message recorded during their own early history by one of their founding fathers. Due to the exact date mentioned, it becomes obvious to whom the expression 'a dark and secret order' is referring:

When the millennium after the millennium begins,
There will be a dark and secret order.
Their law will be hatred, their weapon venom,
They will be insatiably lusting for gold,
Spreading their reign throughout the earth,
And their servants will be sworn to one another
By a kiss of blood.

The just and the weak will obey their rules,
Those in power will be at their service,
The only law will be what they [the secret order]
In shadow dictate.

They will sell their venom even to the Church.
And the world wanders with the scorpion lurking under its soles.
(stanza 19)

Almost nine hundred years ago this pioneer of the Templars described the dark and secret powers of the twentieth century in a manner that no one could have imagined in those days: a global order causing poison and hatred, secretly attempting to monopolize the gold, dictating its course of action to the just and weak as well as to the politicians and the religions. John of Jerusalem, however, warns his lodge brothers of the distant future, telling them that their unscrupulous manipulations will eventually fail. They will end in self-destruction while the earth will complete the final cleansing:

When the millennium after the millennium begins
The earth will quake in several places
And the cities will be laid in ruins.
Everything built without the advice of the wise
Will be threatened and destroyed.
Villages will be buried under mire
And the ground beneath the palaces will split.
Man will be obstinate, being obsessed with pride,
He will not hear the warning
Which the earth calls out to him again and again.
Raging fires will destroy the new Romes,
The destitute and barbarous, despite the legions,
Will plunder deserted wealth. (stanza 22)

When the millennium after the millennium begins
The sun will burn the earth,
The air will no longer protect from fire,
Being only a curtain full of holes,
And the stinging light will burn the eyes and skin […] (stanza 23)

[…] Man will form every living entity
According to his own fancy
And countless numbers of them he will kill.
What will become of man

Who changes the laws of life like this,
Having made a living animal
Into a clump of clay?
Will he be in the image of God or born of the Devil? (stanza 25)

The last ten stanzas of John's Prophecies start off with a new line, '*When the millennium after the millennium comes to its end*, indicating that his visions even encompassed the entire third millennium. These prophecies – just as many visions and channelled sources of today – point out that with the dawning of the new millennium an era of divine insights will begin. Men will be freed from the dark forces and will experience a spiritual and even physical transformation.

When the millennium after the millennium comes to its end
Men will finally have opened their eyes.
They will no longer be imprisoned in their heads
And in their cities,
They will see from one end of the earth to the other,
Understanding each other,
They will know that hurting another
Is hurting oneself.
Men will be one big single body,
Everyone being a part
And together the heart.
There will be one language spoken by all,
And thus, after terrible pains,
It will be born, the greatness of human destiny. (stanza 31)

When the millennium after the millennium comes to its end
Men will know that all living entities are carriers of Light,
All of them being creatures deserving equal respect.
They will found new dwellings
In the heavens, on the earth and within the ocean.

Men will remember what has been
And will know to understand what will be.
They will no longer fear their death,
Having lived several lives in one life,

*And they will know that Light
Will never be extinguished. (stanza 40)*

Thus end the prophecies of John of Jerusalem, one of the first Templars. These few quotes give an idea of the high consciousness these 'Middle Agers' had, being visionaries of a 'New Age'. At the same time they knew that it would take one thousand years and more until these revelations would manifest on earth; and they also had the responsibility of knowing about the degradation, destruction and corruption that would come about in the meantime. It was a burden that only a few initiates were able to carry with transcendental calmness and composure.

Summary and outlook

Modern mystery schools, secret societies and fraternities look back on a long historical development. They evolved from traditions that were committed (1) to keeping sacred knowledge from being lost or distorted, and (2) to keeping the memory of former epochs and past civilizations alive – of their greatness and glory as well as their degradation through misuse of power. Cyclic human history had gone through a catastrophic turning point (from our view about 10,000 years ago), which deprived mankind of most of its previous achievements. Life became a 'primitive' struggle for existence, and time brought about an increased forgetfulness. With the onset of Kali-yuga five thousand years ago, the mentality of exploitation and egotism had become a global phenomenon. Due to the less refined consciousness of the people, matter was experienced to be more binding and grosser in its density.

Only a few individuals and small groups were able to preserve the timeless sacred knowledge and to transmit it through the centuries. In the course of many generations, beings of a less divine mentality began to infiltrate these ancient mystic traditions up to the point of taking over leading positions. In this way, false priests and god-kings established themselves as indisputable authorities who had the power to incite bloodshed through rituals and battles as a means to please or pacify 'God'. Later on, in the slipstream of the world religions, they managed to usurp the real messengers of God and their teachings to serve their own ambitions.

In the course of increased subjugation, exploitation, persecution, inquisition, crusades, colonization and corruption, countless people became victims of the arrogance and violence exerted by these totalitarian forces. Many could not resist the provocation and succumbed to feelings of hatred and revenge. Perpetrators and victims became entangled in fighting each other, involving both their descendants and their own later incarnations. Those who had been tortured, overwhelmed and killed reincarnated as opponents of the evil-doers and built up fronts against them. By giving in to feelings of hatred and revenge, they lost their purity and entered the arena of duality, wanting to become more powerful than the original perpetrators in order to overthrow them. By taking up the fight against the dark forces, some became a dark force themselves, no better than those they wanted to combat.

Nevertheless, some aspects of the original and timeless ideals can still be sensed in today's secret societies and fraternities. Therefore, people feel attracted to them, even certain progressive theologians, priests and Vatican members who no longer support the old dogmatic ways of their own church. With humanistic ideals, these covert revolutionaries hope to reform the confessional tradition they belong to. However, their success has been only ambivalent and partial despite the fact that these efforts have already been going on for centuries. On the one hand, this new input reduced Christianity's absolutism and furthered interreligious dialogue. On the other hand, the antagonism of the Church and the Lodge caused further corruption and infiltration. Again it becomes evident that mixing two half-truths does not produce a higher truth.

In the present phase of world history, the global power game is heading for dramatic challenges and surprises, some being brought about by the dark forces, some by the beings of the Light. Ultimately, the restoration of divine harmony will eliminate all forms of disturbing extremes, just like a healthy body which neutralizes all forms of infectious alien elements.

As unfolded in Part II of this book, there are plausible scenarios regarding the course these dramatic events might take. One thing is for sure: They will concern all of us.

Historical excursus:
From the Templars to Freemasonry

Freemasonry was officially founded in London, on St John's Day, 24 June, 1717. Is it true that the Freemasons are related to the Templars? How, then, were the four hundred years between 1307 and 1717 bridged? Did some Templars really survive the persecution, and did their following generations nurture a revengeful opposition against the Church? Are there traces in history?

As the answers to these questions can validate the historical interpretation given in this chapter, the following excursus is added. At the same time, they provide a further illustration of how devotion degraded into deviation, both in the Church and in the Lodge.

Let us return to the year 1307 when the Gestapo-like death blow against the Templars took place on Friday, 13 October. Today we know that it was not thoroughly crushing. The initial raids only took place in France. In other countries they followed later, which allowed a good number of Templars to flee, to go underground or to change their identities.

It is also known that the Templars possessed a first-class fleet, probably the most advanced of the time. (They were not lacking money!) In the evening of 12 October 1307, the entire fleet lay at anchor in the port of La Rochelle situated on the Atlantic Coast of France. When the royal-papal armies appeared on the scene in the evening of this Black Friday, the docks were found vacant. The fleet consisting of eighteen ships had disappeared and was nowhere to be found. Till today, there is no official conclusion regarding the whereabouts of these ships.

Outside of France the persecution of the Templars was carried out more hesitantly. Scotland even ignored the Vatican's order. At first, England also ignored the order; only when the pope increased his pressure on the king were a few raids conducted. Most of the arrested Templars were later acquitted of their charges. The same happened in Italy, central Europe and Spain. On the Iberian peninsula the Templars had been an essential support in the fight against the Islamic Moors. Understandably, the kings of these countries were not interested in executing war comrades. In Portugal, where the Templars possessed key dock facilities, the order was pro forma disbanded and their property – including ships – confiscated, only to be handed over to the newly founded 'Christus Order'. Looking at the names of its original members, it is obvious that this new order mainly consisted of people who had formerly belonged to the Templars. The 'Christus Order' was dedicated first and foremost to seafaring. Christopher Columbus (1451–1506) was married to the daughter of a Grand Master of this order, and had access to the maps and diaries of his father-in-law.[68]

What was the fate of those Templars who disappeared with their fleet? The lodge authors mentioned in this chapter take great pains to furnish an answer to this question, and they all arrive at the same conclusion: The Templars had fled from their paternal land of origin, France, to their maternal land of origin, Scotland. Stigma-

An amazing monument by 'mythological' humans

In the Indian Himalayas, north of Badrinath, near the border to Tibet, there is a 'wonder of the world' that is practically unknown in the West. One huge block of stone is precisely laid across a gorge that is ten metres wide and twenty metres deep. The topographical surroundings clearly indicate that this stone-bridge is man-made, as it is fit into the only place of the gorge where two opposite ledges are found: one is underneath overhanging rocks, the other is a small recess, about one foot in width, where the face of the rock creates a step. The roughly worked block is about 13 metres long, 9 metres high and 4 metres wide – weight: approximately 1,200 tons! In spite of having most advanced technology, today's engineers cannot even theoretically conceive of a way to put this megalith across a gorge.

View from the north

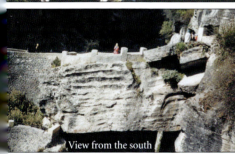

View from the south

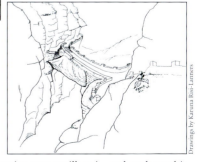

The traditional explanation says that this stone was put there by Bhima, the brother of Arjuna, when they and their other three brothers left their kingdom and went to the Himalayas to 'die'. However, they left the world not by an ordinary death but by a physical ascension (by developing a Light body, see pp. 207, 408). Bhima, who foresaw that the route of their 'march of transformation' would become an important pilgrimage way in the future, used a stone because stone would survive many millennia, and anyhow, this region was far beyond the timberline. Therefore, this bridge is called Bhimpul, 'the bridge of Bhima', since time immemorial.

Drawings by Karuna Risi-Lamers

The amazing monument
of an ancient technological civilization

The biggest stones of the world which were artificially cut and moved are not products of modern technology, but of an unknown ancient civilization. They are found in the Lebanon at a place called Baalbek, fit into a big terrace wall at a height of six metres: three precisely cut blocks, each 20 metres long, 4 metres high and 3.6 metres wide, each weighing 800 tons!

Outside Baalbek lies an even bigger block: 21.36 m × 4.33 m × 4.6 m, weighing nearly 1,200 tons. With his advanced technology, modern man is unable to move and lift such heavy blocks. And here in Baalbek we have no reinforced streets, the land is hilly, and the quarry is several miles away.

One interpretation (given by Zecharia Sitchin in *The Stairway to Heaven*) says that Baalbek is identical with the place called 'Mountain of Cedars' mentioned in the Epic of Gilgamesh, which was the place of the extraterrestrial god Enlil (p. 342). Did he build this wall and terrace to create a wide platform – maybe to have a landing field for the legendary 'flying thrones of the gods', as shown in ancient Sumerian, Accadian and Persian depictions?

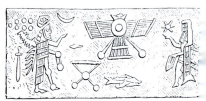

Indian temple pyramid with a cap stone of 80 tons

The Brihadisvara temple of Thanjavur (Tanjore) in Tamil Nadu, South India, is a UNESCO World Heritage Site since 1987. This impressive temple from the eleventh century contains an architectonic mystery. The artistically worked cap stone atop the pyramid, the so-called vimana stone, is one solid block of rock weighing 80 tons! In order to move such a weight today, we would need a special truck with twelve axles, which weighs another 50 tons.

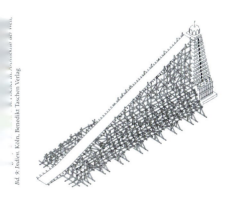
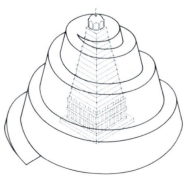

How was it possible for the Indian temple architects to lift a block of 80 tons into a height of 65 metres? Conventional scenarios of today's architects consider a 'solution' with elephants dragging and pushing the stone over a ramp way made of a wood (bamboo) construction or of an earth spiral that covered the entire pyramid. Would these constructions carry a dynamic weight of more than 100 tons? The temple priests indicate that mysteries of this kind have been the feat of mystics with paranormal abilities.

Painting by Urs Amann, Winterthur

Forces from the dark realms of the astral and extraterrestrial parallel worlds are secretly pursuing their agendas on earth (genetic experiments, hybrid breeding, etc.). Some of these forces also have incarnated agents on earth (p. 92). The so-called Greys and their 'bio-robots' belong to the lower levels of the dragon's hierarchy, which influences humanity's mass consciousness by promoting a destructive technology and spreading an atmos-fear of terror, stress and anxiety (pp. 66, 361–2).

In St John's Revelation humanity is warned against a manipulative technology which will lead to the point where nobody is able to buy or sell anything unless he (and she) has the mark of the beast on the right hand or on the forehead (Rev. 13.18).
Nowadays, the idea of people having 'something' on the forehead is no longer anything far-fetched. Rather, it is openly demonstrated in films and even in public advertising.

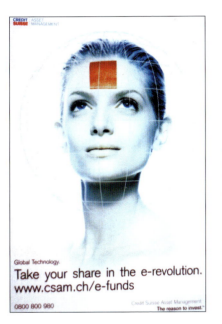

In the year 2000, several European banks used the same picture for advocating the English slogan, 'Take your share in the e-revolution – The reason to invest'. It showed a young woman's head within the globe's grid (symbolizing the 'world-wide grid', the *centralized* global computer web?). Her neck was unnaturally long, and on her forehead she had a mark, namely an enlarged portion of skin. Reduced to the proportion of the face, this mark would have the probable size of the 'mark of the beast'. (pp. 258–9)

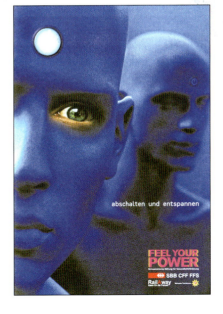

In the year 2001, there was a health campaign in Switzerland which had as its motto, 'Switch off and Relax – Feel Your Power'. As an illustration they chose the picture of two human heads painted blue, with no hair and a lifeless expression – and with a computer button on their foreheads, exactly on the third eye'. These bald, sexless people look like aliens, or like hybrids …

Indian temples as a depiction of the cosmic creation

The temple site of Madurai, Tamil Nadu, South India.

Different forms of pyramids are found all over the world. The form of the temple pyramids (Gopuras) of South India represents the hierarchical order of the cosmic dimensions. The top and bottom sections of these constructions are parallel and are connected by descending levels (heavens), down to level that touches the earth.

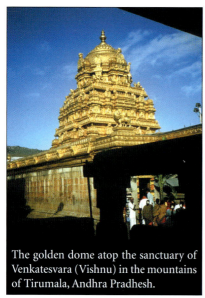

The golden dome atop the sanctuary of Venkatesvara (Vishnu) in the mountains of Tirumala, Andhra Pradhesh.

A testimony of a past golden age? Or a 'light-house' for the next golden age?

The highest temple pyramid of India (120 metres), situated in Rangakshetra, Tamil Nadu.

Transformation of the earth

Drawing: © Karuna Risi-Lanners

In the present age, the earth and mankind are passing through a phase of utmost physical condensation. It was not always like that, and will not always remain like that (pp. 278, 370). The raising of the earth's vibration, and the ascension to come, were initiated by the incarnation of the 'first-born son of God', the cosmic Christ, or *Christos Pantokrator,* called Brahma in Sanskrit. 'And remember, I am with you always, to the end of the age' (Matt. 28.20). As this coming of the Light will mark the end of darkness, the dark forces attack Jesus in various ways: by absolutizing him with Bible dogmatism, by mundane profanation and by Luciferean imitation. 'Beware that no one leads you astray. For many will come in my name, saying, "I am he" [or, "We are the only ones knowing him" …] But those who endure to the end will be saved!' (Matt. 10.22; 24.4, 13; Mark 13.5, 13; Luke 21.8, 19; John 16.1; Rev. 13.10)

For more than twenty years, amazing pictogrammes have been found in crop fields all over the world, most of them in England. They have diameters of up to two hundred metres, some are even bigger (longer). They are created within a short time, probably within seconds, usually during the night. Despite the large number of pictogrammes (approximately 4,000 during the last 25 years), no 'perpetrators' have ever been caught or even seen!

The superficial, or non-existent, coverage by the news media, the additional *intentional faking* of crop circles, and the bluff statements of people claiming to have been the creators of these pictogrammes, have caused the general public to ignore these miracles, or to believe that they are simply the work of some students or old people who want to fool the world.

Who is able to create such designs overnight, all over the world, in a large number and with stunning perfection? Are they the work of planetary and interplanetary Light beings who act unobtrusively? Are these pictogrammes interdimensional mandalas imprinted on power places and chakra points of the earth: as signs for those who have 'the eyes to see', and as an energetic acupuncture for the body of Mother Earth, a preparation for her physical ascension?

tized and ostracized as 'anti-Christians' by brute force on the part of the State and the Church, the Templars were forced to hide, or conceal their membership. In Scotland, however, they were not only tolerated but welcomed because Robert the Bruce, the man spearheading the Scottish struggle for independence from England, had been excommunicated by the pope in 1306. When the pope issued a bull against the Templars in November 1307, it was no longer binding for Scotland.

Evidence of the Templars' presence in Scotland can be found in the battle of Bannockburn in 1314. The Scottish troops were able to defy the English army only by the grace of a mysterious circumstance. Suddenly, in the decisive phase of the battle, a reserve troop of men on horseback appeared. Due to their expert combat strategy, they shocked the English militia, overrunning it, causing it to flee in panic. This battle took place on St John's Day, 24 June 1314. The date so carefully chosen and the tactics exhibited in battle both bear the stamp of the Knights Templars.[69]

Furthermore, researchers in Scotland have discovered typical Templar buildings and anonymous graves of warrior monks from the thirteenth, fourteenth and fifteenth centuries. Hugo de Payens himself had founded one of the first western Templar branches in Scotland in 1130.

The most important Scottish centre of this period is the stone chapel of Rosslyn (built 1440–90), which still exists today. Though officially said to be a Catholic chapel, it was never really considered a site of Christianity but a sacred place of Templar descendants, the first 'Freemasons'. This became evident two hundred years later during the English Civil War (1642–8) when the troops of Oliver Cromwell (1599–1658) devastated Ireland, Wales and Scotland, razing countless royal and clerical properties. Cromwell also reached Rosslyn but he spared this chapel though having destroyed every church along his way. Two years later, Cromwell's troops under the command of General Monk once more invaded Scotland and also came to Rosslyn. They destroyed Rosslyn Castle, but the chapel, though in close vicinity, was again left unscathed. Cromwell and Monk obviously knew the 'unofficial' significance of this chapel, both being top-ranking members of these covert insider societies.

In other words, there were many lodges long before the official foundation of Freemasonry in 1717, but they had been forced to act in secrecy until the power of the Vatican, due to the Reformation, began to dwindle in the sixteenth and seventeenth centuries.

The Freemasonic authors Knight/Lomas cite evidence that the King of Scotland, James I (1566–1625), was initiated into the 'Lodge of Scoon and Perth' in the year 1601. In 1603 he was proclaimed King of all England, taking up residence in London. It was at this time that the famous *King James Bible* was produced. This important work was completed to further England's independence from Rome and its local clergy. The preface to the first edition, written by King James himself, contains remarks on papacy that might easily be considered as polemical or inimical.

In 1598, the same James, at that time King of Scotland, had initiated the organized structuring of Freemasonry. The authors Knight/Lomas state: 'From this point onwards Freemasonry had a Lodge structure which would soon spread to England and eventually the entire Western World.'[70]

James I was succeeded by his son, who became Charles I. Contrary to his father, he considered himself again to be a king 'by the grace of God', thus triggering dissonance in parliament and ultimately provoking the English Civil War.

Oliver Cromwell, a wild figure in this civil war, was a minion of Sir Thomas Fairfax, an imperialistic lodge member to whom Cromwell was indebted for his social advancement.

These few examples show that, in the sixteenth and seventeenth centuries, the neo-Templars already had an effectively operating network of lodge alliances. Only a few decades had to pass before a perfectly organized and unified Grand Lodge would be able to officially announce its existence in world history, on St John's Day of the year 1717.

In this regard, even the English Masonic authors Knight/Lomas have to admit: 'In trying to formalise itself as a regular institution, English Freemasonry was already starting to lose its way.'[71] Using less diplomatic words, the anthroposophical historian Heinz Pfeifer comments:

> From 1717 onwards, Freemasonry became more and more dependent on the British Lodge, and the only thing remaining of original Freemasonry was the variety of external forms. With the corruption and subsequent control of World Freemasonry by the British Grand Lodge the grasp for global power was launched [...] preparing the ground for the future Anglo-American Empire.[72]

Triggered by this starting shot, many other secret organizations sprang up. Among them was the prototypal Illuminati Order founded in 1776 by Adam Weishaupt in Germany, which rapidly gained international influence. Soon, the Illuminati Order also became operational in Scotland. There, the most prominent member was Prof. John Robison, who later left the order and went public (see p. 104). His book *Proofs of a Conspiracy against all the Religions and Governments of Europe*, published in 1797, gives clear evidence of the actual goals of secret organizations such as the Illuminati and falsified Freemasonry.

1776 was also an important year in North American history. It was the year of the Declaration of Independence which, 13 years later, led to the founding of the USA.

> It is no secret that Masonry was a major moving force behind the American Revolution and the founding of the Republic of the United States of America [...] The men who created the United States of America were either Freemasons themselves or had close contact with Freemasons. [...] When George Washington was made First President of the United States of America he had been a member of the Craft for almost thirty-six years and was at the time a member of the Alexandria Lodge, No. 22.[73]

It can hardly be denied that the Freemasons at that time were sincerely endeavouring to live up to their high-set ideals. The Constitution of the United States is proof hereof. Justice and equal rights for all were to be the foundation of the New World as opposed to the Old World. (Later on, for the purpose of pushing on its plans, the 'secret government' had to undertake many cunning actions in order to effect the altering of specific paragraphs of this Constitution.[74])

The involvement in mundane politics, however, soon forfeited the vision and idealism of the original mystery school. Men of purity and honesty had not much chance to stay at the top. There was a continent to be conquered and a 'new world' to be gained. With their superior weapons they were ready to subjugate and annihilate the natives, considering these 'savages' to be inferior humans or even children of the devil. Both the religious and the secular forces had ideologies to justify their doings.

Due to his greed for power, the 'white man' fell deeply into the entanglement of karma. This atmosphere (collective consciousness) allowed a further breakthrough of negative entities, granting them a strong foothold on earth. The traces they left in history speak for themselves: the elimination of the Indians, the enslaving of the Africans, lodge murders, internal rivalry, deception, arrogance, the brutal Civil War, the idolatry of technology and industry. In the twentieth century, the USA became the hub of a new imperialism, carrying on the heritage of the British Empire. It was no longer based on direct colonization but on financial domination.

Despite the propaganda that 'everything is becoming better', exploitation, wars, pollution and other dangers have now become global due the workings of these forces. Global problems pave the way for global control. This 'New World Order' will probably be established first in the New World itself. Being the focus point of world power and world domination, America is also the point where most powerful energies of the Light have to be anchored. Many revolutionary things have already sprung up in the USA, planting the seed for positive and spiritual changes of consciousness. The cultural melting pot of the USA brought about a unique open-mindedness that went beyond petty conservatism and drained traditionalism.

Deep wounds have been inflicted upon the earth by forces based in the USA. Will the healing also come from there, bringing us back to the original idealism inspired by sacred knowledge? What will it take till humanity is willing to transcEnd the global power game? What challenges still lie ahead? These topics will be taken up in Part Two.

Part II
Prophecies and the Revelation – Mankind in the Mirror of Its Future

Where is today's artificial progress leading to?
What are the next steps to be expected?
Who are the forces behind it?

CHAPTER SIX

Moneypulation

Amongst the Vedic scriptures there are some which especially focus on mythological history and prophecy, the most famous being the *Mahabharata* and the *Bhagavata Purana,* also called *Shrimad-Bhagavatam.* They contain amazing information about the onset and subsequent development of our present age, in which materialism, violence and deceit were foreseen to become 'normal'. In Sanskrit the spirit furthering these developments is called Kali, 'the divider', the dia-bolic force that destroys unity, peace and truth. Therefore, the present age was prophetically called 'Kali-yuga', which turned out to be quite accurate.

The Sanskrit scriptures relate that, at the end of the preceding *yuga,* about five thousand years ago, planet earth was suffering because of aggressive military forces led by dark war lords. Seeing this unbearable situation, the higher-dimensional planetary guardians (*devas*) beseeched Brahma, the highest Light being of the universe, for help, who in turn asked the 'Father' on their behalf (see endnote 43 on p. 141 and the quote on pp. 143–4). Their pleas were answered by a divine intervention that culminated in the appearance of Krishna. When the Battle of Kurukshetra, the so-called Mahabharata War, became inevitable, Krishna spoke the *Bhagavad-gita* to his friend and devotee, Arjuna, who at that time was known as the bravest of all warriors.

After this decisive battle, Arjuna and his brothers headed by King Yudhisthira became the rightful leaders of the Bharata Empire. Under their reign people once again lived in peaceful prosperity. Though some first symptoms of Kali-yuga became manifest, society could not be corroded as a whole.

In this not so far distant past ('only' five thousand years ago) the Light beings called *devas* still sporadically appeared on earth. This happened, for example, when Prince Pariksit, the grandson of Arjuna, was enthroned as the next king.[75] Pariksit, born shortly after the Battle of

Kurukshetra, chose the veteran Kripacharya as his spiritual advisor. It was at the celebration of this occasion that some *devas* became visible even to the common man. The *Shrimad-Bhagavatam* (1.16.3) states: *deva-yatrakshi-gocarah.* 'The *devas* appeared on this occasion (*yatra*) within the optical spectrum of the people (*akshi-gocarah*).'

Pariksit was a king who displayed all the magnificent qualities that had been predicted by astrologers on the day of his birth. However, despite a flourishing civilization, King Pariksit noticed that Kali's destructive influence was increasingly visible on earth. In the *Shrimad-Bhagavatam* (1.15.45) the word *bhuvi*, 'throughout the earth', is used to emphasize Kali's *global* impact.

The onset of Kali-yuga, the darkest of the four ages, coincided with King Pariksit's reign. In the course of these ages, spiritual religiosity (*dharma*) gradually declined. It is said that Dharma, personified as a bull, had lost one leg after the other. At the beginning of Kali-yuga, only one leg was left – truthfulness.

> [King Pariksit addressed Dharma the Bull:] In the first age, the age of Satya (truthfulness), you stood on four legs established by the four principles of self-control, purity, mercy (forgiveness) and truthfulness. But it appears that three of your legs are broken due to rampant irreligion in the form of pride, lust and intoxication.
>
> You are now standing on one leg only, which is your truthfulness, and you are somehow or other hobbling along. But quarrel personified [Kali], flourishing by deceit, is trying to destroy that leg also.
>
> The burden of the earth was diminished by the divine incarnation [Krishna] and the ones in His accordance. When He was present, the earth was blessed by His footprints, and thus there was auspiciousness everywhere.
>
> Now she [the earth], the virtuous one, laments her future with tears in her eyes, for now she will be dominated and exploited by base-minded men posing as rulers. (*Shrimad-Bhagavatam* 1.17.24–7)[76]

The attacks on the four pillars of dharma

Once while travelling through his kingdom, Pariksit had the vision of a scene that represented the global state of affairs to come: Kali in the guise of a king attempted to break the last leg of the bull Dharma, truthfulness, so as to gain complete control over the earth. Three of the bull's legs were already broken, and the cow (the earth) was fretfully lowing in pain. Upon seeing this heinous action, Pariksit hastened to protect the bull. Kali, aware of the incorruptible nature of the emperor, immediately surrendered to him, pleading for his protection on the basis of being his citizen. The wise king did not forcefully annul Kali's influence, knowing well that Kali would be effective only when people showed interest in his offers and seductions. In the upcoming age, Kali was to be a challenge for everybody's truthfulness and sincerity. Therefore, Pariksit allotted four particular places to him:

> The king, being requested by Kali, gave him permission to reside in places of animal slaughter, impure sex life, addiction and abuse of wealth. (1.17.30)

As already cited, the first three pillars of *dharma* are broken by pride, lust and intoxication, which are directly connected to the factors mentioned here; the fourth is broken by the abuse of wealth.

Pride destroys modesty and self-control, as a proud person believes the world exists for his enjoyment. The first victims of this arrogance are the animals which such people kill and eat. This especially refers to the killing of cows and bulls, which symbolize the earth and *dharma*.

Lust means wanting to exploit other people for one's own gratification, be it sexually, socially or economically. This mentality destroys the purity of consciousness as it leads to greed, repression and frustration, causing people to become haunted by sexual images (elementals) of egoism, violence and perversion, which take their toll on all levels.

Intoxication refers to all forms of addiction that tune people's consciousness to a low astral frequency, thus rendering these people susceptible to the dictation of negative entities. Those who fall prey to such kinds of influence lose their self-control and mercy because they are on an 'ego trip', being taken over by drugs, stimulants or fanaticism.

Abuse of wealth refers to speculative dealing with gold and money: bribing, cheating, gambling, the taking of interest, etc.

By these factors, the four pillars of *dharma* – mercy (forgiveness), self-control, purity and truthfulness – are undermined, broken and even destroyed. Kali, however, soon had to realize that these forms of abuse and exploitation were not present in Pariksit's kingdom!

> Kali then went back to the king and asked for something more. Due to his begging, the king gave him an additional place to reside, namely those places where gold is hoarded, for wherever there is gold there are also falsity,

intoxication, lust, envy and enmity. [...] Therefore, whoever desires peace and prosperity, especially kings, religious people, public leaders, teachers and priests, should never come in contact with the four above-mentioned principles of irreligiosity. (1.17.39, 41)

Kali, the embodiment of godlessness, then began to exert his influence on those who were accumulating gold to expand their power. Being the father of falsehood and hypocrisy (also mentioned in the Bible, e.g. John 8.44), Kali was able to attack the three already broken legs of Dharma as well as the fourth leg: truthfulness and honesty.

This is the amazing information provided by the ancient prophecy of the Vedic scriptures. It reveals the course of manipulation taking place in Kali-yuga. As we know today, all dealings in this age are factually based on hoarded gold and money. Thus, this prophecy has proven to be true: global manipulation is based on *moneypulation*.

How gold turned into money

Money is the overall decisive factor ruling present-day civilization. Without a monetary system nothing would work. Money is the heart of the Kali-yuga society, and Kali-yuga is the 'age of discord and hypocrisy'. As stated by the Vedic prophecy, manipulation of gold is the main tool that the ulterior forces employ to secure their hegemony on earth. Therefore, if we want to know their next steps, we simply need to follow the trail of gold and money.

The first question to be examined is: How did the present-day monetary system come into being?

Over a long period of time, man lived by trading physical goods. A big change came about when certain interest groups introduced a more systematic payment system to expand trade – the use of silver and gold coins. One now received a commensurate sum of coins for the natural goods delivered. For many centuries, this payment system co-existed with bartering.

With the expansion of transportation and military conquests, the range of trade became international. An increasing number of tradesmen began to send larger consignments over longer distances to achieve higher profits. The system of exchanging physical goods became impractical and also increasingly risky, especially when the goods were coins. Sacks full of gold and silver were very inviting to bandits and pirates.

So what was one to do, being a tradesman who wanted to travel from one place to another in order to purchase and sell large quantities of goods? The easiest and safest way was to avoid the transporting of gold and silver coins by depositing them at the places of destination. And so, trade-offices came into being. They received and guarded the wealth of the tradesmen who went on their way to amass more money. The tradesmen were handed a signed and sealed receipt, a so-called insured letter or voucher.

During the absence of these tradesmen the crates full of gold began to pile up. It did not take very long till other tradesmen approached these gentlemen – not to deposit but to *borrow* gold. 'Listen, a consignment of silk has just arrived from the Orient. If I had more gold I could buy more raw material. If you give me an advance, I will pay it back to you in two months with an additional five gold coins which will be yours.'

The bankers started to consider the matter: 'Actually it is not my gold, and I have firmly vouched for it. The owners have a security. But I think they won't ask for the gold right away. So let me use it and earn some additional percentage.'

This is how the bankers began to lend out other people's gold. In a sense it was cheating from the very beginning, as the gold was already vouched to another person, namely the rightful owner.

Those who first introduced such paper-for-money practices in Europe have already been mentioned in the preceding chapter: 'The Templars [twelfth/thirteenth century] were the first bankers in the Western hemisphere. They were the first multinational business magnates and moneylenders, the first capitalists in the Western world. Whoever issues a cheque nowadays should remember that also this remarkable invention was introduced by the Templars.'[77]

By loaning out another person's gold, the banker became a creditor himself, demanding interest from the coin borrowers. These debtors handed the creditor a receipt stating that they owed him a certain amount of money. In this way, the coin custodians became both issuers and receivers of receipts.

The next step was to make these receipts transferable because it was much more convenient to deal with securities in paper instead of real coins. One tradesman might have said to another: 'Listen, I have gold deposits in Amsterdam (or Paris, Venice, Frankfurt, Constantinople, Baghdad etc.). I'll just give you the receipt. It will be honoured at any of those trade-offices whenever you ask for the money.'

More and more receipts began to circulate, enabling the tradesmen to exchange their own receipts at all trading centres. In this way, the first modern banks came into being, thriving on the issuing and receiving of vouchers. These convertible papers were already transferable, and now they had to become interchangeable as well, so that one bank could process receipts from another bank. The tradesmen did not want to be limited in their transactions, having to go only from Fugger to Fugger or from Rothschild to Rothschild. They expected that, for example, a Fugger bank would also pay out a Rothschild receipt. For this purpose standard bank receipts were required. Paper money was born.

Now, goods and services had to be converted into bank note values. From the eighteenth century onwards, money made of paper and cheap metal was circulating, dominating the entire trading market. Prices and salaries had to be fixed in money value. In this way, the economy and people in general became dependent on money and those controlling the flow of money – the bankers.

In the meantime, banks had also started to issue receipts that were not backed up by sufficient security. They speculated: 'Here we have one thousand crates of gold in custody. We have already loaned them to borrowers – not as gold, however, but as securities in paper. So we have lent out one thousand crates of gold and yet still have one thousand crates of gold! Why not carry on this business and expand the market?'

Both traders and borrowers were convinced of the banks' integrity and their words of honour. They simply believed their paper money to be backed up by gold. It was no longer verifiable because the gold was hardly in circulation anymore.

Soon, it was even authorized *by law* that only a certain amount of the bank-note value had to be backed up by gold. All state banks began to print paper money and declared it to have a specific market value. Nowadays, to a large extent, the money in circulation is not even printed as bank notes. Money has become an imaginary juggling with computer figures. However, this juggling with artificial values is an illusion that can burst like a soap bubble at any given moment.

Money and interest – whose interest?

The present monetary system is based on false values and will keep on working only as long as all participants, the people and the banks, play along. The people are not much of a risk factor because they are always at a disadvantage. After all, they have no power to force the banks to convert their paper into gold. In the case of some crisis or crash, people are left with nothing but paper in their hands. Furthermore, the central banks have the possibility of printing additional paper money or flooding the market with selected stocks, thus causing the exchange rate of these 'values' (currencies, shares) to fall dramatically. In such cases of inflation, many citizens lose a considerable amount of their savings and earnings because money suddenly has less purchasing power. As the history of many First, Second and Third World countries shows, this trick of moneypulation has been used more than once.

Oddly enough, inflation never caused losses for the big banks. Why? Because in most cases it was their own fabrication, as (artificial) economic crises were the 'ideal' means to make competitors and non-insiders insolvent. Through such intermezzos of depression, the finance magnates could buy up bankrupt enterprises for peanuts. Afterwards they increased the market value of their money back to 'normal'. In other words, they built up their financial empire by ruining and swallowing independent enterprises and smaller banks.

Today, we have advanced to a situation in which not only the traders but all citizens deposit their holdings in banks. We have no choice but to trust their promises: 'Give us your money and you will get it back whenever you want. And we will give you back even more than you brought! Give us 100 dollars and in one year it will have turned into 101.35 dollars! Isn't that proof that we are your well-meaning friends? We are serving your interests – by giving you interest!'

'Let money work for you!' This is the modern slogan of the banks, but it should make us suspicious. How does money work for us? We receive an *interest*. But where does this surplus come from?

The explanation is simple: The banks invest our money in their own businesses – which yield far more profit than the total interest paid out to the depositors! Compared to the incredible profit they make, the interest added to the deposits is but a ridiculous tip.

It is no secret where the money of the banks is flowing to: into industrial enterprises (machines, computers, chemicals, arms etc.), insurance companies, real-estate dealings, universities and scientific research (micro and nuclear technologies, pharmaceutical industry, and genetics). Another main field of investment is the exploitation of natural resources. In this regard, an inexhaustible bonanza is found in the allegedly poor countries that once made up the so-called Third World. These 'developing countries', as they are called today, are located in the prolific equatorial belt of Middle and South America, Africa and Asia. Up to one hundred years ago, it would have been impossible to imagine that anyone living in these tropical countries could die of starvation. There was no scarcity as these countries were privileged by nature: they had a rich vegetation, ample harvests and an abundance in natural resources. Even in the desert zones nobody died of hunger.

Today, more than half of the world's nations are counted among the poor and 'underdeveloped' countries, where about 40,000 people (mostly children) die of starvation every day – and this already for decades. What has happened?

How the Third World was created

Beginning in the fifteenth century, the superpowers of the Christian Occident began to found colonies throughout the world, with violence, cheating, war and genocide marking their ways. During the nineteenth and twentieth centuries, colonies were granted a different political status. They now gained 'independence' but not freedom.

The imperialist forces never even thought of actually giving up their colonies. Their humanitarian propaganda was a farce. In reality they simply entered the next phase of their power expansion.

After the declarations of independence, the Third World consisted of raped countries that were in dire need of a new infrastructure in order to survive. For centuries they had been subjected to foreign exploitation that destroyed all their indigenous economic structures. Some had gone through wars of independence, which further increased the inner chaos and destruction.

At this point, the former masters offered technology and education to their ex-colonies. But this 'reparation' was not for free! In order to accept this offer, the Third World countries needed money – which they did not have. Again, help was offered by the same 'generous' source in the form of *loans*. 'We will supply you with money so that you can buy from us. You can invest this money, and with your profits you can pay back the loans.'

With the prospect of lucrative business opportunities, the Third World took the bait or, to be more precise, was hooked to the rod. The banks granted big loans and also provided the blessings of civilization through their industrial associates: machinery, factories, railways, cars and tractors, fuel, chemicals, fertilizers, hybrid seedlings, etc. And to protect the new infrastructure, these nations needed their own armies. Again, the associates of the moneylenders offered assistance. Soon, civil wars started, incited by foreign manipulation and social injustice, because the former masters often chose their own men to become dictators in these countries.

For centuries, the economy of the colonized world has been dictated by the rich countries' greed for consumer goods (coffee, tobacco, cacao, cotton, bananas, soybeans etc.) and industrial raw materials like caoutchouc, copper, iron and uranium; not to forget, of course, the precious stones and metals, especially gold, platinum, diamonds and jewels. Another source of huge profit was, and still is, the cutting down of rainforests for obtaining tropical wood and new land for the meat industry (for growing cattle feed).[78]

Political and economic corruption in the Third World kept the profits in foreign hands, and the only ones benefiting in the respective countries were a few local agents in high positions. People in general never got to see any benefit from the big deals. In agriculture, the enforced single-crop farming caused total dependency on the buyers from abroad, who soon began to bring down the prices. In the meantime, the banks raised the interest rates for the loans given. Thus, despite gigantic profits made from their lands, the Third World countries were encumbered with such high debts that they could not even pay the compound interest, what to speak of the interest or the debts themselves!

Initially the ex-colonies had hoped to pay back the debts with the profits of their production, but it never got that far. The 'poor' countries remained under the full control of the money lords.

All the while, the banks had been playing a similar game at 'home'. That is why many industrial nations such as the USA are now hopelessly indebted, too. To whom? *To the banks of their own country.*

Colonies, superpowers and the dream of a World Empire

Colonial history and the subsequent creation of the Third World demonstrate the mindset of the forces that shaped the course of modern civilization. This phase of history also reveals what their plans really were, plans that are culminating in our present time.

One example among many is the Englishman *Cecil Rhodes* (1853–1902), a renowned exponent of imperialism and the British Empire. After graduating from Oxford University, he moved to South Africa. In 1884 he was appointed Minister of Finance of the Cape Colony. From 1888 onwards he controlled the entire diamond industry of this country, in those days approximately 95% of the global production. Due to his ruthless political and military tactics, which did not shun violence and bloodshed, the colony quickly expanded. One part of it was even named after him: *Rhodesia*. In 1890 he became Prime Minister of South Africa. At the same time, he was a member of the London Parliament and of various secret societies as well – the most important one being founded by himself. He was one of the richest and most influential individuals of his time.

The vision which he was uncompromisingly committed to, in spite of his ailing health, was a global monarchy under British rule. In 1891 Rhodes wrote in a letter to the occultist William T. Stead, in those days one of England's most famous journalists:

> It would have been better for Europe if he [Napoleon] had carried out his idea of a universal monarchy; he might have succeeded if he had hit on the idea of granting self-government to the component parts. Still, I will own, tradition, race and diverse languages acted against his dream; *all these do not exist as to the present English-speaking world,* and, apart from this union, there is *the sacred duty* of taking responsibility for the still uncivilized parts of the world.[79]

Rhodes, being aware that he would not live for long, rewrote and updated several wills, seven in all. In his third will (written in 1888), he requested that his legacy and wealth be used to establish a secret society committed to the hegemony of the British Empire. This society was to be structured according to the statutes of the Jesuit Order, with the term 'Roman Catholic religion' being replaced by 'British Empire'.[80] When Rhodes, despite his wills, did not die, he himself took charge of establishing this society. Thus, in 1891, the 'Secret Society of Cecil Rhodes' came into being. The Society at first consisted of only three members: Cecil Rhodes, William T. Stead and Lord Esher, an advisor and friend of Queen Victoria.

'Soon famous personages such as the Earl of Rosebery, Arthur James Balfour, Nathan Rothschild, Alfred Milner, and H.A.L. Fisher were also initiated into the secrets of this group, which at first was named "The Secret Society of Cecil Rhodes". The aim was not to establish yet another occult Brotherhood. Most of the members, if not all, were already Freemasons anyhow. [...] The actual goal was to establish the "Holy Empire" – an undertaking that demanded furtive support because such "holy aims" had to be pursued without attracting public attention.'[81]

In 1897 Alfred Milner became the new British governor of South Africa, succeeding Rhodes. In this position, he advanced imperialistic racism and furthered the Boer War:

> The British believed that the war against the Boers would be a 'picnic with pig-shooting sport' (*International Herald Tribune,* Philadelphia Public Letter, 24 June, 1902). But contrary to their expectations, the war was drawn out for almost two years and eight months. The Boers were obviously not that easy to beat. As the technology did not yet allow 'carpet bombing', Milner's troops simply jailed 117,000 civilians in concentration camps, which had been erected by Marshal Lord Kitchener in 1901 in order to break the resisting front of the Boers. Winston Churchill, who was to become the great European hero, said back then [as a member of the House of Commons]: 'There is only one way of breaking the Boer resistance – most severe oppression. In other words: We must kill the parents to make the children respect us' (quote documented by Bronder, p. 165).
>
> 5,000 of those men who still resisted fell on the battlefield. About 30,000 civilians died in the 40 concentration camps of Lord Kitchener. A strange coincidence by the way: Lord Kitchener belonged to the circle of friends who sympathized with the 'Ordo Novi Templi' founded by the Viennese occultist Lanz von Liebenfels – where Theosophy, Ariosophy and the Thule Order converged. And Karl Haushofer, who belonged to the mentors of the Third Reich, wrote a Kitchener biography.[82]

After Cecil Rhodes' death in 1902, the Governor of South Africa, Lord Milner, founded another secret society called 'The Round Table'. Within only a few years it spawned scions in all colonies of the British Empire. During the First World War, Lord Milner became England's Minister of Defence. In 1919, after the successful war, 'The Round Table' expanded its Anglo-American reach and led to the foundation of the *Council on Foreign Relations* (CFR) in the USA. Co-founder was President Wilson's ominous counsellor, Colonel Edward M. House.

For decades, this Council remained unknown to the general public despite the prominence of its members – senators, presidents and other men holding key positions in politics, high finance, the military and the media. It was only in the sixties that a larger audience got to hear about the existence of the CFR and the important role it played in the Anglo-American power game. This information came out mainly due to the disclosures first made by Prof. Carroll Quigley (see bibliography).

Leading CFR members, who also belonged to top lodges, formed elitist groupings like the so-called *Bilderberg Group* (1954) and the *Trilateral Commission*. Up to the present day, they function as secret planning units that only serve the interests of those who monitor them.[83] However, these commissions are not yet the top of the pyramid:

> [...] the handful of powerful unelected men who secretly rule America. Through interlocking directorates, they control the debt and destiny of America – they elect and tell presidents what to do. They are above the Council on Foreign Relations, Trilateral Commission, and Federal Reserve System![84]

There are countless examples illustrating how the above-mentioned members of secret power circles have manipulated recent world history. Alfred Milner's name also appears in the context of the Russian Revolution. In the book entitled *Czarism and Revolution,* written by Arsene de Goulevitch, a former general of the 'White' Russian army, several famous politicians and bankers are named as secret financiers of the Revolution and the new communist regime. Goulevitch testifies: 'In private interviews I have been told that over 21 million roubles were spent by Lord [Alfred] Milner in the financing of the Russian Revolution. [...] The financier just mentioned was by no means alone among the British to support the Russian Revolution with large financial donations.'[85]

Approaching the matter from different angles, many critical researchers come to the same conclusions. An American author writes:

> According to Goulevitch, English secret agents were numerous in Russia before and during the Revolution. In fact, some financial support for the Leninist cause was rumored to have come from English banking sources. One of

those rumored sources was Alfred Milner. As we recall, Milner was one of the organizers of the Round Table. He was also a major political figure in South Africa during the Boer War. It was during the Boer War that the English created the modern concentration camp. If Goulevitch's allegation contains any truth, then we might better understand where the Bolsheviks got the idea to establish a massive concentration camp system as part of the new communist economic system: namely, from the English.[86]

Alfred Milner's name also appears in the book *Experiment on Autobiography* by the famous British author Herbert George Wells (1866–1946), written in 1934. H. G. Wells, mostly known for his early works *The Time Machine* (1895) and *The War of the Worlds* (1898), was later introduced into high levels of the Anglo-American oligarchy. This may explain why in his later years he propagated their globalist ideas. In his autobiography he reveals how he was deeply influenced by his pragmatic mentor, Bertrand Russell, and Alfred Milner, whom he personally got to know in elitist circles of the Anglo-American high society, like the Fabian Society and the Coefficient Club. Reflecting their ideas, H. G. Wells published books like *The Open Conspiracy: Blue Prints for a World Revolution* (1928) and *The New World Order* (1940), frankly describing the plans of the ulterior forces from the approving perspective of a supporter (see quote on p. 221).

These are just a few examples dating from the late nineteenth and the early twentieth century. Looking back with the knowledge of today, we can easily detect the outline of the master plan, which back then was inconceivable for most people. What was put into action in those days is now said to be in its final stage.

'Order out of chaos'

Apparently, there are forces that wish to sow discord, plunging people and entire nations into misery and dependency. Those staging these actions are extremely intelligent, and their decisions are far-sighted. They are not merely observing a five-year plan but plans spanning many generations. They are versed in the knowledge of reincarnation and know about the reality of astral energies (and their magical invocation). Therefore, their plans appear illogical and incredible to those of 'normal' education.

The purpose of provoking global chaos can be summarized with the Latin formula *ordo ab chao* ('to establish order out of chaos'), the maxim of the 'illuminati'. The envisioned *ordo* that is to emerge out of the conjured chaos is the 'New World Order' (*novus ordo seclorum*).

The catch-phrase 'New World Order' became openly known to the world from 1935 onwards when the USA or, more precisely, the US Central Bank issued their new one-dollar bill. This occurred in the time between the two world wars and was initiated by the Central Bank, which had passed into private hands, the hands of the bankers, while retaining its federal façade as a so-called state bank. The crucial point of this coup was a historic event which is recorded in all history books, but mostly without reference to its real implications. It was the 'Federal Reserve Act', which became effective on 24 December 1913.

The Federal Reserve Act prepared the ground for the establishment of the *Federal Reserve Bank*, the so-called central bank that now was authorized by law to print bank notes without an equivalent gold value, and to lend this money to the American government with interest. In simplified terms, this law was an official permission to print counterfeit money; however, not everybody was allowed to do this, not even the government. The right was exclusively reserved for the *Reserve Bank*, the private 'national' bank. Due to this Act, the USA became almost totally dependent on the supranational high-finance network.

This 'Federal Reserve conspiracy'[87] was not without opposition. One of the main critics was Congressman Charles Lindbergh senior, the father of the famous aviator, who publicly declared:

> 'This Act establishes the most gigantic trust on Earth. [...] When the President [W. Wilson] signs this Act, the invisible government by the money power, proven to exist by the Money Trust Investigation, will be legalised. The new law will create inflation whenever the trust wants inflation.
>
> 'The Federal Reserve was, and still is, hailed as a victory for democracy over the Money Trust. Nothing could be further from the truth. The whole Central Bank concept was engineered by the very group it was supposed to strip of power.'[88]

'When the President signs this Act ...' He did, of course, guided by respective counselling. A few months later, the world had to accept the start of the First World War.

In 1933, H. G. Wells published his insider knowledge in the book *The*

Shape of Things to Come: The Ultimate Revolution. Therein, he enthusiastically elaborates the plans of constructing a new society on the ruins of all subdued nations. He also predicts a second world war and subsequent wars in which, for example, US airplanes will use 'peace gas' to annihilate opposing 'evil warlords'! The goal is to establish a 'New World Order', the title of the book which he published in 1940.

At the end of *The Shape of Things to Come*, he summarizes what he had learned from his mentors and friends:

> […] it is a theory of world revolution. Plainly the thesis is that history must now continue to be a string of accidents with an increasingly disastrous trend until a comprehensive faith in the modernized World State, socialistic, cosmopolitan and creative, takes hold of the human imagination. When the existing governments and ruling theories of life, the decaying religious and the decaying political forms of today, have sufficiently lost prestige through failure and catastrophe, then and then only will world-wide reconstruction be possible. And it must be the work, first of all, of an aggressive order of religiously devoted men and women who will try out and establish and impose a new pattern of living upon our race. (H.G. Wells, 1933)

'Order out of chaos' – chaos was produced without a doubt, and some forces (always the same!) profited from this chaos, and do so up to the present day.

The pyramid on the one-dollar bill

After the First World War, the ulterior forces decided to globally present the structure of their clandestine hierarchy. They chose a worthy and permanent prospectus that nobody could afford to throw away: the then new one-dollar bill that came into circulation in 1935. For this

important document the men behind the Federal Reserve Bank chose a design which included a pyramid with a magical eye hovering above it. An Egyptian-like pyramid is not the most typical symbol of America. It's like having an igloo on an African bank note.

Since the pre-war era (1935), the design of this bank note has never been changed! In 1957, the wording 'In God We Trust' was added. Since 1963, the back-side of the bill only states ONE DOLLAR, 'in silver payable to the bearer on demand' was removed.

An important clue is found at the base of the pyramid – the number of the year MDCCLXXVI, 1776. This officially refers to the 'Declaration of Independence' on 4 July 1776. Sceptics, however, argue that this was merely a *declaration* of independence on the part of the thirteen colonies which thus seceded from the British government, triggering the outbreak of the War of Independence. The real beginning of the USA was not in 1776 but in 1789, the year the Constitution came into effect, with George Washington becoming the first president of the USA (from 1789 to 1797). 1789, the year 13 after 1776, was also the year of the French Revolution. And, by a strange coincidence, 1776 was also the year in which Adam Weishaupt founded the Illuminati Order.

The number 1776 has a deep numerological significance: it is 4×444, or 2×888. The pyramid is encircled by two Latin mottos: *Novus Ordo Seclorum*, 'new order of the ages' or, in its modern rendering, 'New World Order', and *Annuit Coeptis*, 'It [the hovering eye] has favoured our undertakings'. The verb form *annuit* (third person singular) is both present tense and perfect tense; the subject of the verb has to be supplied. In another interpretation, *novus ordo seclorum* and *annuit coeptis* are taken to be one motto, meaning 'The New World Order is favourable to our undertakings'. When in 1957, 'In God We Trust' was added, the rendering 'He [God] has favoured our undertakings' became the common translation.

The pyramid, the mysterious eye and the two mottos together form what is called 'The Great Seal'.

The pyramid has 13 steps, the eagle is holding 13 arrows and a branch with 13 leaves and 13 fruits. Above the eagle there is a geometrical arrangement of 13 stars forming a six-pointed star.

The one-dollar bill is full of occult Lodge symbols. Why Latin, why a pyramid, why a magical eye, why a Great Seal, why the prominent use of the number 13? Was it only to represent the original thirteen states?

Let us keep in mind that this dollar bill was not conceived in 1776 but after 1930! At this time the USA wanted to be a powerful political unit – so why rehash the fact of once having been only 13 states and monumentalize a date that marked the beginning of a war?

The quadrilateral pyramid with thirteen steps is said to represent the secret power hierarchy. The higher the level, the smaller and more exclusive the elite. Dominating them all, poised above the top step, is a triangle with an 'all-seeing eye'. Considering the actions that have been financed with this money since 1935, one may guess whose supramundane eye it is.

Why not just one crushing blow?

The examples presented so far demonstrate that there are secret forces instigating wars, revolutions and other forms of chaos in order to serve their own purposes. One question which may arise at this point is: Why do these almost all-powerful forces have to take so many intermediate steps? Why don't they just subdue the whole world with one crushing blow and then enforce their totalitarian world order to secure 'peace' once and for all?

The answer is simple: because they are not *all*-powerful. Many power groups dream of a crushing blow, but such a feat is not that easily done. The group itself must be ready for it, the time must be ripe, mankind must have been shaped accordingly, and the required infrastructure has to be in place, particularly a world-wide high-tech network for global communication and transaction. Only then will it be feasible to reach out for total control. (Presently, the said requirements are being perfected at a stunning speed.)

Furthermore, those on the upper levels of the pyramid do not desire a world full of people hating and resisting them. Such an open tyranny would not be lasting, and soon tensions would come about within their own ranks; then, along with the powder keg of a rebellious world population, their plans for extended world power would soon be destroyed from within and without.

Another, less obvious reason is found in the spiritual dimension of existence itself, namely the law of free will. The occult initiates of the top levels know well that they are not alone in this world. There are other hierarchies beyond their influence – the Light beings –, and the dark forces fear their power. Therefore, by spreading fear and by dragging people's attention away from all spiritual perspectives of life, they want to hinder the Light beings from finding any resonance on earth.

Both sides – the God-devoted and the God-averse – bring their influence to bear on earth, and the collective consciousness of mankind decides which influence will prevail. *Asuras,* too, are subjected to the law of free will. For this reason they are intent on programming men's consciousness according to *their* aims in order to prevent people and their governments from pursuing other aims and interests.

To have people get hooked, one needs bait. But the bait alone is not enough. People's attention and interest must be drawn to it (by propaganda, manipulation or force). In the 'ideal' case, those who fall for it even think they want it, or need it.

In summary, the ulterior forces want to induce people to voluntarily do what they want them to do. If necessary, they are also prepared to give a veiled, but vehement push.

'Divide and rule!'

A regime only lasts as long as those controlled acquiesce to the controllers without resistance. The easiest way to set up such a situation is indicated by the old maxim 'divide and rule' (Latin: *divide et impera*), which advises the 'imperators' to divide those they wish to control into two factions, and to make them become enemies. Then, to oppose the external enemy, citizens will willy-nilly gather behind their own politicians, and hardly anybody will suspect that both factions are being controlled by the same backstage powers.

The application of this dia-bolic principle has determined world history to a large extent. A typical example was seen in the twentieth century: the creation of a first and a second world through two world wars. When the world was divided after WW II, the capitalist West headed by the US, and the communist East headed by the SU took the roles of enemies for 44 years. The fact that the communist Revolution in Russia had been financed by certain capitalists of the West indicates that supranational powers wanted to create a second faction. With this new enemy, it was possible to justify any military action, even a second world war and two atom bombs, to increase the 'defence' budget, and to expand the secret services for 'national security'.

After 1945, although the world war was finished, war continued in the Soviet Union. Millions of citizens were killed in massacres and concentration camps. How was it possible for such a blood-soaked state to suddenly be a superpower causing the USA to tremble in fear? Well, the USA – or the 'pyramid', respectively – was not trembling in fear. The population, of course, was, being continually bombarded with the information that behind the 'Iron Curtain' there was the evil communist enemy just waiting for the right moment to strike.[89]

Behind the real curtain, the backstage powers were sitting at their 'round table' helping the SU to procure the new technology. Why? One possible answer is: because they wanted to establish a world-spanning technological infrastructure, the one required for the 'new world order'. After a certain period, the Iron Curtain was pulled open again. The stage was cleared for the next act in the game of 'divide and rule'.

After 1991 the leaders of the US and the (former) SU became official friends again. No one mentioned the massacres and the concentration camps of the Soviet Union, what to speak of compensating the countless victims and their families. Now (in 2003) the two worlds are defined as 'the axis of the good' as opposed to 'the axis of evil'. Either you are with us, or you are against us …

Simultaneously, many confessional camps are intensifying their dogmatic tradition of dividing the world into 'we' and 'the others' (the 'believers' and the 'non-believers', the 'saved' and the 'condemned'). There seems to be no room for reconciliation and mutual acceptance. Will the course into chaos cause an 'Armageddon'? Is a totalitarian 'new world order' the only solution as its propagators believe?

Historical excursus:
Ulterior influence in Russia

The above interpretation of historical facts is admittedly unusual, and many people strongly disbelieve that a secret power would (or could) conspire in such a manner without anybody noticing and publicizing it. The fact is: It has been made public all along. But who takes it seriously? Some are even willing to blame the 'prophets'.

However, a closer look at the network of world politics, secret societies and financial magnates quickly reveals hidden facts and factors, as demonstrated in the following additional analysis.

It has been indicated that the Russian Revolution and the Soviet Union were financed by western interest groups which wanted to divide the world in order to have a 'credible enemy'. In the West, the phantom called 'communist Russia' was used to justify the installation of an all-pervading technical infrastructure serving ulterior purposes, and for the powers of the Eastern Bloc, the phantom of the 'capitalist USA' was similarly useful. Then, at one point, the credible enemies became friends again. Had both sides been monitored by the same brains envisioning a new world order under the centralized directorate of the money lords?

To substantiate the plausibility of such supranational agendas, let us examine once again the phase of world history in which communism became the second world power for half a century. These interactions did not happen by chance but by the plans and doings of 'real people'.

One person that held a key position in the US/SU interaction was the American Ambassador in Russia during the decisive years 1943 to 1946: Averell Harriman (1891–1986). One could name many other famous and less famous (but not less influential) individuals who served the same 'process'. Harriman's biography is one of many typical examples that illustrate how individuals, secret societies and world politics are closely interwoven.

Harriman's father, Edward Harriman (1848–1909), was an American railway magnate who was instrumental in the establishment of the Atlantic-Pacific-Line running across the North American continent.* Harriman also controlled the maritime traffic between America and Japan. After the end of the Russo-Japanese war in mid-1905, Harriman wanted to carry out the next step in his project of a world-spanning railway and shipping-line system. However, 'his dubious business policies led to a congressional investigation in 1906. The main enterprise of the Harriman family was the banking house Brown Brothers, Harriman & Company.'[90]

---

* In those days the railway industry closely co-operated with the producers of steel and arms. The expropriation of the native Americans (which was 'most easily' achieved by killing them) formed an integral part of the smoking advancement of the railway network.

Averell, Edward Harriman's eldest son, was eighteen when his father died. He was predestined to continue his father's legacy, in particular his plans concerning Russia. As befitting a descendant of high society, Averell studied at Yale University. Elitist universities like Harvard and Yale are strongholds of fraternities representing outposts of secret societies. They serve to select and recruit young blood. As most of the future politicians, attorneys, journalists and economists pass through the sluices of these universities, it becomes clear why so many leading people of our present-day society are – directly or indirectly – affiliated to backstage circles.

One of the largest student fraternities is known as 'Skull & Bones' (S&B). Its not very appealing name refers to an initiation ritual of Freemasonry. *Nomen est omen?* Joining such a society is quite attractive because it enables one to make contact with prominent men whom one normally would never meet in person. And there, in these societies and brotherhoods, the big shots are one's 'brothers'. What student with ambitions in this world can afford to disregard such an opportunity?

Averell Harriman became a loyal and respected member of S&B and soon belonged to the influential ulterior levels. In 1920, together with his younger brother Roland, he founded an investment company that profited from the interim war period by large investments in Europe, especially Germany. In 1926 another Yale graduate and S&B member joined the Harriman company: Prescott Bush, the father of George Bush sen.

In 1931, New York's Wall Street saw a big bank fusion: 'Harriman Brothers & Company' and the British-American 'Brown Brothers & Company' merged and became the 'Brown Brothers, Harriman & Company'. Eight of the twelve board directors were S&B members.

Due to intercontinental investments, this joint bank became the largest private bank of North America before and during the Second World War. Investigative authors provide evidence that this bank and its branches in Europe funnelled huge sums of money to Germany to support its rearmament.[91]

After the end of WWI Averell Harriman paid a visit to Berlin, the capital of war-torn Germany. There, he opened a subsidiary in 1922: *W.A. Harriman & Co.*, and he also met Fritz Thyssen. In 1924 the *Union Banking Corporation* was founded as a link between the Harriman Bank and Thyssen's *Bank voor Handel en Scheepvaart* (BHS) in

Holland. Huge sums of money were brought into Germany via this connection.

In 1926, Prescott Bush was appointed vice president of the bank W.A. Harriman & Co. In the same year, Thyssen's *German Steel Trust* was established with a 'little help from some friends'. It is obvious that steel factories are indispensable for military rearmament.

In 1927, Harriman met Mussolini in Italy. This visit also resulted in a co-operation.

In 1929, 1931 and 1933 there were three meetings between the bank magnate James P. Warburg (representing Anglo-American high finance and the oil industry) and Adolf Hitler. During each visit Hitler received sums of money running into many millions.[92] Hitler's Book *Mein Kampf* had already been published. So, his foreign supporters knew very well which plans they were sponsoring.

In 1933 Hitler became chancellor and, soon after, dictator of Germany. Meanwhile, US funds were being pumped into the Reich. The amount was so enormous that (in 1942) US authorities were forced to start an investigation of the *Union Banking Corporation*. Based on the 'Trading with the Enemy Act', securities were confiscated which belonged to Prescott Bush, Roland Harriman and five other business partners, three of them from Germany. Being a delicate top-level issue, the whole affair was handled very discreetly, and the officials quickly dismissed it, probably due to some order from above.

Meanwhile, top banker Averell Harriman, now in the role of a diplomat, frequented England, Europe and Russia. From 1941 to 1943 he was President Roosevelt's special representative in England and Russia in order to co-ordinate the 'Lend-Lease Program'. From 1943 to 1946 he was US Ambassador in Moscow, and from 1946 to 1948 he took the position of USA's Minister of Commerce! Throughout his lifetime he maintained personal contact to the communist leaders, and was again and again sent to the Soviet Union by Truman, Kennedy, Johnson, Nixon and Carter. (The last time he visited Moscow was to meet with Andropov, in 1983, at the age of 92.)

In 1971, Averell Harriman married the 51-year-old Pamela Churchill, the widow of Churchill's son Randolph. Pamela Harriman-Churchill was one of Bill Clinton's most important supporters.

In 1993, Pamela Harriman was appointed American Ambassador to France by Bill Clinton.

Happy summit meeting of Lodge brothers: Winston Churchill, Averell Harriman and Josef Stalin at the Moscow Kremlin, August 1942

Obviously, world politics has many levels, and highlighting just one person is not sufficient to give a full picture. Still, the presented example illustrates that the principle of 'divide and rule' has been factually applied, even on a global scale (through the creation of the two blocs labelled US and SU). The alleged cold war existed only on the level of superficial politics as confirmed by many non-official history books, for example: *National Suicide – Military Aid to the Soviet Union,* written by the already mentioned Prof. Anthony Sutton, published in 1974, during the height of the 'cold war'. This book reports how American companies either directly or indirectly (through international business partners) built arms factories in the Soviet Union as well as chemical works and fertilizer factories that were used for producing explosives. America and Russia were thus threatening each other with weapons produced by the same companies:

'The historical evidence is strong and clear. The United States have built installations for the Soviets [...] This construction work took forty years and was undertaken with full knowledge.' This is the conclusion drawn by Prof. Sutton at the end of his book.

Summary and outlook

Ancient prophecy foresaw the coming of an age in which the dark forces would prevail. As shown in the previous chapters, these forces believe themselves to be enlightened, and entitled to do whatever they consider necessary according to their self-defined 'enlightenment'.

All cultures know mythic descriptions of the 'dark age'. A very profound description of its characteristics is given in the Vedic scriptures, based on the concept of the four ages (*yugas*). Therefore, this chapter started with the information found in these sources, especially the *Mahabharata* and the *Puranas*. They say that the present age is a Kali-yuga, an age of division and discord, being a time in which the decline of the four basic principles of true self-realization (*dharma*) will be advanced more and more.

Dharma is said to have four legs symbolizing self-control, purity, mercy (forgiveness) and truthfulness. They are weakened due to egoism and false pride (= a lack of love and God consciousness), which express themselves in the abuse of wealth, in sexual exploitation, in intoxication and animal slaughter.

In the course of the previous three ages, one leg after the other had been broken. According to the *Shrimad-Bhagavatam*, the only principle still intact at the beginning of Kali-yuga was truthfulness. Even the dark forces considered it to be beneath their dignity to lie, and the many clairvoyant people still present then, five thousand years ago, would have sensed it anyway. Lying became practicable and 'normal' only within the age of materialism when people in general lost their higher capacities. (Is this the reason why a lifestyle is being propagated that undermines these higher capacities, by stress, fun, consumption, intoxication, meat-eating etc.?)

The compromising of truthfulness was effected by those people who started to hoard gold. By furthering untruth, Kali, the father of all lie, managed to increase the other vices that were already existent. Those accepting these seductions became more and more blinded and materialistic, which made them prone to fall victim to further propaganda. In this way, they became cheated and exploited themselves.

This is the prophecy of the ancient Indian scripture known as *Shrimad-Bhagavatam*. Today we can see that this prophecy has proven true. One only needs to follow the trail of hoarded gold ('money') to expose the agents of Kali-yuga, the hidden lords that decide over the lives and deaths of millions of people.

Money has become the blood of modern-day society. Without it, the global players' performance would not work. Money in itself is not bad. Only the *abuse* of it makes it into a destructive tool. Abuse is defined as anything that furthers the destruction of the pillars of *dharma*.

As shown by world history, the decrease of mankind's spirituality and the increase of Kali's influence have been the very essence of the last five thousand years.

In this chapter only a few examples from the nineteenth and twentieth centuries have been mentioned: colonial exploitation and the subsequent creation of the Third World, the staging of the Russian Revolution and the two world wars, the cold war, and the short biography of one of the men who held a key position in it.

These examples were meant to demonstrate that covert forces factually exist. Obviously, the philosophical portrayal of anti-godly and godless ideologies presented in the initial chapters of this book is very relevant, especially regarding the current world situation.

Now, in Kali-yuga, truthfulness is a long-gone factor in power politics. Could a person who speaks the truth about the longstanding moneypulation receive a leading position and survive? 'Truth' becomes established through propaganda (mass media) directed by those having the required amount of money – just as the seers foretold thousands of years ago.

Of course, they did not only foresee a time of rampant materialism, they also foresaw mankind's ascension and the coming of a new Earth, initiated by the blossoming of a revived God consciousness.

At the same time, we are warned not to underestimate the power of propaganda which might increase to unexpected dimensions. The forces of materialism and extremism will not voluntarily abandon their illusion of worldly power. It will be a challenge for every individual to remain strong in God consciousness, regardless of what may happen globally.

Will we allow others to manipulate and intimidate us? Whom do we want to believe? What are our real priorities in life?

Divine prophecy is meant to be a help in finding our way through this tunnel of darkness. It describes the lurking dangers (without playing them down), and it reveals the way out as well. Thus we are encouraged to choose our own destiny in order to shape it according to God's will.

The next chapters will present the most challenging scenario we know of. It can be a mirror of our own fears or a window into the Light, a revelation which inspires and enhances our joy in view of the new Earth.

CHAPTER SEVEN

The End-Time Code 666

The earth, seen in its multidimensional context, is linked with astral dimensions and parallel worlds. From there, many beings incarnate amongst humanity. Some originate from the lower astral levels, bringing their ego-based mentality with them, others originate from the worlds of light and harmony. Even in common language, one speaks of 'incarnate devils' and 'incarnate angels'.

Kali-yuga is a time in which both sides are numerously represented. The dark-minded beings, profiting from the Kali-yuga's reduced frequency and increased density, have taken over many earthly positions of power and are intent on swallowing everything. However, due to the law of balance, also many beings of love and harmony are incarnate, doing their divine service without any ego-motivated ambitions. Many of them may be lacking power and wealth, but a higher vision reveals their true strength of inner peace and contentment. They are the rays of light that expose the existence of darkness through their very presence and difference. The dark forces, therefore, are hostile towards these true illuminators who bring original sanity, uncorrupted truth and natural healing into the world, which they (the dark forces) consider their own.

As unscientific as this multidimensional scenario may appear to modern men, it corresponds to the original knowledge of mankind found in all cultural and mystic traditions. It is not even secret knowledge because it is contained in all holy scriptures of the world, be it the Bible, the Torah, the Koran, the Vedas etc. They all agree to the fact that there are invisible worlds beyond the physical plane, as well as invisible beings ('angels' and 'demons') interacting with mankind through inspiration, manipulation or even incarnation.

In this chapter, we will focus on a prophetic description which is world-famous – thus easily available – and highly relevant to our times. It is the last book of the New Testament entitled *Apocalypse*, or *The Revelation of St John*. Despite being very short, only about twenty pages, it contains extraordinary details about a dramatic future occurrence: the coming of ultimate darkness followed by global decisions leading to a 'new heaven' and a 'new earth'.

Along with the Gospels and the Epistles, the Revelation describes how the forces of the 'great red dragon', after a lost 'battle in heaven', will appear on earth to build up a world-wide totalitarian structure. These banished or fallen angels will display a show of global peace, promoted by 'magic' and 'miracles', while simultaneously persecuting the 'people of God' and establishing a dictatorship which most people will not recognize as such. The exact quotes will be given in this chapter.

By now, however, many people have become fed up with the talk about the Apocalypse* because biblical dogmatists of all kinds have used it as a front for their sectarian and absolutist claims. They believe in a 'last battle' in which their 'church' will be the only one triumphant while all other confessions and creeds will be annihilated with the help of 'God' and the 'returning Christ'. They disapprove of any dialogue amongst religions. They even consider such dialogues to be a tactic of the devil who wants to establish his own, anti-Christian one-world 'religion'. (Such plans do exist, but one has to distinguish between the dead-end version of a so-called one-world religion and the true spiritual unity of God-conscious individuals.)

As shown in the previous chapter, sectarianism is a very efficient trick used by the dia-bolic forces in order to divide and rule. Distorted religion infects the core of people's hearts and makes them divided by dogmatism and self-deluding elitism.

While this one extreme (the too-much) isolates people into heaven-and-hell factions, it additionally drives many others into atheism and agnosticism. Such people, being disgusted and/or disillusioned with 'religion', resort to the opposite extreme – the too-little – and become averse to any religious perspective and, even more so, to all apocalyptic warnings.

---

* Apocalypse is usually understood to mean 'doomsday' and 'the end of the world'; its literal meaning, however, is different. The word is derived from the Greek verb *apo-kalyptein*, 'to reveal, to unveil' and simply means 'revelation', referring to a mystic vision of prophetic dimension.

Fanaticism may generate a certain amount of strength to keep one's faith against all odds and doubts, but it is not a level of mature God consciousness. If all religious people were united, recognizing the unity within the diversity and respecting the diversity within the unity, then the atmosphere of world-wide tension and enmity would vanish like darkness at sunrise.

Truly divine revelations (and interpretations) have two functions: to indicate the shadows and to show the light. In other words, they warn against the pitfalls of both extremes, and they provide a higher vision to help people make up their minds. Such times of decision usually coincide with the earth's transition into a new cycle, and that is again the case in our time.

Prophetic voices of all cultures speak about the same vision – the 'new Earth' to come, the 'New Jerusalem' of the Bible, the new 'age of truthfulness' (Satya-yuga) of the Vedas, the 'Fifth World' of the Native Americans.

All cultures and religions have become influenced by the dark age and need a fundamental purification, an 'apocalyptic' transformation. Therefore, this chapter is an attempt to grasp the essence of the Bible prophecy without Bible absolutism.

What was the purpose of the last sixty years?

The era after the Second World War was marked by local wars and civil wars on all continents along with a 'cold war' between the First and Second World – the US and SU. Academic historians, however, categorically exclude any 'conspiracy' or hidden agenda behind the stage of world politics.

Nevertheless, the question arises: If there are people with plans to achieve world control, what was the purpose of the last sixty years? An answer has already been indicated on p. 92 and p. 223 and can now be expanded to a specific scenario.

While military, political, and economic moves did not result in any decisive change, one crucial change did occur: the explosive technological boom. Many things unknown fifty years ago have by now become common consumer products, especially computers, digital money, chip technology and portable phones. They are part of a world-wide infrastructure based on satellites, wireless communication and centralized data stations.

> Even the Catholic Church of the Middle Ages was tolerant by modern standards. Part of the reason for this was that in the past no government had the power to keep its citizens under constant surveillance.

This statement was written by George Orwell in 1948 in his novel *1984*. He imagined that the constant surveillance of the citizens would be achieved by a dense network of telescreens – both monitors and cameras in one. Orwell obviously failed to foresee the quantum leaps of technology in the second half of the twentieth century. Otherwise he would not have envisioned surveillance to function with such a primitive monitoring system. In this regard reality has long surpassed George Orwell's vision!

'Cameras and satellites, directional aerials and probes [...] The state of surveillance as predicted by George Orwell for 1984 has meanwhile become something quite common. A realistic depiction of how transparent man in our digital age has become is presented in the film *Enemy of the State*.'

Thus reads a review of this film[93] that came into the cinemas at the beginning of 1999. Many were shocked at seeing the ice-cold implementation of technology shown in this thriller. However, surveillance specialist Larry Cox, an adviser to the producers of this film, commented: 'The state of technology shown in the film is one of ten years ago. Today we are much more advanced. The new devices and methods are top secret.'[94]

The technology that makes world-wide control possible is available now, and only now, after decades of progress. The entire infrastructure is in place. The question is only *whether it will be used for this purpose or not*. Where is this progress leading to? We are being told: peace and security.

Why world power?

Real peace depends on the contentment of the individuals, and contentment can never be enforced. Therefore, peace is possible only through the divine harmony of free will, and collective contentment only through *unity in diversity*, based on perceiving God, the absolute Individuality, as the all-embracing, all-unifying centre.

Godless forces, however, are incapable of believing in this higher unity inherent in diversity. They only know of an *imposed unity*. Their aim is a monopoly of exclusive control. Many superpowers of the past have already aspired after this aim – the Babylonians, the Greeks, the Romans, the Arabs, the Mongolians, the Vatican, Napoleon, Hitler, the British with their Empire – but they all have failed.

One day, however, as the prophecy of the Revelation goes, the draconic forces will succeed in gaining world power for a short period.

When will it come about?

Many Bible interpreters have already pondered on the exact date and time the Revelation refers to. There has been a lot of apocalyptic hysteria caused by false alarms and false prophets. Therefore Jesus warned: 'But that day and hour nobody knows, neither the angels of heaven, nor the Son, but only the Father.' (Matt. 24.36)

The exact date is not known. The general date, however, is ascertainable on the basis of its symptoms which Jesus mentioned when he was asked, 'When will this be, and what will be the signs of your coming and of the end of the age [...] when all these things are about to be accomplished?' (Matt. 24.3; Mark 13.4; Luke 17.22; 21.7)

In answering this frequent question asked by both the Apostles and the Pharisees, Jesus mentioned many signs:

- wars 'near and far', 'nation will fight against nation, state against state';
- increasing natural catastrophes such as earthquakes and floods;
- many new diseases and people dying of hunger on a global scale;
- signs in heaven and on earth;
- heresies in the name of God or Jesus; many false prophets promising peace and miracles while 'deceiving the whole world';
- slander and persecution of those believing in God; many will be diverted into fatalism, fanaticism or indifference ('And with the increase of iniquity, the love of many will grow cold.' Matt. 24.12)

In the days of Jesus, it was inconceivable that the nations *of the world* would wage war on each other, or that hunger could become a global problem. Today, however, this list of symptoms reads like the contents of a common newspaper. People know about the two world wars and the ongoing wars, about the exploitation of nature, about the suffering of the poor countries, and about the damage that drugs, smoking and meat-eating (mass breeding) cause both to the world and to one's own health. But who of the leaders and the citizens really cares?

Indifference, hypocrisy and cold-heartedness which lead to wars, violence and exploitation – these are the main characteristics of the 'end times' as prophesied by Jesus. Reading the list of these signs, we cannot deny that it fully fits our present time.

The relevance of the details mentioned in the Gospels becomes even hotter when seen in the context of the Revelation, in which Jesus showed St John many dramatic details of the future.

In other words, it is not impossible to recognize which phase of history these visions refer to. The scriptures contain specific clues. In addition, there is a key passage in the Revelation that allows an even more precise dating of the time frame down to the decade. This key is the figure 666. It is not in fifty or five hundred years to come, but it is *now* that the apocalyptic scenario becomes relevant. As the subsequent analysis will show, the code 666 allows us to date the scenario with a precision of a few years.

The two apocalyptic 'beasts'

The Revelation says about the timing of its scenario: It will come about when the number 666 starts to show up everywhere with such a prominence that nobody will be able to buy or sell anything without having to go through this number. – This is quite a precise statement.

The passage mentioning the number 666 appears in connection with the description of a war in heaven in which Archangel Michael is confronted with a 'great red (fiery-coloured) dragon':

> And war broke out in heaven; Michael and his angels fought against the dragon. The dragon and his angels fought back, but they were defeated, and there was no longer any place for them in heaven. The great dragon was thrown down, that ancient serpent, who is called the Devil or Satan, the deceiver of

the whole world [or: who has led all the world astray] – he was thrown down to the earth, and his angels were thrown down with him. [...] 'For you, earth and sea, disaster is coming, because the devil has come down to you with great wrath, knowing that his time is short.' (Rev. 12.7–9, 12)

'Thrown down to the earth' means that they fell down to the lower astral levels, the dark parallel worlds close to earth. From this invisible base, many fallen angels incarnated amongst mankind in the form of human beings while remaining connected to their occult background, thinking and acting accordingly. This is not only a modern esoteric interpretation but a world-view indicated by the Bible itself: 'Our struggle is not against enemies of flesh and blood, but against the rulers, against the authorities, against the cosmic powers of this present darkness, against the spiritual forces of evil in the heavenly places.' (Eph. 6.12)

The cosmic event of the hosts of Satan being banished from heaven leads to the appearance of two 'beasts' on earth, both of them invested with the power of the dragon. The Revelation emphasizes several times that both 'beasts' succeed in deceiving almost everyone, being empowered by the force that 'has led all the world astray'. In other words, it is not just a madness of a few Satanists but a global phenomenon welcomed or at least accepted (or ignored) by almost everyone.

The first beast appears as a leader or dictator, the second as a religious leader, a false Messiah or prophet. For this reason he is often called the 'Antichrist'. They work hand in hand to establish a global despotism culminating in a mock religion based on leadership cult, fear and false promises:

> The second beast exercised* all the power of the first beast, on its behalf making the world and all its people worship the first beast, whose deadly injury had healed. And it worked great miracles. [...] Through the miracles, which it was allowed to do on behalf of the first beast, it was able to lead astray (deceive) the people of the world and persuade them to put up a statue in honour of the beast [...]. He was allowed to breathe life into this statue, so that the statue of the beast was able to speak [...]. (Rev. 13.12–15)

Then follows the passage mentioning the number 666, which enables us to attach an approximate date to the events described:

---

* The writer of the Revelation uses the past tense because he describes the visions shown to him from the perspective of a witness who saw these scenes as something that had already happened.

> It compelled everyone – small and great alike, rich and poor, slave and citizen – to be marked on the right hand or on the forehead, so that no one could buy or sell anything unless he had the mark, that is, the name of the beast or the number of its name. Here wisdom is needed: anyone with understanding may interpret the number of the beast for it is the number of a human being, and his number is six hundred and sixty-six. (Rev. 13.16–18)

The dragon and its hosts of angels are flung down to the earth, and the land and sea of the earth are cautioned to be wary, for the dragon 'has come down with great wrath, knowing that his time is short'. The dragon does not appear in person, but dispatches two representatives, the two 'beasts', one appearing out of the sea, the other out of the land. The first beast receives its power directly from the dragon, and the second beast introduces a world-wide worship of the first beast.* They unite worldly and religious power, which enables them to obtain control over all people: the poor and the rich, the workers and the bosses. Finally, their global power will be sealed with the number 666 marked either on the right hand or on the forehead of each subordinate. Only those who bear this mark will be able to buy and sell.

The triple six as a magical code

Regarding the world-wide presence of the number 666, we have to clarify the basis of the following analysis as there are strong voices questioning its validity, based on philological criteria. These critical objections are not unjustified because in the original languages, the number six hundred and sixty-six is *not* written as 666. Only the Arabic system of numbers uses a triple six. In Greek it is written with the letters Chi (600), Xi (60) and Stigma (6), in Hebrew with the letters Taw (400), Resh (200), Samech (60) and Waw (6). In Roman numerals it is written as DCLXVI.[95] Therefore, from the philological and numerological point of view, it is erroneous to identify this apocalyptic number with

---

* 'Worship' not only refers to religious ceremonies but to any concentrated and combined effort to serve the interests of the 'beast' with ritual-like repetitions of procedures, body postures and hand movements. For example, to a first-century man like St John, the many millions of people sitting in offices at computers, manning the keyboards and staring at the screens, must have appeared like a congregation of devoted worshippers all executing the same ritual behind a 'speaking statue'.

a triple six. Six hundred and sixty-six is the cabbalistic sum total of the name of a man, the so-called Antichrist.

The analysis given in this chapter, however, does not refer to philology and numerology, but to *symbolism* and *magic*. Therefore, the above-mentioned criticism does not nullify this modern interpretation. Both have their validity in their respective fields of application.

Despite the fact that the original languages did not use a triple six to write the number six hundred and sixty-six, it is undeniable that all modern languages do use a numbering system that writes this ominous number as 666. The same numbering system is also used in the Slavic, Turkic and Caucasian languages, although most of them have Cyrillic or other alphabets. Since the Middle Ages, the 'Arabic' decimal system of numbers has increasingly come into use, with the result that everybody in modern society can read Arabic numbers whereas relatively few can read Greek or Hebrew numbers.

Today, the triple six has become the global symbol for the apocalyptic number. We have to expect, therefore, that certain interest groups will use it to promote their aims, both openly and covertly, for the prediction says that this number will be the key to achieving total power on earth. Those desiring such power will not hesitate to use this magical symbol, ignoring the further contents of the prophecy, namely that the power granted by the force behind this number will only last for a short time; then, it will be destroyed along with those it enchanted and seduced.

Regarding the criticism in question, we can even argue that the philological approach could be turned around! St John was informed that the number of the beast's name would be six hundred and sixty-six, and he got to see that the number six hundred and sixty-six would be written as a triple six (contrary to his own language). He also got to see that this number and its magical code 6-6-6 would be used on a global scale, even independently of its numerical value 666. So we have to assume that he saw the triple six and not the number Chi-Xi-Stigma or Taw-Resh-Samech-Waw. And he was informed that this triple six stood for 'six hundred and sixty-six'. So he just translated it into his own language, using the Greek or Hebrew numbering system of his time.

So, it is certainly legitimate to make an analysis of our present situation by looking for traces of the triple six – the same traces that St John got to see.

6-6-6 is present world-wide

Buying and selling, power over the poor and the rich – it is obvious that the issue is money. And it is *now* that buying and selling is becoming monopolized, centralized and globalized. In all of these developments the code 6-6-6 plays an important role!

In Rev. 13.17 it is said that a time will come when nobody will be able to buy or sell anything without using a specific marking. Even twenty years ago, such an idea was still inconceivable: *every article we buy or want to sell having to be marked with the same 'symbol'?* By now, only a few years later, this compulsory mark has become a common thing. We know it as the bar code, officially called EAN (European Article Number) or UPC (Universal Product Code).

The very fact that there is an ancient prophecy foretelling this global marking of all consumer goods is amazing. But that is not all. Interestingly enough, there is also a triple 6 indicated in this binary bar code! This technical detail is elaborated on the next double page.

In addition to the bar code, world-wide money transactions have increasingly become dependent on the global computer net. There, too, we find a 6-6-6 coding.

In order to see this code, we have to be aware that some languages use letters for numbers. Everybody is familiar with the Roman numerals that consist of the letters I V X L C D M. In Hebrew, St John's mother tongue, there is a full set of symbols that corresponds to both letters and numbers. This means that *every* letter also has a numerical value. The number 6, for instance, correspond to the letter w (as well as to the letter v because there is no difference between v and w in Hebrew). Thus, 6-6-6 is written as www in Hebrew. Today, the letter sequence www is the code demanded for gaining access to the Internet.

The abbreviation www stands for *world-wide web*. The word *web* originally refers to a spider's web. In cyber language the word *net* is much more common: network, Internet, Intranet, Netscape – not webwork, Interweb etc. Is it by chance that all Internet users are forced to operate with the (techno)magical symbol of the 'beast', the triple six?

The bar code and the world-wide computer network – both contain the symbolical element 6-6-6. To what extent money and computers are interconnected is seen in the system of credit cards and other systems of cashless transactions.

Is 666 an evil number?

The whole cosmos is based on harmonics, and harmonics can be expressed in numbers. How, then, could a number be evil?

The Revelation only mentions that there is a satanic force which will *misuse* the number six hundred and sixty-six by making it its worldwide symbol. As shown above, this universally applicable symbol is the triple six in its variegated forms of appearance.

The triple six is a basic number of our physical existence. The bodies of all living entities (plants, animals, humans) consist of organic matter, and the basic element of organic matter is carbon. In the periodic table of chemistry, carbon has the atomic number 6. This means that carbon atoms consist of 6 protons, 6 neutrons, 6 electrons. Our organic body – in its basic ingredient – is vibrating at a nuclear rate of 6-6-6! This in itself is nothing grave or dangerous. However, we are warned that the forces of the 'dragon' will be intent on entrapping mankind's consciousness (by instigating an overwhelming identification with the physical body) in order to further materialism, body cult, sex addiction, dull enjoyment and stupid entertainment and, as the other side of the coin, mental stress, disease, superficial relationships, frustration, fear, and loss of spiritual perspectives. And *that* is certainly grave.

So there is no need to panic if someone has a triple six in his phone number or car license plate. But those who consciously choose to work with this symbol, for whatever reason, are playing with fire.

Some simple games with numbers

Beyond the symbolic use of the triple six, the number six hundred and sixty-six represents the numerological sum total of the letters of the beast's name: 'this mark ... the number of the beast ... is the number of a man.' Thus, with the use of a numerological system, one may be able to identify the 'beast' by his name. However, interpreters are not even clear about which system to use, the Greek alphabet or the Hebrew Cabbala.

The number 666 and the triple six can be found in many numerological and geometrical variations. For example, the number 18 is relevant, being the result of both 6+6+6 and 3×6. Another interesting

Is there a triple six hidden in the bar code?

Bar-coding is a very practical system to identify articles and to compute them into the cash register. There is no longer any need of manually typing each price. It only takes a short scan, and everything is registered both in the machine and on the sales receipt. The bar code can even be held upside-down, and still the scanner reads it properly.

The EAN standard bar code can be read irrespective of its position because it is laid out in two parts, a left side and a right side, each containing six numbers (separated by a double line in the middle). In these two parts, different sets of bar-coding are used. The scanner, being programmed to recognize these sets, immediately 'knows' which numbers constitute the left side and which the right, even if the two sides appear vice-versa.

A bar code consists of a series of black bars and white spaces of varying widths, which represents a series of numbers, each number being depicted by two bars. Each of these two-bar modules consists of seven basic space units, of which some are empty and some 'black'. In the binary computer language, the scanner reads 'empty' as 0 and black as 1 and thus identifies each group of seven space units as one particular number.

There are three sets of bar-code definitions for each number. In the standard bar code, sets A and B are used on the left side, set C on the right side. Sets A and C are like positive and negative (black becomes white, white becomes black). Set B is the mirrored version of set C. The mirrored version of set A is not (yet) implemented in the bar-coding system but could be used to create a new, expanded form of bar-coding.

For example, the definition of the number 3 in set A is 0111101, consisting of the thickest bar possible (four units) along with the thinnest bar (of one unit). Amongst these sets of bar-coded numbers, only one number contains two one-unit bars with a one-unit space: 0000101 and 1010000. It is the number 6 in the sets B and C.

In other words, the binary coding element 101 only appears in the bar-coding of the number six. Exactly these one-unit parallel lines are placed additionally on the left, in the middle and on the right of every standard bar code. They are longer than the other bar-code modules and do not stand for a number. Although these three parallel lines are not read as 6-6-6 by the scanner, they still contain the binary coding element 101, which is only found in the B and C modules of the number 6.

Again there is the question: Is it by chance that the 101 coding element was used to define the number 6? This definition was arbitrary and could have been easily used to designate any other number. Then, the three one-unit parallel lines would have no reference to the triple six. In the definition chosen, however, they 'coincidentally' contain the coding element 6-6-6.

The EAN-13 bar code with all binary units (seven per module of each number), which are normally invisible. The UPC symbology is a subset of this standard bar code.

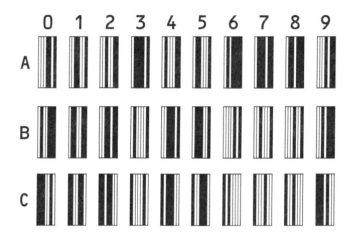

The bar-coding sets A, B and C.

'Nobody shall be able to buy or sell anything unless he has been marked with the number 666' (Rev. 13.18). Is a two-thousand-year-old vision becoming true? Till now, only articles have been marked. Will a time come when also human beings will have a personal bar code, at one point even 'tattooed' as an invisible mark on their bodies?

number is 36: it expresses the symbol of the triple six (three 6), and – when adding up the numbers 1 to 36 (1+2+3 … +36) – it results in 666. A triple six can also be hidden in geometry, for example in equilateral triangles: 60 + 60 + 60 degrees; sum of their digits: 18 ($\times$ 2 = 36).

As the number 6 is the basic component of the beast's name and symbol, a key that suggests itself is the additive alphabet of the number 6: A=6, B=12, C=18, etc. This is a simple game with numbers and has nothing to do with Cabbala (Cabbala is much more complex, and the order of letters in the Hebrew and Greek alphabets are different from today's common ABC). Still, being based on this modern alphabet, which now, in the 'end time', is globally used and understood, the additive alphabet of the number 6 can be expected to also provide some additional insights – and it does!

The additive alphabet of the number six

A = 6	N = 84	C = 18	N = 84
B = 12	O = 90	O = 90	E = 30
C = 18	P = 96	M = 78	W = 138
D = 24	Q = 102	P = 96	
E = 30	R = 108	U = 126	Y = 150
F = 36	S = 114	T = 120	O = 90
G = 42	T = 120	E = 30	R = 108
H = 48	U = 126	R = 108	K = 66
I = 54	V = 132	666	666
J = 60	W = 138		
K = 66	X = 144		
L = 72	Y = 150		
M = 78	Z = 156		

We can choose any word and substitute the letters for numbers. The result is astonishing: one word of global impact having the numerical value 666 is COMPUTER. Interestingly enough, the numerical value of NEW YORK is also 666. And names like 'Kissinger' and 'Monsanto' have the same value. Again, this is simply a game with numbers which should not be overestimated.

Summary and outlook

On its last pages, the most popular book of the Occident, the Bible, predicts that there will be a time when a long-thriving (draconic) force comes to global power, its key being the number 666. Although the Hebrew and Greek ways of writing numbers are different from the system of Arabic numbers, it is the latter that is globally known and used. Therefore, groups interested in obtaining global power might be tempted to use the number six hundred and sixty-six and its modern symbol – the triple six – in order to invoke the desired success at whatever cost. The appearance of this ominous code on the global market of buying and selling will indicate when the time frame of the apocalyptic scenario has come.

What St John foresaw was a globalization of trade and monetary monopoly: 'to lead astray the people *of the world* [...] he compelled *everyone* to be marked' (Rev. 13.13, 18) and: 'The *merchants of the earth* have grown rich from the power of Babylon's shameless luxury [...] your merchants were *the top ranking men (the magnates) of the earth*' (Rev. 18.3, 23). It is quite remarkable that today's globalization was foreseen by a 90-year-old Jewish-Christian man in the first century AD.

Since the middle of the twentieth century (after the two world wars), the globalization of trade and monetary monopoly has become a strongly propagated idea, along with the covert and open use of the number 666 and its symbol. The binary-coding element of the triple six is hidden in the UPC bar code. The triple six is encoded in the Internet abbreviation www. 666 is the numerical value of the word 'computer'. It is there in codified names, addresses, official forms and numbers, and it appears in advertising and entertainment. Alert observers will detect its traces again and again.

Almost two thousand years ago, St John foresaw a (techno)magical boom based on the number 666, and he mentioned several times that it would enchant and seduce the whole world. Today we can see that the world economy has become fully dependent on the global computer web and the bar-coding system. Therefore, we come up with two hypotheses: (1) that the vision of the Revelation refers to our present-day society and (2) that the *entire* vision should be taken seriously as it might not only be correct in regard to the number of the 'beast'.

Most people tend to ignore or deride this warning. The only ones who still take it seriously are Bible-fundamentalist authors and groups. Unfortunately, however, their preaching is so zealous and biased that it turns off all people except their own followers. It seems that those coming in the name of Jesus and Christ are very good at (involuntarily) distorting or even ridiculing this information, thus keeping it bound to sectarian circles. This is a pity because the Revelation contains not only warnings but also spiritual insights and inspiring perspectives of the earth's future, which today are more relevant and important than ever before.

The future is never predestined, and every individual is free to live in a divine way, regardless of what the 'rest of the world' may choose to do. Already now, many seeds of the new Earth are being planted.

> The Pharisees asked when the kingdom of God was to come. And Jesus answered: 'The kingdom of God is not coming with things that can be observed [like a mundane kingdom]. And there will be no one to say: "Look, it is here", or "it is there!" For, in fact, the kingdom of God is already here – right in your midst [or: 'the kingdom of God within you', according to other translations].' (Luke 17.20–1)

CHAPTER EIGHT

Unlimited Technological Progress – to What End?

Through the introduction of paper money, the money-pulators were able to handle immense sums and to create phantom wealth. With these resources they could grant loans and make individuals, companies and entire nations indebted to them and, thus, dependent on them. If 'required' they could also financially ruin them.

However, as long as cash money exists, there remains a certain independence for people, because it is *anonymous*. In this regard, too, the apocalyptic scenario is ultra-modern, if not 'science fiction'. Let us examine what it actually predicts.

Up to now, all consumer goods have become marked with a bar code, the standard version consisting of two times six numbers. At the same time, a global computer infrastructure (designated as www, 'world-wide web') is being installed, making cash money more and more outdated. Where is this technological progress heading towards?

The apocalyptic scenario says: At one point people will be able to buy and sell (and to earn money) only if they are 'marked' on their right hand or on their forehead. Only nowadays, with the technology seen at the beginning of the twenty-first century, do we have the required horizon to interpret what St John got to see in the first century: people being marked with a kind of (invisible) bar code on their body which is used to identify them and to register all their transactions in a central computer. Practically, this would mean that both the consumers and the consumer goods become bar-coded.

From a certain viewpoint such a system would have many advantages. There would no longer be illicit work or any chance of evading taxes. One would no longer have to fear burglars or pickpockets. One would not even have to fill out a tax declaration because the central computer would do it automatically and just deduce the calculated tax amount from one's personal account. And it would be more difficult for terrorists to organize any attacks. This new world order promises 'peace' and 'security' – for all those who fall in line.

Regarding the computer identification of the world population there are already projected bar-code systems in the form of an invisible laser tattoo. One system involves personal ID bar codes consisting of 18 numbers: *three times six numbers,* or three groups of six numbers (again 6-6-6)! In other words, people would simply get an expanded UPC code – 12 digits for goods, 18 digits for people. (For the third group of 6 numbers, the mirrored version of set A, which is still in store unused, could be implemented.)

The trend heading towards the complete abolishment of cash money is obvious to see. With the increased use of computer money, ready cash becomes unwelcome and unpractical, even suspicious. In more and more countries people are becoming equipped with all kinds of plastic cards: ID cards, credit cards, cash cards, post-bank cards, driver's license cards, insurance cards, railway cards, telephone cards, bus cards, customer cards, health insurance cards, etc. And in addition, people still have to carry paper money and coins with them.

Once, gold was replaced by paper money, and now the paper is being replaced by plastic cards and computer numbers. Will the flood of personal cards one day be replaced by a body-worn bar code?

That is the question investigated in this chapter.

Abolishment of cash money – fact or fiction?

It is no secret that bankers in the upper ranks consider cash money a 'luxury that the world can no longer afford'. Therefore, cash money transactions through one's bank or post office are becoming increasingly expensive. Apparently, the use of cash money is being 'punished' with high charges while account transactions are being furthered and supported on all levels. Who still receives his salary in cash money?

Step by step, the introduction of a global cashless society is being prepared, and through the mass media, it is presented to be the normal and consequent direction of progress. On the following pages, the

Unlimited Technological Progress – to What End? 251

Farewell to Cash Money
New cash cards are pushing out coins and notes

Headline on the cover of the Swiss news magazine FACTS, *edition 33/1996. The plan of abolishing cash money already exists and is being implemented step by step, one step having been the introduction of cash cards.*

examples quoted are mostly from the German-speaking countries. If it is propagated here in Europe, we can deduce that the Anglo-American world is even further immersed in this progress and 'process'.

As early as in 1996, the Swiss news magazine *Facts* announced: 'Farewell to Cash Money!' The corresponding article left no doubt about the plans and aims:

> Plastic cards with chips will supersede coins and bank notes as a means of payment. The new money will consist of bits and bytes [...] Banks, credit-card organizations and software experts are working on a solution to dematerialize money [...] Electric purses are merely an intermediate stage in the development towards a digital currency in the third millennium. (*Facts* 33/1996, t.AR)

Referring to the progress made, the German Press Agency (dpa) reported at the end of the year 1998:

> Triumphant advance of the chip card: *Farewell to wallet and purse* [...] What may remind the layman of 'Starship Enterprise' has been made possible by computer scientists: 'We are equipped with the necessary technology. This revolutionary change is no longer something utopian or a thing of the distant future', says Sabine Belling, spokeswoman for Gemplus, manufacturer of magnetic strips and chip cards [...] (12/13 December 1998, t.AR)

Obviously, the directors of technological progress have already said farewell to cash. We can therefore assume that it is only a question of time until their vision will be materialized, most probably through the staging of a financial crash. A crash, and no more cash ...

Everything put on one card?

Many people, faced with the flood of plastic cards, have already voiced the desire of having all information on one card. This idea, of course, is nothing new, and the system is already there. It is called 'smart card'.

However, the more information is stored on a card, the more disastrous it is to lose it. The loss of such a card cuts the owner completely off from all services. In the time it takes to replace it, one can neither buy nor sell!

> Imagine somebody losing this multifunctional chip card with all the vital data it contains! Wouldn't that be like an existential black-out? After all, one has lost one's total identity! Is it recommendable to put everything on one card? In order to prevent unauthorized use of the card, is it necessary to have a personal code number for every single purpose? But who will be able to memorize all these numbers?[96]

The solution to all these problems that come along with a smart card is not yet presented openly, but it is no secret either. Actually, it is quite obvious, being the logical consequence of the direction progress has been given. And it has already been foreseen! Instead of having the information of all people distributed on many cards, the final solution entails the registration of all information about people in a central computer, with each person being able to access his or her account through the corresponding unique ('personal') bar code. This bar code could be imprinted on a personal card or – lossproof and foolproof – on one's hand or forehead as a kind of invisible laser tattoo. No more fear of loss or theft!

The technology is available. The vision is there in the heads of many influential global players. And people have seen the entire scenario in films like *Enemy of the State*, *Matrix* and *Dark Angel*. So is it really that far-fetched? One big step in that direction might have been the launching of implantable microchips for animals – and for humans.

Implantable microchips for humans: just a temporary fashion?

In December 1999, the American enterprise ADS (Applied Digital Solutions) presented a commercial microchip for humans called 'Digital Angel'. The person having such a microchip in his or her body can be located anywhere on the planet by the GPS satellite system. This is especially relevant for children and for prominent people who fear to be kidnapped. In March 2002, an American family by the name of Jacobs appeared in the headlines because they had volunteered for a pilot project of chip implantation. The microchip also stores medical information which can be retrieved in the case of an accident. 'With such a facility lives can be saved. This gives me a feeling of safety and peace of mind', to quote Mrs Jacobs (according to the news release).

Today, it has become fashionable for the young generation to have body piercings. Has the promotion of piercings simply been a warm-up for the 'ultimate' piercing – the implantation of a microchip?

In the case of domestic animals, microchips as ID tags have already become quite normal. In more and more countries, it is even becoming compulsory. For example, in December 1996 microchips for dogs became obligatory in Hong Kong. In a television broadcast by the international Hong Kong station, the official placard was shown: *Have your dog microchipped – get your pet an identity!* The viewers got to see happy dogs and happy owners. Those privileged with being TV-interviewed were bursting with enthusiasm and praised the microchip to the skies: 'Extremely practical! Harmless! Painless! Reliable! Safe! Prevents illegal dog dealing!' – And in a way they were even right. It was not explicitly mentioned, but the idea suggested itself: an implanted chip would be the ideal ID tag for human beings as well (TV-CNBC News, 25 November 1996). According to the world-view of certain people, there is no essential difference between animals and people anyway!

Admittedly, this technical 'miracle' in itself is practical and probably harmless, and there would be no need to condemn it – if it stopped here. But obviously, this is not the case. As mentioned in the quote about the farewell to cash, *'electric purses [and implantable microchips] are merely an intermediate stage in the development towards a digital currency [and ID system] in the third millennium'.*

A digital currency and ID system is based on microchip technology.

And sure enough, the idea of microchipping citizens has already been around for years, and it has never been a secret. In 1993 (11 October), an article published in the *Washington Times* had the headline 'High-tech National Tattoo' and reported the following information:

> [...] there is an identification system made by the Hughes Aircraft Company that you can't lose. It's the syringe implantable transponder. According to promotional literature it is an 'ingenious, safe, inexpensive, foolproof and permanent method of [...] identification using radio waves'. A tiny microchip, the size of a grain of rice, is simply placed under the skin. It is so designed as to be injected simultaneously with a vaccination or alone.

A similar piece of news was published in 1995 by the magazine *Tucson Weekly* (Vol. 11, No. 14, June 15–June 21, 1995), with the headline 'Electronic Leash: The Implantable Bio-Chip Is Already Here':

> When inserted underneath the skin, this chip can link an individual to a computer database, or it can track a person's location via satellite. [...] Once implanted, the chip is virtually impossible to remove. [...] even surgical removal using advanced radiograph techniques is extremely difficult. This is because fibrous tissue adheres to grooves in the glass surrounding the chip to prevent migration of the chip.

In the news and in TV reality shows, people are told about children disappearing, many of them never to be found again. And often it is hinted: If the children had an implantable transponder chip, we could easily find out where they are! – However, there is no guarantee. If criminals know that their victims have a microchip, they will not hesitate to remove it by whatever means. If they are ready to kidnap and kill, they will not refrain from adding another atrocity. In other words, the implantation of chips will induce (and force!) criminals to become even more brutal.

Nevertheless, under the catchword of so-called security, Big Brother once again resorts to his well-proven method: causing fear and intimidation. Facing the unwillingness of many adults to accept a chip under their skin, he simply aims at the next generation, with the 'permission' of the intimidated parents. (We might be reminded of the propaganda when vaccination was made compulsory, either by law or by social pressure.)

In the autumn of 1998, the world was informed about the experiment of an English Professor, Kevin Warwick, who had wanted to be microchipped in order to test 'the interactive link between man and machine'. (If we remember that the letters v and w are equivalent to the number 6, we detect that this man's name contains a triple six in symmetric two digit intervals. This is a strange coincidence, of course, but there are not that many names having this particularity.)

Only a few years later, in 2002, the implantable microchip for humans became commercially available for the common man, woman and child.

Globalization of the Web

Most probably, the abolishment of cash money will be effected by some financial crash like another Black Friday. When will this occurrence come about?

To make a prediction is not very difficult. Cash money can only be abolished when the global infrastructure required for the new system is extant. Is this the reason why a world-wide network ('web') of computer communication is being established as a top priority, with almost unlimited funds?

In January 2000, right after the Y2K panic, representatives of the political, economic and financial world elite assembled in the town named Davos situated in a remote mountain valley of Switzerland. It was the annual reunion of the World Economic Forum (WEF), which was attended by Bill Clinton, then President of the USA, along with Bill Gates and many others. In his one-hour speech, President Clinton glorified the importance of the Internet and the necessity of its worldwide installation. Only two weeks after this meeting, a press release went around the world, indicating the immediate and stepped-up implementation of this strategy:

> Tokyo – A branch of the World Bank starts a joint venture together with the Japanese computer enterprise Softbank Corporation to further new Internet firms in around 100 countries of the Third World. The goal is to decrease the 'global digital gap' between the rich and poor countries and to improve the Internet access for 4.8 billion people in poor countries, as stated yesterday by World Bank president James Wolfensohn. This is to be the 'starting of the globalization of education' and the 'starting of the globalization of the Internet', said Wolfensohn. (15 February 2000)

The most advanced and most expensive technology is being used to create a world-wide web in order to unite computer- and telecommunications through a satellite-based system. Once installed, this infrastructure will allow (and force?) people all over the world to pay by card, even in a jungle village or desert oasis. The push towards such a technology is nothing new. For example, in March 1998, *Der Spiegel* (12/1998, p. 237) reported: 'It is planned that in the future, mobile phones should function even in remote regions such as the North Pole or Mongolia. For this special purpose, *Iridium* (an international consortium of associated telecommunication companies) will launch 66 satellites into space by the end of this year' (t.AR). In the meantime, this technology is again outdated, and more advanced systems are being installed.

Why are such huge amounts of money being spent while thousands of people are dying of hunger every day? Is it all just to give yet greater comfort to the consumer? Are billions of dollars being spent just to enable some Mongolian nomads and North-Pole Inuits to use a portable phone? Are the investors of these billions really that selfless and humanitarian?

In the edition of *Der Spiegel* quoted above, it is admitted that we actually do not need all of this perfectionism and globalization of technology:

> Customers insist on their simple needs. [...] They don't need any 3-D graphical chips with turbo function. Such devices are not helping the computer industry to expand, at least not in the traditional way. [...] For Nathan Brookwood, economic researcher employed with Dataquest, the next step is obvious: 'The industry urgently has to come up with a hardware-oriented solution that will enrapture the people.' (p. 206, t.AR)

'... *a hardware-oriented solution that will enrapture the people*'?! In practical terms this means: new possibilities of applying sensors, microchips, transponders, satellites and globally inter-linked computer systems. When adding up the information of this chapter, we can imagine possible applications, the most extreme scenario including the marking of all individuals by microchips on ID cards, later to be replaced by a laser tattoo on one's hand or forehead. This 'hardware-oriented solution' would indeed open up an almost unlimited global market for data-processing products. Therefore it is not surprising to see that the idea of having 'something' on one's forehead is already there in the heads of some economic 666 enthusiasts, and experiments have already been conducted:

> A few years ago, in 1988, Singapore tested this system for three months on ten thousand people! The magazine *Science et Foi* (Nr. 10, p. 37) wrote that this city with millions of inhabitants wanted to test how people react when credit cards are replaced by an individual bar code readable by a laser scanner. The code was partly marked on the wrist and partly on the forehead.[97]

The danger of the mark

For almost two thousand years, mankind has been warned about the dangers of materialistic progress. The fact that spiritual sources emphasize this particular point so much indicates the importance of this warning. Being 'branded' will be detrimental physically and spiritually: 'All those who worship the beast and its image, or have had themselves branded on the hand or forehead, will be made to drink the wine of God's wrath. [...] There will be no rest day or night for those who worship the beast or its image or accept the mark of its name. [...] and a foul and painful sore came on those who had the mark of the beast or who worshipped its image.' (Rev. 14.9–11; 16.2)

A similar vision is reported by the author Dannion Brinkley. In 1975, after having been part of a killer commando in the Vietnam war, he had a near-death experience during which he foresaw things to come in the near future. Afterwards he was able to remember 117 of his visions, and published them in a book. From 1978 onwards, one vision after the other proved true. By 1993, 95 of them had happened exactly as foreseen in his OBE (out-of-body experience), such as the Chernobyl disaster, the fall of the Iron Curtain in 1989, the Gulf War, the massacres of the Yugoslavian War, the increasing financial debt of the USA, and other details referring to economic crises in all parts of the world.

During his near-death experience, he also saw a gene manipulator in the Middle East who succeeded in changing the human DNA structure; this invention enabled him to generate a virus that was used in a new kind of implantable computer bio-chip.

> His method of rule was unique. Everyone was mandated by law to have one of his computer chips inserted under his or her skin. This chip contained all of an individual's personal information. [...] There was an even more

sinister side to this chip. A person's lifetime could be limited by programming this chip to dissolve and kill him with the viral substance it was made from. Lifetimes were controlled like this to avoid the cost that 'growing old' places on the government. It was also used as a means of eliminating people with chronic illnesses that put a drain on the medical system.[98]

Again, we have to remember that the implanted chip is not the final stage of this process, as microchips are not very practical. When the chip is implanted, one can no longer access it to update its content. Therefore, much more 'practical' would be having all the information stored in a central computer and having each person identified through an ID bar code. Then, every buying and selling transaction could easily be registered, processed and monitored. According to the Bible, the implantation of a microchip is just an intermediate step towards the marking of (almost) all people on their right hand or their forehead.

What might the next steps be?

In the manifestation of the apocalyptic scenario, we still 'lack' the financial collapse that leads to the introduction of a cashless money system. As the entire infrastructure is being completed now, we must reckon with unexpected things happening in the near future.

> In all likelihood this surprise take-over will no longer be triggered by a world war, as probably originally planned, but by a feigned global collapse of currency. [...] Then, cash money can be presented as the root of all problems, and the immediate global introduction of an electronic currency can be presented as the only solution. Thus, nothing would even faintly look like a conspiracy for the majority of the world population, and for this reason the last-minute resistance still dreaded by the 'Synagogue of Satan'* would not even arise.[99]

For people to be identified by a personal bar code, a centralized global computer system is required. Nowadays it would be technically possible to have one single supercomputer with the capacity of processing all people's data communicated by connected computers. This thought, too, is no longer taboo, and it is already being materialized:

---

* This expression is explicitly used in the Revelation (2.9 and 3.9).

Scientists are heading for the Internet of the future. [...] From the simple data storing machine called 'world-wide web', a global super brain shall arise, linking all computer systems to provide any kind of information and any desired amount of storage capacity. [...] This octopus-like computer net is called 'The Grid' [...] the 'World-wide Grid'. [...] Since the beginning of November [2000] the European Union (EU) has been supporting the development of this Grid infrastructure with an investment of 80 million Euro. The intended goal is the installation of a new high-speed data net. In the USA, the work on the Grid has been going on already for quite some time.

This was reported by *Der Spiegel* in its edition 49/2000 (t.AR). Apparently, as these few media quotes reveal, we are witnessing the development of a technological infrastructure that could be 666-compatible.

Summary and outlook

In the fields of economy and banking, the hailed progress is heading for the abolishment of anonymous cash money and for the implementation of digital money. Today, people increasingly use money cards for all their buying and selling transactions. Will the cards at one point be abolished, too? Will the ID code be placed on people's bodies so as to avoid the danger (and the annoyance) of citizens losing their access to the centralized data processor? We do not know. But there is the apocalyptic vision indicating this possibility. And thus, we are warned.

If cash money were actually withdrawn and replaced by digital money, nobody would be able to buy or sell anything without being identified. 'Of course, this system will allow total control', the official justification will admit, 'but what is the problem? It serves the social security of the citizen. Honest people do not have anything to hide and won't have to fear this control. The only ones fearing it will be the criminals and terrorists, the tax evaders, the drug dealers and the cults. But these are the very disturbers that we all – the world government and you, the citizens – wish to jointly combat and eliminate. Then, finally, global peace and security will no longer be threatened.'

However, who will define what is 'criminal' and 'dangerous'? Let us not forget: Up to three hundred years ago, people in Christian countries were considered criminals if they believed in karma, reincarnation and higher-dimensional worlds. Later, under communist dictatorship,

Christians and other religious people were considered criminal or mentally deranged and were persecuted, arrested, tortured and/or killed. Nowadays, natural healers and social critics are increasingly restricted or even criminalized by new laws. Those who try to be independent and self-sufficient are cornered by high financial demands of ever-increasing taxes and insurance obligations. Neighbourhood watch is turning every citizen into a spy and into a 'potential terrorist', and potential terrorists have no rights, just like the real ones. And those refusing to accept the mark of the beast will also be called criminals ...

That is the apocalyptic scenario.

The more criminality, terror and insanity increase, the more total control can be enforced. Should things come to a head, a crisis might be conjured up (a financial crash, riots of the unemployed masses, staged or real terrorism, war mobilization etc.), leading to a state of 'national emergency', which implies an *all-pervading police state;* all citizens would immediately have to acquiesce to absolute dictatorship. According to the already existing law, offering resistance in such a situation can be punished on the spot with execution without legal proceedings, also in former democratic or republican states.

Admittedly, this scenario is quite sobering, probably even frightening. It is a challenge beyond false promises or naive hopes, for *spiritual* optimism and confidence are not dependent on external conditions. The bigger the material challenge, the bigger the spiritual help offered to all those who seek and believe (as will be pointed out in the following chapters). In this sense, we are heading for exciting times – the adventure of crucial decisions.

CHAPTER NINE

People Cannot Say They Did Not Know

The scenario of the Apocalypse is a prophetic description of the time when the present materialistic civilization will come to its end, and of the succeeding new age. This prophecy is not an isolated prospect; it stands in the line of earlier visions of prophets such as Daniel, Ezekiel and Isaiah as well as the end-time statements made by Jesus himself, recorded in the gospels of Matthew, Mark and Luke. 'These words are to remain secret and sealed until the time of the end.' (Dan. 12.9)

Radical changes have also been foreseen by many other cultures, for example by the Hopi Indians, who speak about the end of the 'fourth world' and the beginning of the 'fifth world'. The change from the third to the fourth world was effected by water; the change from the fourth to the fifth world will be effected by fire. This may refer to earthquakes and volcanoes but also to the white men's fire weapons as preluded by the atomic bombs thrown upon Hiroshima and Nagasaki.

Similarly, the ancient Sanskrit scriptures indicate the onset of a 'golden age' after five thousand years of an Iron Age (Kali-yuga). Then, finally, the dark influence on earth will be overcome.

Briefly summarized, the Revelation describes the course of events during the phases before the end of times, the end of times itself as well as the time thereafter. The phases just before the end of times are described as the 'opening of the seven seals'. When the seventh seal is opened, seven angels appear one after the other, each sounding his trumpet. The sounding of the seventh trumpet opens up the end of times. Then, through divine intervention, the 'kingdom of 1000 years' will come about, marking the transition to the time of the 'new heaven' and the 'new Earth', the 'new Jerusalem'.

The Apocalypse is like a complex kaleidoscope of visions with manifold levels of interpretation addressing the people of John's time, the following generations and, particularly, those people destined to experience the predicted end of times. 'Now write down all that you have seen of what is now and what is still to come. [...] Come up here, and I will show you what is to take place in the future.' (Rev. 1.19; 4.1)

Occurrences as never experienced before

The Revelation contains some obvious parallels to the scenario envisioned by the prophet Daniel about five hundred years BC: 'At that time Michael will arise, the great leader of the angels, defender of your people. That will be a time of great distress, unparalleled since nations first came into existence. [...] I hear the man speak who was dressed in linen, standing further up the stream: he raised his right hand and his left to heaven and swore by him who lives forever. A time and two times and half a time; and all these things will come true, once the crushing of the holy people's power is over [...] These words are to remain secret and sealed until the time of the end.' (Dan. 12.1, 7, 9)

A similar statement was made by Jesus: 'For then there will be great distress, unparalleled since the world began, and such as will never be again.' (Matt. 24.21)

At the same time, inconceivable forms of divine help and intervention will occur, also 'unparalleled since the world began'!

The two halves of Tribulation

Seven is a sacred number in the Revelation (7 churches, 7 candle-sticks, 7 stars, 7 spirits of God, 7 seals, 7 trumpets, 7 vials, 7 thunders, etc.). Similarly, the 'end of times' lasts for 7 years, a time span which is divided into two halves of 42 months, or 1260 days. Whether the words 'years', 'months' and 'days' are to be taken literally remains to be seen.

In the middle, after the first half, the two 'beasts' will appear, establishing their short 666 dictatorship: 'They will trample on the holy city for forty-two months. But I shall send my two witnesses to prophesy for twelve hundred and sixty days ...' (Rev. 11.2–3)

This description refers to the first half. During the period of the sixth trumpet, the beast makes its first appearance and kills the two witnesses. After three and a half days, God breathes life into these two witnesses, and they ascend to heaven in front of everybody's eyes.

Then follows the vision of the cosmic woman who is about to give birth to a child; a dragon appears, trying to devour the child, but the new-born child is 'carried up to heaven' while the dragon and its hosts are thrown down to the earth for the final decision.

With the beginning of the second half, the first beast appears out of the sea (13.1). One of his seven heads has a wound but it is healed. This wound is mentioned three times (13.3, 12, 14) and is described as a deadly wound. One interpretation says that this person might have been saved from seeming death by some kind of miraculous healing. Should this be the case, then he was called back to life through the magical power of the dragon as an imitation of the resurrection of Jesus and the two witnesses. Many will interpret this magical resurrection as the last confirmation of the beast's alleged divine mission (Rev. 13.3–4).

The beast's reign marks the second half of the end time and also lasts three and a half years. The woman, whose new-born son had been attacked by the dragon, 'escaped into the desert, where God had prepared a place for her to be looked after for twelve hundred and sixty days. [...] The beast was allowed to mouth its boasts and blasphemies and to be active for forty-two months.' (Rev. 12.6; 13.5)

Forty-two months are the same as 1260 days (42×30) and represent the three and a half years. The seven years consist of two times 1260 days, 2520 days. This is a sacred number which signifies perfection, being the first number divisible by 2, 3, 4, 5, 6, 7, 8, 9 and 10. So it might well be that these numbers are to be taken symbolically.

The second half of Tribulation

With the opening of the seals and the blowing of the trumpets in the first half of Tribulation, St John perceived images of war and death which he described in words typical of a man of the first century. Nowadays, from our point of view, we can easily understand what he saw: the technological warfare of our time, the destruction of the environment, and natural catastrophes. 'But the rest of humankind, those who were not killed by these plagues, refused to change themselves.' (Rev. 9.20)

At this point, an angel descends from heaven, placing one foot on the sea and the other on the land, and proclaims: 'The time of waiting is over; at the time when the seventh angel is to blow his trumpet, the mystery of God's plan will be fulfilled, just as he announced it to his servants the prophets.' (Rev. 10.6–7)

Thus begins the second half of Tribulation, a dramatic time of decision polarized by the appearance of the two beasts. In the fifteenth chapter of the Revelation, it is described how all those who resisted bearing the mark of the beast attain God's mercy. At the same time, three impure spirits dispatched by the dragon and the two beasts instigate the godless kings of the world to start the war of Armageddon. With the pouring of the seventh vial, the whole earth trembles and the cities of all countries are destroyed. Islands disappear, and mountains are effaced, but men still persist to curse God, not wanting to understand why all of these things are coming to pass. Then, all of a sudden, a divine rider appears, followed by his divine hosts:

> I saw the heavens open, and a white horse appeared; its rider was called *Trustworthy and True;* in uprightness he judged and fought. His eyes were flames of fire, and he was crowned with many coronets; the name written on him was known only to himself, his cloak was soaked in blood. He is known by the name *The Word of God*. Behind him, dressed in linen of dazzling white, rode the armies of heaven on white horses. [...]
>
> Then I saw the beast and the kings of the earth with their armies gathered together to fight against the Rider and his army. But the beast was captured, and with it the false prophet who had worked miracles on the beast's behalf, by which he deceived all those who had accepted the mark of the beast and those who had worshipped its image. (Rev. 19.11–13, 19–20)

The two beasts are 'thrown alive into the fiery lake of burning sulphur', and an angel binds the dragon and locks him away for 1000 years. During this time, those who had been 'killed due to their testimony to Jesus and the word of God ... come to life', and they 'reign' alongside with 'those who refused to worship the beast or its image, and who had not accepted the brand-mark on their foreheads or hands.' (Rev. 20.4)

After Satan's last and final revolt, 'a new heaven and a new earth' emerge (Rev. 21.1). With this wonderful prospect and prophecy, the Apocalypse ends – and, thus, the New Testament and the entire Bible.

The army of two-hundred million soldiers

Another astonishing but realistic factor to be mentioned is the huge army that St John got to see in connection with the sounding of the sixth trumpet:

> The voice told the sixth angel, who had sounded his trumpet: 'Release the four angels who have been held back at the shore of the Euphrates, the big river. [...]' And I was told the number of their troops on horse, it was two hundred million. [...] The horses had heads like lions; fire and smoke and sulphur came out of their mouths. [...] The deadly effect of the horses came about from their mouths and tails. (Rev. 9.14–19)
>
> The sixth angel poured his vial into the Euphrates, the big river, which then dried up. Thus the way was opened to the kings who came from the countries of the rising sun. (Rev. 16.12)

The region of the Euphrates is today's Iraq! The troops mentioned in this vision belong to the 'kings of the East' or, according to other translations, 'the kings from the countries of the rising sun'.

Although it was totally inconceivable to him, St John reported authentically: 'And I was told the number of their troops on horse, it was twice ten thousand times ten thousand.' Only today, 1,900 years later, is there a nation that has grown to such a size as to be able to come up with an army of so many men. And it is exactly there where St John saw this army come from – the Far East: China, the giant in outback Asia.

In a documentary about Red China, entitled 'The Voice of the Dragon', the Chinese pride themselves with being capable of mobilizing a national army of 200 million people[100] – precisely the number given in the Apocalypse!

In modern China, the number of the unemployed alone would suffice to form such a huge army. '120 million people looking for work, often entire families, are itinerant in this vast country and migrate to the cities, bringing down the salaries. Pessimists are awaiting the induced unemployment of at least 100 million, possibly even double this amount.'[101] Double the amount? Again the number 200 million!

The China factor also popped up in a big scandal exposed in the USA in 1999. The general public got to know about a strange case that must have seemed absurd to every 'non-illuminated' citizen: President Bill Clinton had given his consent for a secret transaction which supplied the latest US nuclear technology to China! In the second week of March 1999, an article by the well-known political journalist Michael Kelly was published in the *Washington Post*, entitled 'Lies about China':

> Notra Trulock, the department's chief of intelligence, had uncovered evidence that showed China had learned how to miniaturize nuclear bombs, allowing for smaller, more lethal missile warheads. [...] The White House's secret would have remained secret had it not been for a select investigative committee headed by the Republican Christopher Cox. Cox's committee unearthed a pattern of more than two decades of Chinese nuclear spying, including the Los Alamos case.

On 6 March 1999, the *New York Times* published a drawing showing the latest W-88 nuclear warhead – weight: 150 kg, i.e. thirty times lighter than the Hiroshima bomb. The latter measured more than three metres in length. W-88 is only 70 cm long but has an impact ten times more devastating than the Hiroshima bomb. W-88 is one of those secret US-missiles of which China now possesses all construction plans!

The rage and uproar of the American people was expressed by the Republican Senator of Oklahoma, James Inhofe. His speech in front of the Senate, delivered on 15 March 1999, in the presence of Vice President Al Gore, was widely spread (also through the Internet):

> I am going to tell you a story of espionage, conspiracy, deception and cover-up, a story with life and death implications for millions of Americans. [...]
> I am stating that the President withheld information and covered up the Chinese theft of our technology. The President misled the American people on numerous occasions about the threat posed by strategic nuclear missiles in the post cold war era. [...] During this period of time, President Clinton made statements on over 130 separate occasions, such as the following: 'For the first time since the dawn of the nuclear age, there is not a single solitary nuclear missile pointed at an American child tonight. Not one. Not a single one.' During this period of time, he knew that China was targeting up to 18 intercontinental ballistic missiles at American children. [...] the motive for aiding and abetting our adversaries could be money, or it could be some kind of perverted allegiance to these countries, or it could be a total indifference to the security of the lives of Americans. The motive is not important. The fact is President Clinton did it and he knew exactly what he was doing. [...] Of all the lies this president has told, this is the most egregious of all. He repeated this misleading, deceptive lie over 130 times between 1995 and 1997.
> The likely suspect spy was identified in early 1997, and the FBI urged that he at least be transferred to a less sensitive position. But inexplicably, he was

allowed to keep his sensitive job at Los Alamos for another year and a half. This was the spy responsible for the theft and President Clinton kept him in that sensitive job for another year and half. Finally, he was fired by Energy Secretary Richardson last Monday [8 March 1999], but only after he was publicly identified in news reports as having failed two previous lie detector tests. [...] I am convinced we have not yet scratched the surface of this national security scandal exposed by these most recent revelations.

Even the conservative Senator Inhofe could not help speaking of these facts as a 'conspiracy' and 'some kind of perverted allegiance'. This reminds us of a statement by the American author G. Edward Griffin, published in 1994 in his book *The Creature from Jekyll Island:*

> Those at the top of the structure are now working to maneuver both Russia and the United States into a world government which they expect to control. War and threats of war are powerful tools to prod the masses toward the acceptance of that goal. It is essential, therefore, that the United States and the industrialized nations of the world have a credible enemy. [...] U.S. government and megabank funding, first of Russian, and now of Chinese military capabilities, cannot be understood without that insight.'[102]

Soon after this espionage scandal, which might have led to the exposure of many other dubious insider activities, public attention was diverted to Bill Clinton's sex affair with Monica Lewinsky. Furthermore, it was exactly at this point when NATO decided to begin its war in Yugoslavia.[103] The China scandal quickly disappeared from the news.

The construction of the third Temple in Jerusalem

The signs of the imminent 'end of times' were described by Jesus as follows: people misusing his name, threats of war and ongoing wars 'near and far', earthquakes and floods, people throughout the world dying of hunger, new diseases, and people falling into materialism or fanaticism. And he mentions that the Jewish people will be living in Israel again, and that the temple will be reconstructed.

Of all the points mentioned above, the one listed last is the most obscure. Jesus predicted that the Temple of Jerusalem would be razed to the ground within the life-span of the generation of his time. And so it was: In the year AD 70, the Romans conquered Jerusalem and destroyed the Temple as a punitive action against the long-standing local rebellion. Thus, two prophecies came true simultaneously: the destruction of the Temple and the dispersion of the Jews, called Diaspora.

> Yahweh will scatter you throughout every people, from one end of the earth to the other; [...] Among these nations there will be no repose to you. [...] Yahweh will bring you back in ships to Egypt. [...] And there you shall offer yourselves for sale to your enemies as serving men and women, but no one will buy you. (Deut. 28.64–8)

The Romans committed an enormous massacre in Jerusalem, and the inhabitants that survived were shipped to Egypt to be sold as slaves – so many that the supply of slaves came to exceed its demand, just as Moses had prophesied one thousand years before.

> Many days will pass before you [the inimical power named Gog] are given orders; in the final years you will march on this country, whose inhabitants will have been living in confidence, remote from other peoples, since they escaped the sword and were gathered in from various nations, here in the mountains of Israel, which had long lain waste. (Ezek. 38.8)

This prophecy states that in 'the final years', a military campaign against Israel will take place, that is, when the Jewish people, who had been dispersed, will have returned to Israel. For the people of Ezekiel's time (sixth century BC), it was inconceivable to imagine that they would once be dispersed all over the world, to say nothing of the need for 'escaping the sword' and a later 'gathering in from various nations'.

It was not until the twentieth century that the Jewish people could finally return to the land of their forefathers. On 15 May 1948, the new State of Israel was proclaimed. In 1998, Israel celebrated its fiftieth anniversary. The young generation of 1948 is today's old generation. 'In truth I tell you, before this generation has passed away, all these things will have taken place.' (Matt. 24.34)

After stating that the destruction of the then new Temple was near, Jesus predicted that – in the end time – the Jews would again have gathered in Israel with the Temple being rebuilt (Matt. 24.15).

In the Revelation, too, it is mentioned that during the time of Tribulation the Temple of Jerusalem will exist again (Rev. 11.1–2).

Today, the Temple Mount of Jerusalem is a major holy place of

Islam, and a large mosque stands on the site of the ancient Temple. Should indeed a third temple be constructed, then it will be accompanied by evil omens, and it will not stand for long, if the predictions of the Apocalypse hold true. An earthquake unprecedented in its impact (Rev. 16.17–19) will devastate the entire region.

Construction plans for a new temple do exist. After the end of the Six-Day War in 1967, the well-known Jewish historian Israel Eldad announced in an interview: 'When the Jewish people took over Jerusalem the first time, under King David, only one generation passed before they built the Temple, and so shall it be with us!'[104]

According to the Old Testament (Num. 19.2), part of the inaugural ceremony of the Temple is a red cow that is to be slaughtered for this special occasion. For outsiders, this detail may appear irrelevant; for those inside, it is indispensable.

> And yet the construction of a third Temple is essential to the view that many Orthodox Jews have of salvation and the coming of the Messiah. Without the Temple, there is no way to fulfill many of the religious obligations, such as ritual sacrifices that the Torah requires. In Orthodox theology, that means that all Jews are stuck in a state of impurity, and are therefore unable to be in the presence of God. [...] According to the rabbis, the only way that Jews could become pure again was by being sprinkled with the ashes of a red heifer that has been mixed with water traditionally drawn from the pool of Siloam. According to the Mishnah, the written version of the oral tradition, the ceremony of the red heifer sacrifice has only been performed nine times in the history of the Jewish people. When the tenth heifer appears, the Messiah will finally come.[105]

This was reported in July 1998 when five hundred pregnant cows of the Red Angus breed were to be delivered from Nebraska to the Jordan Valley – a clear sign that the search for a red heifer was being intensified.

Some Christians, as Lawrence Wright points out, are also very interested in matters concerning a third Temple construction, in particular Bible fundamentalists: 'Christians have also helped to fund some of the radical Temple activists [...]. In Christian theology, the holiness of the Temple was supposed to have been replaced by the divinity of Christ. [...] When Jews speak of their Messiah, Evangelicals interpret that to mean the false Messiah, or the Antichrist. It is the Antichrist, Evangelicals believe, who will occupy the Third Temple.'

In 1999, Randall Price, Professor for Old Testament Studies and

Semitic Languages, published a voluminous book (736 pages) entitled *The Latest Developments in Bible Prophecy – The Coming Last Days Temple*. On the back cover, we are informed:

> Right now in Israel, plans are well underway to construct a new Temple. From drawing up the blueprints to detailing the furnishings to preparing for the new priesthood, much is being done for what could be the most significant building effort of our time.

Will this temple be the epitome of final peace on earth or the cause of an escalating war? The construction of the new Temple inevitably entails the destruction of the two sanctuaries of Islam situated on the Temple Mount for more than one thousand years. These in turn were built on the ruins of a Christian basilica, which the Arabian conquerors had destroyed in the eighth century.

Prof. Price states in his book (p. 175): 'It was not until AD 1187 – when the Crusaders were finally dislodged by Saladin – that Jerusalem was said to be the third holiest place in Islam (after Mecca and Medina). In fact, in AD 1225 the Arab geographer Yakut wrote that the city of Jerusalem was holy to Jews and Christians, as it had been for 3,000 and 2,000 years respectively, but in contrast noted that only Mecca was holy to the Muslims. [...] By contrast, the Temple Mount is the one and only holy place in Judaism, and is backed by at least 3,000 years of recorded history. Despite the fact that Islam has dominated the Temple Mount for 1,300 years, Jews have continued to direct their daily prayers toward it and to look forward to the day when the Temple could be rebuilt.'

Finding a solution to the dilemma of three religions claiming rights to the same place is not easy. Apparently, none of them is ready for a compromise.

The crucial element of the scenario

The fact that the Revelation contains so many relevant points that have come true should invite even sceptical minds to take a closer look at its further contents.

The crucial element of the apocalyptic scenario is the one which is described to wind up the end time, initiating the emergence of a 'new earth' and a 'new heaven'. This element should not be withheld even though it may be against modern convictions: it is the visible return of Jesus. What does that mean?

Right at the beginning of his report, St John highlights the culmination of his visions: 'Look, he is coming on/with the clouds; everyone will see him, even those who pierced him.' (Rev. 1.7)

According to the prophecies made by Jesus himself (Matt. 24.30; 25.31; 26.64; Mark 13.26; 14.62; Luke 21.27; John 8.23), by the prophets (Dan. 7.13–14), and by the Apostles (Phil. 3.20; 1 Thess. 4.16–17; 2 Thess. 1.6–7; 2 Pet. 3.10), the return of Jesus Christ 'in/on/with the clouds' will be visible to all!

'And then the sign of the Son of man will appear in heaven, and then all the peoples of the earth will beat their breasts; and they will see the Son of man coming on the clouds of heaven with power and great glory. And he will send his angels with a loud trumpet call [the seventh and last trumpet] to gather his elect from the four winds, from one end of heaven to the other.' (Matt. 24.30–1)

Almost identical statements are found in the Gospel according to Mark (13.24–7) and in the Gospel according to Luke: '... men fainting away with terror and fear at what is coming upon the world, for the powers of the heavens will be shaken. And then they will see the Son of man coming in a cloud with power and great glory. When these things begin to take place, stand up and raise your heads, because your liberation is near at hand.' (Luke 21.26–8)

For the Apostles, the prophesied end of times was an indisputable reality. And they were deeply convinced that, with the end of times, Jesus would return, as expressed many times in their Epistles:

> For God's justice will surely mean hardship being inflicted on those who are now inflicting hardship on you; but you who are now suffering hardship, will be liberated together with us, when Jesus our Lord appears from heaven with his mighty angels in flaming fire. (2 Thess. 1.6–7)

> About the coming of our Lord Jesus Christ, and our being gathered together to him: we beg you, brothers and sisters, do not be easily thrown into confusion or alarmed by any manifestation of the spirit or any statement or any letter claiming to come from us, suggesting that the Day of the Lord has already arrived. [First many other things will come to pass ...] Let no one deceive you in any way; for that day will not come until the Great Revolt has taken place and there has appeared the wicked one, the bringer of destruction. He is the adversary [i.e. the beast described in the Apocalypse] and will take his seat in God's sanctuary, declaring himself to be God. (2 Thess. 2.1–4)

At the time when Paul wrote this epistle, the Apocalypse had not yet been revealed to John. Nevertheless, both predictions are quite identical, especially regarding the appearance of the 'adversary' and the help granted by the divine hosts of heaven.

God's seal, the new song and the everlasting gospel

'All this is but the beginning of the birth pangs' (Matt. 24.8). 'And with the increase of iniquity, the love of many will grow cold; but anyone who stands firm till the end will be saved. And this good news of the kingdom will be proclaimed to the whole world as testimony to all the nations. And then the end will come.' (Matt. 24.12–14)

This quotation briefly summarizes the succession of events during the end of the present civilization. When the first prophesied signs begin to manifest – with the first seals being opened and the first trumpets being sounded – the 'end of times' will not yet have come, as it is only the 'beginning of the birth pangs'. The end of civilization will be brought about by the appearance of the beast.

Before this big incision, however, God's message will be spread throughout the world. At the same time, all religions will compete, believing their message to be the only true one. But they are all deluded, as further details of the prophecy reveal. Coming from the East, an angel appears (Rev. 7.2–3):

> And I saw another angel ascending from the rising sun, having the seal of the living God, and he called in a powerful voice to the four angels who had been given power to shake up earth and sea, saying: 'Wait before you do any damage on the land or at sea or to the trees, until we have put the seal on the foreheads of the servants of our God.'

Those marked with the sign of protection are symbolically numbered at 144,000. After envisioning this first group, John sees yet another, much larger group, 'a great multitude that no one could count, from every nation, from all peoples and races and languages, standing before the throne and before the Lamb, robed in white' (Rev. 7.9). 'They all had his name and his Father's name written on their foreheads' (14.1). In front of the throne, they sing a song that nobody knows except those who sing it themselves. At that time, another angel appears, 'flying high in heaven, sent to announce the gospel of eternity to all who live on the earth, every nation, race, language and tribe'. (Rev. 14.6)

It has to be noted that the people of God will consist of God-devoted individuals of *all* nations, peoples and tribes. This also means: of all religions! The common denominator is their heart-felt commitment to God, which is not confined to any religious confession.

The 'good news of the kingdom which will be proclaimed to the whole world' is the same as the 'gospel of eternity'. Obviously, it cannot be just the Bible or another holy text of any existing religion. The gospel of eternity is described to be new to this world. It is beyond written texts and dogmas. It is the essence of religion that every individual receives in his/her heart, inspired by 'the angel high in heaven'.

The prophets have made it clear that the meaning of these visions will remain concealed until the 'end of times' has come. Only then will everything be revealed, seal by seal. All religious traditions will be given fresh and liberating impulses, which are symbolically represented by the Apocalyptic angels who offer God's seal, the new song and the gospel of eternity to mankind. Another important indication is the 'Lamb', which will be the centre of the gathering of God's people during this time of transformation.

In other words, it is not a new cult or religion but a *new consciousness* manifested by all receptive people independent of their nationality, race and creed. It is this universal truth which will enhance a new spirituality and a new understanding of God and one's true self, leading people to a heart-felt form of prayer, meditation and togetherness.

Summary and outlook:
Prophecies and the individual's free will

Are prophecies an infringement upon people's free will? Do they state inevitable facts? If so, what would be the role of our free will? Is it possible to change this global scenario?

First of all, no prophecy in itself states a fact. Prophecies are insights into probable scenarios of the future. Whether a particular scenario becomes reality depends on the direction of people's consciousness. The present and future generations are given the opportunity to hear these warnings and to react accordingly, using their free will. If the course is changed, then prophesied blows of destiny can be staved off. Nothing in the future is absolutely fixed or inevitable. But if people fail to correct the course of their destiny, then at one point the avoidable becomes unavoidable.

Therefore, the crucial question is: How will people use their free will? Will the collective mass change its course and see through the imposed manipulation? Will it benefit from the knowledge that is provided? This, again, is predictable! For this reason it is not only possible but probable that some prophecies will come true. In divine prophecy, possibility and probability come together as a true insight into the future, and every individual is free to choose what and whom to believe. Even if the general course of events is not changed, we still have the full freedom to choose our *individual* quality of life (regardless of the external circumstances). The apocalyptic scenario does not say *who* will be deceived, only that *many* will be. So it is up to us to choose our destiny. This individual decision is not predestined at all, even if the external situation may take on the form foreseen in the Apocalypse.

Every change starts with pioneering individuals believing in the vision of the new Earth that will come about through people unfolding their natural, inherent God consciousness. 'Coming from the East an angel appears [...] bringing the gospel of eternity to all who live on the earth' (Rev. 7.2; 14.6) – inspiration is always there, may it come from the East (Asia? Russia?), from divine revelations, or from signs in heaven and on earth. Even warnings and catastrophes can have a positive effect, the effect of shaking people out of indifference, routine and stress. This perspective, too, is part of many prophecies.

CHAPTER TEN

Divine Protection and Intervention

One of the main contents of ancient and contemporary prophecy is the announcement of a decisive turning point in history, unparalleled in its impact, when man will be confronted with occurrences that will exceed all experiences of his former 'normal' daily life. This refers to occurrences of a *destructive nature* (natural catastrophes and actions by inhuman forces) as well as to occurrences of a positive, *transformative nature:* divine inspiration and protection, even miraculous rescuing actions 'from above'.

The world order based on the 666 dictatorship will not last long, if it can be established at all. Prophet Daniel said about the ten-horned beast: 'He will speak words against the Most High, and he will persecute the holy ones, those who believe in God. He will intend to change the holy days and the law, and the people of God will be exposed to him for a time, two times and half a time. Then the court will sit in judgement, and he will be stripped of his royal authority, which will be finally destroyed and reduced to nothing.' (Dan. 7.25–6)

Those who live in true God consciousness will stay firm and remain fearless. The forces of the dragon are allowed 'to attack only those who are without God's seal on their foreheads' (Rev. 9.4). *God's seal* shines on the foreheads of all those who understand the divine signs, and is not to be confused with the mark of the beast. The latter is only a lifeless and godless imitation, materialized through an artificial system of technology.

Throughout the times of Tribulation, we will witness *divine* signs never seen before, at least not within the known history of mankind. In these situations of extreme suffering and danger, celestial help will be offered to all those who reach for it: 'And they will see the Son of man coming on the clouds of heaven with power and great glory. And he will send his angels with a loud trumpet to gather his elect from the four winds, from one end of heaven to the other. [...] This is what it will be like when the Son of man comes. Then of two men in the field, one is taken, one left; of two women working at the mill, one is taken, one is left.' (Matt. 24.30–1, 39–41)

Thus goes the description of the divine intervention that is said to be unparalleled in the history of the world and of all nations (Dan. 12.1, Matt. 24.21).

What does 'chosen' mean?

'But shortened that time shall be, for the sake of those who are chosen. [...] And he will send his angels with a loud trumpet to gather his elect ...' (Matt. 24.22, 31)

These statements indicate that there are ways to liberation and ways limited to duality, and it is up to us to choose which way we want to go. This is our free will, and our responsibility as well. Those choosing a way to liberation are naturally on the road of the chosen ones. In other words, there *are* chosen people, but it is not God who decides who is chosen; we ourselves decide. The chosen ones are those who choose to select themselves by being truly divine: 'Love God the Omni-Present with all thy heart and soul, and thus love all creation as you love yourself.' This is the essence of Christ's teaching, which is the essence of all religions.

To belong to the 'elect' has yet an additional meaning. Ascension to a higher level of material existence is not the final goal in life. The final goal is the attainment of unity in love with God, the absolute Individuality. In some traditions, this is called the 'return to God' or 'the attainment of God's kingdom'. Now, in the end time, God-conscious men and women have different tasks and vocations. Some of them have the task of physically accompanying the earth during her ascension, and they will experience their own physical transformation alongside with that of the earth. Those having this particular task are chosen for the path of ascension. Other God-conscious individuals will not necessarily go through a physical transformation, having other vocations. They are not chosen *for ascension* but still, they are chosen in the absolute sense. Some of them may simply die and leave the material world once and for all, as they all belong to those who are gathered 'from the four winds, from one end of heaven to the other'.

Protection by ascension

With the sounding of the seventh trumpet, hosts of angels will be sent out in all directions to gather 'the elect'. This corresponds to the description of the men working in the fields and the women working at the mill, some of whom will be accepted (or 'taken') and some not. These two examples indicate that both men and women will be saved alike, an important detail which Jesus especially emphasized, because in the patriarchal society of those days, this was not a matter of course.

The 'gathering of his elect from the four winds, from one end of heaven to the other' – this occurrence is said to be unparalleled in history. Due to a total lack of comparable experiences, Bible interpreters have great difficulties in understanding this passage. The usual explanation says that the phenomenon of 'ascension' is a moral or theological allegory for the Day of Judgement, when it will be decided who may pass before God and who not.

However, a closer study of these passages shows that the occurrence described has nothing to do with the Day of Judgement. It is not an allegory for the hereafter. Rather, it is a phase during the time of the earthly Tribulation when many warnings are given, which most people will tend to ignore. Then, at some point, certain men and women are said to be 'taken' or to be 'gathered by the angels'. This passage does not describe a judgement, it describes an unprecedented *act of protection!* It indicates a kind of ascension.

In Rev. 13.6, it is stated that these people will 'dwell in heaven' and that the dictator will not have the power to harm them. The only thing he will be able to do is deride and blaspheme them.

The scenario of ascension is not meant to induce people to passively await 'help from above'. Quite the contrary: Considering the whole apocalyptic situation, we see that it demands detachment from all material and confessional bindings, perseverance and fearless self-responsibility.

The gateway to transformation

With the onset of the dark age, mankind has sunk deeply into condensed matter and limited consciousness. Time, however, is cyclic, and space, being intrinsically connected to time, is subject to cyclic changes, too. Therefore, the earth is not static and will not remain in a state of stagnating material condensation. Soon, it will transform itself to a higher level of material vibration again. This will also change the individual experience of death, as *physical* death is only a part of the three-dimensional world.

Most entities of the higher-dimensional worlds do not undergo physical death. They do not have to leave their bodies and reincarnate in another body while forgetting their previous existence. For them, death means a conscious transformation of physical existence. In the Sanskrit language, they are therefore called *amara*: immortal.

Only an incarnate being from a higher, or the highest, dimension is able to initiate a physical transformation of earth and mankind. This was one of the reasons why the 'first-born' son of God came down into this world. The indication that it was him who appeared as the Redeemer shows that we are not just dealing with a minor sub-cycle, but with a most extraordinary turning point in history that has been prepared for the last two thousand years.

With the gateway now open, many people will be able to accomplish their ascension. This was Jesus' cryptic message when he said that he would leave the earth to prepare a place for the 'elect', and that he would return to take them to him:

> Do not let your hearts be troubled. You trust in God, trust also in me. In my Father's house there are many mansions. Otherwise I would not have told you that I go to prepare a place for you; and after I have gone and prepared you a place, I shall return to take you to myself, so that you may be with me where I am. (John 14.1–3)

While most people of today lack any practical and comparable experience, those who were privileged to personally witness the mystery of Jesus, got a glimpse of what he meant:

> After his suffering he presented himself alive to them by many convincing proofs, appearing to them during forty days and speaking about the kingdom of God. [...] They asked him, 'Lord, is this the time when you will restore the

kingdom to Israel?' He replied, 'It is not for you to know the times or the periods that the Father has set by his own authority. But you will receive power when the Holy Spirit has come upon you; and you will be my witnesses in Jerusalem, in all Judaea and Samaria, and to the ends of the earth.'

When he said this, as they were watching, he was lifted up, and *a cloud took him out of their sight*. While he was going and they were gazing up towards heaven, suddenly two men in white robes stood by them. They said: 'Men of Galilee, why do you stand here looking up towards heaven? This Jesus, who has been *taken up* from you into heaven, will come back in *the same way as you saw him go into heaven*.' (Acts 1.3–11)

After the crucifixion, Jesus appeared to various individuals and groups of followers, manifesting himself in a half-physical body, sometimes even passing through walls. After forty days, he vanished in a Light body through ascension. Ten days after the ascension, on Whitsunday, the mystical empowerment of his followers took place.

Did these things really happen? If they were only fictitious accounts of some later scribes, then it would be difficult to explain the sudden commitment and fearlessness of Jesus' followers. Throughout the time of their personal association with Jesus (and Mary Magdalene!), they had often succumbed to doubting, and when he was crucified, they fearfully hid away behind closed doors. But it is a fact that, all of a sudden, these same men were fully convinced and prepared to go out into the world. This miraculous change *after* the crucifixion was certainly not caused by mere nostalgic 'memories of the past'.

Regarding the inner conflicts tormenting the followers of Jesus, who were torn between believing and rejecting him, there is a very telling passage in John 6.60–2. Some followers of Jesus, upon witnessing his revolutionary words and deeds, had become bewildered and upset: 'What he says is too much! Who can listen to such a speech?' And Jesus answered them: 'Does this alone disturb you? What, then, will you say when you see the Son of man ascend to where he was before?'

Developing a Light body

Jesus, in his transfigured body, also appeared to Saul, who was to become known as the Apostle Paul. Repenting his former actions against the followers of Jesus, Paul became a fervent believer himself, and a witness of the promised transformation.

Through inner revelations, Paul was able to perceive the cosmic identity of Jesus as the first-born son of God, the primeval being of the universe – in Sanskrit called *Brahma* – who had incarnated* as the 'Son of man'. Therefore, he also understood the higher purpose of why Jesus had appeared on earth, namely to initiate the ascension of mankind and to lead it back into a deathless (*amara*) state of Light existence. Paul had never met Jesus in person, which had the advantage that he did not limit Jesus to his external activities as the 'son of Mary'. Seeing the spiritual background of these historic events, Paul enthusiastically and zealously emphasized the higher identity of 'our Lord Jesus Christ'.

For this reason, it is not surprising that the present-day propaganda which disparages Jesus, also defames Paul with vehemence.

Admittedly, Paul as presented in the Bible is a very controversial figure. Did he impose an erroneous interpretation upon the historical Jesus? Did he found a Church that Jesus did not want? (Some critics even call Christianity 'Paulinism'.) Or was Paul different from the figure presented by the Church? Was the name of 'St Paul' misused by those who wanted to claim a monopoly on Jesus? History indicates that this is exactly what happened.[106]

Contrary to sectarian dogmas, the Gospels, the Revelation and also Paul maintain that all human beings who love God and God's creation like themselves are qualified to receive God's mercy; they are the true (= universal) followers of Jesus. And, in the end times, they will be the 'elect' and the ones chosen to ascend.

> But our homeland is in heaven, and it is from there that we are expecting a Saviour, the Lord Jesus Christ, who will transfigure the wretched body of ours into the mould of his glorious body [like his body of ascension], through the working of the power which he has, even to bring all things [including our mortal bodies and planet earth] under his mastery.

This was written by the Apostles Paul and Timothy in their Epistle to the Philippians (3.20–1). The phenomenon that nowadays – with the dawning of the new age – is known as the 'spiritualization of matter'

---

* The words 'to incarnate' and 'incarnation' are derived from the Latin word *carnis*, 'flesh' (*in carne:* 'into the flesh'). The biblical statement about the original *logos* 'having become flesh' (John 1.14) indicates that the highest Light being ('he who was with God from the very beginning, he through him everything was created', John 1.2–3) took on a physical body. See also endnote 43.

and the 'elevation to the fifth dimension', was initiated by Jesus, the first who overcame the physical bondage of this age. The transformation of matter will ultimately result in both heaven and earth radiating in new glory: 'Then I saw a new heaven and a new earth; the first heaven and the first earth had disappeared ...' (Rev. 21.1)

It is important to note what these quotes actually say: our condensed and transient ('wretched') body will undergo a physical transformation so that it will become as 'glorious' as the body of Jesus when he rose from the dead. The ascension of Jesus was something unprecedented, but not unique. It was something that happened *for the first time* (at least in our present age, the Kali-yuga). It opened the way for the future transformation of all those who would choose to be chosen. At the given time, Jesus – as the cosmic Christ – will intervene together with his angels in order to effect our own ascension. 'And look, I am with you always, till the end of time.' (Matt. 28.20)

In his Epistles, Paul mentions apocalyptic elements (the trumpets of God, the Archangel) that John, in his visions, got to see about forty years later. For example, in 1 Cor. 15.51 he writes:

> Listen, I will tell you a mystery: we are not all going to pass away asleep, but we are all going to be changed, instantly, in the twinkling of an eye, when the last trumpet sounds.

In the Epistle to the Thessalonians, further details are depicted:

> At the signal given by the voice of the Archangel and the trumpet of God, the Lord himself will come down from heaven; those who have died in Christ will be the first to rise, and only after that shall we who remain alive be *taken up in the clouds,* together with them, to meet the Lord *in the air.* This is the way we shall be with the Lord for ever. (1 Thess. 4.16–17)

Statements such as 'being taken up in the clouds' and 'meeting the Lord in the air' reveal that the ascension is not merely a symbolical act. Rather, they indicate something very physical, as shown in the next chapter of this book. The ascension is not symbolical, but the word 'cloud' certainly is. Or did they use it only as a meteorological term? A 'cloud' was also instrumental in the ascension of Jesus: 'And they witnessed how he was taken up by a cloud, so that they no longer could see him.'

Something similar is said about the two invulnerable witnesses mentioned in the Revelation. After the first half of the end time, God allows them to be killed by the beast, but only for the purpose of revealing the most incredible of all miracles before the eyes of the whole world: they, too, will experience resurrection and ascension! 'Then they heard a loud voice from heaven say to them, "Come up here", and while their enemies were watching, they went up to heaven in a cloud' (Rev. 11.12). Again, a 'cloud'! Apparently, ascension is always connected with the presence of some 'cloud'.

From the biblical context we can conclude that the ascension of the two witnesses coincides with the ascension of a vast number of people all over the world, because shortly after this incident the beast will come forward to enforce his world domination. At the same time, he will blaspheme those who 'are sheltered' in heaven.

'Sheltered in heaven'

'The beast was allowed to mouth his boasts and blasphemies and to be active for forty-two months; and he mouthed his blasphemies against God, against his name, his heavenly Tent and all those who are sheltered there.' (Rev. 13.5–6)

Why does the dictator bother about those sheltered in heaven? Why does he mention them at all? He and his Union are busy establishing a global dictatorship. For them, God and God's kingdom are irrelevant and fictitious. Nonetheless it is stated that the beast will mainly speak about God and, in this connection, about those dwelling in heaven!

According to the two most frequent interpretations of this passage, those dwelling in heaven are (1) *people who have faith in God*, as their minds are already focussed on the celestial plane, or (2) *the angels in heaven*, for it was them who had checked the dragon's influence.

However, both interpretations fall short of the actual description given in the text. Regarding the first interpretation, the dictator will not *speak about* those who have faith in God, he will *persecute* them as stated right in the following sentence (13.7): 'He was allowed to make war against the saints and conquer them, and given power over every race, people, language and nation.'

Regarding the second interpretation: why should the dictator care about blaspheming the angels in heaven? If he at all knows that his patron, the dragon, has been defeated by the Archangel Michael and his hosts, he will certainly avoid this embarrassing topic and suppress it with all means. And still, it is said that he will mainly talk about God and those sheltered in heaven! Why? Because he is *forced* to! Those who are 'sheltered in heaven' obviously figure as something spectacular. Have many people become elevated and physically transformed – all of a sudden, instantly, in the twinkling of an eye, with the sounding of the last trumpet indicating the beginning of the second half of Tribulation?

With the whole world speaking about those sheltered in heaven, the dictator has to react. He will do so by defaming them and by lying. He cannot admit, 'The long-promised ascension has now come to pass; I am the predicted beast and will be destroyed in three years.' Rather, he will call the New Testament a mere collection of falsified propaganda writings of early Christianity. And he will come up with a heinous lie in order to explain what has happened. For example, he might say these people have committed mass suicide, driven by apocalyptic hysteria. Using the methods shown in the film *Wag the Dog*, he could 'document' this breaking news with images of burnt 'suicide corpses' – produced with little effort in some film studio. And he could say that this 'mass suicide' has been religiously motivated: 'Therefore, from now on, all terror-breeding forms of religion will be strictly prohibited.'

Today, most people tend to ignore such warnings. If they happen to hear about them, they react cynically or even aggressively, not realizing that they are fulfilling *yet another prophecy* with their very reaction:

> First of all, do not forget that in the final days there will come sarcastic scoffers whose life is ruled by their passions. 'What has happened to the promise of his coming?' they will say, 'Since our father died everything has gone on just as it has since the beginning of creation!' [...] But there is one thing, my dear friends, that you must never forget: that with the Lord, a day is like a thousand years, and a thousand years are like a day. The Lord is not being slow in carrying out his promises, as some people think he is; rather is he being patient with you, wanting nobody to be lost and everybody to be brought to repentance. The Day of the Lord will come like a thief, and then the heavens will pass away with a loud noise, and the elements will be dissolved with fire, and the earth and all that it contains will be burned up. (2 Peter 3.3–4, 8–11)

According to the Revelation (6.9; 7.14; 11.11), those who are chosen to ascend are individuals who, in earlier times, have stood up for the word of God and given their lives in His name. In the run-up to the end time, these souls again reincarnate on earth so as to be present in this difficult time, inspiring and encouraging all those who do not want to be deceived by the 'Big Brother'. By their ascension, these former martyrs will be spared from renewed persecution and murder.

How can we avoid being 666-marked?

'Take care that no one deceives you. [...] Anyone who stands firm to the end will be saved.'[107]

If the prophesied Tribulation actually comes to pass, there will be global chaos causing wide-spread, total bewilderment – as people will be confronted with overwhelming things happening all at once: natural catastrophes, economic collapses, unknown diseases, and wars, along with mysterious phenomena appearing in the sky and on earth, shattering all 'normal' world-views.

In this scene, the Revelation says, a dictator will appear, posing to be the world's saviour and the bringer of peace. In response to the general yearning for someone to come and 'clean up the mess', he will establish his own new world order based on a technomagical, godless tyranny. At one point, everybody will be called upon to surrender to the dragon by accepting the mark of the beast, the code of its name.

We do not know whether this will factually happen. However, if it *does* happen, the crucial question is: How can we avoid being marked with the code 666?

First of all, we have to be aware that we should not accept it. At the present moment, this may appear to be a matter of course. The marking would constitute a total infringement on privacy. It would mean giving away one's power and freedom. From the spiritual point of view, it would be a surrender to fear, even a selling of one's soul, leading to an astral ('hellish') imprisonment after death. And Satan's seal, as the Bible calls it, will soon cause a painful death (Rev. 14.9–12; 15.2; 16.2; 19.20).

However, if things get worse, then many might be intimidated into accepting the new system, thinking it to be the last step required for attaining personal safety, economic stability and a terror-free society. Those who refuse to accept it will be threatened with harsh punishment. Obviously, it will be an imposed procedure, and that is always an alarming symptom. Would a true helper act like that?

The marking of the people will occur at the beginning of the second half of Tribulation. By then, according to this scenario, the breaking of the seven seals and the blowing of the seven trumpets will already be a thing of the (recent) past. It will be a chaotic time: More than half of mankind will have died in wars and catastrophes; even the controversial phenomenon of 'ascension' will have taken place. Therefore, the agents of the newly established world government will no longer know who is still alive and who not. Only in such a situation will the marking of each individual become compulsory. But let us not forget: The prophecy only says that, without the mark, one will be unable 'to buy or sell'. It does not say that one will not be able to survive.

Those 'chosen ones' who are still present at this time will simply not step forward. Thus, they will be factually 'dead' (non-existent) for the system. In any case, they will not let themselves be marked with the 666. With divine guidance, they will be able to survive this short 'end time'. It is not a question of hiding away for decades.

The earth herself will be at the edge of her big quantum leap. In this connection, we are assured that the 'paranormal' potential of each receptive person will be activated more and more, as we are heading towards a personal quantum leap, too. If required, we will even be able to live on light and *prana* (cosmic life energy), and then, we will no longer need to buy or sell anything. Of course, it takes a physical and mental transformation, but we are not alone in this process. We are supported by higher-dimensional Light beings (the guardian angels), who can be instrumental in many ways.

When the new regime enforces the marking of all people, many who had been in doubt, or 'too busy', will suddenly understand what is going on. These newly awakened people will not be left in the lurch either. Even if a wave of ascension is to happen, there will be some who remain in this chaos and hell to continue serving as emissaries of the Light. They will exemplify fearlessness and faith in God, knowing well that divine protection is always present (see, for example, how the Apostle Peter was freed from prison by an angel, Acts 12.7–11, 18–19).

The protection promised for the time 'before all this happens' will become even more intense during the culmination of the end time.

> But before all this happens, you will be seized and persecuted; you will be handed over to the synagogues and to imprisonment, and brought before kings and governors because of my name – and that will be your opportunity

to bear witness. Therefore settle in your hearts not to worry about your defence, for I myself shall give you an eloquence and wisdom that none of your opponents will be able to refute or contradict. You will be denounced even by parents and brothers, relatives and friends; and some of you will be put to death. You will be hated by all because of my name. And yet not a hair of your head will be harmed.* Your perseverance will win you your true lives. (Luke 21.12–19)

These words of Jesus referring to the time before the 'end' apply even more so to the time comprising the second '1260 days'. In this phase, all God-conscious people who are still present will be blessed with expanded abilities, as they are in resonance with the ascending earth. They will have a telepathic connection to the invisible Light worlds and Light beings as well as to the 'first-born Son of God', the highest Light being: 'I myself shall give you an eloquence and wisdom.' In other words, they (we?) will be guided and protected by divine inspiration, which might even include a physical transformation.

Examples of former ascensions and evacuations

The indication of a physical ascension or 'evacuation' as found in the Bible is unique in its way, but it is not an exclusively biblical phenomenon. Similar occurrences have already come to pass in former times on a local scale, as reported by the mythological history of other cultures: accounts of God-conscious individuals or groups of people being rescued from a great danger by simply disappearing to another location (through a paranormal ability or some extraterrestrial intervention). This adds another realistic aspect to the enigmatic Bible words about being 'taken up in the clouds, to meet the Lord in the air'.

The ascension, though being 'mystical', is a (meta)physical effect and therefore has a (meta)physical cause. In practical terms, ascension means physically entering into a higher dimension or level of existence.

---

* 'Some will be put to death': some of the newly awakened might die as martyrs. 'Others will not have one hair harmed on their heads': This refers in particular to those who, even though being qualified for ascension, will stay on earth in fulfilment of their vocation. These last ones will be the first ones to populate the new Earth.

Divine Protection and Intervention 287

In science fiction, this is known as de-materialization, teleportation or 'beaming up'. In the Bible, it is described as an effect caused by angels. Another physical aspect often associated with ascensions and revelations is the phenomenon of the 'cloud'. The Old Testament contains detailed descriptions of such extraordinary occurrences, indicating some high-tech and/or metaphysical presence. One example is the 'close encounter' experienced by the prophet Ezekiel:

> I looked; a stormy wind blew from the north, *a great cloud* with flashing fire and brilliant light around it, and in the middle, in the heart of the fire, a brilliance like that of amber, and in the middle what seemed to be *four living creatures*. [...] Now, as I looked at the living creatures, I saw a wheel touching the ground beside each of the four-faced living creatures. [...] Over the heads of the living creatures was what looked like *a solid surface* glittering like crystal. [...] The spirit *lifted me up,* and behind me I heard a great vibrating sound, 'Blessed be the glory of Yahweh in his dwelling-place!' This was the sound of the living creatures' wings beating against each other, and the sound of the wheels beside them: a great vibrating sound. The spirit *lifted me up and took me* [...]' (Ezek. 1.4, 15, 22; 3.12–14)

This unusually detailed description as given by Ezekiel was minutely analysed by Josef Blumrich (1913–2002), a renowned NASA engineer and colleague of Wernher von Braun. He had read about the technical interpretation of Ezekiel's account in Erich von Däniken's first book, *Chariots of the Gods* (1969), and initially intended to refute this 'nonsense'. However, upon closer examination, Blumrich had to admit the plausibility of the technical interpretation – and reconstructed a flying machine by strictly following the biblical description! He even made several inventions based on Ezekiel's report, and had them patented. In 1972 he published a daring book in his own name, presenting practical evidence of Ezekiel having had an 'encounter with an extraterrestrial intelligence'.[108]

One of the most impressive accounts of an evacuation comes from the Hopis, a native American tribe with an oral tradition reaching far back into the past. They describe the different ages as 'worlds', and they still remember how they entered the 'third world' approximately 800,000 years ago. It is interesting to note that this date is identical to the Vedic dating of the *yugas*. Presently, we are living in the fourth *yuga*, the Kali-yuga. The previous, third *yuga* – just like the 'third world' of the Hopis – began about 800,000 years ago.

During the time of the 'third world', the Hopis relate, their ancestors lived on a continent situated in the west of the present Americas. In these lands, known as Kásskara in their language, they lived in harmony with all of creation for hundreds of thousands of years, and they had open contact with divine beings, whom they called *Kachinas*.

About 100,000 years ago, Kásskara began to sink gradually. When it became necessary to evacuate the land, the Kachinas told the people of Kásskara that new land was rising amidst the Eastern Sea. With the help of their flying shields, the Kachinas brought the first groups of pioneers to this new land. Up to the present day, the Hopis remember and venerate these angelic helpers who had once taken them 'up into the air'.

> During the period of the third world and actually since the beginning of the first world, we have always been in contact with the Kachinas. Kachina means 'high-esteemed knowers'. [...] Kachinas can appear visible to the eye, but sometimes they also remain invisible. They come to us from outer space. They are not from our own planetary system but from other, more distant planets. [...] Being space travellers, the Kachinas knew where the new land was, and thus they brought them [the first groups from Kásskara] there. Only the Kachinas were able to do this because they possessed flying shields, contrary to our people. We were not able to construct them. But the people of Atlantis possessed flying shields. They had not obtained them from the Kachinas, who had deserted them. Rather, the Atlanteans themselves had constructed them with their evil powers [...][109]

This history of the Hopis was only recently written down and published, again by Josef Blumrich (in continuation of his research after the Ezekiel study). The story he got to hear was amazing: In a previous age, groups of people were evacuated from a sinking continent by extraterrestrial beings who possessed 'flying shields'! These beings, the Kachinas, also built the first living facilities on the new land, the present-day South America. According to this historical tradition, the North and South American continents are not as old as modern geologists believe. (Like the theory of evolution, the continental-drift theory is not proven either, despite all claims of official geology.)

Following the description given by the Hopis, Blumrich was able to identify this ancient Kachina site as the mysterious city known as Tiahuanaco, situated on the shore of Lake Titicaca high up in the Andes. It is connected to the even more mysterious site named Puma Punku, a field full of huge slabs of andesite (harder than granite) weighing up to

1,000 tons. Today, these slabs are broken, and scattered as ruins, despite consisting of such a hard material. Even the Incas knew Puma Punku only in the form of ruins. Obviously, these slabs are very old, but the way they were worked indicates an extraordinary (extraterrestrial?) technology. They are precisely cut on all sides; some have small edges and grooves that are perfectly straight over a length of up to 20 metres, others have fine, many-levelled geometrical incisions and depressions. If we today wanted to make the same clean cuts in andesite, we would have to use the most advanced stone cutting technology.

A further example of an evacuation is found in the Sanskrit scriptures. In comparison to the Hopi record, this incident did not take place that long ago – 'only' about 3000 BC.[110] It is still well-known in India because it was recorded in several holy books, having been quite spectacular. The circumstances were as follows: There was a powerful king named Jarasandha who made several attempts to conquer the city of Mathura, in which the then young hero Krishna resided. As Krishna succeeded in repelling all of these attacks, the aggressor made an alliance with other kings and recruited a gigantic army consisting of many legions. With this ocean of soldiers, horses, and elephants, they approached Mathura from all sides.

In the original texts, the war of Mathura and its startling outcome are described as follows:

> Hearing that his friend had been defeated several times, the very powerful king Kalayavana became angry. He quickly marched on Mathura to support the king of Magadha [Jarasandha], leading millions of arrogant, very strong and brave warriors. [...] For the welfare of his citizens, Krishna then had a safe shelter appear far away in the ocean: the wonderful city of Dvaraka. (*Padma Purana* 6.246.37–9)

> Krishna saw the entire city besieged by Kalayavana's huge army that filled up the entire horizon on all sides [...] and Jarasandha was to come the next day or the day after. Krishna, therefore, decided to manifest a fortress which no human force could penetrate. It was built within the sea, having a circumference of 12 *yojanas* [about 100 miles]. [...] Lord Indra, the leader of the gods, brought an assembly hall, standing within which a mortal man is not subject to the laws of mortality. [...] And different *loka-palah* (rulers of planets) came to offer similarly wonderful gifts. (*Bhagavata Purana* 10.50.44–55)

When the city of Mathura was surrounded by these blood-thirsty kings, it appeared as if the inhabitants led by Krishna were desperately lost, with no means of escape. At this point, Krishna accomplished a feat that nobody had expected:

> At night [the night before the decisive battle], Krishna suddenly lifted the people that were asleep, and by his divine power carried them to that wonderful city of Dvaraka, situated in the ocean. When the men with their wives and children woke up, they were amazed to find themselves in golden mansions, far away from the enemies. Surrounded by magnificent houses full of wealth, food, garments and ornaments, they felt like the hosts of gods who live in heaven. At the same time, Krishna, the unlimitedly powerful *avatara,* amazed the huge army with his appearance. (*Padma Purana* 6.246.44–6)

Krishna evacuated the city of Mathura by employing spiritual powers, without resorting to 'flying shields'. Still, such flying devices, called *vimanas,* are mentioned in many Sanskrit scriptures. They are said to exist on all levels of the universe, from the dark worlds up to the highest realms. Corresponding to each particular level and dimension, the *vimanas* have their respective quality and nature. Some are products of a lifeless interdimensional technology, others are conscious lightships, and again others are spiritual energy fields used as a means of transmaterial trans-portation, as indicated in the following quote:

> From one moment to the next, Krishna left his earthly surroundings, and, together with his children and wives, rose up in a splendid *vimana* and returned to the spiritual world. (*Padma Purana* 7.16.2–3)

Apparently, the terms 'ascension' and 'evacuation' can refer to various forms of interdimensional intervention. Not all noisy flying objects ('clouds') are of a dark origin, and not all noiseless ones of a divine origin.

Babylon and beyond

In the centuries running up to the 'end of times', occult and pseudo-religious organizations were foreseen to become more and more influential, for example, those called 'Synagogue of Satan' (Rev. 2.9; 3.9) and 'whore of Babylon' (Rev. 17–19).

Regarding the latter, it is said that 'the kings of the earth' and 'the merchants of the earth' are made rich by her (Rev. 18.9, 11, 23). She keeps mankind under her spell by a kind of 'sorcery' which deceives the people of the world (Rev. 18.23). While giving false promises, the force of Babylon indirectly kills many people throughout the world:

> Your merchants were the magnates of the earth, and all the nations were deceived by your sorcery. And in you was found the blood of prophets and saints, and the blood of all those who have been killed on earth [of all those who died an unnatural death]. (Rev. 18.23–4)

This passage of the Bible indicates that the magnates of globalism have become rich by 'sorcery' – the English translation of the Greek words *pharmakon* and *pharmakiai* (as used in Rev. 9.21; 18.23)! Are these familiar Greek words hinting at the verification of yet another apocalyptic prophecy?

The use of the name 'Babylon' indicates a dark force whose roots go back to Babylon, and even further into the remote past. Some call it the 'Babylonian priesthood', the Brotherhood of the serpent, of the dragon, of the gods of Eden – those forces that had invaded the earth in a former age.*

In the First Book of Moses, we can still find a fragmentary report about this antediluvian phase of human history:

> When men started to grow in numbers on the surface of the earth, and daughters were born to them, the 'sons of the gods', looking at the women, saw how beautiful they were; and they took as wives all those whom they wanted to take. [...] The Nephilim were on earth in those days, and also after that, when the sons of the gods continued to have relations with the daughters of men, and they had children by them. (Genesis 6.1–4)

In the course of the many millennia that followed, these groups have split themselves up into multifarious factions. Some have remained allies, some have become competitors and opponents, and again others have chosen to leave the endless power game for good. All entities are evolving – some towards the Light, others deeper into the darkness.

We may take these ancient stories seriously or not, in any case it remains a fact that these gods of the past still move the masses, either directly or indirectly, through the channels of religious fanaticism,

---

* In the Sumerian language they are called Anunnaki ('those who came down from heaven [*anu*] to earth [*ki*]); in Hebrew this term is translated as 'Nephilim', the fallen angels, literally 'the fellers', 'those who cause others to fall down'.

materialistic mammonism and occult elitism. Some of these entities have been attempting to expand their influence on earth by incarnating amongst men, by subtle manipulation and, increasingly, by a renewed physical presence. Are the 'gods' preparing their return?

Today, we know of many reports about encounters with non-terrestrial and higher-dimensional entities, ranging from illuminating contacts with Light beings down to contacts with less spiritual entities, some of them being neutral, others materialistic and aggressive. Some are simply observing and examining mankind and the planet, some are manipulating or abducting people, and some are said to be doing things that are even worse.

The perspective that today's religions, secret politics and wars have a 'mythological' background, expands the spectrum of relevant topics beyond the earthly horizon. This delicate and complex matter will be unfolded in Part III.

Summary and outlook

Regarding the problematic world situation, many people ask: What is going on? What do the global players really want? Where is 'their' progress leading to? Who are 'they'?

These were the questions investigated in Part II. Amongst the many possible scenarios, the one foreseen by St John on Patmos is the most famous and probably the most accurate prophecy. It frankly says who the background forces are: the 'dragon and his hosts', a satanic intelligence which 'deludes and deceives the whole world'. It also reveals what their goals are: establishing a world-wide structure of artificial peace and order based on a totalitarian global dictatorship, culminating in the marking of all people. Accepting this mark symbolizes the ultimate surrender of one's soul to the dark forces.

The scenario of the Apocalypse, however, does not end here. It repeatedly emphasizes that the fearless and truthful will remain protected spiritually and even physically. They will 'gain their true life', and they will be the ones to inherit the new Earth.

There are countless opinions pro and contra. Some feel powerless against these forces. Others sympathize with them, and again others ignore or deride all warnings, calling them the paranoia of 'conspiracy nuts' and 'doomsday invokers'. Both of these paranoid types of people certainly exist. And yet, it is a fact that ancient prophets and visionaries foresaw amazing and even shocking details of the future, which are now becoming true.

The final vision, however, is optimistic and exciting. Ancient and contemporary sources alike confirm that a new age is about to set in. There will be 'a new heaven and a new earth'.

An integral aspect of this new reality is the renewed contact with higher-dimensional Light and Star beings, our cosmic brothers and sisters. They can be called 'angels' – but ultimately we are all angels. As incarnated Light beings, we are invited to reawaken to the consciousness of our real, eternal identity. All of our former lives on earth have been preparations for the life in the present turning point of history. A full cycle along with its many subcycles is being completed, all coming to an end – an end which will transform itself into a new beginning on a higher level.

If we choose to go this way, we are chosen.

> For it is not against human enemies that we have to struggle, but against the principalities and the ruling forces who are masters of the darkness in this world, the spirits of evil in the heavens.*
> This is why you must take up the complete suit of armour from God, or you will not be able to resist on the evil day, or stand your ground even though you exert yourselves to the full. So stand your ground, with truth a belt round your waist, and uprightness a breastplate, wearing for shoes on your feet the eagerness to spread the gospel of peace. Above all things, take up the large shield of faith, with which you will be able to quench the burning arrows of the Evil One. And then, take salvation as your helmet and the word of God as your sword granted by the Spirit. Pray in the Spirit at all times in every prayer and supplication. (Eph. 6.12–18)

---

* Or, according to another translation: 'For our struggle is not against enemies of flesh and blood, but against the rulers, against the authorities, against the cosmic powers of this present darkness, against the spiritual forces of evil in the heavenly places.' (*The HarperCollins Study Bible*)

Part III

The Cosmic Background of Past and Present History

Terrestrial and extraterrestrial forces –
how are they linked?
Who are the 'gods', 'angels' and 'demons'?
'Ye are gods'* – what does that mean?

* John 10.34

CHAPTER ELEVEN

Interdimensional Contacts Rediscovered

The Sanskrit word for a living physical body is *kshetra*, 'field'. This is the literal meaning, which is applicable to the entire spectrum of physics. On the gross-material level, *kshetra* refers to any kind of designated field or land. For example, the most famous battlefield of Vedic history is called Kurukshetra, 'the field of the Kuru dynasty'. When referring to the subtle-material level, *kshetra* has the same meaning which the word 'field' still rudimentarily has when today's physicists speak of 'energy fields' and 'field theories'.

Interestingly enough, also the body is called a *kshetra*, an energy field! With the choosing of this term, the speakers of Sanskrit indicated that every form of body can be defined as 'the physical domain in which the consciousness of a living entity is present'.

A monocellular being has a very limited *kshetra*. Intestinal bacteria, for example, will never perceive that they are situated within the body of a more evolved living entity which animates this superior organic unit. As soon as the living entity passes away, the body is left behind without the co-ordinating life factor, and the inner micro-organisms are no longer subordinate to it. They begin to live independently, and the dead body (which is no longer a *kshetra!*) is taken over by these smaller units of micro-organisms. That is the explanation why only a dead body decomposes – a simple fact which is not that simple after all. It visibly demonstrates the existence of a non-material life factor, its presence or absence causing a difference which could not be more drastic. Therefore, the most drastic pair of words is used to describe these two different conditions: alive and dead.

Micro-organisms are totally unable to comprehend their position and function within the physical unit of the bigger *kshetra*, to say nothing of the fact that this bigger *kshetra,* too, is positioned within yet higher structures of planetary and cosmic dimensions. For bacteria, our body is *a universe,* and we humans are something so alien and unknown to them that they do not even perceive us. For them, we do not exist! Similarly, is not mankind, too, living like blind, ignorant bacteria within the organism of the multi-dimensional cosmos?

Undeniably, man's consciousness is very limited and only capable of perceiving those things that lie within the scope of its *kshetra,* which interacts with the world through the senses of smell, taste, touch, hearing and sight. Those who identify themselves with matter are therefore limited to the reach and perception of their senses, even in their thinking, feeling and endeavouring, and in the contents of their world-view.

Our consciousness, however, being non-material, is not limited to matter. Just as light exists independently of shadows and darkness, consciousness is independent of matter. The consciousness of each human being has the potential of going beyond the limitations of material sense perception, even beyond the limitations of the body.* Flashes of this potential may manifest as occasional telepathy, as a case of spontaneous healing, or as a sudden thrust of superhuman power (mostly in moments of shock or desperation) when, for example, a mother can lift a car away from her child. Later on, such a person can hardly remember the incident. It is like having been under hypnosis. And, indeed, hypnotical acts can serve as a spectacular illustration of the actual potential dormant in our mental and causal bodies. Still, hypnosis is not the recommended way to activate such powers, as it depends on orders suggested or even imposed by another person.

The potential of consciousness ('mind over matter') does not always present itself in a spectacular manner. From a higher point of view, every living entity is 'spectacular', be it a light-seeking plant, a flying insect, a swimming fish, a colour-changing chameleon, a running leopard, etc. A body of gross matter, which otherwise would be lifeless, is being animated to do wonderful things: growing, moving, procreating, perceiving, communicating. *Life* itself is the biggest miracle! And we as human beings are invited to appreciate it, beginning with ourselves ...

---

*An example of people who consciously activate these potential powers are the masters of Asian martial arts who are able to break bricks with the naked hand, to knock over someone without touching him, to fight blindfolded, to display certain aspects of invulnerability, etc.

Cosmic hierarchy

Those whose consciousness reaches beyond the limitations of the physical senses are said to have a 'good intuition', a 'magical touch', a 'third eye' or a 'sixth sense'. Having paranormal or psychic abilities simply means that one's energy centres (*chakras*) are less blocked than those of the average human, which allows one to connect to sources that lie beyond the ordinary sense perception.

The human body is three-dimensionally condensed and consists of approximately 80 % water. Many people on earth believe that the only 'intelligent species' in this universe is the one whose bodies consist of 80 % water – namely they themselves. But why should the vast variety of cosmic life be limited to beings with bodies of 80 % water? How can we exclude the existence of beings with bodies of 80 % fire, air or ether, or any other kind of mixing ratio? Not to speak of beings with bodies that do not consist of gross-material elements.

A holistic world-view allows us to perceive the cosmos as a material field in which non-material beings ('souls') manifest themselves in subtle, ethereal, astral, semi-physical or gross bodies. All of these living entities constitute a many-levelled cosmic hierarchy. From the viewpoint of 'Terra', most of them are situated on a higher-dimensional level of existence. They have bodies which are less condensed and less limited. Obviously, their *kshetras* (fields of consciousness) are much wider than those of us humans, which means that the reach of their awareness and sense perception goes far beyond gross matter.

Our human consciousness pervades and animates an earthly body. Similarly, there are beings whose *kshetras* comprise an entire planet. As we are earthly beings, they are *planetary beings*. Every living planet is animated by the consciousness of a planetary being, who is like the soul of this celestial body with all its gross and subtle levels of life.

Above the planetary beings are the *solar beings* whose consciousness animates a star and its corresponding solar system. It was not simply superstition when the ancient mythological cultures spoke of a 'god or goddess of the earth', of a 'sun god', etc. Rather, it was true esoteric and divine knowledge – or some remnant of it.

Above the planetary and solar beings are the *galactic beings* – beings with a consciousness encompassing an entire galaxy including its many billions of solar systems.

Above the galactic beings are the *central-solar beings* who live 'on' the galactic central suns, having the function of synchronizing their respective galaxy according to its many interlinked orbital cycles of multidimensional space and time.

And there are *intergalactic beings* inhabiting yet wider and vaster dimensions of existence. Being intergalactic, they can tune into any galaxy, solar system and planet within their 'jurisdiction'.

Above all of them – and encompassing all of them – is the *universal Being*, the cosmic mind or logos whom many call God. And 'he' is, from a certain perspective, as the entire cosmos has been created and manifested through this Being's consciousness. All other beings in the universe live within the *kshetra* of this universal god. In the Vedic scriptures, 'he' is identified as Brahma. He is the first and highest Light being in the universe. There are as many Brahmas as there are universes, but there is only one Brahma in each universe.

The totality of the innumerable material universes is situated within an unlimited, non-material background – the eternal spiritual world beyond space and time, beyond all duality. This space- and timeless origin is all-pervading and omnipresent. It is the ever-present (absolute) and life-giving reality beyond duality, which can be called the *kshetra* ('kingdom') of God, the absolute Individuality, all relative individuals being like rays or parts of God. Thus, with true enlightenment, we can perceive the presence of God also in the material world.

This multidimensional perspective allows a conclusive definition of the term 'energy'. All forms of energy are *fluxes of consciousness within the kshetras of respective living beings*. Energy is not something abstract or mechanical or 'material'. In reality, it is always the emanation of some conscious entity. Ultimately, all energies within the universe emanate from the consciousness of the universal Being, Brahma, and all other beings can use parts of this energy to form their own worlds.

Man's position in the multidimensional cosmos

Planets and solar systems are like atoms and molecules within the *kshetras* of the respective galactic and intergalactic beings. Contrary to human beings who, in most cases, do not consciously relate to the atoms and molecules within their bodies, these higher-dimensional beings are fully aware of all aspects of their cosmic 'territories', including all creatures living therein. In other words, man always moves within the *kshetras* of various beings. We may not see them, but they see us.

Only in Kali-yuga have contacts to higher-dimensional worlds become something unknown or unusual. Still, through parapsychological phenomena (near-death experiences, astral travels, etc.), modern man has the possibility of at least hearing about the perspective that life is not limited to gross matter.

True enlightenment leads to an awareness of the spiritual reality and of the Light beings, our cosmic brothers and sisters. What appears to be a book of seven seals to us humans is an open book to them, and they are only waiting to share their knowledge with us. They are waiting because they fully respect people's free will, which is the typical (and natural) characteristic of a divine mentality. They are free from any desire to impose their superiority – if they are real Light beings. Still, according to God's will, they occasionally intervene and always inform, and those who have ears to hear can hear them.

In other words, we are never alone, nor are we ever helplessly lost in tribulation. This is the deeper meaning of the words of Jesus spoken in the Sermon on the Mount: 'Ask, and it will be given to you; seek, and you will find; knock, and the door will be opened to you. For everyone who asks receives; everyone who seeks finds; and to everyone who knocks the door will be opened.' (Matt. 7.7–8)

The revival of higher abilities

In all times, mankind receives prophecies and revelations from the Light worlds, especially in times of impending global changes: 'Surely God the Almighty does nothing, without revealing his secret to his servants the prophets.' (Amos 3.7)

Apart from disasters and troubles, the ancient prophets also predicted many wonderful and enthusing occurrences for the 'end time'. These descriptions also refer to our present day:

> Then afterward I will pour out my spirit on all flesh. Your sons and daughters shall prophesy, your old people shall have dreams, and your young people see visions. Even on the menservants and the maidservants shall I pour out my spirit in those days. I will show portents in the sky and on earth, blood and

fire and columns of smoke. The sun will be turned into darkness, and the moon into blood, before the great and terrible Day of the Lord comes. And everyone who calls on the name of God will be saved. (Joel 2.28–32)

These prophetic statements are of great significance: When the time of transformation is near, the spirit of God will be poured upon all flesh; man's consciousness will no longer be limited to dense matter and locked *chakras*. As a consequence, men and women of all social levels will be able to hear the inner word, to perceive their spiritual guides and to revive their individual God consciousness.

Furthermore, Joel foresaw wondrous signs appearing in the sky and on earth. Other sources, too, have indicated that men must be prepared for unexpected manifestations of this kind.[111]

In the end of times, the border between the visible and invisible worlds will gradually fall away, and beings of the light and beings of darkness will appear in the world of man. In both cases, this lifting of the veil indicates that 'the day of the Lord' is near.

Obviously, not all psychic messages are fictitious or 'evil', as critics and religionists maintain. Quite the contrary: biblical statements like the one given by Joel, as well as many revelations and 'inner words' of today, prove that the spirit of God has not only spoken to man in the past but is continuing to do so up to the present day. The increasing number of people open to the esoteric and spiritual aspects of life is not merely a New Age phenomenon, it is *a divine sign* prophesied for the final time of the present cycle. In order to help people be prepared and fearless in view of a troubled future, the spirit of God continues to transmit knowledge and inspiration. Mundane education, unfortunately, does not inform us about these crucial matters. Therefore, we need other sources – and those who seek will find.

Communication with higher dimensions

The Book of Joel (2.28–9) proclaims that a time will come when those receptive to the spirit of God will regain a state of expanded consciousness and universal awareness. This will happen previous to the 'great and terrible day of the Lord'. In the countdown to this finale, many people will become enlightened through their inner contact with the family of Light beings (the 'hosts of heaven'), and will thus awaken to the fact that they themselves are rays of God who incarnated on earth. Some have forgotten it, and some have denied it, but in 'the day of the Lord', all incarnated angels, both the fallen and non-fallen ones, will have to pass the same test of living in the original consciousness of oneness (divine love).

This vision of a new age is not an isolated prophecy. Jesus himself said to his apostles: 'I still have many things to say to you, but they would be too much for you to bear now. However, when the Spirit of truth comes, he will lead you to the complete truth, for he will not speak on his own, but will say only what he has been told; and he will reveal to you the things to come.' (John 16.12–13)

Obviously, the Spirit of truth mentioned by Jesus is the same as the spirit that shall be poured out 'on all flesh', as mentioned by Joel. From these words of the Old and New Testament, we can conclude what the term 'Spirit of truth' refers to: the reconnection of man to the spiritual reality through divine mercy. This will be a revelation and experience unique in its kind, perceived by those who are awakened and receptive. It is made possible by the Spirit of truth transmitted by the universal Being (the 'first-born') who is one with the Source, the 'Father'. Everything that exists in the universe comes through the medium of this being whose *kshetra* is the entire universe. Only for that reason could he speak the way he did:

> However, when the Spirit of truth comes he will lead you to the complete truth, for he will not speak on his own, but will say only what he has been told; and he will reveal to you the things to come. He will glorify me, since all he reveals to you will come from me. Everything the Father has also belongs to me. That is why I said: all that he reveals to you will come from me. (John 16.13–15)

According to these words, it might even be that Jesus himself will speak through the Spirit of truth, as he had 'still many things to say' which he could not say two thousand years ago:

> I have been telling you these things in veiled language. The hour is coming when I shall no longer speak to you in veiled language but tell you about the Father in plain words. (John 16.25)

The standard exegesis of the statement 'I still have many things to say to you but they would be too much for you to bear now' maintains that the word 'now' refers only to the time up to the day of Pentecost*; on this day, the promised spirit of God came upon the Apostles, who thus received the complete truth; afterwards, the spirit was handed down to the following generations only through the 'apostolic' line.

So let us read what exactly happened on Whitsunday, the day of Pentecost:

> And there appeared to them tongues of fire; these separated and came to rest on the heads of each of them. They were all filled with the Holy Spirit and began to speak different languages as the Spirit gave them power to express themselves. Now there were devout men living in Jerusalem from every nation under heaven, and at this sound they all assembled, and each one was bewildered to hear these men speaking their own language. They were amazed and astonished. 'Surely', they said, 'all these men speaking are Galileans. How does it happen that each of us hears them in his own native language? […]' Everyone was amazed and perplexed; they asked one another what it all meant. Some, however, laughed it off. 'They have been drinking too much sweet wine,' they said. Then Peter stood up with the Eleven and addressed them in a loud voice: 'Men of Judaea, and all you who live in Jerusalem, make no mistake about this, but listen carefully to what I say. These men are not drunk, as you imagine; it is only the third hour of the day [9 a.m.]. Rather, this is what the prophet was saying: 'In the last days – the Lord declares – I shall pour out my spirit on all humanity. Your sons and daughters shall prophesy, your young people shall see visions, your old people have dreams. Even on the slaves, men and women, shall I pour out my spirit.' (Acts 2.3–18)

As revealed by Peter in his spontaneous speech, the Apostles understood the prediction of Jesus – that the Spirit of truth would come to man – to be a verification of Joel's prophecy, and Peter explicitly quoted it in his response to the laughing onlookers. Based on these words, and the reaction of the Apostles, we can conclude that the event of Pentecost was the opening of the inner connection to the higher worlds, initiated by Jesus, whose ascension had taken place just ten days before. This incident shows that the Spirit of truth was not a privilege granted to the Apostles, or the 'apostolic line', alone.

Speaking a foreign language in an altered state of consciousness is neither impossible nor unheard of. It is a known fact that trance medi-

---

* Pentecost: celebrated ten days after Jesus' translation ('ascension'), i.e. fifty days after his resurrection (therefore 'Pentecost', from Grk. *pentêkostê*, the fiftieth).

ums may happen to speak in a language unknown to them.[112] For astral and higher-dimensional beings, language barriers do not exist.

The people who assembled to celebrate Pentecost were in a state of trance and spoke 'channelled' messages. The scoffing onlookers first thought that the speakers were drunk, which is an interesting detail that was kept in writing because it proved that these community members were not in their usual state of consciousness. The expression 'drunk' was simply an ignorant description of an altered state of consciousness, in modern terms: a mediumistic trance.

Obviously, this experience was nothing extraordinary for the Apostles. They defended those in trance by quoting the Book of Joel. We may even assume that some of the Apostles themselves, and later also Paul, were endowed with the gifts of the spirit. Receiving sermons through the inner word was natural for the initiates of those times. During the first three centuries, there were many confidential circles of original Christians who experienced this ever-new inspiration, which was the secret reason why the Good News spread so quickly: Religion was no longer limited to the written word and the autocracy of high priests; the Spirit of truth, the living God and divine love revealed a totally new quality of life.

Only when the Church of Rome took over the Jesus movement did a new tyranny of the written word start, established by the foundation of an ecclesiastical hierarchy. Immediately, the agents of this new institution began to preach against those having the inner word or the gift of telepathy (with slogans like, 'Beware of the voice of the devil!'). Many of these gifted people were killed or anathemized, and professional members of the Church monopolized Christianity by taking the positions of 'authorized' priests, bishops and popes. Only those having gone through the Church-monitored schools were entitled to preach and lead communities. The reason was obvious: hierarchical positions could easily be manned with institutionally chosen people, whereas those chosen by the Spirit of truth could not be recruited by schooling and appointment; and people were not to know about the 'alternative', original form of Christianity, what to speak of comparing it to the new, 'only' Church. Therefore, everything became controlled by clerical men, and all others were degraded to the status of laymen and laywomen. The persecution soon expanded to all forms of 'heretics' through the 'Holy Inquisition' and to all 'pagans' through colonization.

Paul, foreseeing these deviations and falsifications, warned all following generations about any form of lifeless and heartless dogmatism, and as a criterion he mentioned the individual use of the 'spirit':

> Always be joyful; pray constantly; and for all things give thanks; this is the will of God for you in Christ Jesus. Do not stifle the spirit, or despise the gift of prophecy with contempt; but *test everything and hold on to what is good* and abstain from every form of evil. (1 Thess. 5.16–22)

This is the verdict given by Paul regarding the gift of prophecy. The often-quoted statement 'test everything and hold on to what is good' originally referred to channelled messages, new revelations and the inner word! Paul instructs us not to reject such divine inspirations wholesale, but to test them. He knows that there are always some that originate from the Spirit of truth – and to these good gifts one should hold on. At the same time, one should 'abstain from every form of evil', especially those forms of evil which 'stifle the spirit'.

The mystery of the 'inner word'

Many religionists strongly condemn and demonize every kind of psychic or paranormal revelation. They are convinced that only satanic spirits can be at work behind such speaking and writing; only the Bible prophets, who spoke the 'word of God', and the Bible writers, who wrote under the 'dictate of God', were genuine channels. Everybody else is considered to be a channel of the devil, especially those receiving messages today.

Nevertheless, even these absolutistic claims acknowledge that speaking and writing under the inspiration of God is possible. Actually, the entire Bible is said to be a product of such paranormal contacts. Also the Koran was manifested through the dictate of an angel, as well as many other texts. Considering the fact that such holy books, in their turn, have been dictating world history to a large extent, we realize how much mankind has been influenced by paranormal sources, be they divine or less divine. However, only a small part of the 'private' revelations has been written down and included in the official scriptures.

Those who explore the history of the early Jesus movement will soon notice that inspired speech, trance contacts, 'channelling' and spiritual healing were integral parts of the inner communities. The first generations after Jesus had no tangible record of his teaching and personality, no pictures and, initially, not even written words. Many were illiterate anyway. Still, the Jesus movement spread like 'wildfire' throughout the Mediterranean countries and Middle Asia, reaching even India and the Himalayan region.

What was the empowering and driving spirit behind this new movement which, after all, did not contain crucial new elements of philosophy? Compassion for all living beings (non-violence) and a pure life according to principles similar to the Ten Commandments had already been taught by Buddha, by Pythagoras and other enlightened teachers. Love of God, prayer and the revelation of God's kingdom were already part of the Vedas and the traditions of the ancient spiritual mystery schools. Obviously, there must have been an additional driving force within the movement of Jesus and his followers. What was it?

First of all, it was the mystery of the Light body and, secondly, the 'Spirit of truth'. Both factors caused a new dimension of practical spirituality as initiated by the experience on Whitsunday.

The cosmic Christ, the first-born in God's creation, had appeared as Jesus, as stated at the beginning of John's Gospel: the original logos of the universe had 'become flesh'. In other words, the universal Being incarnated[113] in an earthly body that became fully spiritualized through the impact of this most powerful Light being. The enlightened Apostles and their followers knew about the cosmic hierarchy and the all-pervading presence of Christ's logos. Therefore, they were able to connect themselves to this divine presence, the Spirit of truth.

When these early followers came together, they did so in the name of Jesus, who had told them: 'As the Father loves me, I love you; abide in my love. If you truly follow my words you will abide in my love, just as I have truly followed the words of my Father and abide in his love. These things I have spoken to you so that my joy may be in you and your joy may be complete. This is my commandment, that you love one another as I have loved you.' (John 15.9–12)

In their inner circles, the believers experienced love and joy that was sublime and 'complete'. When these groups of enthusiastic men and women met, they created a most powerful energy field in perfect resonance with the field of Christ's consciousness. They experienced pure and unconditional love among themselves and were thus able to receive and reflect the universal love of Christ. Within this unique field of pure energy, some were able to utter the inner word ('inspired speech'), and some were able to 'speak in tongues' (in trance) or to serve as telepathic channels. Others worked as healers and aura interpreters with empathic intuition, again others could perceive and discern astral entities, etc. These were the gifts of the spirit as promised by Jesus, who had said: 'For where two or three meet in my name, I am there among them.' (Matt. 18.20)

In their gatherings, they often experienced a direct and personal revelation – the inner word – which was more impressive than any written word. This was the life and soul of the Jesus movement of the first two centuries. The living Christ empowered many simple men and women (the 'menservants and maidservants' mentioned by Joel) to become divine instruments. In a chain reaction, more and more Jesus groups came into life, inspired by the spirit of Christ speaking to these circles through the inner word.

Being a non-institutional system, it had the advantage that it could not be misused by ambitious people looking for power and prestige. It was impossible to imitate the inner word by a show of devotion or by having a position. The spirit empowered only those who were truly receptive and resonant to Christ's love. It could not be grasped or usurped. It only came through mercy.

In short, these self-purifying circles were immune against infiltration and worldly ambitions. Therefore, the dark forces became frustrated and envious, but they also realized the big potential of this spontaneously increasing movement. Being unable to usurp it, they had to destroy it and to replace it with another system.

Soon, competitors started to further the institutionalization of the movement, as well as the creation of an official priesthood. Some even became known as 'church fathers'. They became rigid, dogmatic holders ('pillars') of a mundane structure, and as such they are mentioned and glorified in the chronicles of the institution they created. At the same time, some pioneers of the early movement became 'integrated' into Church history, others were condemned, and again others – in particular the many receivers of the inner word – were simply ignored. The writers of Church history were convinced, or wanted to create the impression, that the Jesus movement had always existed in the form presented by those who supported the institutionalization.

Nevertheless, also in the official Bible we can still find passages indicating that inspired speech, psychic trance, spiritual healing and other gifts of the spirit had been essential factors in the life of the early communities. The most important testimony is found in the First Epistle to the Corinthians, chapters 12 through 14.

> There are many different gifts, but there is the same spirit imparting them; and there are many different ways of serving, but they are all on behalf of the same Lord; and there are many different forms of ability, but in everybody it is the same God working through them. The particular manifestation of the spirit granted to each one is to be used for the general good. To one is given through the spirit the speech of wisdom; to another, speech of knowledge of God, in accordance with the same spirit; to another, faith, given by the same spirit; and to another, the gifts of healing by that one spirit; to another, the working of miracles; to another, words of prophecy; to another, the discernment of inspired utterances [or: discernment of spirits; distinguishing between words coming from a divine source and those not]; to another, the gift of speaking in different tongues, and to another, the interpretation of tongues. But all are activated by one and the same spirit, who allots the gifts to each one individually just as the spirit chooses. (1 Cor. 12.4–11)

'Speaking in tongues' refers to speaking in a state of trance or religious ecstasy, sometimes in an incoherent manner which has to be interpreted. The respective man or woman is either overwhelmed by a vision or by some kind of astral entity.[114] The Apostles emphasize that 'inspired speech' (the inner word; speaking through divine inspiration, so-called 'prophesying') is rated higher than speaking in tongues: 'However, he who prophesies speaks to other people, inspiring them and giving them encouragement and reassurance. Those who speak in tongues may inspire themselves, but those who prophesy inspire the community. Now I would like all of you to speak in tongues, but even more to prophesy. Indeed, those who prophesy are of greater importance than those who speak in tongues.' (1 Cor. 14.3–5)

Furthermore, this Epistle reveals that the author himself was endowed with the gifts of the spirit:

> Now suppose, brothers, I [Paul] came to you and spoke in tongues, what good would I do you if my speaking provided no revelation or knowledge or prophecy or instruction? [...] That is why anybody who speaks in a tongue must pray that he may be given the interpretation. [...] I can do both: praying with the gift of the spirit and also praying with my mind. I can sing praise

with the gift of the spirit but I can also sing praise with my mind. Otherwise, if you offer praise through the spirit, how will the ordinary person say 'Amen' to your praying or speaking since he does not understand what you say? […] But in an assembly I would rather speak five words with my mind to instruct others as well [without inspired speech], than ten thousand words in a tongue.' (1 Cor. 14.6, 13–19)

In this Epistle, Paul addresses the members of the inner circles of Corinth, instructing them how to speak to people who are not (yet) ready or mature enough to participate in the circle of pure believers. They shall also be instructed without any secrets, but the means shall be different. Instead of bewildering the outsiders with inspired speech, it is better to instruct them with one's own words, which is what Paul meant by 'praying and praising with one's mind'.

The Spirit of truth in modern times

The inner word was soon replaced by the *written* word, which became a means of manipulating people on the authority of so-called Scripture. This was an especially effective trick because at that time, most people were not able to read. In the Middle Ages, only the priestly class was allowed to read the Bible. Lay citizens and academics were forbidden to read it or even to possess it. In some countries, 'unauthorized' reading or possession of the Bible was punished by death. This totalitarian arrogance of the Roman Church, along with its decadence, provoked the Reformation in Europe, which was followed by a Counter-Reformation and fierce religious wars that continued over several centuries.

One important aspect of the Reformation was Luther's translation of the Bible into German (1522: publication of the New Testament, 1534 of the entire Bible). This was revolutionary as the Bible contained many crucial truths that contradicted the practices of the Church, starting with the commandments 'Thou shall not kill', 'Thou shall not lie' and 'Thou shall not steal'. Furthermore, people got to hear what Jesus said about the arrogance of the priests, about the 'truth that will set you free', and about the Spirit of truth that was to manifest in the revelation of the 'complete truth'. Obviously, the 'sheep' of the Church were not meant to hear anything about these aspects of spirituality.

And yet, the spirit always remained accessible. In the secret inner core of monastic orders and secular mystery schools, some initiates continued to receive the inner word and speeches in trance. Also mystics and hermits kept up the spirit, in the literal sense of the word.

John of Jerusalem, one of the founders of the Templars (mentioned in Chapter Five), bears testimony to this fact. At the end of his *Book of Prophecies,* he cryptically writes: 'I see and I know. My eyes see in heaven what will be, and I leave the time with one stride. A hand leads me to the place that you do not see and of which you know nothing.'

The more the power of the Church increased, the more it became dangerous to belong to spiritual circles. Many enlightened people who lived in the 'heretical' knowledge of the higher worlds, the inner word, reincarnation etc. were killed. But the knowledge itself could not be eradicated because reincarnation is a fact. And so it came to pass that many of these initiates were born again in later generations. Indeed, those who lost their lives actually found it (Matt. 10.39, Rev. 14.13), and they are the spiritual pioneers in the 'end of times', wearing the symbolical white robes of transformation (Rev. 7.14).

The harmony of unlimited points of view

In researching and comparing the many revelations received during the last two thousand years, we find that biblical, metaphysical and spiritual themes have been explained in a vast variety of ways. Some may even seem to contradict each other.

Many revelations – many truths? Should the contents not always be the same if the source is the same? No. The *essence* is always the same. But the way in which this essence is presented is absolutely individual. The desire for a predefined 'truth' is typical of immature people who wish to be told what to believe, what to do, whom to follow and whom to consider as evil. It means giving away one's self-responsibility.

In talking about God and the absolute, we have to be aware that we are dealing with topics we cannot really grasp. The Unlimited is inconceivable to our limited minds. How can our mind, which is conditioned by the frames of space and time, imagine that which is spaceless and timeless? The spiritual reality cannot be imagined and understood by our mind, it has to be experienced and realized by our self – because, in our true identity, we are spiritual ourselves ...

Words and theories are always relative and limited. Therefore, it would be wrong to assume that there is only one true and valid belief system to explain the Unlimited and the unlimited number of topics it entails, for example: matter and spirit, the kingdom of God, the beginning of time within eternity, the creation of the limited out of the Unlimited, the cause of eternal souls being born in the worlds of matter, the fall of the angels, the origin of evil, the role of the different religions, the history of the planet and the universe, life after death, etc.

None of these topics can be limited to one single set of explanations. Whatever is expressed with words and dualistic concepts is, by definition, relative and limited because the human being is conditioned to approach the Truth from a particular point of view. And there are as many points of view as there are individuals. This refers not only to the receivers of a particular explanation but also the givers, be they incarnate on earth or situated in a higher dimension.

Divine sources may give different kinds of information regarding their wording and perspective, but in their essence they always indicate the same truths: life after death, the existence of higher realms, the oneness beyond duality, the reality of God, and the inspiration to live in divine love. In the course of history, these contents were revealed in different manners and with different priorities according to the time, the place, and the people involved. It is therefore not amazing that Vedic and Buddhist seers received revelations of a different content than native shamans or ancient Jewish prophets. And the early Christian communities received yet again different revelations – different not in the sense of 'contradictory' or 'excluding'. The knowledge in school given on primary, secondary and university levels is not contradictory but different nonetheless. In the same way, all revelations are imbued with the same spirit – always provided that they are of a divine origin.

Those who do not limit themselves to one single point of view are able to handle many 'different' explanations. They are not stuck in one particular system of doctrines while excluding all others as false or 'satanic'. Rather, they are able to perceive the good within all teachings. At the same time, they carefully avoid the diabolic spirit which tries to destroy this very harmony of understanding. They are able to *differentiate without judging*.

In other words, we should not be bewildered by the variety of perspectives found in divine revelations. The realms of Light are characterized by oneness in diversity and diversity in oneness, and it is only natural that the Light beings speak about the same essential truths in their own individual ways. It is up to us to decide what is good for us in the respective situations of our lives. That is the *freedom of self-responsibility.*

Furthermore, and most importantly, revealed information is always adapted to the person who receives it. According to the law of resonance, divine sources always respect the mental concepts and even the vocabulary of the person serving as a medium. They will never give more than the receiver can handle, digest or accept. Therefore, a person of an earlier century living in a Christian country was only given information in reference to the Bible. If, for example, the absolute historicity of the Old Testament's stories had been questioned, the receiver would have blocked the contact due to his, or her, confessional conditioning, thinking that now the devil was talking. In such cases, the sources imparted visions of biblical scenes to enhance the person's faith and devotion, and not necessarily to prove the historicity of these scenes (e.g. Adam and Eve, Noah's family as the only survivors of the Great Flood, or Egypt as the place of enslavement).

The Light beings know that revelation is a dynamic and ongoing process. Contrary to that, the diabolic spirit is rigid and dogmatic. That is why clutching to one single point of view and absolutizing it through dogmas is so detrimental to finding the truth.

The same applies for new revelations. If one is singled out and declared to be the only truth, then it becomes distorted, even if the revelation itself was good. And there were many good revelations all over the world.

False love and light

In their attempts to achieve power and control, the forces of darkness always try to imitate the Light by presenting themselves as enlightened knowers, leaders or saviours. This may be done in a blunt and violent manner (as in dictatorships) or in a subtle and 'esoteric' manner. In the latter case, words like 'God' and 'love and light' are used, too, but due to the sectarian or pseudo-spiritual context, they create an atmosphere of exclusivity and dependence based on unconscious fear.

If misused, concepts of 'love and light' can be a powerful means to cause fear. This happens when – in the name of God, Jesus etc. – people are made to believe: 'We are the only ones in love and light, and we can tell you who is of the light and who is not; if you leave us, then you have left the forces of love and light; you have missed your chance; whatever you will do from now on will be God-forsaken and doomed to failure.'

People who speak in this manner are convinced they are acting in God's will, and their followers desperately believe that this is the case. Otherwise, these followers would have to realize that they have fallen into a binding dependence and that in reality, their group and belief system is not as perfect as they think.

As long as we are able to 'test everything and to hold on to what is good', we are immune against the diabolic spirit, and we will never fall into the trap of 'religious' or atheistic absolutism, knowing well what is really absolute and what is relative. Guided by this Spirit of truth, we will be able to differentiate with clear intelligence and intuition, perceiving the good in everything we encounter – even in the negative – while immediately sensing any dia-bolic influence wherever it appears, even in the 'positive'.

Differentiating without judging is simple but not easy. It is much 'easier' to think, 'We are right, and the others are wrong.' It is much 'easier' to accept a set of doctrines of the too-much or the too-little: doctrines of some 'religion' or doctrines of materialism presented as accepted scientific knowledge. It is 'easier' to follow some group dynamics and to go with the stream – up to the point of the waterfall.

During the Kali-yuga, the flow of things goes downwards into deeper condensation, conflict and chaos. To reach the source, we have to swim 'against' the stream. Therefore, we are called to find the real sources of Light through our inner connection, which is most easily activated when 'two or three gather in my name'.

Summary and outlook

Physical matter is the most condensed form of energy, and energy is always formed and directed (animated) by a conscious entity. According to karma – the result of simultaneous predestination and free will – a living entity assembles matter within its *kshetra*, or 'field of consciousness', thus causing matter to take on a temporary form which is called 'body' in the widest sense of the term (from a physical body up to a galactic and universal energy field).

In all of these processes, the living entities are not independent creators; they simply use already existing elements (matter and its inherent laws) that are created and permeated by the absolute consciousness, the Creator God, in Sanskrit called Vishnu, 'the All-pervading One', or Paramatma, 'the absolute *atma*'.

In other words, all material forms have at some time been assembled and shaped through the influence of consciousness emanated by a living entity, and are continually being formed by consciousness. And to take the mytho-logic even further: all things – individual bodies, bodies of water, celestial bodies, etc. – are animated and maintained by the consciousness of some particular individual. Matter in its innermost aspect is kept together by the *atomos*, the indivisible *atma*, and its emanating consciousness – under the karmic supervision of the Paramatma.[115]

Every material body is animated by a spiritual being, an absolutely unique individual; that is why no two people have identical features, fingerprints etc. Our body, having been assembled under the 'matrix' of our projected consciousness, perfectly mirrors our individual mode of consciousness. The physiognomy of the body, the structure of the iris (and of the ear, the skull, the hands etc.), the lines of the palms and the fingerprints and even the date of birth are determined by the consciousness that built the body in its particular shape and condition. They are physical expressions of our individuality which are beyond our direct control. They are *given* to us by the omniscient arrangements of the Paramatma according to our karma.

Through divine awareness, we can detect the wonders of consciousness and of God's creation everywhere, not least in our own bodies. The principle of consciousness animating a material energy field ('body') applies to all levels of existence. We as human beings permeate our body with our projected consciousness. Similarly, planetary beings animate a planetary body, solar beings an entire solar system, galactic beings an entire galaxy, intergalactic beings many galaxies, interdimensional beings many dimensions, and the universal Being the entire universe. The universal Being ('Brahma') is the cosmic logos, the supreme interdimensional Light being within the universe. He is the first-created entity or, in biblical terms, the 'first-born Son of God' (the cosmic *christos*).

The words spoken by Jesus two-thousand years ago, 'I still have many things to say to you but they would be too much for you to bear', were also relevant in the later centuries. The revelations continued to be gradual and successive. Not everything could be given at once, because the full truth about God, the ungodly forces and the cosmic power game would have been 'too much' for most people, and still is even today.

The simple and natural way of living a God-conscious life has been lost for a long time, especially since the beginning of Kali-yuga five thousand years ago. When it was lost, so-called religion became a means of power to dominate all those who were willing to follow. These dominating forces also moulded the memory of mankind's past and created a censored, manipulated 'history'. People were no longer meant to know their true origins and their individual vocations.

Now, with a renewed access to higher-dimensional sources, we can also gain a new, more complete understanding of our past and future. Two examples of such contemporary revelations are presented in the next chapter.

CHAPTER TWELVE

The Hidden History of Mankind Newly Revealed

Higher-dimensional sources can offer insights that would be difficult to obtain otherwise, if at all. Let us remember that all holy scriptures of the world describe themselves as being revelations of such higher, divine sources. But, thank God, these sources were not only active in the remote past. They are still flowing today, even more than ever before, as they are continuing to lead us 'to the complete truth …' (John 16.13)

Whatever attitude we have towards paranormal sources, one thing cannot be denied, namely the highly unusual and revolutionary nature of their messages. Even if a terrestrial author were found to be the hidden 'perpetrator' of such texts, they would still remain unusual and revolutionary.

The text quoted on the next pages is an example hereof. It was received by *Tom H. Smith* (1942–93) in 1992 through telepathic writing. Tom lived in Kentucky and remained quite unknown as a channel because he wrote only for two years; his texts were never published in book form.

By 'chance' or providence, a world-travelling friend of mine brought some of Tom Smith's texts to me in Switzerland (in summer 1993). Since 1981 I had been living in a Vedic monastery, and was immersed in a cultural and religious tradition that was quite different from the contents conveyed in these channelled texts, which I had to read in secrecy (as such material was not 'authorized' by the monastic surrounding I lived in).

The texts I received were mostly spoken by the 'sun-god' of our solar system. Reading these words was like an inner communication with divine beings, and I felt challenged and moved at the same time. Following a spontaneous impulse, I wrote an airmail letter to 'Mr Smith', asking him whether he had any more such channellings, and whether he planned to translate them into other languages, German 'for example'. I just wanted to know more about this man who wrote down such extraordinary texts.

Three weeks later I received Tom's answer, a letter of five pages:

> Dear Armin,
> Thank you very much for having such an interest in the sun-god and 'his' powerful words. Thank you also for taking your time to read the book [manuscript] and to write me. I am quite pleased and thrilled that someone as far away as Switzerland would not only receive these texts and find meaning in them, but also would write me about it.

Also included was a channelled text – a personal letter to me from the sun-god! Another such message followed in Tom's next letter. The contents of these two 'space-mailed' sun letters was seemingly general but very personal at the same time, indicating that the sender knew me very well. From these two messages it became evident once more that Tom's abilities were genuine.

We exchanged a few cordial letters, discussing many topics including a possible translation into German. Then, in October, I received a parcel from Kentucky containing a file with the print-outs of all the texts that Tom had received. There was only a short letter included, saying that he, Tom, had 'been told' to send these texts to Armin. While looking through the file, I saw a few hand-written notes by Tom. It was his personal collection, and probably the only complete collection of print-outs (more than 500 pages). On the front page he had written: 'Complete Set of Translated Material – Feel Free to Browse / This set is not for sale.'

I wrote back in deep gratitude, with no answer this time.

Two months later, I was informed that Tom had died …

Lost knowledge from new sources

It is a physical law that energy is never lost. Similarly, human experiences are never lost as they are recorded in the conscious or subconscious memory of the many observers and participants. As shown in the following excerpts, the higher-dimensional witnesses have a lot to say about the hidden past (and future!) of mankind. The past was totally different than official history and anthropology proclaim, and the future will be different as well. These texts have an explosive potential because they reveal essential truths which indicate ...

- that many things happening in the world today are due to origins that lie far back in the past;
- that some earthly developments are not limited to earthly factors;
- that mankind has been exposed to the influence of dark forces for a relatively long time;
- that the original human beings came down to earth from higher universal levels through physical condensation (and not through an evolution from matter to animals to human beings; life forms did not evolve from matter);
- that five thousand years ago,[116] certain negative forces gained reinforced access to planet earth;
- that humanity has arrived at a crucial turning point – with every individual having to decide whom to believe and whom to follow, as the paths leading deeper into the darkness and those leading further into the Light are both wide open now;
- that the path to the Light will include an ascension of the earth and of those human beings who develop a similar resonance;
- that the earth is our 'home far from home', as we are all parts of God or, in Tom's wording, 'the God Source'.

Right from the beginning, Tom emphasized that channelled texts, no matter how good they were, could never be a 'substitute for our own knowing and our own higher sources of guidance and information'. In his first letter to me, he clearly stated:

> As you seem to know, the best source of truth comes from within. All the answers to our concerns can be found from our own knowing and discernment. The positive energies that I have channeled have told others on numerous occasions that it is better to go within for your truths than to read a particular channeled message from them. They encourage us to go within, through prayer, meditation or whatever is best for us. Each of us cannot know everything, or we can often use some guidance or education on certain issues. Consequently, mine and other channelings can be very meaningful when used in this regard. But they are no substitute for our own knowing and our own higher sources of guidance and information.

'The Human Experience – Then and Now'
(as received by Tom H. Smith)

[**Planet Earth in the days of yore:**] In your terms of time, a long time ago the Earth was inhabited by a humankind that lived very close to the Earth. This humankind was in constant contact with its own inner awareness, its own higher self. This was not a human who was advanced by today's scientific standards. But in fact this human was more advanced, as this human could communicate directly and at any time with those from other planets. Humankind was allowed to travel through space in the space friends' crafts and see the universe. Humans communicated with the spirit realm in a way that was so instinctive that it was part of their daily life.

Humans communicated with all things around them. There were no wheels for traveling or moving heavy objects and large loads. Yet this humankind could move the largest of objects without any physical effort. There was communication with all energies, including those in large stones, the trees, the flowers – everything. And this was a loving communication. And with love, the stones would move on their own.

Humanity was advanced in many other ways as well. They communed with the Earth, and humans asked the Earth how they could help. The Earth in turn provided humans with all the food they needed. Humankind did not have to work for this. It was a gift.

This species of humankind was overseen by many space friends. It was agreed that the space brothers would be there to help when they were asked to, but would not infringe upon their choices. This arrangement worked quite well as humankind knew that it was on this planet to develop its own gifts and to work in harmony with the Earth and all of nature to develop and grow in the physical and the spiritual sense. So the space friends did not intrude in any way and humankind did not make unreasonable requests either, such as certain technologies to make life easier.

Humankind knew why it was on this planet and did not wish to avoid any of its pleasurable growth. […]

[**Good and evil in this universe:**] It is no secret to humankind that there is 'good' and there is 'evil' or 'bad'. Humanity's understanding of this, in general, is based on the teachings from the Bible and other, similar sources. It should be no surprise to humankind, then, that the universe as a whole contains good and 'bad', or as we say, positive and negative. We say this also with the understanding that humankind as a whole may be able to accept some form of existence beyond the physical realm.

There are many kinds of negative energies. Some of these have extraterrestrial existences, and many of these are very advanced by human standards.

But they too are of the One Creator. They simply are on a path that is not pleasing to the God Source. Keep in mind we say this as a general statement.

There are those extraterrestrials who feel, in fact believe, that to allow the Earth and humankind a freedom of choice, a free will to pursue their own path, is not in the best interest of these particular ETs or beings. For they wish to draw on the energies of humankind and the Earth, to the extent they can. These human energies can 'feed' these ETs and even be a part of their livelihood. Also by controlling humans in certain ways, it allows other energies that humans would have utilized, to be accepted by these other beings.

[... Next] I wish to talk about the controls, the viruses, the memory-fading practices, and some of the events and circumstances that have directly led humankind to where it is today. In doing this I recognize the danger that some may say that I am degrading and even judging certain aspects of humankind. Neither of these is true. Even though humankind was subjected to certain events somewhat 'beyond' its control, humans did agree to it and participated at a certain level. Humankind was a partner to this with some misgivings, but a partner nevertheless. Humanity wished to experience certain emotions as a species. We all recognize this and respect it. At the same time we are intimately aware of what this has done for humankind and the Earth.

The human species was clearly a total partner with the Earth as both were evolving. They were very close to complete harmony between humankind and nature. It was very obvious to all the high-level energies that this marriage was exactly what was needed for the human species on the Earth. The 'time period' I am referring to here was after the Atlantean catastrophe. Humankind was aware of the spiritual 'problems' that had led to the destruction of Atlantis and was determined not to repeat them. This was not a modern or high-tech human. Most of the high technology went 'down the tubes' with Atlantis. Besides, the human of this time did not need nor want such diversions.

Humankind recognized in its own way the path that it and the Earth were taking, and was extraordinarily aware of when and how it was to go, even the approximate time frame. How could this be so? Simple. Humankind was completely in touch with its total being – the current physical being and its higher self. There was open and accepted communication and knowing. There was open communication with the space brothers and sisters. There was no desire to follow a path similar to Atlantis or even Lemuria.

There had been another planet on which many of these same people [souls] had lived. This particular planet's energies had made many of the same choices as the Atlanteans had, which in fact led to that planet's destruction. Here I refer to Maldek. As many are now aware, Maldek was destroyed with such force that all that remains are fragments of its mass. This is identified as an asteroid belt that orbits the sun. Again, the Earth's inhabitants did not wish to repeat that process as well.

So humankind and the Earth had much going for themselves, especially the recollections of what not to do. It was with renewed focus that humankind was setting out to 'balance' the imbalances it had created.

There were those energies on other planets who did not wish to share the Sun's total energies and who at the same time did not want the Earth to gain a status equal to or greater than their own planetary systems. They recognized that this could only be done by redirecting the focus of humanity, and by interfering with the growth, evolution and energy fields of the Earth. [...]

[How negative influences reached the Earth:] They knew that humankind was very aware of any 'outside' interferences, for they recalled Atlantis, Maldek and Lemuria. Venus and Mars too had been through a similar process. These lords or other beings could not simply physically destroy the human species for there were other space beings of a loving nature who watched over the Earth out of love. These star beings were not only of a superior love level to the lords just mentioned, they also were vastly superior in technical means that prohibited any kind of physical harm from occurring. But, this was all they allowed themselves to do as they had total respect for humanity's free will. They could not infringe in any way, such as forcing their own beliefs upon humans. And humankind did not want this either.

It was then a challenge for the 'war lords', as I will call them, to learn how to defeat humankind and the planet as well. The war lords were very experienced at this as they have had millions of your years to perfect their styles of dominance – whether it is through direct conflict or through more subtle ways. But humankind was determined in its path.

Over the next 10,000–15,000 years many different types of approaches were made to change the focus of those on the Earth. There was considerable success with certain individuals and even certain groups, but these did not meet with the total affect the war lords had wanted. One thing was happening though. The human resolve was weakening somewhat as it was experimenting with certain emotional systems and even certain belief systems. Understand that this humankind knew full well the power of the mind and the spiritual connections to the universe and the Infinite Creator. It knew and practiced the creating of its own realities. But it was becoming more daring and began to experiment on its own. However, this did not deter humankind from its ultimate objective. It was creating some diversion for humanity.

The war lords were also aware of the DNA, or basic structure of humankind as a physical being. There were experiments in this regard with some small-scale success. Approximately 5,000 years ago the incessant experiments and probes by the war lords began to show certain progress. They found that a certain alteration in the DNA structure could create a very subtle filtering effect on humans as related to their total being. It was like a very slight 'memory loss'.

Now these war lords had also determined that they were more allowed to operate if they too could incarnate as humans. This they did, even though there was a risk that the incarnate agent would forget its ties to them. They took these risks without any regard to the human side of them. After working with their own incarnate agents over extended periods of time, they had those on the Earth who could teach their own truths. The loving space friends could not interfere in this process. Humankind was now faced with other humans who might full well convince them of a 'better way'. At the same time the DNA 'virus' was taking hold. While it was not a complete filter and did not obstruct the total physical self from the spiritual self, it was becoming quite effective when used in conjunction with the teachings of certain high priests. Soon a battle ensued, a war of teachings. This also caused some physical fighting as well. Humankind was starting to doubt itself.

Then a brilliant idea was introduced – religion – controlled worship. Soon the concepts of a 'good God' and a 'bad God' (hell) were introduced. Separatism was alive and well and flourishing. Humans, God and the spirit realm were now separate and distinct and not part of the One. With these concepts came 'guilt and need to repent' for your sins and evil ways, lest you be cast into the eternal flames of the evil gods. Religion in itself was a virus, a self-perpetuating virus. The agents were gaining such a stronghold that they began to physically purge those who could not accept their ways.

So the 'die was cast', as there was a clear split between those who were able to go within and maintain their knowing, and those who turned that aspect of themselves over to the agents or high priests. It was not long before truly sincere humans felt the call to the priesthood as well. These had lost complete sight of their total self. Unknowingly, they became puppets for the agents from the dark side.

The creativity of the war lords did not end here. They introduced concepts that further enhanced their control over humankind. Commerce and industry were introduced with the ideas of reward, wealth and power. Materialism then became a focus for a species that previously knew there was no need to focus on those things that were not spiritually connected – things that did not enhance spiritual development. […]

There were many who recognized their own self-worth and their own place in the universe. But these were becoming fewer and fewer. Each civilization had their own visionaries who attempted to keep the focus on the spiritual self, the harmony with the Earth. Names that you know, and some you may not, tried to teach the truths. There is a long list, so I will mention only a few – Buddha, Elijah, Mohammed, Confucius, Christ, Abraham, Jacob,

Moses, and so on. Some of these had very deliberately God-directed incarnations – Jesus and Buddha for instance. But the genius of the war lords, and the greed and gullibility of humankind allowed the teachings of these same individuals to be misinterpreted and even totally erroneously stated. In doing this the system self-perpetuated, and little to no outside interference was needed. Humankind had learned to completely limit itself in practically all aspects of spiritual development and other ways as well. Humankind guaranteed a consistent and continuous harm to the Earth as its thirst for more and greater industry and technology occurred. […]

What lies ahead? This too will be explained, although be aware that very little is absolute due to your free will.

The human species is at a true crossroads in its evolvement as an inhabitant on the Earth and as a spiritual brother and sister and equal within the universe. Each and all of you have choices to make that will absolutely affect your continuation as a species, or discontinuation, depending on your decisions.

Your development is separate from Earth, yet it is one with it as well. The Earth has decided that it wishes to move into the fifth dimension and support a light-bodied human as her inhabitants. It is now up to humankind to make the journey in concert with the Mother Earth, or to continue the harm that manifests as both physical and vibrational.

Regardless of the decisions of the human mass consciousness, you will experience certain events that you do not think possible. The degree of these experiences is a choice of each and everyone on the Earth. There is nothing to fear but extreme caution is advised.

I and others have already mentioned that the DNA of the human species has been altered. But even more important has been the introduction and acceptance of such controls and limitations as religion, industrialization, separatism and many facets of these areas. This obviously has been the work of certain technologically superior forces. If you can believe what these have done for the human race and the Earth, then it is just as easy to realize these 'superior' forces are not acting in the best interests of either humankind or the Earth. These forces are in fact of the 'negative type' or from the dark side of the light. It should not take a mental giant to also realize their tasks are not finished as humankind and Earth are on the verge of escaping their grip and moving into a higher love level.

There is now, and will continue to be, diligent efforts by these dark-side agents to assure that their controls are permanent. I will say they have lost their hold on the Earth. It will graduate to the fifth dimension. But the way can be made more difficult or pleasant, depending on humanity's choices.

So what can these agents of the dark do for or to humanity? First of all, there are many of these agents currently incarnate. Some of these are consciously aware of their path and their 'history' and others are not. Many, many of these are part of your government as well as others [other governments]. But your government is such an influential body, that more are concentrated with it. Other governments also have these agents or 'high priests', among them Russia, Japan, China, Germany, Peru, France, England, Iraq, Iran. Essentially all countries have these representatives in some form or another. But not all in government are such agents. Most in fact are not. These agents have been most influential as they have learned to usurp the power given them by the mass consciousness. They are quite intent on their goals, as they have invited the disease known as 'indifference', which allows them to move about and produce their desired results. Lest someone in government read this and fear they are guilty, I say keep this in mind. Most of you are not from the dark side. You have only allowed yourselves to become puppets of them, just as the high priests 5,000 years ago did. You have allowed the greed and power interests of many to control and even own you. You have allowed the secret and covert actions of your government to create the 'national security' myth so that it can function without the knowledge of the public. You have allowed public interest programs to be established that in effect have caused millions of people to be dependent on you and even addicted to your power. I can easily continue this, but you should begin to understand the point. [...]

Humankind's DNA has been altered, but this alteration is easily bypassed when each individual realizes and recognizes its own spiritual being. Here I speak of the human oneness with itself, the spirits of the Earth, the God Source, the space friends – all within the universe. It is not the spiritualism as depicted with the authority and even rigidity of religions as generally understood. So, when the spiritual being is recognized, the effects of the changes to the human DNA are countered.

What is all this leading to? Why make such a big issue out of certain aspects of the human being? Simple. With information and knowing, each of you is better prepared to make your choices. What might you expect? I shall now tell you.

The agents and 'aliens' will not surrender their control without a fight. They will use every trick at their disposal. Brothers will turn against brothers, sons against fathers – do these words sound familiar? The coming times are what these words were referencing. But it need not be. It is not a time of fear, as fear attracts fear. It is a time for love and acceptance [of yourselves and others].

Your government (and others), if allowed to, will begin to take more and greater control over you, its citizens. You will begin to hear of more laws giving the government more absolute control under 'certain circumstances'. There will be a movement towards centralized records of each – a big computer. This will be done in the name of efficiency. Its real purpose is centralized tracking to assure each person is accounted for and to assure total support for whatever the government does. The move towards smaller but more sophisticated armed forces. Smaller because it will be easier to control, easier to train. Some of the technologies being developed are not in the best interest of any citizen of the entire planet. This technology would not be possible without the direct assistance of the agents, in the form of those from space, other planets. Your government has been working with these 'negative' ETs for some 35–40 years. This is another story, but they have assisted you in development of weapon systems and craft. In turn, they have been given free reign to carry out their own needs on the human race. [...]

Along the way your government made certain alliances or treaties with some unexpected guests – UFOs, space beings, those from distant planets. But your government and the Soviet Union had the opportunity to move in a different direction than each took. Ambassadors from the Pleiades and other star systems arranged for and in fact visited with representatives of your respective governments – your heads of state – President Truman [and others] and Joseph Stalin. [...] They offered these two governments their help out of love for humankind and the Earth. But they came in peace and would assist only in peaceful and loving ways. The governments must give up the arms race and work towards completely peaceful and nonmilitaristic solutions to world problems. But both governments were suspicious of the other and therefore refused. Both governments spoke for their citizens and refused the help of these star beings. Both countries spoke for their citizens and said you preferred their approach. So these positive and loving beings from other dimensions could not infringe and interfere and therefore 'withdrew' from the planet. They had seen the destructive power of nuclear weapons both on Earth and in other planetary systems. But they recognized an even greater destructive power, that of negative thinking [because it causes all other destructive things to happen].

These appearances by the benevolent star beings allowed for the eventual intervention by those space beings who had been working behind the scenes for so long. They too made offers to the respective governments, only they knew what was wanted. They knew that power and weapons were the key. So your government in particular has been working with these dark-side space beings. Russia did not join in as much, as they had their own civil unrest to deal with, although they have benefited from the alliances.

More detail will be forthcoming on these circumstances and activities. For now this gives you a general idea of how your government has come by certain technologies. Keep in mind, neither trusted the other – agents or government. This is always the case in an 'unholy' alliance. Consequently, the space aliens were never willing to give total technology to the humans for fear of having it used against them. Likewise, the US government would hold back on some of its promises and certain freedoms for the same reasons. Yet there has been tremendous activity and interaction among the appropriate organizations.

The space agents have not been completely truthful with your government. Most humans involved [the agents of the secret government] could not properly comprehend many of the future events, anyway. The government is not aware of the future directions of the planet Earth. They are aware of certain levels of potential activity but this is all.

So this brings us to now, again, but from a slightly different perspective. Many in your government are preparing to initiate certain activities to preserve themselves under certain circumstances. More will soon be available on this. But this will all be done in the name of 'national security' and the preservation of certain leaders and power brokers. The government will acknowledge the existence of the space agents but will deny any wrongdoing. The space beings will be introduced as being here to help humankind. In your marketing terms, you will be sold a 'package', and many will buy it as they do not believe the government would harm its citizens. But there are alternatives.

I anticipate this occurring in the near future. Keep in mind, the ultimate aim of the agents from the dark side is to continue and even reinforce control over the people. They are well aware of parts of the Master Plan and know the future of this planet will be moving. They cannot stop this [the Earth] as it has the blessing of the sun-god and the God Source. But they can continue their focus on humankind, if you allow them to do so. This [allowing] has been, is, and will be most important for each to know. Your collective consciousness can allow or disallow what you choose.

[A scenario which we can 'allow or disallow':] To reinforce their position, the space beings will be making special physical appearances in the future. The lords, who have similar control over those beings who have been working directly on Earth, will visit. They are indeed powerful, as they use their thoughts to empower themselves. They too are from the dark side and they are the ones responsible for altering your DNA and introducing the different control systems. They know the human race inside and out, so there is no fooling them.

These lords will appear to come in peace and love. They will be coming to 'save' humankind. They will even do some very beneficial things for humankind. This will include such things as teaching new medical technologies as well as other technologies. They will cure certain diseases that they brought to humankind in the first place. But this will look good for them. It will endear humankind to them. They will speak of love and truths. This will create much confusion in the minds of many, as the benevolent and loving space beings will also be presenting themselves. To those who can discern, this will present no difficulties. To those who have developed their self-awareness, this will not present difficulties. But to the masses who still cling to their old ways by endorsing their own limitations, to these there will be potential difficulties.

These 'negative' space beings will give humankind a very attractive alternative to your current situations. This is a complete illusion but those who accept it will not realize this until it is too late for them.

There are choices that each can make and that the mass consciousness acting as one can make. Every human on this planet has been given the same opportunity, the same knowledge for their self-determination. There is absolutely no one who can say they did not know. Each of you have incarnated with the same ability to self-empowerment, to being aware of your oneness, to being able to discern what is love and what is illusion. You have chosen your own kinds of programming to conceal your knowledge of your self and the universe. You can reverse this as well.

I have explained in some detail events of the past, present and future, as you call it. Yet there will be volumes of details on this same subject. […]

There is no intent to characterize those space beings from the dark side as other than belonging to the One Creator. For we are all part of the One. But the Father of us all is not pleased with those whose path is not that of love. The One Creator loves all for Its love is perfect. But the Creator also says that for every harmful act there must be an offsetting or balancing act of love. Eventually, in the realm of timelessness, those from the dark side must come to terms with the love that the God Source offers to all. They can only do this in a loving way that will balance all harm or non-love each has done. *[… And the same is true for all of us!]*

Apocalypse now?

The prophetic words spoken by Joel and the beginning of their fulfilment on the day of Pentecost indicate that it is possible for man to access divine sources of guidance and higher information. Jesus himself stated that he had yet many things to say and that the time would come when he would no longer speak in allegories and veiled language but in plain words, in order to explain what he really meant. Jesus said this shortly before he was arrested and crucified. Obviously his prediction was not fulfilled during his physical presence on earth. The unveiled information was to be revealed later, at the given time, through the Spirit of truth. This is only natural because great events are always announced in advance, both by renewed spiritual information and by warnings and prophecies.

Looking back over the past two thousand years, it becomes evident that in our times, starting from the nineteenth century, the number of people endowed with the gifts of the spirit has rapidly increased. Despite the quality and purity of the 'paranormal' phenomena being quite varied, the very fact prophesied by Joel can be observed: young and old men and women, mostly from the working class ('menservants' and 'maidservants'), suddenly do 'prophesy', 'have dreams' and 'see visions'. As stated in the same passage (Joel 2.28–32), this was foreseen to happen prior to 'the day of the Lord'.

This crucial turning point in history is also mentioned by many contemporary revelations, for example in the following text, spoken in 'plain words', as Jesus himself promised. These plain words are all the more exposing as the chosen passage unveils the hidden meaning of a main theme of the Apocalypse: the dragon forces. Fifty years after his ascension, Jesus – in his Revelation to St John – had still used a form of communication that was mostly veiled and symbolic. The explanation in plain words was to be given at a much later date, namely in the time when these prophecies were to come true.

Undeniably, the unveiled explanations are given now. According to the logic of the prophets, this means that the described event is imminent. And only now are the people addressed able to handle such mind-boggling information about the cosmic background of earthly history, past and present.

The following channelled text refers to a scene of the Apocalypse, 'the woman and the dragon' (Rev. 12.1–6; 13–17). This mysterious passage of the Bible entails two obvious questions: What does this 'woman' symbolize? And who is the 'dragon'? As we are now told, these words were not only symbolical but also realistic, when seen from a perspective which includes the astral dimensions.

The beings of light and love do not play down the workings of the dark forces. Being situated beyond all shadows, they are able to see and identify the factors that block out the light. The clarity of discernment and the sublime love felt in these words lend credence to the claim that it is indeed the ascended Jesus who is speaking, further revealing some of the many things he still has to say:

During our past gatherings we have spoken about events that are to come and that, to a great extent, have already come to pass. Today I would like to give you information about the connection between the things prophesied to you in the remote past and those which have now begun to fulfil themselves. You have been told everything before. [...]

There was a pregnant woman crying aloud in the pangs of childbirth. And a dragon was waiting for the child to be born, for it wished to devour the child. Then the child was born, and a hand came down from heaven to lift it up so that the dragon could not devour it.

Please understand these words in depth! The pregnant woman crying aloud in the pangs of childbirth is your planet earth. It is the earth presently moving in great pain while giving birth to the new kingdom. The dragon is a symbol for the unified forces on earth that are being manipulated by entities from a far-distant solar system, entities originating from the lineage of the Beast. The entities symbolized by the serpent, the dragon, are manifestations of a development that took place outside the human race. They have their origin in the dimensions of the lizards and snakes [astral reptoids] that, over a long period of time, have developed into entities able to dispose over magical knowledge and dark powers. They are entities that have no emotions because the evolution of their species was limited to the one-sided expansion of intelligence and strength. They have established energy bases under the earth, and through them they are connected to their far distant home planet. They have used their intelligence and knowledge to manipulate those people on earth who direct global destiny.

The dragon represents the power and intelligence from without, that attempts to devour the child that is about to be born. And this child is the 'New Jerusalem', the new kingdom, the coming new Earth. The hand that appears from the clouds to save the new-born child is a symbol for the star sisters and brothers who have taken position to lift up the seeds of the new Earth, those whom the dragon wants to devour. Several of you will be able to ascend on your own, to raise yourselves and to attain the celebration hall without the help of the spaceships.

In this way, all who are called upon will be gathered together. And while you lovingly and joyously reunite with your sisters and brothers, the cleansing of the earth will be accomplished. The inner worlds of the planet will turn inside out, and all domains will be renewed. The earth will be born anew and you, in these moments, will be dwelling in the celebration hall.

Therefore, you who have gathered here, know that your presence is of great significance. Many times have I spoken these words to you. You have walked on various thorns and thistles that were and still are a part of your destiny on earth. I once told you that the select are bought from the earth with a price.* All that you have borne in times of the past due to inflicted pains, diseases, wars, the heavy yoke of oppression – it is all this I meant when

---

* see I Cor. 6.20 and 7.23

I said that those who are mine have been bought with a price. All past humiliation, all the thorns and thistles were part of the price that you have paid. This was necessary for you to acquire insight, wisdom and knowledge so that no temptation would ever be able to reach your hearts again. On earth you have been walking on the thorns and thistles of adverse life circumstances. But on your heads – invisible to you – you carry crowns that are brightly radiating in the spiritual realm. The crowns of some are inscribed with the word 'mercy', others with the word 'love', yet others with the words 'humility', 'perseverance', 'friendliness' and 'kindness'.

The serpent is aware of your importance, your power and your potentials. Therefore, be prepared, take heed, for it will never cease to devise of ways to snare your feet to make you fall. Hold fast your crowns! Hold them fast and know: darkness will grow even more. You, however, remember your crowns when everything turns so dense that you may think to never see the light again! Then the hand of the Father will reach into time and lift you up from this globe. […]

The dark forces have again plotted a big tribulation. They are gathering in their bases to unify their forces, for it is their plan to bring about the downfall of those bearing the invisible crowns. Not wanting to abandon their empire on this planet, they are striving to prevent the new kingdom from coming. Therefore, take heed, remain true, and know: *Everything that nourishes doubts within you and cools off your hearts are seeds from their realm.* Weed them out and always endeavour to purify and renew the circumstances of your life! Grow in your love with every breath, and become evermore absorbed in love!

The empire from without that is still also in your world has no capacity to love. Therefore, let love be your protection. Take the sword of love and never give it out of your hand! It is given to you who are called upon, chosen and faithful. Throughout all times the knowledge of the things to come was given to you before they came to pass. It will also be given to you in the future. You have seen in the past that all words came true, and verily, all further words will also come true. […]

While you are in safety, protected by the hand that stretched out from heaven, the war will begin. The dragon will persecute the woman, and mankind will be exposed to the danger of being deceived. From outer regions other nations and other civilizations will rush in and also fight for this planet, the earth, intending to claim their right to power. But the Father will end this war, and a great cleansing will take place through inundation.

When the elements and the waves of fear begin to rise, remain within your inner stillness and peace! For what is being realized is the will of God! Every single action is observed and every single motion in the earthly world is registered. If someone happens to be endangered, he or she will be taken up. And the hand will reach down from heaven above, which is the realm of angels in the form of the star sisters and brothers.

Do not fear anything! The physical world will be born anew. Do not be attached! The house of the Father is spacious. The earth is positioned in the lower heavens, but her heart and soul have now called out to be elevated into the higher heaven. Therefore, you will soon take leave of the physical world and enter into a higher dimension of existence.[117]

Summary and outlook

The two texts quoted in this chapter are examples of messages received through contemporary sources of prophecy and 'channelling'. They were quoted at length so as to show the extent of disclosure and inspiration that such sources can offer.

These two texts were received by individuals – one in the USA, the other in Germany – who knew nothing of each other. And yet, they both describe the same scenario in a complementary way. As shown in the next chapter, they are substantiated by sources of Vedic, biblical and native backgrounds as well as by other contemporary seers and investigative researchers. Thus, we are given an overall view that also takes astral and extraterrestrial factors into account.

Although channelled messages should not be taken as absolute either (by claiming one of them to be the one and only truth), they do certainly convey perspectives and explanations that broaden our horizon. They deserve to be considered and heard, no less than the writings and opinions of terrestrial authors, journalists etc.

CHAPTER THIRTEEN

How Much Truth Is There in Science Fiction?

Regarding the depth and quality of their contents, contemporary revelations are certainly not unholier than canonized texts of the Bible and other religious books. Rather, they are the fruits of an increased spiritual 'output' containing many topics which could not be told earlier, or which had been deleted by some 'representatives of God'.

The texts quoted in the previous chapter have illustrated the broad spectrum of these topics in their interwoven complexity: the spiritual origins of mankind, the existence of advanced civilizations in the past, the *yuga* cycles, the role of extraterrestrial beings in past and present human history, the infiltration of religions and governments by dark forces, psychophysical and genetic manipulation of the human race, the transfer of secret technology for ulterior motives, the presence of godless and God-devoted beings, etc.

Are the psychics who claim to receive such information simply 'contaminated' by science fiction and fantasy products? How, then, could ancient writers and prophets come up with similar themes? Could it be that today's producers of such films and novels are 'inspired', too? Are they – and their fans – spellbound by such topics due to a subconscious resonance? Have they been connected to these dimensions in their past lifetimes, and are they now simply projecting their suppressed fears, hopes and traumatic experiences? Tele-vision as a substitute for psychic visions of extraterrestrial worlds and star wars ...?

St John's Revelation speaks about a war in heaven provoked by the dragon, Satan personified. What is this dragon in its original form? The answer to this question, with its multi-faceted implications, was one of the things that were to be revealed later, when the people were prepared to grasp it. This is now the case, only since twenty or thirty years (not least due to the many presentations designated as fantasy and science fiction). In plain words, the 'dragon' symbolizes the force behind the destructive rulers on earth who are instrumentalized by non-terrestrial entities – 'manifestations of a development that took place outside the human race; they have their origin in the dimensions of the [astral] lizards and snakes' (p. 330). Being intellectually very advanced, they possess technomagical means of manipulation, but they are devoid of positive emotions and are spiritually impoverished. Symbolically, they are cold-blooded. This reptoid force ('the dragon ...') is attempting to hold off the transformation of the earth ('... will try to devour the new-born child'). However, there will be startling divine interventions: 'a hand reaching down from heaven will save the child'.

Reptoid influence at the beginning of Kali-yuga

Dragon-like powers are mentioned in contemporary and biblical texts and also in all other religions and native traditions. A lot of detailed information is found in the ancient scriptures of India. One example is the description of how the present dark age (Kali-yuga) began five thousand years ago, written down in the last of the twelve cantos of the *Shrimad-Bhagavatam*. This amazing story goes as follows:

At the end of the preceding age (Dvapara-yuga), the dark forces wanted to kill Maharaja Pariksit, the holy king of Bharata (India), because he maintained a divine atmosphere which prevented Kali's influence from manifesting on earth. Using a human agent, in this case the proud son of a priest (*brahmana*), they managed to curse the king, who now became vulnerable and thus exposed to magical attacks. It was at this moment that an astral entity of the lineage of the Nagas ('snakes': the Draconians or Reptoids) went into action. Nagas are semi-physical beings with immense magical abilities. For example, they can alter their bodily shape and appear as humans among humans, maintaining their form under certain conditions or for a certain time.[118]

With this ability, the said Naga entity called Takshaka* took on a materialized human body. By bribing a high priest, he gained access to

---

* Takshaka: (Skr.) 'biter; injurer'; name of a reptoid, vampire-like being; consisting of the words *ta*–body; *kshan*–to hurt, to wound (*kshana*–to kill); and *ka*–doer.

this last Dvapara-king, whom he killed with his fiery poison. However, due to the extreme exertion of materializing and spending himself, the mutated Naga agent could no longer maintain his human form and fell back into his Naga shape – a sudden macabre 'shape-shifting' in front of everyone's eyes. With his last strength he managed to escape by teleporting himself to his lair-base.

Seeing the murdered king, the assembled priests wanted to punish the heinous killer by death through fire. They began to use magical mantras to forcibly drag him back to the scene. Being pulled by their invisible energies, Takshaka was no longer able to withstand this superior power, and in great desperation he fled to Indra, the king of the celestial realms. Indra, being neutral and seeing the workings of Providence, allowed him to take refuge in his spaceship. In the meantime, the priests' act of revenge was stopped due to the intervention of the heavenly sage Brihaspati.

This is neither a science-fiction story nor a Star Wars episode, but a chapter from an epic Sanskrit scripture describing how, five thousand years ago, godless reptoid forces managed to gain a strong foothold on planet earth. In this connection, the Sanskrit word *vimana* is used twice. This word is well known in ufology, as it simply means 'flying chariot', 'aircraft' or 'spaceship'. The original texts are so clear in this regard that even conventional Sanskrit scholars are unanimous about the meaning of this word. The standard Sanskrit-English Dictionary by Sir M. Monier-Williams, first published 1899 by the Oxford University Press, explains the word *vimana* as follows (p. 980):

> from *vi-man,* measuring out, traversing; a car or chariot of the gods, any mythical self-moving aerial car (sometimes serving as a seat or throne, sometimes self-moving and carrying its occupant through the air […])

Let us now read the unabridged description of this terrorist attack that marked the beginning of Kali-yuga, in its original wording as found in the *Shrimad-Bhagavatam* (12.6.11–28):

> [Listen, how Kali-yuga made its entrance on earth.] O learned *brahmanas,* when the flying snake-being, the Naga named Takshaka, who had been sent by the angry son of a *brahmana,* came down to the earth to kill the king, he met Kashyapa Muni on the path./ Takshaka flattered the high priest Kashyapa by presenting him with valuable gifts and thereby stopped the sage, who was

expert in counteracting poison, from protecting Maharaja Pariksit. Then the Naga, who could assume any form he wished (*kama-rupa*), took on the form of a human *brahmana*, approached the king and killed him through the poison of his bite.

While beings all over the universe looked on, the body of the great self-realized royal sage (*raja-rishi*) went up in flames by the fire of the snake's poison. There arose a terrible cry of lamentation in all directions on the earth (*bhuvi*) and in the heavens (*khe*), and all the demigods, demons, human beings and other creatures were shocked. [...]

Hearing that his father had been fatally bitten by a Naga agent, Maharaja Janamejaya became extremely angry and had *brahmanas* perform a mighty sacrifice by which he began to burn all the snakes of the world.

When Takshaka saw even the most powerful serpents being burned in the blazing fire of the snake sacrifice, he was overwhelmed with fear and approached Indra, the leader of the demigods, for shelter.

When King Janamejaya did not see Takshaka entering his sacrificial fire, he asked the *brahmanas*: 'Why is not Takshaka, the lowest of all serpents, burning in this fire?'

The *brahmanas* replied: 'O best of kings, the snake Takshaka has not fallen into the fire because he is being protected by Indra, whom he has approached for shelter. Indra is holding him back from the fire.'

King Janamejaya, hearing these words, replied: 'Then, o revered *brahmanas*, why not make Takshaka fall into the fire along with his protector, Indra?'

Hearing this, the priests chanted the following mantra: *takshakashu patasveha sahendrena marutvata* [...] 'O Takshaka, fall immediately into this fire, together with Indra and his entire host of demigods!'

At this time, Indra was in his spaceship together with Takshaka (*savimanah sa-takshakah*). Suddenly, he was thrown from his position by the penetrating words of the *brahmanas*, and he became very disturbed.

Brihaspati [the teacher of the demigods], seeing Indra falling through the universe (*ambarat*) in his spaceship along with Takshaka (*vimanena sahatakshakam*), approached King Janamejaya and spoke to him as follows:

'O King among men (*manushya-indra*, 'human Indra'), it is not fitting that this king of snakes meet death at your hands, for he has drunk the nectar of the immortal demigods. Consequently, he is not subject to the ordinary workings of old age and death. [...] Therefore, my dear King, please stop this sacrifice of serpents (*sarpa-satra*), which was initiated with the intent of doing harm to others. Many innocent snakes have already been burned to death. Indeed, all people must suffer the unforeseen consequences of their past activities.'

Advised in this manner, Maharaja Janamejaya replied, 'So be it.' Honouring the words of the great sage (*maha-rishi*), he desisted from continuing the snake sacrifice and honoured Brihaspati, the most eloquent of sages.

A testimony from Borneo

Unexpectedly, the word 'Naga' also popped up on my journey to Borneo in 1999. Together with a small group of friends I wanted to meet native people in this exotic world who did not know about contemporary esoterics, ufology and secret politics. What do *such* people know about today's ruling powers, about paranormal phenomena, about the origin of men, about astral and extraterrestrial influence? This promising prospect prompted us to leave all common tourist paths in order to meet fellow men who were as 'uncivilized' as possible.

Borneo, the fourth biggest island in the world, is today politically divided, one part belonging to Malaysia, the other to Indonesia. Both governments support a strong Islamization. Global industry is cutting down the rain forest, especially in Sabah and Sarawak, and modern civilization with all its facets is being promoted, forcing the native people into a world of technology, salary work, taxes, military etc. Their next generation will be totally cut off from the roots of its tradition.

Since time immemorial women have been the keepers of the esoteric tradition in the native tribes of Borneo. As animistic shamans (called Bobolyan or Boboleezan in the local languages of North Borneo) they fulfilled manifold tasks within the social and religious structures of the former jungle tribes. Today, authentic Bobolyans have become few in number, because the tradition is on the decline due to external influence and internal deterioration. Furthermore, missionaries and religionists have been fighting these spiritistic women since the nineteenth century, calling them 'witches' and 'devil worshippers'.

A friend from Germany who had been living in Sabah for several years, supporting the natives, introduced us to an indigenous tribal community he knew. We were welcome and could live with them, but there was no Bobolyan in sight. We did not insist on meeting one, but just stayed there, thankful for their cordial hospitality.

The Naga totem-pole (detail) shown to the author in Borneo.

Then, in the evening of the eighth day, they surprised us with a festive ceremony in which they accepted us as trustworthy friends. That night, an old and skinny Bobolyan lady appeared seemingly from nowhere, and I was allowed to ask her all my questions. A young woman translated her words from the Rungu language into Malay, and our friend did the further translation into German. And thus it went on for hours, far into the night, with the whole village, about fifty people, listening with rapt attention. Initially, they even felt a little uneasy about this unusual revival of mythology, knowing that officially they were expected to be 'liberated' from such 'pagan' world-views. Way out in the wilderness, in the darkness of the night, this tribe's last forest-dwelling generation once again got a glimpse of their timeless tradition. And here, at the end of the world, I asked: 'Who rules the world?'

The old Bobolyan stated that she had never left the local area and that she did not know how to read and write. Still, 'we all know who is ruling'. But she did not start a political discussion. She immediately, and naturally, talked about the bigger picture. Beyond the world of man are the worlds of the spirits, with good spirits and evil spirits. The good ones do no harm, that is why she is not too concerned with them. Her 'real work' concerns the evil spirits whom she has to appease or neutralize. This has become very difficult nowadays, and limited to a few basic tasks on a local level. Beyond that, they all feel powerless as these evil spirits have come in the shape of men, sending their foreign servants to do all kinds of horrible work, like cutting down the jungle trees.

And then she said: 'This destruction is the work of the Nagas.' I was taken aback – it was the only word I could make out in all she said. Here we were far away from India, and the same word was used to name the

The discarded totem-poles at the edge of a jungle in North Borneo ...

astral forces that want to possess mankind and the planet. She went on to relate that some of them incarnate as humans, that she herself had seen people appear in a Naga form, and that these forces have been influencing mankind for a long time, and so on, and so forth.

Some days later we even got to see a ghastly illustration in the form of a totem-pole. A local craftsman had carved it about thirty or forty years ago as an expression of his vision of the world's situation. (It was lying amongst several other poles that had been discarded by the natives themselves, because the state religion does not like totemism and animism.)

This particular pole, made of ironwood and about two metres high, showed a man standing upright with a big moustache and typical western features, wearing the attributes of a rich and powerful man – a turban and big earrings, the equivalent of a crown in western traditions. His head was disproportionately large, his face without emotion. There was a strange (astral?) beast sitting on his head,

sucking at his forehead chakra depicted as a spiral on a lying crescent. And even worse: he held a naked, pregnant woman, one hand on her left breast, the other on her womb, *feeding her to a dragon!* The woman (with native features) was smaller than the man, her head shaven – the

... *with the Naga totem-pole depicting an astral vision of today's global exploitation.*

sign of a slave. The message of this artwork was shocking and obvious: a high-ranking western man was callously sacrificing a pregnant indigenous woman to a cold-blooded man-eating force. What an answer to my question![119]

Traces in Sumerian mythology

The so-called 'demons' (*asuras*) are not unified in a cosmic conspiracy but split into different factions, ranging from moderate and ethical groupings to radical and totalitarian wings. This rivalry affects all subordinate levels, down to our planet earth.

A closer look at history from this point of view indicates that many escalations on earth may have had invisible backgrounds. Even in modern times, most war lords and terrorists are moved by religions and scriptures that are said to be of a non-terrestrial origin. Are invisible worlds reaching into world history through these channels? The earth as a battlefield of the demons and the gods?

In addition to this, most ancient records report that in former times, today called the mythological times, the 'gods' were even visibly present on earth.

> When people began to multiply on the face of the ground, and daughters were born to them, the sons of God saw that they were fair; and they took wives for themselves of all that they chose. Then the Lord said, 'My spirit shall not abide in mortals forever, for they are flesh; their days shall be one hundred twenty years.' The Nephilim were on the earth in those days – and also afterwards – when the sons of God went in to the daughters of humans, who bore children to them. These were the heroes that were of old, warriors of renown. (Gen. 6.1–4)

This passage of the Old Testament is quite puzzling and has been interpreted in different ways. Who are the 'sons of God'? Who is the 'Lord'? Who are the 'Nephilim'?

One interpretation, taking the historical perspective, examines the parallels to other ancient legends of the Middle East. All of them mention different gods, giants and demigods as offspring of the sexual union of gods and humans. In the new Torah edition *Etz Hayim*, this passage is entitled 'Celestial-terrestrial intermarriage' (p. 33): 'Legends about relationships among gods and mortal women and among goddesses and men, resulting in the propagation of demigods, are widespread and familiar subjects of pagan mythology. The version presented here, highly condensed from what was once a well-known and fuller story, adds to the ancient myths the Israelite notion that the offspring of such unnatural unions may possess heroic stature but are devoid of divine qualities.'

In the above-quoted verses taken from the *HarperCollins Study Bible*, the wording 'began to multiply on the face of the ground' conveys a perspective that one might call extraterrestrial. The terms 'sons of God' and 'Nephilim' could also be interpreted along these lines.

What was going on in those days of old? The *HarperCollins Study Bible* comments: 'The *sons of God* – explained in later eras as renegade angels – resemble many figures of ancient mythology who recognize no border between heaven and earth. The term is perhaps synonymous with *Nephilim*, a word possibly related to the Hebrew root "to fall". These are called *heroes ... of old, warriors of renown* with some irony – their legacy is now faint, nearly forgotten.'

In Hebrew, the words for 'sons of God' are *b'nei elohim*, literally 'the sons of the Elohim' as *elohim* is the plural of *el* ('God', also found in names like Micha-el, Dani-el, Immanu-el etc.). *Etz Hayim* explains: 'The word *b'nei* often means "members of a category", so that the Hebrew phrase here means "members of the category of divine beings" (*elohim*).'

Other interpretations take *b'nei elohim* to be a symbolical expression for terrestrial men (males) as they are descendants of Adam, the first created 'son of God'. According to some, this passage indicates the beginning of mixed marriages (Israelites marrying pagan women), according to others, the beginning of polygamy. In this context, the word 'Nephilim' is seen as a description of tall earthly warriors like Goliath who were still around in the times of Joshua and David. In the fourth book of Moses, the author sees the land of Canaan still full of Nephilim, 'giants': 'All the people we saw there were of enormous size. We saw giants there, too: the Anakim descended from the Nephilim. We felt like grasshoppers, and so we seemed to them.' (Num. 13.33–4)

The *New Jerusalem Bible* says about Gen. 6.1–4: 'An obscure passage (from the Yahwistic tradition). The author uses a popular story of a race of giants, in Hebr. *nephilim*, the Titans of eastern legend, born of the union between gods and mortals. The author does not present this episode as a myth nor, on the other hand, does he deliver judgement on its actual occurrence; he records the anecdote of a superhuman race simply to serve as an example of the increase in human wickedness which was to provoke the Flood.'

The historical approach, which considers non-biblical texts as well, is further supported by the fact that the passage in question is the direct introduction to the story of the Great Flood, a motif also found in many other, more ancient sources.

Very relevant in this context are the Sumerian cuneiform tablets, as they contain passages describing a 'myth' similar to Genesis 6–9. However, the older version contains remarkable differences. It describes an archaic conflict between Enki and Enlil, the two leaders of the extraterrestrial Anunnaki; these are described as colonizers who used the dimensional gates of the Middle East to gain access to the earth. Why did they come? The Sumerian texts make it quite clear: to exploit the planet's resources and to find slaves. (Being propagandistic, these texts describe the former population of the earth as primitive and stupid, and suggest that these alleged subhumans became intelligent, productive and civilized only due to the intervention of the 'gods'.)

The main base of these alien colonizers was the land that was later to become known as Sumer and Babylon, situated in today's Iraq. From there, they established 'branches' throughout the Middle East up to the Lebanon (Baalbek). The cuneiform texts, especially the Epic of Gilgamesh, relate that the Anunnaki were still present at the time of the Deluge and that they wanted to let the human race be destroyed by this cataclysm. Enki, however, warned some of his favourite humans and instructed them how to build a boat to survive. Later, a monotheistic version of this event was included in the Old Testament.[120]

After the Deluge, the Anunnaki* delegated their authority to select human agents – high priests, kings and pharaohs. Some modern interpretations claim that these colonizers, the 'gods of Eden', even founded the bloodlines of the ominous Babylonian Brotherhood, which later on evolved into certain secret societies, clerical institutions, and circles of nobility, some of them extant to the present day.[121]

---

* There might be a connection to the similar-sounding name 'Anakim' mentioned in Num. 13.34 ('the Anakim descended from the Nephilim').

The children of the feather and the children of the serpent

Only recently have the Native Americans started to speak openly about their ancient knowledge, as most white men still have difficulty with their 'wild' world-views.

The following testimony was given by an Apache-Hopi ambassador known as Robert Morningsky, because his tribal name means 'morning sky'. The author was fortunate enough to meet him during an UFO congress in Zurich in 1997, which gave ample opportunity to discuss hot topics in a small circle.

Since the early nineties, Robert Morningsky has been publicly active, passing on the prophetic, alerting knowledge of his people, and speaking about the existence of our cosmic kin. He confirms, for example, that they know about the crashing of several UFOs in their lands, having witnessed it with their own eyes. Up to the present day, many American 'Indians' still spend their nights under the open sky, especially during the summer months – like in July 1947 when a UFO crashed in Roswell, New Mexico. 'We have always known about these things but the white man never bothered to ask his "primitive" red brother.'

In the minutes of the 'International New Age Meeting' held in Maleny, Queensland (Australia), on 8 February 1992, Robert's presentation is summarized as follows:

> [...] The Greys said that they were a dying race and needed help to get their bodies genetically stronger and healthier. An agency MJ-12 was brought into effect, to monitor this programme of experiments and implantations. Negotiations were completed and a treaty was signed in California. In Florida another body of Aliens arrived, called 'the Blues' by Robert Morningsky. They offered other advice, not to deal with the Greys, it would only lead to disaster. They [the Blues] would teach with peace and harmony if men disarmed and listened. The military said no deal! So they left, but a few decided to remain and stayed in Northern Mexico and Arizona and made a treaty with the Hopi Indians. These Aliens are known by the Hopi as Star Warriors. [...] The Hopi legend is that there were two races, *the children of the feather,* who came from the skies, and *the children of the serpent,* who came from under the earth. The children of the serpent chased the Hopi Indians out of the earth; these evil under-grounders were also called two-hearts. The government has signed a treaty with the children of the serpent. The Hopi have signed a treaty with the children of the feather.

In his lectures and seminars Robert Morningsky hands out a written manifesto (also published in the Internet) in which he shares the Hopi knowledge about spirituality and history. Amongst many other points, he also mentions the reptoid, semi-physical race that has interrelated with humanity in a non-divine way:

> The Lizard People: The Reptile is cold-blooded, the warmth of passion is not found within. They seek warmth outside themselves, and survive by stealing the warmth of the fire of other beings. This is the way of the Reptile.
> The Children of the Reptile [serpent] have also left their tracks on Mankind's history. Where there have been deceit and lies, where there have been fear and turmoil [...] therein, the Children of the Reptile have resided. Seeking to emerge into the World of the Sun, they feed upon the fire of others. Never forget this! Keep your fire under your control.
> Seek the Path of the Reptile and you shall find one of the greatest deceits of all time. It was the serpent that aspired to Godhood. It was the serpent that wanted Man's adulation and it was the serpent that wanted man's soul. Those who seek your passion, your spirit, or your soul – these are the Children of the Reptile. [...]
> Unknown to the humans of the time [to those who made the treaty], the Greys already had connection with the Children of the Reptile. Underground bases would permit easier contact and give the Children of the Reptile direct monitoring of all activities. [...]
> The weakness of the Greys is that they are emotionless. They feed upon our emotions that we willingly give up. When consumed with fear and insecurity, lack of confidence in ourselves, we give up our passion to the feeding frenzy of those devouring sharks.
> In other words, the Children of the Reptile must not be forgotten in the equation of earthly events. Their alliance with the Greys poses a formidable force. It will do researchers and all who study the Greys well to remember that the true power behind them are the Children of the Reptile.[122]

UFOs – an age-old phenomenon?

The above-quoted examples from ancient and native testimonies indicate the same basic contents that are mentioned in contemporary channellings and psychic insights. They all agree on the point that there are dark forces as well as hosts of the Light, both of them having their respective influence on humanity, not only in the present age but since time immemorial.

As documented by many researchers, all ancient cultures spoke about gods who came from heaven, some being angels, others being oppressors and exploiters. But they all had some form of aircraft described as *'vimanas'*, 'heavenly chariots', 'clouds', 'fiery pillars', 'flying shields', etc. The expressions used today, such as 'flying saucers', 'cigar-shaped aircraft' and 'unidentified flying objects' (UFOs), are not really more enlightened.

Do these terms all refer to the same phenomenon? If these 'flying shields' were here in the past, they should be here also today.

And they are.

In the following elaboration, we can cite only a few selected key events and quotations to give an overview of the facts, reports and testimonies – sightings, recorded incidents, and people claiming to have inside knowledge, some of them being high-ranking officers. Referring to this information, different researchers have given their interpretations, ranging from doubts and denials to science-fiction-like scenarios. There is a big quantity of relevant literature and Internet articles about these topics, making it easy for everybody to find further amazing documents, reports of personal experiences, and official testimonies. Newcomers are usually overwhelmed, and astounded, by the amount of available material. In the present age of information, nothing can be kept totally secret, especially when thousands of people have seen 'something'. And, some pieces of information always leak out. Furthermore, many documents, some official and some controversial, have been provided by former insiders or obtained by researchers through the 'Freedom of Information Act'. A lot of investigation and research has been done in the past fifty years, and now it appears that the phenomenon has entered another stage.

Strange flying objects after WWII

Rumours about unidentified flying objects have existed throughout the centuries, with a culmination around the end of the nineteenth century (mostly on the US west coast). But all of these observations are minor in comparison to what happened after 1945.

Suddenly, the UFOs were there. Did they appear as a reaction to the Second World War, or maybe to the dropping of the two atom bombs? It started in Europe – with waves of strange objects appearing over

Scandinavia. But soon a much bigger wave was seen in the skies above the USA, particularly in June and July 1947. On 24 June 1947, Kenneth Arnold, a 32-year-old businessman and respected rescue pilot, reported that while flying above Mount Rainier, he had seen nine objects that flew at a speed of approximately 2000 kilometres per hour, a speed three times faster than the fastest pursuit planes of that time.

In the following weeks, hundreds and thousands of citizens, amongst them many pilots and members of the Army, reported similar observations: round flying objects which suddenly appeared and disappeared, either alone or in formation. And, interestingly, they often appeared above Army and Air Force bases. On 28 June 1947, three days after Arnold's report, UFOs were sighted over Maxwell AFB (Air Force Base) in Montgomery, Alabama, and one day later over White Sands AFB in New Mexico, the prohibited missile testing ground. On 8 July, there was a flock of UFOs over Muroc AFB (today Edwards AFB) in the Mojave Desert in southern California.

'Flying Saucers now sighted in most US States' was a headline in the *San Francisco Chronicle* of 7 July 1947.

The phenomenon was obviously something completely novel, and the US military officers (initially!) handled the matter like any other public issue. Proof of this was a press release written by Lieutenant Walter Haut on the instructions of Colonel William Blanchard, the Commander of the Air Force base in Roswell, New Mexico, where Bomber Squadron 509 was stationed, the squadron that had dropped the atom bombs on Hiroshima and Nagasaki.

In the night of 2 to 3 July 1947, an object crashed into the fields of a remote ranch near Corona, a small village out in the middle of nowhere, about 100 miles northwest of Roswell. The rancher, William 'Mac' Brazel, found parts of the wreckage (consisting of an unknown material that was thin but highly resilient) and brought them to Roswell with his pick-up truck on Sunday, 6 July – for him a one-way trip of four hours. He contacted the sheriff, who in turn informed the nearby AFB. Immediately, on the same Sunday, a group of Air Force experts under the command of Major Jesse Marcel went to Corona to check out the situation. Mac Brazel's report had arrived amidst the nation-wide wave of flying-saucer sightings.

The next morning Lieutenant Haut wrote the following statement to the press:

> The many rumors regarding the flying disc became a reality yesterday when the intelligence office of the 509th Bomb Group of the Eighth Air Force, Roswell Army Air Field, was fortunate enough to gain possession of a disc through the co-operation of one of the local ranchers and the Sheriff's office of Chaves county. The flying object landed [crashed] on a ranch near Roswell sometime last week. Not having phone facilities, the rancher stored the disc until such time as he was able to contact the Sheriff's office, who in turn notified Major Jesse A. Marcel, of the 509th Bomb Group Intelligence office. Action was immediately taken and the disc was picked up at the rancher's home. It was inspected at the Roswell Army Air Field and subsequently loaned by Major Marcel to higher headquarters.

Those newspapers that were printed in the afternoon instantly took up the news and published it in their Tuesday editions, with front page headlines like 'RAAF Captures Flying Saucer on Ranch in Roswell Region' (*Roswell Daily Record*, 8 July 1947).

While these papers were being printed and distributed, top-level offices reacted with an immediate dementi. General Roger M. Ramey moved heaven and earth to prevent the statement from receiving further publicity. The whole nation had seen, or heard about, these strange objects. Therefore, referring to the sensational Roswell statement, the *San Francisco Chronicle* wrote on 9 July: 'A platter-puzzled Nation thought it was about to get the answer to the mystery of the "flying discs" yesterday.'

And, on 10 July 1947, the same newspaper reported:

> '*Flying Saucer*' Find Turns Out to Be a Weather Balloon – (Ramey Broadcast) There was immediately much telephoning from the Pentagon in Washington, and then Brigadier General Roger M. Ramey, commanding the Eighth Air Force at Fort Worth, said the object had been identified as the wreckage of a high-altitude weather observation device.

While the nation was being told that everything was just a false alarm due to a crashed weather balloon, the ranch in the middle of nowhere was immediately isolated by the military. When Mac Brazel returned, he was not allowed to enter his fields for one week. He and his family were forced to stay silent about all they had seen.

This incident marked a decisive turning point. Until the beginning of July 1947, the US Air Force had apparently never been challenged to deal with a crashed flying disc and had not yet issued any instructions about how to proceed in such a case. Otherwise, the commanding officers of Roswell AFB, the place that had been instrumental in the top-secret atom-bomb project, would not have gone public that innocently. This indicates that they were dealing with such matters *for the first time,* and did not know what was going on.

Now, however, the highest US authorities immediately ordered absolute discretion, and an immense censorship apparatus was built up. Further coverage of this matter was impeded (by ridicule and 'private' threats) and then suppressed. It took thirty years before independent researchers again became aware of this case (along with other cases).

Regarding the Roswell incident, more than three hundred reliable witnesses were found even thirty years later, amongst them Jesse Marcel, Walter Haut, rancher Mac Brazel and Sheriff Wilcox (who had been first contacted by Mac Brazel). Another witness was General DuBose, Ramey's superior! Having retired in the meantime, they all felt free to give their honest testimonies, stating that they still maintained their original opinion: the debris they had found and seen had not been part of any US weather balloon.

General DuBose, for example, testified that the original material of the wreckage had been exchanged with the material of a weather balloon, which was then presented to the press. This he also confirmed in an affidavit in 1991:

> My name is Thomas Jefferson DuBose. [...] I retired from the U.S. Air Force in 1959 with the rank of Brigadier General. In July 1947, I was stationed at Fort Worth Army Air Field (later Carswell Air Force Base) in Fort Worth, Texas. I served as Chief of Staff to Major General Roger Ramey, Commander, Eighth Air Force. [...] The material shown in the photographs taken in Maj. Gen. Ramey's office was a weather balloon. The weather balloon explanation for the material was a cover story to divert the attention of the press.

In July 1947, General DuBose had co-ordinated the transport of the wreckage material from Roswell via Fort Worth to Washington and to the Air Material Command at Wright Field, later Wright Patterson AFB. DuBose in his affidavit: 'The entire operation was conducted under strictest secrecy.'

One of the people present at Wright Field when the material from Roswell came in was Lt. Col. Arthur E. Exon. He retired as a brigadier general, and in 1990 he testified to the authors Kevin Randle and Don Schmitt: 'The metal and material was unknown to anyone I talked to.

Whatever they found, I never heard what the results were. A couple of guys thought it might be Russian, but the overall consensus was that the pieces were from outer space.'¹²³

Based on the 'Freedom of Information Act', researchers obtained an FBI memorandum which revealed that – right on 9 July 1947 – the Pentagon, through Brigadier General George F. Schulgen, had requested the FBI to participate in the investigation of the crashed flying discs (it says *discs* – indicating there was more than one):

> Colonel Forsey indicated that it was his attitude that inasmuch as it has been established that the flying disks are not the result of any Army or Navy experiments, the matter is of interest to the FBI. He stated that he was of the opinion that the Bureau, if at all possible, should accede to General Schulgen's request.

At the bottom of this FBI memorandum¹²⁴ the legendary FBI chief J. Edgar Hoover had responded with a hand-written note, stating: 'I would do it but before agreeing to it we must insist upon full access to [the] discs recovered.'

And so it came to pass that top-ranking officers who only a few hours ago had been convinced that the debris recovered had been something *completely unknown,* all of sudden could no longer remember anything. They appeared confused and intimidated. Although it was highly unlikely that the aviation experts of Roswell AFB had mistaken a weather balloon for a UFO, the press printed the official denial without further questions. A top-secret cover-up had started.

In the following years, UFOs were also seen in other countries and continents. The next big UFO wave, however, again took place over the USA, in the summer of 1952, culminating in UFOs appearing in formation above the White House in the nights of two consecutive Saturdays (19 July and 26 July 1952).¹²⁵ Interestingly enough, these parades over Washington had been announced by the psychic UFO-contactee George van Tassel, one of those early 'weirdos' who claimed to be in telepathic contact with the ufonauts. These contactees received telepathic messages with 'urgent warnings to mankind' regarding the dangers of nuclear experiments, and messages with spiritual topics. George van Tassel published these announcements in his newsletter *Proceedings,* which he sent to the Pentagon and the FBI headquarters. Soon after, the parades factually took place!¹²⁶

From May to August 1952, more than a hundred sightings witnessed by military staff and/or radar were recorded, not to speak of the many other sightings reported by civilians.

The situation was flabbergasting. UFO contactees appeared, transcommunicating warnings against any further usage of nuclear weapons, and UFOs supported these protests with two 'peace demonstrations' above the White House. And there were no crashes.

After this paranormal summer, the 'official' attitude towards the UFO topic again changed remarkably. Denying or covering up the phenomenon was no longer possible. But heeding the warnings and changing the chosen course of destruction was apparently out of question, too, at least for the secret government. Therefore, in January 1953, Air Force Major General John A. Samford and Air Force General (and secret MJ-12 member) Hoyt S. Vandenberg founded a committee headed by CIA member Dr H. P. Robertson, called the 'Robertson Panel'. Documents now available reveal that this Panel was meant to monitor the public presentation of all UFO matters with the intended purpose of debunking and ridiculing everything in this regard.

The new strategy had instant legal consequences. The US Ministry of Defence issued an order binding for all Air Force members, the *Air Force Regulation* 200-2. According to this regulation, the public was only to be informed about a UFO sighting when it could be presented to have been an illusion. All other accounts were to be handled as top secret. Towards the end of the year, an even stricter regulation was decreed: *The Joint Army Navy Air Force Publication* 146 (*Janap* 146), issued by the joint command of the Army, the Navy and the Air Force. Now, the passing-on of information about UFOs of any kind was categorized as spying and was punishable with either prison of up to ten years or a fine of up to $10,000.

The Robertson strategy and the new regulations had their desired effect. From 1954 onwards, the number of UFO reports submitted by pilots and military personnel drastically decreased. Why did the secret services no longer need such official reports? This sudden lack of interest may have had several reasons. One speculation says that 'they' no longer needed such reports because they had done clandestine investigations of their own, and had come up with tangible results – or even contacts – that were to be kept in topmost secrecy! The topic itself was delegated to Hollywood and 'science fiction'.

The suppression of public research

Nevertheless, not all information could be suppressed, mainly due to the 'ufonauts' themselves, who did not follow the strategy of the earthly secret government. In the early sixties there were new waves of unidentified flying objects over the USA, inciting a public interest so intense that the head of the Republicans of those days, Gerald Ford, the later US President, made a petition for a congressional hearing, which then took place on 5 April 1966. The result of this hearing was the foundation of a scientific committee led by Prof. Edward Condon, a known sceptic (and debunker) of the entire UFO phenomenon. Those who did not follow the line of Condon and his superiors were soon fired, for example Dr David Saunders and Dr Norman Levine. The official reason: 'insubordination'.

At the same time, Major Coleman VonKeviczky, an American UN official, compiled an extensive documentation about the UFO phenomenon and the ongoing sightings, and presented it to the General Secretary of the UNO, U Thant, who met with him for a personal interview on 9 February 1966. Right after this half-private initiative, Major VonKeviczky was suspended from his UN post at the instigation of certain US authorities. Still, U Thant (1909–74) kept up his involvement, as reported by the *New York Post* in its edition of 27 June 1967:

> U Thant and UFO's – In the very middle of the Near East crisis, UN Secretary General Thant took time to do a very significant thing. He arranged to have one of the top advocates of the theory that flying saucers – UFOs – are from another planet, speak before the Outer Space Affairs Committee of the UN. […] On June 7 Dr. James E. McDonald of the University of Arizona, a firm believer in UFOs, spoke before the UN outer space committee. Dr. McDonald believes that UFOs are extraterrestrial spaceships on reconnaissance missions to explore the earth. […] Interesting fact is that U Thant has confided to friends that he considers UFOs the most important problem facing the UN next to the war in Vietnam.

However, a systematic investigation by the UN was blocked. The UN ambassador of the Soviet Union, Nikolai Fedorenko, commented that UFOs were nothing but 'the nightmares of imperialistic and capitalistic nations', and US representatives emphasized that there was already a 'scientific' investigation going on, led by Prof. Condon; a separate UN committee was therefore declared to be unnecessary.

In December 1968, the so-called Condon Report, the 'official study' on UFOs by the University of Colorado and the National Academy of Science, was published, concluding that the entire UFO phenomenon was unsubstantiated; therefore, a further investigation was said to be no longer justified.

Still, the sightings continued. On 14 July 1978, there was even a special UN conference about UFOs, headed by the Secretary General Kurt Waldheim. Amongst the ten experts and scientists that had been invited were the astronaut Gordon Cooper and Lawrence Coyne, a colonel of the US army, who both had witnessed spectacular sightings. However, the scientists headed by Jacques Vallée and J. Allen Hynek prevented this conference from founding an independent UN committee that was meant to investigate the UFO phenomenon on a global basis.[127]

In this way, the hopes for an official investigation that was not monitored by some 'secret government' were destroyed once again.

What did the astronauts see?

Since the beginning of space exploration it has been rumoured that some astronauts have seen UFOs or experienced paranormal things. These rumours have been confirmed (to some extent) by some former astronauts themselves, and by members of the NASA. A very important testimony was given by Gordon Cooper, one of the first men in outer space. In May 1963, he was the man aboard the legendary *Faith 7* which orbited the earth 22 times in 34 hours and 20 minutes. In 1965 he was aboard *Gemini* 5 together with Charles Conrad, staying in space for 190 hours, orbiting the earth 120 times.

Soon after, Gordon Cooper started to go public with his UFO experiences. For example, in an interview published in the *Los Angeles Herald Examiner* on 15 August 1976, he clearly stated that he had seen several alien spaceships during his flights in outer space.

Again and again, he recounted that he had seen formations of UFOs as early as in 1951, when he had been stationed in Germany. Later, while serving at Edwards Air Force Base in California, he and his crew had seen such objects on several occasions. One such object was even filmed while it landed and took off (in May 1957). When Cooper sent the film to Washington, it disappeared somewhere in the Pentagon.

In an open letter to Grenada's UN ambassador Griffith, dated 9 November 1978, Gordon Cooper stated:

> I believe that these extra-terrestrial vehicles and their crews are visiting this planet from other planets, which obviously are a little more technically advanced than we are here on earth. I feel that we need to have a top level, coordinated program to scientifically collect and analyse data from all over the earth concerning any type of encounter, and to determine how best to interface with these visitors in a friendly fashion. We may first have to show them that we have learned to resolve our problems by peaceful means, rather than warfare, before we are accepted as fully qualified universal team members. This acceptance would have tremendous possibilities of advancing our world in all areas. [...] I also like to point out that most astronauts are very reluctant to even discuss UFOs due to the great numbers of people who have indiscriminately sold fake stories and forged documents abusing their names and reputations without hesitation. Those few astronauts who have continued to have a participation in the UFO field have had to do so very cautiously. There are several of us who believe in UFOs and who have had occasion to see a UFO [...]

In 1996, a ten minute TV feature with 69-year-old Gordon Cooper was produced that went around the world. *'Gordon Cooper, a highly decorated pilot and astronaut: he wants the people to finally know the truth.'* That was the tenor of this astounding and exceptional report.

And Gordon Cooper was no the only pre-Apollo astronaut who observed unidentifiable flying objects in outer space. The already mentioned 'Condon Report' also contained an examination of the UFO sightings by the early astronauts. Despite its purpose of debunking the UFO issue once and for all, even this Report had to admit that there were at least three visual observations made by astronauts while orbiting the earth that could not be sufficiently explained. This referred to the space missions *Gemini* 4 and *Gemini* 7.

The ex-astronaut Gordon Cooper during his 1996 TV feature, as shown in Germany by the station PRO 7 on 16 January 1997.

The 'Condon Report' was concluded in December 1968, i.e. before the Apollo missions. Starting with 1969, more astronauts got the opportunity to experience the fact that 'there are more things in heaven and earth'. Two astronauts who, later on, chose to speak publicly about these topics were Brian O'Leary and Edgar Mitchell.

Edgar Mitchell was a crew member of the Apollo missions 10 and 16, and was Chief Pilot of Apollo 14. Moved by his experiences in outer space, he began a spiritual journey and founded the 'Institute of Noetic Sciences'.

> In publicly made statements, Mitchell confessed that he no longer doubted the existence of UFOs. 'It's not whether I believe they are real or not, but we still have to find out where they are coming from.'[128]

In 1996, Edgar Mitchell published a book entitled *The Way of the Explorer – An Apollo Astronaut's Journey through Material and Mystical Worlds*. Therein he describes, from the viewpoint of an extraterrestrial, how mankind's exploration of outer and inner space will be the next epoch of advancement.

A similar transformation was experienced by Brian O'Leary, who became a prominent author and lecturer about holistic science and parapsychology. The titles of his books speak for themselves, for example: *Exploring Inner and Outer Space – A Scientist's Perspective on Personal and Planetary Transformation* (1989), *The Second Coming of Science – An Intimate Report on the New Science* (1989) and *Miracle in the Void – Free Energy, Ufos and Other Scientific Revelations* (1996).

During a press conference in 1991 Brian O'Leary said:

> 'I do not know the truth of the matter of alleged UFO cover-ups. What I do know from my own experience and from scientific investigations and experiments is that UFO phenomena and a range of other paranormal events (ESP, near-death experience, etc.) are part of our reality – as incredible as it may seem. These phenomena are not at all hoaxes as the sceptics claim. [...] Part of that new reality is embracing the unknown and the possibility that we have visitors beyond Earth or beyond our dimensions of time and space.'[129]

From 12 to 14 January 1997, 'Televisione Svizzera Italiana' (TSI), the TV station of the Italian-speaking part of Switzerland, broadcast a high-class documentary on UFOs in four parts, produced by Guido Ferrari. Part 4 was a live discussion with astronomers and UFO researchers,

How Much Truth Is There in Science Fiction? 355

Prof. Dino Dini from Pisa, Italy, during the TV live discussion on TSI, 14 January 1997.

among them Prof. Dino Dini (born 1921) from the University of Pisa, a spacecraft engineer who had been working for NASA since the mid-fifties.

The viewers of this live presentation expected Prof. Dini to represent the conservative NASA standpoint. Instead, this 76-year-old scientist made sensational statements that shook up even the other experts present in the studio:

> Now, the fact is: What Armstrong saw was real. For wherever there is confusion, be it during the Gulf War, the last war, wherever tumult breaks out, these *dischi volanti* [flying discs] appear. They emerge from bases positioned near the earth. [...] Neil Armstrong saw objects following them, spacecraft that was following the Apollo – and also living beings. Apollo was followed by other spaceships. This is a fact that was observed during various expeditions.

Furthermore, Prof. Dini openly admitted that there had been a cover-up of the topic by NASA and that he had participated in it:

> That was us who had suppressed the global discussion of the issue because we had received orders to this effect. We were extremely shocked upon seeing which gap of difference there was between our technology and science and that of the UFOs. Therefore it is evident that this caused us to give negative assessments about UFOs. [...] Without a doubt, it is very sobering to admit the fact that we have no explanations, as our level of science is still primitive when compared to that of those planets where these spacecraft come from.

Was he serious about what he said? The author (A.R.) contacted this witness and got the opportunity to meet him in his office at the

University of Pisa, Department of Engineering, where he had been the dean for many years.

In 1954, as a young professor of engineering and technical physics, he had been called to the Jet Propulsion Laboratory of the California Institute of Technology (*Caltech*) in Pasadena, where he worked for the famous rocket engineers Tsien Hsue-she, Theodore von Karman and Wernher von Braun. In 1966, he also became Italy's national co-ordinator for the Propulsion and Energetics Panel within the Advisory Group for Aerospace Research and Development (PEP-AGARD), a division of NATO. At the time of our interview, he still worked in this position for the military, for the University and for the motor industry; he also was president of the technical commission of Italy's motoring organization (A.C.I.), and had been so for more than twenty years.

Armin Risi and Prof Dino Dini during the interview in Pisa, July 1997.

This respected and distinguished gentleman confirmed everything he had said on TV, and added further information, for example:

> The astronauts were never allowed to forget that they worked on behalf of an organization, and this organization did not want to ruin its reputation with dubious stories. If it had become known that the space-flight missions were followed by alien spacecraft – with alien beings aboard! – then the entire mission would have lost its scientific nature, and these UFOs and extraterrestrials would have been the central topic. The astronauts were immediately ordered to deny everything. But they had already talked about it. Therefore, they had to add that everything had been the product of some sensory illusion, which is certainly possible in outer space. When I was there, working for NASA, I often had to give public statements, and in certain points, these statements were not true. […] Neil Armstrong, for example, was warned to be more cautious in what he said because his observations had the potential of creating a public tumult. I was there witnessing it. These things were internally published in several memorandum papers. […]
>
> The idea that we are alone in the universe is not very old. It has been the

Catholic Church which spread this doctrine: that human beings only exist on this one planet, this one being so special and unique that life originated here. But already 6,000 years ago, the Sumerians knew that the earth was not the centre of the universe. Apparently they knew even more. In the year 1600, Giordano Bruno was burned alive in Rome because he believed that there were many inhabited planets in the universe. The Catholic Church says that Jesus Christ is the only Son of God. This may be true in regard to the earth. But Jesus has *many millions of brothers and sisters!* He is not the only Son of God in the universe. I think if we can leave behind such outdated opinions of the Middle Ages, then we have come closer to peace on earth.[130]

Universal team or interplanetary war?

Many other testimonies and documents could be quoted as well. Some mention UFO crashes, cover-ups and dark forces, others speak about inner awakening and cosmic consciousness. From a multidimensional perspective, these seeming contradictions are easily resolved. Obviously, there are higher-dimensional beings who communicate with humans in a friendly, even divine way, in most cases invisibly through telepathy and inner inspiration. This would explain why some astronauts experienced a spiritual transformation, even without direct contact with UFOs and Light beings.

At the same time, we also hear about other aliens. These, while being technically very advanced, are atheistic and materialistic, some even 'satanic'. As indicated by several UFO researchers and secret documents, the earthly secret government rejected the help of the divine beings and preferred to deal with less divine beings who offered technological rewards. Later on, some agents of the secret government may have realized that they had entered a very unholy alliance. But obviously they did not mind, or hoped for the best.

Was this the reason why Douglas MacArthur, one of the most respected US generals during WWII, happened to make statements as strange as this one (quoted in the *New York Times,* 9 October 1955)?

> 'The nations of the world will have to unite – for the next war will be an interplanetary war. The nations of the earth must someday make a common front against attack by people from other planets.'

This statement also appeared in an article entitled 'Gen. MacArthur knew of UFOs – General's huge UFO files suppressed by U.S. govt' by

John R. Frick, published in the newspaper *The World News* (New York, 7 August 1982). In the end phase of WW II, General MacArthur had seen UFOs himself, and in April 1945 – still during the war! – he founded an organization named 'Interplanetary Phenomenon Unit'. After retiring from the Army, he tried to find some public platform for sharing his opinion about UFOs, but he was silenced by the already established infrastructure of secrecy.

Contrary to statements about an 'interplanetary war' and attacks 'by people from other planets', Gordon Cooper wrote in his letter to the UN in 1978 (see p. 353): 'We may first have to show them that we have learned to resolve our problems by peaceful means, rather than warfare, before we are accepted as fully qualified universal team members.'

Obviously, these voices did not refer to the same 'teams'. Not only the contactees, also astronauts and other respected individuals spoke about global transformation and universal understanding. However, these individuals were forced aside or ridiculed. Those who indicated the dark aspects of the phenomenon suffered the same fate. Thus, we have to suspect that 'somebody' wanted to keep out the knowledge of the Light beings and cover up the presence of the dark beings ...

Disclosures and misinformation

Why, after the initial bewilderment (until the beginning of July 1947) and the subsequent meticulous investigation, was the UFO issue suddenly (from 1953 onwards) passed over in silence or even debunked and ridiculed? Why was there no longer any interest in getting reports from pilots, military personnel and other qualified people?

For many years, such questions were not even asked because hardly anybody knew about these topics. Only in the late seventies and in the eighties could the official secrecy no longer be maintained. The continued UFO sightings and other – presumably correlated – riddles such as animal mutilations and human abductions had aroused the interest of many private investigators, who founded their own research groups independent of any government liaisons.

In 1978, the author William Moore heard from his researcher colleague, nuclear physicist Dr Stanton Friedman, about a rumoured flying-saucer crash near Roswell in July 1947. By chance, Friedman had met a man who knew Jesse Marcel, the former AF Major from Roswell; this man told Friedman that his friend Jesse had privately mentioned to him something he was not supposed to tell anybody ...

This spark ignited an additional fire in the already extensive field of ufology. And indeed, the story could be confirmed. It had been published in some newspapers, and most witnesses mentioned in the articles were still alive. In 1980, William Moore and the best-selling author Charles Berlitz published a book entitled *The Roswell Incident,* the first investigative publication about this long-suppressed issue. Although written in a sensational style and not thoroughly accurate in all its assumptions, it made an impact on the public and encouraged other witnesses to finally speak out.

In the following years, many incredible, even shocking theories and testimonies began to go round, building up a momentum of disclosure after disclosure. The mass media, which had ignored or ridiculed the UFO topic over the past twenty years, were thrilled, too, and could no longer withstand the temptation of giving it serious coverage. A historic TV event took place in the USA on 14 October 1988: a live two-hour documentary entitled *UFO Cover-Up Live* was broadcast nationwide, reaching and shaking up millions of people. The basic information given was outrageous for those times. (Today, even kids have seen the plot in TV series like 'The X-Files' and 'Dark Skies'.) It stated that the secret government had made contact with some alien force in the early fifties, allowing these creatures to conduct their experiments on earth, while agreeing to cover up their presence. In return, the secret government was to receive advanced technologies which they could use to push on their own agendas. Different witnesses spoke about crashed discs and recovered alien bodies. Some even spoke of secret underground bases and ghastly genetic experiments including hybrid breeding.

It was in those years that other researchers went public with similar reports, for example the famous pilot John Lear, holder of many aviation world records (and the son of William P. Lear, the engineer of the Lear-Jet). Many important statements came from witnesses who were military veterans, such as ex-Navy officer Milton William (Bill) Cooper, retired AF Lt. Col. Wendelle Stevens, ex-CIA member Virgil Armstrong, retired NATO officer Robert O'Dean, who had seen a 'Cosmic Top Secret' NATO assessment concerning UFOs, or Phil Schneider, a geologist and engineer who claimed to have been involved in the construction of several joint human/alien underground bases (he was killed in 1996, soon after he had gone public). Another prolific source to be mentioned is the Internet writer named 'Branton', the compiler of the controversial *Omega files* (about secret underground bases, reptoid aliens and occultism, lodges and the UFO secrecy, the Denver airport, etc.). Parallel to these investigative disclosures, many channelled messages indicated the same basic scenario: negative alien contacts on the one hand, positive Star and Light beings on the other.

Nowadays, there are countless books and Internet articles covering these topics pro and contra. The above-mentioned names are good keys to enter the limitless field of ufology, which contains topics ranging from a cosmic conspiracy to cosmic consciousness to the Cosmic Christ.

A speculative scenario

The course of history as well as many channelled sources indicate that the atom bombs marked a crucial turning point in the earth's occult history. They can be interpreted as a technomagical dark rite based on the simultaneous sacrifice of 200,000 and 100,000 human victims. On the subtle-energetic levels, these two mass killings opened up an interdimensional gateway for like-minded entities, allowing them to physically access the earth again. And so it happened that they suddenly appeared, visible to the whole 'nuclear nation', while casually crashing a few discs with bio-robots aboard in order to present their terrestrial counterparts with the first samples of seductive technology.

Some years later, in the early fifties, positive Star and Light beings started to contact humanity and the world leaders in order to warn them against the 'grey' ETs and their masters. At the same time they offered universal help, provided that the world leaders stopped all nuclear armament and experimentation. The secret government rejected these offers and tried to contact the Greys through a project called SIGMA. By 1953 this project had been established and, at one point, succeeded in contacting them, resulting in the clandestine agreement already mentioned (humans in exchange for micro- and bio-technology).

In the following years, mysterious abductions of humans began to take place. As these individuals were not able to remember the incidents, it took some time before the first cases became publicly known. In 1963, the couple Betty and Barney Hill began a series of therapeutic (hypnotic) regressions which revealed an abduction by a UFO during a period of 'missing time' they had experienced in 1961.

In 1965, the case of Antonius Villas Boas, the son of a Brazilian rancher, received short publicity. He recounted an incident that had taken place in 1957: while working in the field one night, he saw a strange flying object approaching him, and was taken aboard for genetic and sexual experimentation. These aspects of the UFO phenomenon were totally unknown back in 1965, and still he described an incident that corresponded to the scenarios that were to become revealed *en masse* only twenty years later.[131]

On 9 September 1967, the first case of an animal mutilation became known. In southern Colorado a dead horse was found, with its head reduced to a clean skull, while the rest of the corpse was well preserved, with no signs of decay. However, the body was drained of all its blood, several organs and the spine were missing, cut out with an unidentifiable technique. There were no traces of blood on the ground, no footprints and no tire-tracks. But there were other traces: fifteen flat circles impressed on the ground, a broken bush and, next to this bush, a circle of eight holes, each about four inches wide and three to four inches deep. Measurements with a Geiger counter showed increased values at the site. In the following months and years, thousands of similar cases became known, mainly from North and South America.[132]

According to this scenario, the objects sighted in 1947 belonged to the dark side. And sure enough, the crashed discs increased the greed of those who took the bait, prompting them to expand their pyramid of secret services by adding new, top-secret levels such as the committee 'Majestic 12' or the NSA (National Security Agency). Through this expanded infrastructure, it became possible to organize the cover-ups as well as the development of a parallel technology intended for their world control.

On the other hand, those appearing in 1952 were the positive beings who wanted to warn humanity. When their offers were rejected by the secret government, they chose to contact civilians (the 'contactees') and open-minded individuals, apparently also some of the astronauts, in order to inspire an expanded consciousness amongst humanity, including love for the creation and the Creator.

The negative ETs were not in the position to simply land and conquer earth, because every planet is guarded by divine beings who serve God's will and the creation. Being divine, they are *neutral* and respect the free will of all beings, including the free will of the dark forces. When the earthly inhabitants and their leaders 'invited' these forces by expressing a strong desire for their technologies, the planetary guardians reacted according to the law of karma and the law of resonance, letting them in. At the same time, for the sake of balance, they started their own operations to inform all those who wanted to see and listen.

The above-mentioned principle of planetary guarding and individual free will explains why those who wanted to shape the karmic destiny of humanity had to make a mutual agreement. The incarnate entities from the dark worlds had made a 'timely' entrance onto the earthly stage and were now, after WW II, in the position of inviting their peers and rejecting the divine offers, even on the level of the UN.

In doing so, they not only made decisions in an autocratic way, they also reflected the mood of the majority of the world population. Is it not a fact that most people euphorically desire and embrace the technical boom along with all of the diversions it offers: TV, computer games, cellular phones, microwaves and microchip technology (which includes almost all products of modern technology, from household appliances to computers to credit cards to satellites)?

According to this speculative scenario, the development of the last fifty years, which was focussed on the establishment of a world-wide infrastructure of '666 technology', has been covertly inspired by the dark forces, the 'fallen angels' mentioned in the Apocalypse.

Reminiscent of the Apocalypse

One of the aforementioned authors, Milton William Cooper (killed in 2001), wrote a book with the title *Behold a Pale Horse,* which is a reference to the Apocalypse (6.8): 'And I looked, and beheld a pale horse. And the one seated upon it had the name Death, and Hell followed him.' In Bill Cooper's interpretation, this Bible text refers to the negative alien force behind the destructive earthly forces. Cooper writes:

> Most of this knowledge comes directly from, or is a result of my own research into the TOP SECRET/MAJIC material which I saw and read between the

years 1970 and 1973 as a member of the Intelligence Briefing Team of the Commander in Chief of the Pacific Fleet. Since some of this information was derived from sources that I cannot divulge for obvious reasons, and from published sources which I cannot vouch for, this chapter must be termed a hypothesis. I firmly believe that if aliens are real, this is the true nature of the Beast. It is the only scenario that has been able to bind all the diverse elements. It is the only scenario that answers all the questions and places the various fundamental mysteries in an arena that makes sense. It is the only explanation which shows the chronology of events and demonstrates that the chronologies, when assembled, match perfectly. The bulk of this I believe to be true if the material that I viewed in the Navy is authentic. As for the rest, I do not know, and that is why this paper must be termed a hypothesis. Most historic and current available evidence supports this hypothesis.[133]

To continue this hypothesis, one has to ask why the negative ETs would need genetic engineering based on organic resources 'harvested' on planet earth. Lyssa Royal, a well-known medium who is said to be one of the few channels having contact with the grey species, communicated the following explanation:

> We needed an existing genetic structure from which we could take the DNA and splice it back into our own, to reestablish the chemical reactions for us to feel emotions again. [...] Please understand that we are not doing anything against anyone's will or wishes. You have invited us, whether you know it consciously or not. We have always assumed your subconscious was the voice of your conscious. [...]
> We view your collective soul as being a part of ours and therefore by that unification, permission is granted. [...] Permission is there. If we were not able to carry it out, then there would have been no permission. [...]
> As you know, the fetuses are either implanted or are naturally conceived and later worked on genetically. Anywhere from one to four months (usually not later) they need to be taken out of the human embryonic environment for the next stage of work to be done on them. [...]
> Some of the unsuccessful strains were much smaller and much more fragile. Some of them had craniums too large to be supported by their bodies, and as they grew they would frequently experience what you call a broken neck or deformed neck vertebrae supporting a head disproportionate to the body.[134]

If this account is authentic, then it is another example of pragmatic self-justification. Due to their materialistic experiments (hybrid breeding, cloning etc.), the Greys have genetically and physically degenerated into a state of infertile bio-roboterism, but still they adhere to this method. Instead of seeking assistance from the divine agents of creation, they want to save their race 'off their own bat' by further encroachments upon another species. They see nothing wrong or evil in their doings because they simply execute what they consider necessary. Furthermore, they follow the fatalistic version of atheistic deism, thinking that they are 'invited' and authorized to access the earth simply due to the fact that they are able to do it. ('If we were not able to carry it out, then there would have been no permission.') Obviously, they have undertaken something to obtain this 'invitation'.

Nevertheless, the grey species quoted above does not belong to the most powerful groups of 'Greys' and 'fallen angels'. They themselves mention other entities whose intentions – even from their point of view – are negative:

> These negative extraterrestrials would range from the negatively oriented Zeta Reticuli (which some call the Greys), to any type of Orion interaction – whether it be with physical extraterrestrials, telepathic contact, or holographic projections. There are also other mixed humanoids who are of a negative orientation. Generally, it is for the purpose of gathering data about the human psyche to use at a later date to perhaps exert control or power over the human species.[135]

Opinions about the abduction phenomenon are divided. Some say that this genetic harvesting is beneficial for mankind as more and more male humans are becoming sterile; at one point, the new race resulting from the hybrid interbreeding of men and Greys will start to populate the earth and will be the teachers of mankind.

Other researchers are not that optimistic and have serious doubts about these entities and their motives: '[The Greys and their superiors] state that we are destroying the planet; so we need to be controlled, that we should surrender to them for they are our creators. *Here is the great deception.* The Confederation [on the other hand] does not go against free will because they recognise it as an essential part of the Universal Law, and they offer clear advice which shows that we were *not* created by the fallen programmers or cultures.'[136]

Who is behind the Greys? Some abductees mention having met reptoid-looking beings as commanders of the Greys. In this connection we are reminded of Robert Morningsky's statement that 'it will do researchers and all who study the Greys well to remember that the true power behind them are the Children of the Reptile'.

The question we all have to ask is: Will the real, spiritual awakening of mankind be the product of some genetic breeding, or will each individual have to first transform his/her consciousness, thus effecting the transformation of the physical body as a natural side-effect? If life is seen as nothing but a complex expression of organic matter, then genetic manipulation is the only means of advancing 'human evolution'. Obviously, there are many groups who firmly believe in this materialistic interpretation of life. One of these groups even promotes human cloning as a means to 'physical immortality'.

However, if individuality is not just a product of material duality, then reality looks quite different.

Summary and outlook

From ancient and contemporary sources we can deduce that the UFO phenomenon is a multidimensional, and permanent, aspect of our world. The fact that UFOs became a world-wide phenomenon only after the end of the Second World War does not mean that they came into existence at that time. Rather, it means that – fifty years ago – this phenomenon entered a *decisive new phase*.

Any serious and non-biased research on UFOs requires a multi-dimensional world-view that takes both modern and ancient sources into account. Otherwise one will end up with one-sided interpretations that only serve ideological motives of the pro or contra camps.

Modern ufology is a collection of vastly contradictory opinions. There are ufologists who mutually claim that the others have fallen prey to false information spread by secret services, sensationalists or lunatics.

Some say that the UFO talk about extraterrestrials is deliberately spread by certain secret services in order to conceal the *terrestrial* origin of these flying objects (meaning: the secret technology developed by the USA or by some other furtively operating power). Therefore, all rumours concerning negative ETs, to say nothing of grey or reptoid beings, are merely grotesque aberrations of human fantasy.

Others say that the rumours about secret earthly technology are false information deliberately spread by certain secret services in order to divert people's attention away from the *extraterrestrial* background.

Why? To avoid panic, to maintain their materialistic world-view, to continue their cover-ups, and to conceal even darker aspects of this 'cosmic conspiracy'.

Others doubt the reality of these phenomena altogether and claim *all* reports about UFOs, abductions and channelled contacts to be fakes, fallacies or false conclusions due to hallucination, ignorance or madness; if people actually saw something in the skies, then it could easily be explained with some rational fact like planet Venus, meteors, weather balloons, satellites, rare atmospheric conditions, etc. Reports about nocturnal abductions by ETs are seen as merely neurotic dreams triggered by undigested childhood traumata, such as sexual abuse by some close relative, the suppressed memory now being projected on anonymous nightmare Greys.

Others say that UFOs are visitors from our future who have mastered time travel. Others claim UFOs to be objects coming from deep-underground caves and extensive ancient tunnel systems. One theory describes them to be survivors of Atlantis who, along with their advanced technology, withdrew into these subterranean worlds; now that humanity is about to destroy the planet, they (their descendants) have decided to emerge again. According to another theory, the earth is hollow, and the UFOs are said to be spaceships from this inner-terrestrial civilization. Again another theory maintains UFOs to be the technical achievement of secret societies of the German Reich, namely of those that had allegedly fled (to South America, to the Antarctic, to Iraq?) before the end of WWII, thus being able to preserve their advanced knowledge and to continue secretly with their agenda.

Others say there are no extraterrestrials or, at least, no evil extraterrestrials; all hysteria about 'negative ETs' attacking the earth is nothing but propaganda which is being built up to enforce a totalitarian world government on humanity; the film *Independence Day* was a prelude from Hollywood, preparing the field for later 'disclosures' and 'alarms'.

What is serious, and what is false information?

One thing we know for sure: All ancient civilizations and indigenous people mention astral and extraterrestrial 'demons', 'spirits', and 'gods' who possess flying shields, flying chariots, *vimanas* etc. This fact alone is sufficient to exclude the assumption that UFOs are only the products of a secret modern technology. Still, the aspect of hidden earthly technologies should not be underrated. The entire matter is obviously very complex, and it is veiled in many wraps. Any one-sided approach will miss out on important aspects of the bigger picture.

Military spokesmen of several countries have already admitted that they have known about UFOs for quite some time. For example, renowned generals of the former Soviet Union have made official statements and have come out with detailed reports about sightings witnessed by qualified personnel.

In 1996, Nick Pope, a member of the British Ministry of Defence, published a book entitled *Open Skies, Closed Minds* (see bibliography) with the MoD's authorization, in which he described this ministry's UFO research. In his own words, Nick Pope was 'the Ministry of Defence official who was responsible for researching and investigating UFOs, alien abductions, crop circles, cattle mutilations and other strange phenomena'. He had been a sceptic who did not believe that any of these so-called strange phenomena were really strange or inexplicable, but 'my unique access to new data and old government files convinced me that the UFO phenomenon raised serious defence and national security issues. [...] Strong evidence emerged suggesting the presence of structured craft capable of speeds and manoeuvres beyond the capability of even the most advanced prototype craft operated by the Royal Air Force or the United States Air Force. [...] All this led me to believe that an extraterrestrial explanation for some sightings could not be ruled out' (quoted from Nick Pope's personal website).

Reports of UFO sightings have been officially (and partially?) released by government offices of Belgium – as a consequence of the spectacular series of UFO sightings in 1989–92 – as well as by respective offices of Spain, Switzerland, Mexico and a few other countries. Besides these official releases, which are usually not very informative, many former government and army insiders have unofficially spoken out (some have been mentioned in this chapter). The testimonies and statements they give may be contradictory in various regards due to their different levels of information, and due to their different personal convictions, in some cases also due to covert tasks of information and misinformation. But they all agree in stating that there was, and is, 'something' out there …

When 'the time is ripe' some hitherto secret agencies may even step forward to confirm that they have contacts with aliens. Most probably, they will present everything as beneficial to mankind.

In films, we have already seen the story of aliens presenting themselves to the public, stating that they are our friends *and creators* and that they have now returned to save us from our self-induced calamities. Similar visions and (false?) promises have already been communicated to abductees, who later recalled these 'prophetic' encounters in hypnotic regressions.

If there is any truth to this scenario, then let us not forget the warning quoted in the previous chapter: 'They are from the dark side and they are the ones responsible for altering your DNA and introducing the different control systems. [...] They will cure certain diseases that they brought to humankind in the first place. [...] They will speak of love and truths. This will create much confusion in the minds of many, as the benevolent and loving space beings will also be presenting themselves. To those who can discern, this will present no difficulties.'

In any case, we have to expect public disclosures and 'fantastic' revelations in the next few years to come.

In order to stay untouched by false hopes, rash euphoria and dogmatic prejudices, spiritual intuition and inner guidance are most important – in the future, now, and always.

CHAPTER FOURTEEN

The Future That Is Now

The essential teachings of all religions and mystery schools lead to a multidimensional world-view and to a spiritual 'life-view'. From such a perspective, we have examined different ways of explaining the origin of duality and evil. We have looked into the reality beyond duality: individuality, free will and divine love (the oneness of twoness) as the perfection of free will. And we have analysed the different false concepts that arise when the principles of individuality and self-responsibility are misunderstood due to a standpoint in darkness. It became evident that it is impossible to define light in terms of darkness (because light is a reality totally different from any abstract concept of non-darkness). Furthermore, light is never a product of darkness. Similarly, life and consciousness, being spiritual (non-material), cannot simply be a product of 'self-organizing' matter, as postulated by the materialistic theories of evolution.

Now, in the last chapter, the many strands of this big picture will be taken up again and put together for a practical conclusion. The main goal is getting a sense for 'the truth that will set you free' (John 8.32), which implies that mankind is presently not free. Free of what? Free of absolutist claims and misunderstandings of the Absolute, free of alien dictation and alienation from one's real self, free of separation from the Source, ultimately free of fear and godlessness.

Over the ages, humanity has fallen into the extremes of the too-much and the too-little, the two faces of the same dia-bolic spirit. Humanity demonstrated some resonance, and there were those who profited from it. Some of them were visible, others stayed behind the stage, and again others preferred to remain invisible to terrestrial eyes.

Nevertheless, the drama 'on stage' indicated that the symptoms were effected by deep-rooted, hidden causes. One strong indication was, and still is, the simultaneous presence of harmonious and destructive elements on earth. Most people consider this co-existence of good and evil to be normal and natural, being unable to imagine that matters could be different. 'Wars and murder have always existed.' That is a standard phrase of resignation (and false programming), a phrase which is not even true as it applies only to the dark age, the last five thousand years. However, in these five thousand years, violence and non-love have indeed been the overriding factors of history. But where did these inhuman impulses come from? What, or who, opposed the light and caused shadows to be cast? Who 'created' darkness?

Light is free of darkness, and within the bounds of darkness there is no light. They are mutually exclusive. Still, there is a borderline where darkness ends and light 'begins'. The same principle applies to the worlds of light and the worlds of darkness. Although separate, they verge on each other, and planet earth happens to be situated in this cosmic border zone. (It was not always like that and will not always remain like that.) The circumstance of being a planet where light and darkness are present side by side makes the earth a very special place. It is a passage way from darkness to the Light and a place where Light beings can contact their fallen brothers and sisters.

The ancient seers and prophets foresaw a time of decision when the dark side would be exposed to the Light in an apocalyptic epiphany concerning and confronting everybody on earth. For two thousand years and more, humanity in all cultures has been informed about this upcoming 'open air' event …

In our present time, many interlinked time cycles are heading for a rare common meeting point, which will mark a global turning point in history. Through this synchronicity, interdimensional time windows will be opened, and mankind will be confronted with its mythological past. The things happening today have a long pre-history both on the individual and the collective level, going back to the incidents in human and natural history that marked the previous turning point. These incidents have left their traces in the subconsciousness of many people, and now they are surfacing again, as they need to be balanced and neutralized. All the wounds need to be healed, and all misdeeds forgiven. Forgiving oneself and each other clears the collective field for the transition into the next big cycle – the time of the 'new heaven' and the 'new earth'. Understanding everything means forgiving everything.

It is not by chance that we are here at this time.

The approaching turning point entails many challenges, and present world history indicates that we have not yet reached the darkest point of illusion and destruction. Right before a point on a wheel starts to go up again, it 'hits the bottom'.

From manifestation to incarnation

Once upon a time, the earth was fully in the realm of the Light. In Sanskrit, this primeval age is called *Satya-yuga*, the 'age of truthfulness', which has a deep meaning, as will be explained later in this chapter. The Satya-yuga is the same as the 'First World' mentioned by the Amerindian cultures.

The difference between each *yuga* is so epochal that speaking of different 'Worlds' is no exaggeration. Not only time was different in the past, but also space, because space and time cannot be separated. The past of the earth consisted of different 'space-time ages', and also the present space-time experience will change again. As everything is interconnected, all cosmic cycles and sub-cycles are reflected on the earth, from fractal day-units up to the level of the *yugas*, each *yuga* causing different material living conditions.

On its course through space and time, the earth gradually moved into the borderline zone of light and darkness. Or, to describe it from the perspective of the light, shadows began to reach the earth, cast by beings who did not belong to the earth (as the earth itself was fully in the light). At first, the shadows were only tangential, but once having reached the earth, they quickly grew.

In the early phase of Satya-yuga, the earthly Light beings lived in their respective parallel dimensions and interacted with the physical world only through creative impulses on an energetic level. In due course of time, some of these Light beings manifested themselves on earth in a three-dimensional body, which they created through a 'paranormal' condensation of their higher-dimensional bodies. 'Let us make humankind in our image, according to our likeness' (Gen. 1.26, not to be confused with Gen. 2.7).

The first human beings in three-dimensional (physical) bodies were not primitive descendants of animals, but self-manifested Light beings who appeared as human arche-types within the space-time continuum of the physical earth. They acted according to the will of the Creator, as it was the natural next step within the ongoing creation of the earth. There were no tinges of selfishness or ego. 'God (*elohim*) saw everything that he had made, and indeed, it was very good. And there was evening and there was morning, the sixth day.' (Gen. 1.31)[137]

Before the appearance of these arche-types of physical man, the earth had already been inhabited by intelligent life-forms, but they were higher-dimensional. (Even nowadays, the earth co-exists with populations in parallel dimensions: the astral, elemental and elfish worlds as well as all the higher worlds up to the world of Brahma.)

In the early phase of their earth-mission, the Light beings appeared through self-manifestation (condensation of a body). Later on, they came through incarnation and birth, which entailed an increased forgetfulness of their previous existence in the higher worlds. Again, there was a deep and divine reason for this step – a step which initiated a creative process that has not yet been concluded.

The more earth-bound the early humans became, the more they were exposed to attacks and encroachments, and thus, legendary and modern history began.

With this broader horizon in mind, it becomes possible to make a rough outline of the mythological history of mankind, which extends back to the antediluvian civilizations and further back to the multidimensional origins of humanity, as described in ancient and contemporary revelations.

Mythological history of mankind (part 1)

In the remote past, humanity consisted of individuals endowed with mental and spiritual capacities which people of today call paranormal. The energetic vortexes (*chakras*) of their ethereal and subtle bodies were fully active, and their mental focus was consciously directed by their spiritual self, the *atma*. They were connected to the Star and Light beings of the higher dimensions who protected the earth according to the pure resonance of these original humans.

In the course of time, the 'serpent' entered the paradise that the Adamic species was manifesting. The original humans were not of terrestrial origin, and neither were the intruders. They were aggressive and imperialistic, or pragmatic at best. Even according to modern standards they possessed an incredible technology, but they had chosen a path away from God. Therefore, they saw nothing wrong in their attempts to exploit the terrestrial resources – and inhabitants. And so it happened that the earth became a target of their operations.

Only when the big global 'blackout' occurred about ten thousand years ago did these dark forces leave again, but not voluntarily. They had to flee because their ground bases were being destroyed by the forces of nature, as graphically described in the Epic of Gilgamesh. Furthermore, due to the decree of the solar and galactic beings, they were not allowed to return to the earth with their superior technology. A new round in the cosmic power game was starting, with new rules and changed conditions according to the then imminent Kali-yuga.

However, the former lords were allowed to act according to their free will, and their will was unchanged. They again wanted to increase their influence on earth up to the point of a total take-over. They understood that they could no longer use the means adopted before. So they had to come up with a new tactic.

And it was devilishly ingenious: Rather than *forcing* people to serve them, they schemed out a method to make their subjects *voluntarily* serve them. In this way, the harvest of life energy was to be even bigger than before, because the energy flow was no longer restricted by aversion and unwilling surrender. If people participate voluntarily, there is no longer any need of forcing them.

What is the most powerful form of 'voluntary' energy flow? It is *fear* and *worship*.

About five thousand years ago, when the humans had recovered from the global cataclysm that had struck their ancestors, these later generations were 'free' again to build up power structures and military forces. In this way, humanity went in resonance with those invisible forces that were just waiting for this new situation to arise. As a responce, they influenced man's psychical and astral conditioning and thereby also his genetic structure and gross-material body. Their method of manipulation was psychosomatic, so to speak.

Through actions of this kind, they prepared the field for their next step: incarnating themselves. When they started to appear as humans among humans, they eagerly took up leading roles as kings and high priests. Being agents of duality and hatred, they started to preach their own doctrines which incited fear and 'worship' in the name of God. They told their subordinates that the big inundation had been the punishment of mankind due to the wrath of God, because mankind had been reluctant to worship God by sacrifice and surrender. 'So if you want to avoid another punishment, you have to pacify God by offering sacrifices of blood.' As this was preached in all traditions, people started to hate and fight each other, all of them thinking that they were the only ones favoured by God. It was perfect propaganda, and it worked ...

The rest is recorded history.

Invisible helpers

While modern civilization, blind to any kind of higher-dimensional existence, continues to exploit the earth, polluting and destroying it more and more, there are Light beings who invisibly intervene both on the individual and global level. Admittedly, it is difficult to ascertain an act of help which was invisible and successful. For example, after a safe journey, how do we know that there was not any problem or danger being prevented without us even noticing it?

The invisible helpers are truly selfless. They have no inclination to impress us with the fact that they are helping. Of course, those who are sensitive or clairvoyant are aware of this additional reality, and they may even inform us about some intervention which took place, although it is difficult to prove such a claim, because on our level of awareness 'nothing happened', or it was just 'good luck'.

Schoolhouse earth has already been saved more than once by the invisible helpers when some stupid pupils or teachers, or intruders, were about to destroy it. For example, hundreds of atomic bombs have been detonated in the name of 'science' and 'national security', and those responsible, when challenged, bluff high-handedly, saying: 'See, nothing has happened!'[138]

We will never know how many meteorites have been deflected, how much radioactivity has been neutralized, how often some natural catastrophe has been prevented or assuaged. 'Do not harm the earth or the sea or the trees, until we have put the seal on the foreheads of the servants of our God.' (Rev. 7.3)

The following report describes one of the many preventive measures taken by the invisible helpers, one which is very credible in the light of the circumstantial evidence: In July 1979, mankind was threatened by yet another self-induced danger. The US Space Laboratory 'Skylab' had gone out of control and was hurtling back towards the earth. The news even spoke about calculations indicating that Skylab might crash on North America. Only a few hours after the release of this news, Skylab hit the *southern hemisphere*. It crashed into the Indian Ocean and onto uninhabited land in western Australia! Simply good luck? Or had there been a mysterious change of Skylab's trajectory?

Yes, there had, says Prof. Kyriacos Markides from the University of Maine. In 1979, he visited Cyprus for several months to study the work and personality of the great mystic known as Daskalos. He was also there when, on 11 July 1979, Skylab was about to enter the earth's atmosphere. Daskalos, as an incarnated member of the planetary White Brotherhood, reacted to the imminent danger caused by Skylab. He left his gross-material body and, in his subtle-material body, went up to the damaged spacecraft in order to influence its course with the use of his mental power. However, despite several attempts, he failed. After another attempt in trance, he opened his eyes and described what he had just experienced:

> 'I just saw three [higher-dimensional] flying saucers. The entities inside communicated with me [...] These entities are really advanced. They live in the higher noetic world and have no form [...] These superintelligences are working very hard. We are so insignificant in comparison to them. [...] "We are the guardians of garden Earth" they said [...] They seemed as if they were working in groups which gave me the impression of flying saucers. I asked them whether they in fact were flying saucers but they seemed to ignore my question. Their response instead was that they are "space people." They live around our planet. [...] They truly love us. [...] I felt as if they were a form of light with vibrating intensity. They are innumerable [...] Had it not been for these superintelligences, Skylab would most probably have crashed over Canada.'[139]

Do human terrestrials who physically go into outer space also contact the invisible 'higher noetic world' and subconsciously communicate with these 'superintelligences'? Did the first astronauts have psychic experiences of a similar kind when they left the earth's gravitational field? During sleep or altered states of consciousness, they may have felt the presence of these higher-dimensional beings. 'As he hurtled earthward through the abyss between the worlds, Mitchell became engulfed by a profound sensation – a sense of universal connectedness. He intuitively sensed that his presence, that of his fellow astronauts, and that of the planet in the window were all a part of a deliberate, universal process.'[140]

Later on, back in the 'normal' state of consciousness, they may have doubted their own experiences and the seriousness of their telepathic dreams. But still, the moving impression remained, and their lives were changed, at least the lives of the more sensitive space travellers. And, in a higher sense, we are all space travellers, although presently serving as ground-crew members on planet earth.

Mythological history of mankind (part 2)

Talking about the invisible helpers also means talking about ourselves. Some of us may have realized that we are Light beings and rays of God while others may have forgotten it, and still others may still be mistaking darkness for light. Nevertheless, even the darkest forces – in their true, original identity – are eternal parts of God. They are cut off from the Light, but once they dissolve and transcend their self-constructed walls of ego, they will be in the Light again.

As mentioned in the section 'From manifestation to incarnation', there was a time when non-fallen Light beings decided to come to the earth in order to become the first physical humans. The earth as a planetary being already hosted a three-dimensional scenery with plants and animals, but humans had 'only' been higher-dimensional. The planetary being knew that sometime in the future, the earth was to ascend as a whole, including the transformation of its condensed matter, and that this would be possible only through consciousness – and not just any state of consciousness, but only through the purest, most divine consciousness: unconditional love. Therefore, the earth desired that beings of this highest vibration of consciousness would come down into her world of matter in order to light up and 'resurrect' the entire earthly existence. The divine hierarchy, starting with the planetary and solar beings, knew that the creation of physical mankind would also invite beings from the worlds of darkness, but they knew that ultimately the initial purpose would prevail due to divine help.

Thus, before any paradise was lost, the plan for recovering the paradise was already thought of and initiated. Hosts of Adamic Light beings projected themselves into the world of physical matter, manifesting an earthly body while maintaining full knowledge of their higher identity. The goal, however, was to maintain the consciousness of pure love without the back-up, or 'safety net', of knowing, *'Actually, I am an angel'*. The ultimate test, and perfection, was to live in pure love in the Here and Now – on earth, in a physical body, without any earthly or celestial identification. That was to be a perfection never attained before. Of course, unconditional God consciousness was already there, but only in the higher-dimensional worlds. Now, manifesting it within the densest form of matter was to become the highest miracle of creation: transformation of darkness into Light. Those who had fallen into separation from the Light could never be forced to 'come back'. Only the purest, selfless love which even withstood the worst onslaughts of darkness could indicate to them the reality of the Light, because by themselves, they would never be able to fathom that there is another reality beyond darkness, not to speak of them realizing that their 'reality' is only an illusion, a vicious circle of self-deception.

The earth – as a 'relay station' of the Light – was to become a place of mercy where even the darkest forces could receive a new chance of actually using their free will, for in darkness there is only darkness to choose from.

Light always, and instantly, returns into any space of darkness whenever there is an opportunity; that is the inner nature of light. Similarly, God and all God-conscious Light beings cannot help shining forth their unconditional love, and that is their mercy – which is exhibited the most within the realm of the earth, because it is here where the Light directly contacts darkness.

It takes real love to touch the dark forces and impress upon them that there is a power far greater than theirs, even though initially they will react with anger, frustration and aggression. Nevertheless, despite their negative attitude, they have come in contact with the Light simply by living on the earth.

For all these reasons, the manifestation of highest love within the world of densest matter was simultaneously a necessity and an act of mercy.

That was, and still is, the divine plan of creation.

Knowing this plan and consenting to it, many Light beings volunteered for the 'experiment' of living highest love within densest matter. And they knew that, at one point, even the supreme Light being would appear on earth in order to conclude the entire cycle.

First, they descended to earth through physical manifestation, and later through incarnation. By subjecting themselves to birth, they became able to live in the Here and Now, with a 'blank' state of consciousness uninfluenced by the memory of their former existence in higher worlds. '... male and female he (*elohim*) created them, and blessed them', says Genesis (1.27-8).

Being telepathic and 'paranormal', these early humans lived without 'civilization' and even without the use of spoken words. Fossil remnants of early humans do not show traces of developed vocal cords, but this is not necessarily the sign of a primitive, ape-like state of human 'evolution'. Maybe these humans were so advanced that they did *not need* vocal cords! History has shown that words – and, especially, the written word – brought about the basis of confusion, misunderstanding and manipulation. In the former 'telepathic age', modern social habits such as diplomacy, hypocrisy and lying were non-existent.

But then, as outlined in Chapter Twelve, something happened: Less divine beings became attracted to paradise earth and wanted to harvest the humans' powerful energy. Using technical means, they adapted themselves to the earthly conditions and, centuries later, enslaved many of the 'unproductive' and naive early humans, subjugating them with physical force and – in later generations – with subtle means of mental and genetic manipulation. The incarnated Light beings (who no longer knew that they were Light beings) were confronted with the extreme forces of duality. As humans, they all reacted differently. Some maintained their pure consciousness, and others gave in to the provocation by taking up the role of victims, by wanting to fight these dark forces, by starting to hate them; some even went over to the other side. In this way, they became entangled in long chains of karma.

Some of those who were not captured started to found their own civilizations, using their telepathy and reactivated former knowledge to call their higher-dimensional brothers and sisters to assist them. (The ages of Lemuria and Atlantis began.) Others kept up their 'primitive' way of life. But in the course of time, over thousands and thousands of years, they were all affected by different cataclysms, by conflicts and by the increase of materialism, which caused rivalry, brutalization and exploitation and, above all, identification with material things.

Now, at the beginning of the twenty-first century, we find ourselves in an atmosphere denser than ever before. At the same time, the perfection attainable today is even higher than it was in paradise when physical incarnation started. Therefore, most of those who were present then are still (or again) here today in order to complete the earthly challenge in its ultimate consequence – facing deepest darkness, the 'dragon'.

The illusion of division

Many warnings speak about 'the forces that deceive the world'. Indeed, deception is typical of the age of Kali, as it is possible *only* in the age of Kali. Kali means 'dividing; diabolic' in the broadest sense of the word, even in the sense of physics. Under the influence of Kali, people live in the illusion that space and time are divided, and due to this illusion they experience space and time as divided. But space and time are never divided, and modern physics has started to sense this truth, at least in its material implication.

In earlier ages, space and time were not experienced as divided. In the higher-dimensional worlds, and in higher states of consciousness, they are still – and always – perceived as non-divided. When space and time are not divided by illusion, the seeming difference between inner and external reality is no longer existent. Thoughts, then, are directly perceived, and they become an immediate reality. Imagine if this were the case today! All of our thoughts and the thoughts of all people an immediate reality – what a mess, what a hell!

In the present age, we have time to think before acting, which is quite an advantage. Not every thought is an immediate reality. We can correct and select our thoughts and decide what we actually want to do.

However, this situation also entails a particularity which is *the* seduction of the age, namely *one can hide one's thoughts*. One can think one thing and say another, which means: One can lie and pretend. Therefore, Kali-yuga is called the 'age of conflict and hypocrisy'. At the turning point of the Kali-yuga – the 'bottom point of the wheel' – the most extreme forms of deception will be possible, and we are warned not to be seduced or deceived.

Removing the veil

'Do not fear them; for there is nothing covered up that will not become uncovered, and there is nothing secret that will not become known.'
— Matthew 10.26

The closer the age of division comes to an end, the more difficult it becomes to maintain the façade of lying and deceiving. With the ongoing transformation, the veil of division and illusion will be removed. We will become more and more sensitive, and one of the first capacities to be reactivated will be the discernment of truth from untruth. We will immediately sense when someone is lying to us or to the public in general. Lying is a conscious act of hiding or distorting the truth, and this dia-bolic division of realities is easily seen in the aura of the respective person as it blocks the flow of his or her subtle energies.

Already today, it is possible to find out whether, and in what regard, a person's energy flow is blocked or impeded, both on conscious and unconscious levels. The body does not lie, as the saying goes, and that is true. Natural methods like kinesiology are based on this principle. In Switzerland, there is even an alternative political party which publicly checks the integrity of its board members by such a method. No ulterior motives allowed! (How many politicians and economists would pass this test?)

At one point, hiding behind one's body will no longer be possible. The time of 'poker faces' and diplomatic 'friendships' will be over, and the harmony of inner and external life will be restored. Outer appearance and mental conscience will no longer be separate manifestations. This holistic state of being was once natural for all humanity; it was our original condition in the primeval age, which is therefore called the 'age of truthfulness' (p. 371). It was destroyed through violence and physical force employed by intruders from the dark worlds. They were free to commit such encroachments because the earth is the polarized zone of free will where light and darkness meet.

The Light beings who had decided to enter the danger zone of duality called Earth had done so by free will, and thus it became their karma ('destiny') to be confronted with the dark forces. From the non-judging viewpoint of the Light beings, the situations imposed by the dark forces were nothing but chances to maintain their unconditional love, or to restore it if they had fallen into feelings of hopelessness, hatred or revenge.

The dark forces, being motivated by the ego, were totally unable to fathom the motives of the Light beings, and they still are. Darkness can never understand light. As soon as it does, it is no longer darkness. It has become light, which entails the total, absolute annihilation of any darkness, including the (false) ego. This reality, however, is impossible to conceive as long as one is in duality. Hence, those in darkness need the mercy of those in the Light who testify that the end of darkness is not the end of existence, but the beginning of real life – life beyond duality and illusion.

Experiencing the Spirit of truth

'I still have many things to say to you but they would be too much for you to bear now. However, when the Spirit of truth comes, he will lead you to the complete truth …'

— John 16.12–13

The Spirit of truth will remove everything that casts shadows. Those blessed in this way will no longer even think of lying to others or to themselves because integrity will be only natural for them.

Long before reaching the political level, the Spirit of truth will reach our private lives. And, indeed, more and more people are realizing that even the slightest lies, spoken to save some last fragment of the ego's façade, are immediately exposed by the arrangements of destiny.

The sources that inform us about the new Earth and the 'end of times' (the end of division and deception) also inform us about our practical possibilities of being in the Light and experiencing the Spirit of truth. The basic method they suggest is universal and its application absolutely individual. Otherwise, it would not be divine and unconditional but sectarian and dogmatic. It has already been mentioned in previous chapters, and it is further unfolded here as the 'happy end' of this book.

The suggestion given by the Light beings is nothing spectacular or cultish. In these last pages, no method for quick enlightenment is being unveiled and offered for sale. No particular master or religion is being advocated as the 'only way', and no world teacher has been kept hidden to now appear as a *deus ex machina* with promises of peace and prosperity.

As predicted for more than two thousand years, the Spirit of truth will be poured mainly upon the common and simple people. To receive this shower of mercy, one has to be connected to the Source, and the expression of this spiritual oneness is divine love. People who truly love themselves for what they are, are also able to love all others for what they are: eternal, divine individuals, rays of God. Men and women with this consciousness are truly whole and 'holy'.

When such holystic individuals come together in unconditional love, they create a most powerful energy field which brings them into natural resonance and union with the highest Light beings, who themselves are pure channels of the Absolute.

> '[God] said, you are gods.' Those who heard the word of God are called gods [...] The Father is in me and I am in the Father. [...] Remain in union with me as I remain in union with you. Just as the branch cannot bear fruit by itself unless it is in union with the vine, neither can you unless you remain in union with me. (John 10.34–8; 15.4)

Union with the Light beings cannot be reached through means of magic or dogmatic religion. The only connection is divine love, and this love is manifested in the most conscious way when 'two or three meet in my name, for there I am in their midst' (Matt. 18.20). 'Two or three [or four or five] meeting in my name' is the simple but most efficient method to practically realize our inner connection to God and God's family.

As Light beings we were all originally united within the oneness of God's love, and now, within the world of densest matter, we can reunite again to complete our inner, spiritual perfection. In such a reunion, the union with God and the countless God-devoted beings enhances all forms of prayer and meditation. We can still continue to pray and meditate alone or in larger groups; whatever we do will be enriched by the spiritual experience received through this small circle of people we really love and trust. In larger groups, this harmony is never the same as there are always people one does not really know or not really like. On the other hand, meditating alone bears the risk of complacency or some form of ego trip.

In a small 'Light circle', however, there is no need and no room for any ego presentation. Everybody is a ray of Light, and together they manifest a unique atmosphere in which everything can be addressed and discussed, above all, spiritual topics. Such people will not need psychiatrists or material diversions. If they happen to be lovers and couples, they will never become tired of each other. Rather, every aspect of practical life – friendship, family, self-responsibility, creativity, intimacy, inspiration, intuition – will gain a new spiritual dimension.

If we want to enter this supremely spiritual experience, we simply need to find a few people with whom we can come together in God consciousness on a regular basis, once every one, two or four weeks, for example. In such a sacred association, we can study a scripture, discuss, pray, sing and meditate. We can even activate the inner word and thus experience the factual presence of those Light beings we resonate with. We live in their field of consciousness anyway. They see us and communicate with us even though we may not be aware of them. It is up to us to expand our consciousness and to perceive their presence.

Inspired by the spiritual energy field of our 'Light circle', we can begin to feel the divine oneness – our inner connection with the Source and the Light beings – and the inspiration may even take on the form of spoken words, which can be called 'inspired speech' or 'the inner word'. In this connection, a nice exercise is to simply start speaking in the way we 'think' these higher-dimensional brothers and sisters would speak. What would our guardian angel, one of the ascended saints or the Cosmic Christ say to us in this sacred moment? Just start and let go, and after a few words it is no longer your mind that is speaking. And even if it is you who is speaking, what would be the harm? You are a Light being, too. 'You are all gods.'

In a small 'Light circle', such experiences can never be staged by the ego. Rather, the ego disappears just like shadows in the light. It sounds simple, and it is. But it is not easy because it is not an initiative undertaken by the ego. Many are enthusiastic when hearing this proposal, but not that many start to actually put it into practice. The ego comes up with so many excuses like 'no time', 'I am not interested', 'I cannot do it', 'I am not holy', or 'Come on, that's childish'. And one continues to spend one's time talking about other matters or watching TV.

All those, however, who believe in the words regarding two or three 'meeting in my name', and actually do it, can have an immediate and direct experience of the spiritual reality, eternity and pure love. It is a revelation of intimacy with God, which is kept in the sanctum of one's heart. It is not used to impress others or to recruit members. Such Light circles do not look for increased membership, as too many people ruin the atmosphere of confidential union (and sometimes even one additional person is already one too many). There is no need of trying to convert others or becoming 'holier' or 'bigger' than other groups. No new sect. No competition. No dogmas.

Real spirituality is based on the oneness of individuality (= love), which everybody longs for. Therefore, we will naturally speak about our experiences when we meet others who are open to such forms of inspiration, and we can encourage them to initiate their own circles of 'two or three meeting in my name'. In Sanskrit, this is called *sankirtan*, literally 'being together (*san-*) for spiritual expression (*kirtan*)', and is said to be the *yuga-dharma*, the religious practice recommended for this age. The divine sources of all cultures have indicated this open secret in one way or another, and contemporary revelations envision a 'chain reaction of love' when people start to detect this inner adventure.

A 'Light circle' means to be in union with both incarnate and invisible God-devoted individuals. We do not have to become 'enlightened' first, or to undergo some ritualistic 'initiation'. It is possible to experience the oneness with God whenever we connect to it, because it is beyond material limitations and conditions.

Being in the association (union) with spiritual friends is an inspiration that immediately sparks our own God consciousness. This is religion in the true sense of the word: *religio,* the 're-linking with God', which is synonymous with the Sanskrit word *yoga*. Both mean the same: the oneness of the part and the Whole in divine love.

As shown in a previous chapter, this form of religion has been the core of the inspiration provided by Jesus, the incarnated Cosmic Christ, who came to transmit 'the truth that sets you free'. And people experienced it as such.

> Religion was no longer limited to the written word and the autocracy of high priests. The Spirit of truth, the living God and divine Love revealed a totally new quality of life. Whenever they gathered they experienced a direct and personal revelation – the inner word – which was more impressive than any recorded word.[141] This was the life and soul of the Jesus movement of the first two centuries. Through this inspiration, many simple men and women (the

'menservants and maidservants' mentioned by Joel) received the inner word and thus became instruments of the Spirit of truth. In a divine chain reaction more and more Jesus groups came into life, all being animated by the spirit of Christ.

We have been told not to stifle the spirit nor to neglect the gift of prophecy (1 Thess. 5.19–20). Nevertheless, the fire of the spirit has been put out and the gift of 'prophecy' (inspired visions and words) has been lost.

Now, we are free again to receive the Spirit of truth in its ever-fresh form and to build cores of real Love and Light. Out of that, everything else will come: intact families, holistic education, natural life, inner satisfaction and a new spiritual consciousness. This is the key to transcEnd the global power game, both on a private and collective level.

Fighting against darkness will never produce light. So let us work for the Light and not fight against darkness. 'Working' for the Light means, first and foremost, simply being the ray of God we are anyhow. A ray naturally emanates light, and our main task is to make sure that nobody buries our light. And, as indicated in this book, that is already 'work' enough, especially here on earth during these times of division and decision.

'Near is, and difficult to grasp, the God. But where danger threatens, that which saves from it also grows.'[1]

EPILOGUE

'When the monsoon comes, the sage builds a hut.'

(Indian proverb)

Hearing about the rainy season with its tropical downpours, a tourist has different ways to react.

For example, he could ignore the warning by applying the popular logic that states, 'Till now there has been no rain; all this talk about monsoons and typhoons is probably just apocalyptic hysteria of pessimists and paranoiacs.' So he may go out sailing or surfing – and meet his personal 'end of the world'.

As another option, he could believe in the reality of the monsoon and consider it a threat which he has to fight against: 'The monsoon is harmful and it must be prevented. Let me order anti-rain missiles.'

Or he could take an 'esoteric' approach and start a global anti-monsoon meditation: 'Let us pray and meditate so that no monsoon will come.'

Or he could go to a church or a prophet's group that promises: 'If you follow us, then you will be saved, and you will be chosen to survive the monsoon flood while all others have to die.'

Or he himself could start to preach: 'There are so many prophets and psychics nowadays channelling so many things. But I tell you: God only speaks through rare selected prophets, usually only one per generation. And now, by divine mercy, the revelation comes to you that this prophet is me [or the avatar or the master I represent]. Trust no scriptures or channelled messages. Trust me, and I say unto you: The monsoon will come! Wait and you will see that I speak the truth.'

And when the monsoon comes, his believers will lose their last doubts and say: 'He predicted everything, and see, it has all come to pass. Therefore, everything else he says must also be true.'

The same monsoon – and so many ways of reacting! Considering all the possible fallacies and false tracks, we can appreciate the wisdom contained in the quoted proverb, which otherwise might sound like a truism: 'When the monsoon comes, the sage builds a hut.'

We could ignore the monsoon or become afraid of it. We could try to fight against it. We could panic and overestimate it. We could join forces with those who claim to have the 'only truth'. We could wait for the 'big saviour' and 'world teacher' who tells us what to believe and what to do. We could even try to exploit the situation for ourselves by becoming sensationalists, false prophets or sellers of 'anti-rain missiles'. Or we could simply resign in frustration because we cannot prevent the monsoon. *But who told us that we must prevent it?*

Even if the monsoon comes, we do not have to be helplessly exposed. The water may inundate the land, but that does not mean that we have to drown. When the monsoon comes, those who are wise simply build a hut. They know the rain will come, and they know the rain will go again. And they protect themselves without fear. They do not become absorbed in artificial endeavours that entail never-ending entanglements in 'further improvements', one patchwork always calling for the next, while simply furthering destruction in the long run.

The parallels to the global situation are obvious: The 'monsoon' that is imminent, once avoidable, has become unavoidable. It *could* be avoided, but for this end, modern men (we) would have to do certain things, and not do other things. We cannot directly change the power structures of politics and high finance, but there are a few things everybody could do, for example to become free from mass-media consumption, legal and illegal drugs, and meat-eating. These simple things alone would suffice to completely change the face of the world (and of world economics).

What is the probability that such a mass awakening will take place in the next few months? Will global diplomacy and anti-evil campaigns manage to create an atmosphere that furthers *true* peace? Or will they increasingly blur any clear view of the real, honest solutions?

Of course, **at one point, new spiritual factors will cause a quantum leap in global economics and politics.** But these interventions will not 'spare' mankind from having to look into its own mirror, which includes recognizing and correcting the course of egoism, exploitation and indifference. 'See, nothing happened' will no longer work as an excuse.

A realistic assessment of the world situation indicates that there will be downpours of aggression as they have been building up over long periods of time. There will be cleansing and transformation on all levels. These changes on earth cannot be avoided and do not need to be avoided because they are preparatory to the spiritual quantum leap.

Praying or meditating to prevent the monsoon from coming is an expression of fear, based on the mindset, 'My will be done.' (Why should these things not happen? Because I do not like them? Because they would thwart my personal ambitions in this world?)

Divine prayers in the consciousness of love and fearlessness are in the spirit of 'Thy will be done'! If people prayed for the strengthening of love, truth and self-less harmony, peace and prosperity would naturally follow. Praying or demonstrating for peace without this higher consciousness invokes the danger of getting false peace and becoming deceived by false promises.

We cannot say we did not know. We have been told for a long time, and everybody senses, 'It cannot go on like that.' Thus, the question is: *How* do we want to go on? Will we react according to the ego (with fear, indifference, helplessness etc.) or according to divine inspiration?

The spiritual view of the world situation is very encouraging. It reveals that many Light beings have incarnated, or are about to incarnate, and that they (we) are all offered the perfection of divine consciousness after a long journey through the highs and lows of this physical world. The keys to this enlightenment are given to us by arrangements of divine mercy, usually through a contact with individuals who already live in this consciousness, be they incarnate or 'invisible'. Through such a real, inner initiation we realize that we ourselves are Light beings and eternal rays of God, and we can begin to experience the spiritual reality in meditation, inner revelation and inspired communication (alone, in twos, and in a 'Light circle').

In this way, we build our symbolical hut. Whatever monsoon may come, we will not become inundated (influenced) by it. We may become wet, but this will not disturb us.

And we know, the monsoon will not last forever. And we also know that nature never looks as splendid and refreshing as after the purifying rainy season.

Endnotes

Quote references and literature relevant to the topic in question are indicated by the name(s) of the author(s) and, if required, by the respective page numbers. The full titles, as well as the details of publication, of the quoted or recommended sources are given in the bibliography.

The abbreviation t.AR indicates an original German quote translated by Armin Risi (in cases where no other English translation exists).

The abbreviation bt.AR indicates an original English quote back-translated by Armin Risi (when only the German translation of the quote was available).

The abbreviation *ibid.* means 'same as above' and indicates that a quote was taken from the source mentioned in the previous endnote (from Lat. *ibidem,* 'in the same place').

1) These are the famous opening lines of the poetical hymn *Patmos* by Friedrich Hölderlin (1770–1843), a visionary German poet who, long before any New Age movement, sensitively perceived the dawning of the 'new day' as well as the 'danger' that was yet to increase dramatically during the last phases of the 'night'. In his time, this was a future of still more than two hundred years. The title of this poem, *Patmos,* is relevant to our book, too, as it refers to the island in the Aegean Sea where John the Apostle received his divine visions that were later to become known as the Apocalypse, or Revelation. 'I, John, … was on the island of Patmos on account of [preaching] the Word of God and of bearing witness to Jesus.' (Rev. 1.9)

2) Taken from Lasker's appreciations of Pillsbury, one published in *The New York Times,* the other in *Lasker's Chess Magazine,* quoted in Harold C. Schonberg, *The Grandmasters of Chess,* Philadelphia: J. B. Lippincott, 1973, pp. 147-8.

3) Today's world record in simultaneous blind chess is 52 games, established by the Hungarian Janos Flesch in 1960, a performance (31 games won, 18 drawn, 3 lost, in 13 hours) that has not been surpassed by anyone up to the present day. In summary, Pillsbury's example has been mentioned because it is instructive in two ways: It demonstrates how far the mind and even the physical body can be influenced by one's consciousness, and it shows the extent of man's dormant inner potentials.

4) The world-view of holistic science is summarized, for example, by Bohm, Sheldrake, Talbot, Wolf.

5) The terms 'higher dimensions' and 'higher-dimensional levels' are used as synonyms referring to worlds of matter in less-condensed, or subtle, forms invisible to the physical eye of human beings. These terms refer to *material*

and not to spiritual categories. Being 'higher-dimensional', therefore, does not necessarily mean being on a high spiritual level of consciousness. The worlds of darkness are also 'higher-dimensional' from the terrestrial point of view.

6) The term 'astral' refers to the higher-dimensional aspects of three-dimensional ('physical') planets and stars. Each celestial body (Grk. *astron*) has subtle-material parallel levels, or astral realms. Literally, 'astral' means 'planetary' or 'stellar', in a subtle-energetic sense. In the higher dimensions of the universe, the astral levels of related celestial bodies are joined together and are thus connected to even higher cosmic units, comparable to apples which are joined together on the next higher level called 'branch', to which they are connected by their stalk, and through the branch they are interconnected to even higher units – the tree, the grove and the entire planet. Starting with their astral 'stalks', planets and solar systems are hierarchically interrelated on respective higher-dimensional (metaphysical) levels. This multidimensional cosmic structure expands up to the most subtle material dimension of the universe from where it emanated and through which all dimensions are interconnected as one universal unit. (In Sanskrit, this highest and most subtle dimension of the universe is called the 'world of Brahma'.)

Being a fractal part of the universal unit, the physical body of the human being is also connected to different parallel ('astral') bodies and *chakras* (subtle energy centres) which, on their part, are linked to the respective cosmic dimensions. Due to these various contexts, the word 'astral' today is used in a more general sense and has become a synonym for 'subtle-material' as differentiated from the term 'gross-material', which refers to the physically condensed form of material energy (= physical matter).

In different esoteric systems, the word 'astral' is used to designate a particular level of subtle energy within the higher-dimensional hierarchy of worlds and elements – categorized as ethereal, astral, mental, emotional, causal, spiritual, or whatever words are used according to language and tradition.

7) The term 'extraterrestrial' is used to indicate life forms, interactions and information originating from sources that are not terrestrial in the ordinary sense. It can refer to astral levels of the earth, parallel worlds or other (semi-)physical worlds. From a higher-dimensional point of view, it is possible that earthly humans are contacted by beings from subtle or semi-physical spheres of 'Terra' itself, or of Venus, Mars, Sirius, the Pleiades etc. Such beings are not limited to means of transportation within three-dimensional physics. But, as indicated in Part III of this book, not all UFOs are 'extraterrestrial'.

8) The concept of 'what we really are' may not be a common topic, but our language is actually rich in terms describing the reality beyond duality: non-material, transcendental, spiritual, eternal, timeless, spaceless, divine. These are more or less synonyms describing different aspects of our original 'being-ness' as parts of God – qualities that the parts and the Whole have in common. In quality, we are equal, in quantity, we are different, because the Whole is absolute: unlimited, omniscient and all-encompassing, including matter and

relativity. The far-reaching consequence of this understanding, and of the possible misunderstandings thereof, will be elaborated in the following pages and chapters.

9) Thinking that evil originates from us humans alone is a very limited concept that entails several problems.

1. It can cause people to ignore the existence of the negative forces and, consequently, to ignore the influence that these forces exert on the collective and individual levels.

2. It can lead to self-pity, inferiority complexes or resignation. 'I am evil, weak and sinful, what can I do?' Self-accusation can lead to religious fanaticism and dependence on institutions, dogmas and/or leading figures.

3. Most people, however, do not believe that they are evil or bad. Ignoring their own resonance to evil influence, and ignoring evil itself, they maintain an attitude of self-complacency. Usually they laugh at all those who talk about 'conspiracies' and 'satanic forces'.

All of these possible effects – ignorance, self-accusation, fanaticism, self-complacency – make people blind to the real mercy of God, causing them to believe that such a mercy is non-existent or irrelevant to their lives, or that they do not deserve it, already have it, or do not need it.

10) The state of remaining beyond the traps of duality is a constant and conscious expression of divine love. But how long does one 'have to' stay in the testing ground of the material world? This question is justified because the universe of polarity is a place of space and time. So the question 'how long' has relevance for those who identify themselves with the linear flow of time, forgetting that they are eternal. The question of time does not arise for the Light beings who live in pure divine consciousness. Still, at some point the universe will be dissolved, and then all beings who did not fall (and those who transcEnded their fall) will ascend into the eternity beyond polarity, beyond space and time, into the 'kingdom of God'. In other words, life in the dimensions of polarity is not the final, eternal state of being. For those living in God consciousness, however, it does not really matter where they live because they live in real oneness (love), in the eternal Now, and are able to 'see God everywhere'.

11) These negative emotions are the cause of all psychological problems. Not to be underestimated is the seemingly harmless set of 'self-consoling' sentiments called *self-pity*. In tracing down the root of all negative emotions, one ends up with this 'Luciferean' self-pity. It means considering oneself to be innocent, thinking that everything one does is good and justified. Therefore one is unable to accept the fact that negative reactions have been caused by one's own actions, and one thinks, 'I am suffering unjustly', which is a projection of guilt upon others, ultimately upon God. By this self-delusion all feelings of humility, gratitude, forgiveness and love are strangled. Self-pity means refusing *to love and be loved* – an unfortunate mentality which is the breeding ground of all other negative emotions. Unable to love and be loved, one becomes frustrated, angry, hateful, and envious of others, especially of those who are able to

love and be loved. In this way, the dark forces fall into a godless (= emotionless, careless, loveless) attitude: 'Leave me alone!', 'I don't care.' On a global scale this attitude causes exploitation of nature, animals and people, up to genocide and ecocide. 'Okay, let's do it. Even if we go to hell – so what!'

12) Lorber, *Die Haushaltung Gottes,* vol. 1, chapter 5, verse 12, t.AR
13) There are many Light beings who incarnate within the realms of duality out of unconditional love in order to 'reclaim the fallen' by inspiring them or by challenging them. Some perform revolutionary feats through creativity in music, art, philosophy, spiritual healing, etc. Others are present in an inconspicuous manner. Despite all troubles and human weaknesses, they are *in* but not *of* the world of duality as they have not *fallen* into it. Their 'diving down' into the worlds of dense matter is just another aspect of their free will, and that is why they naturally respect the free will of others. They are not fervent missionaries or imposing 'peacemakers'.
14) The two forms of negativity are comparable to the 'modes of material resonance' (Skr. *gunas,* lit. 'string; cord; category') described in Vedic psychology as *rajo-guna* ('passion'; restlessness, addiction) and *tamo-guna* ('darkness'; short-sightedness, non-sensibility). The middle course is the path of *sattva-guna* ('goodness'; contentedness, inner balance) leading to *shuddha-sattva* ('pure/selfless goodness'; loving and active God consciousness).
15) The expression 'lord (or prince) of the world' is not to be confused with the 'king of the world' who is also mentioned in the Bible under the name Melchizedek. This title is derived from the Hebrew word *malkuth,* 'the earthly kingdom', which is one of the branches (Sephiroth) of the cabbalistic Tree of Life. The same word is used in the 'Our Father' that says 'Thy kingdom come' (*tete malkuthach*). *Tsedeq* or *Zadok* is the title of the 'king of Salem' and the 'priest of the Most High God' (Gen. 14.18 and Psalm 110.4). This name is also mentioned in the New Testament, in Hebrews, chapters 5 to 7. It is interesting to note that in Eastern traditions the same title, 'king of the world', is mentioned in connection with the mystical kingdom Shambhalla. Many Christians think that this is the place of 'Satan'. Are they confusing the 'lord of the world' with the 'king of the world'?
16) Quoted from the anthroposophical author Wolfgang Greiner, *Christus und Luzifer,* p. 18, t.AR
17) *ibid.,* p. 19, t.AR
18) Greiner, *Das Antlitz des Bösen,* pp. 44, 53, t.AR
19) Quoted in: *FOCUS* 52/1996, p. 145, bt.AR
20) Sagan, *Entities: Parasites of the Body of Energy,* pp. 6ff. Dr Samuel Sagan is a physician, psychologist, Sanskrit expert and metaphysician. Since the eighties he has been running his *Clairvision School* in Australia and has succeeded in healing diseases such as cancer and tumours by liberating patients from astral influence.
21) This was stated by Rudolf Steiner, the later founder of Anthroposophy, in a lecture given on 17 October 1905.

22) Greiner, *Das Antlitz des Bösen,* p. 29, t.AR
23) Daskalos: *The Esoteric Teachings,* p. 155-6. This is a quote by the famous healer and metaphysician Dr Stylianos Atteshlis (1912–95) from Cyprus, known as *Daskalos.* Being a master of what he called 'psychonoetic' (ethereal and mental) energies, he was able to dissolve elementals, recognize and release astral beings who had attached themselves to human beings, heal and even 'operate' people without touching them, project himself with his astral body into parallel worlds, 'bilocate' himself, etc.
24) Daskalos, quoted in: Markides, *The Magus of Strovolos,* p. 42 (Strovolos is the part of Nikosìa where Daskalos lived.)
25) This sentence was handed down by Augustine in his work *De Civitate Dei.*
26) Erdmann, p. 232, t.AR
27) All books about WWII mention the atrocities that happened in the German concentration camps, and the following information is not meant to deny or play down this gruesome aspect of history. Rather, it shows how incredible and inhuman this war really was. Namely, as revealed officially only in the recent past, incredible atrocities were also committed against the people of Germany. More than one thousand cities were bombed. One million tons of bombs were thrown down upon 30 million civilians (around 30 kg of bombs upon each German citizen, including babies, children and old people). 'Operation Gomorrah' killed 40,000 people in Hamburg. Regarding the bombing of Dresden, 'the number of casualties is not known. Official reports mention 80,000 to 90,000. Others mention numbers up to 245,000, as the city was overcrowded with home-coming inhabitants, with injured and recovering people, as well as with thousands of refugees from the east zone, who were not registered […] 410,000 civilians died in Germany due to the Anglo-American aerial bombardment. The number of missing persons is many hundreds of thousands […] 3.6 million houses were destroyed in Germany, 7.5 million civilians were made homeless.' (Kurowski, pp. 310, 315, t.AR)
The Canadian historian James Bacque published two books, *Crimes and Mercies: The Fate of German Civilians under Allied Occupation* 1944-1950 (1997), and *Other Losses: The Shocking Truth behind the Mass Deaths of Disarmed German Soldiers and Civilians under General Eisenhower's Command* (1999), in which he documents how one million disarmed German men were starved to death in American and French concentration camps *after the war* (see bibliography: Bacque). He also shows how Eisenhower, and others, deliberately suppressed available food supplies and medical aid for Germany during 1945–50, entailing the deaths of about 9 million civilians! See also: Friedrich, 2002; Knopp, 2003; Overmans, 2002; or Vealey, *Advance to Barbarism* (1953/1968) as an early voice against Churchill's one-sided version of history; and Richard J. Evans (2002), who investigated the extent of the bombing massacres in Germany.
28) There are many sources about the supranational backgrounds of Trotsky's mission and the Communist take-over in Russia, for example, Prof. A. Sutton: *Wall Street and the Bolshevik Revolution,* or G. Edward Griffin, *The Creature of*

Jekyll Island. The latter contains telling subtitles such as 'Trotsky was Schiff's agent', 'Schiff was not alone', 'The secret society', and 'Round table agents in Russia'. Griffin states (p. 263): 'One of the greatest myths of contemporary history is that the Bolshevik Revolution in Russia was a popular uprising of the downtrodden masses against the hated ruling class of the Tsars. As we shall see, however, the planning, the leadership, and especially the financing came entirely from outside Russia, mostly from financiers in Germany, Britain, and the United States.'

A detailed description of the historical events is given, for example, by Orlando Figes, *A People's Tragedy: The Russian Revolution 1891-1924* (1996).

29) Farkas, *Wer beherrscht die Welt?* ['Who Rules the World?'], p. 42, t.AR
30) For example, Simpson; Farkas, pp. 28–38; Icke: *The Robot's Rebellion*, pp. 162–4; again, a well-referenced source is G. E. Griffin's book, chapter 12, 'Sink the Lusitania!' with the subtitles, 'A secret agreement to get the U.S. into war', 'Selling war to the American people', 'Morgan control over the shipping', 'The Lusitania', 'Churchill sets a trap', 'A floating munitions depot', 'The final voyage', 'A hurried cover-up', 'The cry for war'. Griffin also mentions British Commander Joseph Kenworthy, an eyewitness of the sinking of the Lusitania, 'who previously had been called upon by Churchill to submit a paper on what would be the political results of an ocean liner being sunk with American passengers aboard. He left the [high-command] room in disgust at the cynicism of his superiors. In 1929, in his book, *The Freedom of the Seas*, p. 211, he wrote without further comment: "The *Lusitania* was sent at considerably reduced speed into an area where a U-boat was known to be waiting, and with her escorts withdrawn." Further comment is not needed.' (Griffin, pp. 252f.)
31) Encyclopaedia *Brockhaus*, 1993, 'Sezessionskrieg' (t.AR incl. emphases).
32) K. Algemissen, 'Freimaurer' ['Freemasons'] in: *Lexikon für Theologie und Kirche*, Freiburg/Breisgau 1960.
33) Pfeifer, 'The Brothers of the Shadow', pp. 37, 65, t.AR
34) quoted from: http://www.biblebelievers.org.au/jesuits.htm
35) quoted from: http://www.freedomdomain.com/illumin.html
36) Hölderlin, *Hyperion*, in: The German Library, vol. 22, New York 1990
37) The word *cosmos* perfectly conveys the idea of balance and harmony within the created universe. The Greek word *kosmos* literally means 'arrangement, order, ornament' with the inherent understanding that there is a higher, universal intelligence creating this order and yielding beauty. *Kosmos* has the same root as the verb *kosmein*, 'to bring into order, to arrange in fullness, to complete, to decorate'. (The latter meaning is even found in the word 'cosmetics'!)
38) Again it has to be emphasized that the expression 'illuminati' is not meant to designate any particular group or institution. Rather, it refers to a certain ideology and mentality just like the terms 'racist', 'egotist' or 'philanthropist'. It is the mentality of Luciferean self-justification based on the argument 'what we did to others was necessary'. This way of thinking can be found everywhere, in all ranks and factions, ultimately within each individual. The question is:

to what degree? How far does it dominate the character of a person? There are not that many who fully embody this ideology, and even fewer are those who have the opportunity of applying it on a global level. Those few who do, however, are the ulterior forces who think themselves to be the creators of the world's destiny.

39) Ernest Scott, *People of the Secret*, pp. 233-4. The first sentence was taken from the second chapter, entitled 'A secret directorate?', in which the author theorizes about how mankind evolved from primitive forms up to the point of being challenged to reach 'the second highest galactic energy level: the unifying energy of love'. If love is the second highest energy level within the galaxy, then what is the highest? As revealed in the passage quoted, the 'people of the secret' think that *necessity* is the highest reality of the god-less 'universe'.

40) As mentioned in Chapter One, to be in-dividual means that we are not part of duality, neither of time (past and future) nor of space (creation, dissolution). Linear time is an aspect of the material world and is intrinsically interwoven with space. Being spiritual individuals, we are not products of some material process in the past. Individuality is eternal because it is never part of duality. It refers to the ever-present 'beingness' beyond time and space. Time which is not projected into duality is not time but *eternity*, and this is the spaceless, timeless reality which we all are parts of – even though we may project our consciousness into the worlds of duality and start identifying ourselves with them. But this is *maya*, illusion, 'that which is not'. If materialistic propaganda says, 'You are a product of matter that evolved into living entities, your identity is your mortal body, there is no spiritual, eternal soul', then it says nothing but 'you are not an individual'. The radical application of this diabolic 'truth' is illustrated by the philosophy of the illuminati.

41) quoted in: Michel, p. 69, t.AR

42) The law of action and reaction shows how the past influences our present and future. The past was once the 'present', and our seeming 'present' is immediately sucked into the past. In reality, however, we as spiritual beings are eternal (timeless), which indicates that we, while living in the world of matter, pass from one temporary situation to the next, ultimately from one body to the next (usually called 'reincarnation'). We lived before the present birth and will continue to live after leaving the present body. Karma and reincarnation do not imply endless and merciless cycles of predestination heading for some kind of godless self-redemption. Rather, all theistic sources explain that one's bondage to the seemingly endless chain of actions and reactions can be transcEnded by love and forgiveness based on God consciousness.

43) There was the historical Jesus as a human being, and there is the spiritual being who incarnated as Jesus, described as the original 'logos' becoming flesh (see John 1.1–14: 'In the beginning there was the *logos*', usually translated as 'In the beginning there was the word'). The inner identity of Jesus was revealed to several Apostles and to many mystics throughout the past twenty centuries, and they all recognized him to be God's 'first-born son', who existed before

everything else existed, and through whom everything and all creatures, including the angels, were created. This description perfectly matches the Vedic description of God's (Vishnu's) first created 'son', the supreme Light being of the universe, named *Brahma* in Sanskrit. In biblical and apocryphal sources we can find many parallels, for example:

'God has given me all might in heaven and on earth.' (Matt. 28.18)

'Truly, I tell you, before Abraham was, I am.' (John 8.58)

'Now, Father, grant me again that glory I had in your presence, before the world existed.' (John 17.5)

'I am the Light above everything. I am the cosmos. The cosmos has emanated from me, and the cosmos has attained its purpose within me.' (Gospel of Thomas, 77.1)

'In the beginning there was the Word (*logos*), and the Word was with the God, and the Word was a god. ['A god', from the Greek original *theos,* is used in contrast to the term *ton theon,* 'the God', which is used in the same sentence; another possible translation: 'He who was the Word was with God and was in the full likeness of God.'] From the very beginning he was with God. All things came into being through him. Nothing came into being without him. [...] And the Word became flesh ['in-carnated'] and lived among us, and we have seen his glory [majesty], the glory as of a father's only son. [...] No one has ever seen God; it is the only-begotten Son who is close to the Father's heart who has made Him known.' (John 1.1–3, 14, 18)

'He is the perfect image of the invisible God, the first-born of all creation; for in him all things in heaven and on earth were created, everything visible and everything invisible, whether thrones or dominions or rulers or powers – all things have been created through him and towards him as their goal. He himself is before all things, and all things are sustained by him.' (Col. 1.15–17)

'... God's son, whom He appointed heir of all things, through whom He also created the worlds. He is the reflection of God's glory. He perfectly embodies God's being and sustains all things through his powerful word.' (Heb. 1.2–3)

44) Music is one of the most intense expressions of creativity. Therefore, the change of epochs was always accompanied, if not initiated, by new styles of music. One lasting example was seen in the fifties when some young men refused to accept their given roles within the existing male-dominated society. They intuitively rejected the hypocritical façade of 'good citizenship' and shocked the high-handed winner nation of WWII with a new style of music they called *rock 'n' roll,* a term coined by Bill Haley around 1953/4. The pioneers of this new style were talented and intelligent young men, but they chose to sing simple texts about their lives and dreams, honestly expressing the burning desire of wanting to love and be loved; there was nothing intellectual or poetic in the classical sense. They had no sophisticated ambitions. Rather it was a shift from the 'left brain half' to the right, from the intellectual and stiff male side to the intuitive, instinctive female side, which activated the wild and impulsive aspects within people. And it was no secret that they were inspired

by the *rhythm 'n' blues* of the black 'outcastes' – again something 'unbecoming' for young white men. Elvis Presley was nineteen, Buddy Holly seventeen and Ritchie Valens fifteen when they started to go on stage with three or four fellow musicians of the same age. Initially, there was real idealism and some kind of naive purity – which soon became infiltrated or replaced by less pure and destructive elements. Still, these pioneers had a special charisma and influence. Were they 'starseeds' born on earth to give an impulse to initiate a new epoch? Did they feel the lack of love on earth so strongly because they came from a world where love was a natural reality? Was this the reason why they longed for this love and never really felt at home 'down here'? Buddy Holly (born 7 September 1936) was twenty-two and Ritchie Valens (born 13 May 1941) seventeen when they died in an airplane crash on 3 February 1959, along with another star, Jiles P. Richardson called 'the Big Bopper' (born 24 October 1930). Elvis 'had to' stay a little longer, until 1977, Bill Haley until 1981.

Of course, this music in itself was not yet a form of enlightenment. It simply opened a door that led from the extreme of superficial materialism and puritanism to a more open-minded, free life-style, which soon reached the other extreme – decadent hedonism and nihilism. But within this opened field of both extremes, the golden mean was easier accessible, and people were given the possibility to go beyond social and dogmatic impositions. They were free to enter new dimensions of consciousness, love and spirituality not limited to mundane fun and entertainment. Many were invited, but only a few chose to grasp the chance of this new freedom, especially regarding the man-woman relationship (after five thousand years of oppression).

45) These quotes are taken from http://www.gnosis.org/naghamm/gop.html and from *Das Neue Testament und frühchristliche Schriften,* translated by Klaus Berger and Christiane Nord, two distinguished German philologists (t.AR).

Mary from Magdala, the place where the Egyptians once had one of their sanctuaries of Isis, was not an ordinary prostitute as presented by the Church's Bible. Several points of evidence indicate that she was an initiated priestess of Isis, and that 'prostitute' was only an abusive nickname given to her by those Jews and Christians who hated everything related to the Egyptian gods. The authors Picknett/Prince confirm (*The Templar Revelation,* p. 441): 'The Mandaean view of Jesus – that he was a liar, a deceiver and evil sorcerer – agrees with that of the Jewish *Talmud,* in which he is condemned for "leading astray" the Jews, and in which his death sentence is ascribed to him having been condemned as an occultist' – a sorcerer practising *Egyptian* occultism!

46) The theories of hyperspace and parallel worlds have become integral parts of advanced holistic physics and are discussed by many authors, for example, Gribbin, Herbert, Kaku, Pickover, Talbot, Wolf (see bibliography).

47) The existence of 'parallel' or subtle bodies is a known secret in all esoteric schools, although the names they use may differ: etheric body, auric body, astral body, mental body, causal body, etc. These bodies are overlapping energy fields with a gradation of density. Most metaphysical sources mention a

basic scale of seven bodies. The seventh, most dense body is the physical body, also called the mortal body. The condition of the finer bodies influences the condition of the denser bodies, and vice versa. Some aspects of these complex mutual connections are also acknowledged by modern medicine in terms of 'psychosomatic diseases'.

48) See, for example, Allan/Delair, Berlitz, Childress, Hancock, Tollmann, Velikovsky, Zillmer.

49) There are many open questions regarding the sudden appearance of agriculture along with new forms of 'economically useful' plants and animals 8,000 to 5,000 years ago. A very controversial but sound analysis of these questions, especially regarding the genetic altering, is given by Prof. Arthur David Horn in his book *Humanity's Extraterrestrial Origins – ET Influences on Biological and Cultural Evolution* (1994). Arthur Horn received his degree from the prestigious Yale University of Connecticut in 1976 and was professor of physical anthropology until 1990, mostly at the Colorado State University. Then, he entered the field of spiritual research, inspired by his wife Lynette, to whom he dedicated the above-mentioned book.

Other authors dealing with these questions from different points of view are, for example, Blumrich, Bramley, Childress, Cremo/Thompson, Hurtak, Icke, Rudgley, Sitchin.

50) In 2001, Israel Finkelstein, director of the Archaeological Institute at the University of Tel Aviv, and Neil Silberman, co-editor of the renowned *Archaeology Magazine*, published a book entitled *The Bible Unearthed – Archaeology's New Vision of Ancient Israel and the Origin of Its Sacred Texts*, in which they present the facts regarding biblical archaeology, and the resulting unorthodox conclusions: For example, there was no historical exodus and no violent conquering of Canaan. In the time of the alleged exodus, Egypt was at the height of its power and maintained many administrative and military bases throughout the Middle East. Leaving Egypt through the Red Sea would have been no escape as the Egyptian forces were stationed on the other side, too. Furthermore, it would have been impossible to conquer any land in Canaan without confronting the Egyptian army. But the Old Testament does not mention anything like that. Rather, it says that the people of Moses were attacked by the King of Arad and that they met the resistance of the Amorites and the nations of Moab, Edom and Ammon. However, archaeology has proven that these nations had not yet existed in the eleventh and tenth century BC! These nations and their fortified cities were founded only centuries later. (It would have been the same as saying that Columbus had to fight the US army when he wanted to enter the New World.) Obviously, these accounts were written much later when the scribes no longer knew the exact chronologies.

Actually, this news is not really new, but simply confirms what philologists have already known for quite some time. Therefore, some religious circles are no longer making a secret out of it. For example, the Rabbinical Assembly (the international association of Conservative Rabbis) and the United Synagogue of Conservative Judaism published an excellent work: a new, complete translation of their Holy Scripture, the Torah, in 2001, entitled *Etz Hayim*, Hebrew for 'Tree of Life', edited by Rabbi David L. Lieber, Professor of Biblical Literature and Thought at the University of Judaism, Los Angeles. It is the new standard edition for millions of Jews, both for reading in the Synagogue and for private study. This impressive book (1,560 pages) includes 41 essays written by highly esteemed exponents of Judaism, both men and women, taking an objective and critical standpoint based on the many years of source research and biblical archaeology. What has come about is a Scripture with a potential that could help in the transcEnding of religious separatism and dogmatism. Being relevant for Judaism and Christianity alike (the Torah is part of the Old Testament), *Etz Hayim* has attracted extraordinary attention world-wide.

On 9 March 2002, the *New York Times* published an extensive article entitled 'As Rabbis Face Facts, Bible Tales Are Wilting'. The writer, Michael Massing, describes the provocative anti-dogmatism of this new Torah edition, and the controversies it ignited:

'Abraham, the Jewish patriarch, probably never existed. Nor did Moses. The entire Exodus story as recounted in the Bible probably never occurred. The same is true of the tumbling of the walls of Jericho. And David, far from being the fearless king who built Jerusalem into a mighty capital, was more likely a provincial leader whose reputation was later magnified to provide a rallying point for a fledgling nation.

'Such startling propositions – the product of findings by archaeologists digging in Israel and its environs over the last 25 years – have gained wide acceptance among non-Orthodox rabbis. But there has been no attempt to disseminate these ideas or to discuss them with laity – until now. [...] Since the fall [2001], when *Etz Hayim* was issued, more than 100,000 copies have been sold. [...]

'For instance, an essay on "Ancient Near Eastern Mythology," by Robert Wexler, president of the University of Judaism in Los Angeles, states that on the basis of modern scholarship, it seems unlikely that the story of Genesis originated in Palestine. [...] The story of Noah, Mr. Wexler adds, was probably borrowed from the Mesopotamian Epic of Gilgamesh.

'Equally striking for many readers will be the essay "Biblical Archaeology," by Lee I. Levine, a professor at the Hebrew University in Jerusalem. "There is no reference in Egyptian sources to Israel's sojourn in that country," he writes, "and the evidence that does exist is negligible and indirect." [...] What's more, he says, there is an "almost total absence of archaeological evidence" backing up the Bible's grand descriptions of the Jerusalem of David and Solomon.

'The notion that the Bible is not literally true "is more or less settled and understood among most Conservative rabbis," observed David Wolpe, a rabbi at Sinai Temple in Los Angeles, and a contributor to *Etz Hayim*.

But some congregants, he said, "may not like the stark airing of it." Last Passover, in a sermon to 2,200 congregants at his synagogue, Rabbi Wolpe frankly said that "virtually every modern archaeologist" agrees "that the way the Bible describes the Exodus is not the way it happened, if it happened at all." The rabbi offered what he called a "litany of disillusion" about the narrative, including contradictions, improbabilities, chronological lapses and the absence of corroborating evidence. [...]
'Even some Conservative rabbis feel uncomfortable with the depth of the doubting. "I think the basic historicity of the text is valid and verifiable," said Susan Grossman, the rabbi of Beth Shalom Congregation in Columbia, Md., and a co-editor of *Etz Hayim*. As for the mounting of archaeological evidence suggesting the contrary, Rabbi Grossman said: "There's no evidence that it didn't happen. Most of the 'evidence' is evidence from silence./ The real issue for me is the eternal truths that are in the text," she added. "How do we apply this hallowed text to the 21st century?"'

Thus far some excerpts from *The New York Times*' article. The question of application is certainly crucial. After all, what factually counts is not an endless discussion about evidence and historicity, but the practical result.
Etz Hayim does not absolutize the text. Rather it attempts to distinguish the absolute from the relative truths, first of all by recognizing that not all parts of the text are absolute. Still, they have their relative value and significance. Rabbi Lieber, Senior Editor of *Etz Hayim*, explains in the Introduction:

'Conservative Judaism is based on Rabbinic Judaism. It differs, however, in the recognition that all texts were composed in given historical contexts. The Conservative Movement, in short, applies historical, critical methods to the study of the biblical text. It views the Torah as the product of generations of inspired prophets, priests and teachers, beginning with the time of Moses but not reaching its present form until the postexilic age, in the 6th or 5th century B.C.E. The Torah is viewed by us, in the words of Harold Kushner, as "God's first word, not God's last".'

The *Etz Hayim* edition is based on the oldest complete manuscript of the Torah extant today, called the Leningrad Manuscript. It dates from 1009 and is in itself a copy from the manuscripts of the Masoretes of Tiberias. 'There is, therefore, a gap of as much as 2,000 years between the original writing of the document and the earliest complete copy to which we have access,' states Benjamin Edidin Scolnic in his essay 'Modern Methods of Bible Study'. And he adds: 'The Torah may seem to present a unified account of Israelite history and law during the patriarchal and Mosaic periods. Detailed study of the text, however, has led modern critical scholarship to theorize that the Torah is a compilation of several sources, different streams of literary traditions, that were composed and collected over the course of the biblical period (ca. 1200 – ca. 400 B.C.E.). Because the Torah, from this perspective, is an amalgam of the

works of different authors and schools, it contains an abundance of factual inconsistencies; contradictory regulations; and differences in style, vocabulary, and even theology.'
How should Jews and Christians deal with this diagnosis by non-dogmatic scholars? How should critics react? It is not possible to just reject a scripture that has been, and still is, sacred to millions of people. Rather, as pointed out by Susan Grossman, it is a question of how to interpret and practically adapt the written content in practical life. In this connection, Rabbi Lieber's description (in the Introduction) of their attitude towards the Torah is very important, also for non-Jews:

> 'In keeping with our commitment to Conservative Judaism, we have sought to learn from the Torah rather than to judge it. There are passages that challenge our moral conscience, a conscience informed by Torah values. Among them, for example, are verses about the treatment of non-Israelite nations and the legal and social standing of women in ancient Israel; and the commentary [in Etz Hayim] reflects our discomfort. The *d'rash* commentary has approached the text with reverence, asking not 'Do we approve of this passage?' but 'Because this was sacred to our ancestors, what can it teach us?'

The question 'What can it teach us?' is the key to respectful reading, and can help us to access the text's deeper dimensions beyond the superficial story. Regarding the Torah and the Old Testament, there are many different explanations of what it can teach us. A very promising version is given in *Etz Hayim*. Another example, and probably the most revolutionary, is the book *The Keys of Enoch* by Prof. J. Hurtak, founder of the 'Academy for Future Science', published in 1973. Here, from the perspective of multidimensional language, the Old Testament is perceived as a Light scripture that is not limited to the external meaning of the words written by men. *'The key languages connecting mind-time warps to interconnecting civilizations and manifestations of "Higher Evolution" in our time-zone are Egyptian-Hebrew-Sanskrit-Tibetan-Chinese.'* (*Key of Enoch* 1.1.0) *'The key to the future of living sciences is Torah, the "Creative Language Mathematics" of all the living creations that went into the creations of Man. In the Torah are revealed the language transparencies of the "Higher Evolution." Torah is the key to Kaballah, the wisdom of the many universes, and the key to "The Scriptures of the Luminaries to Come." [...]'* (*Key of Enoch* 2.0.6)
It is amazing to see what the Torah, when read with this higher vision, can teach and reveal. Through this higher vision we can understand all revelations in their universal context, interconnected on a spiritual level, because the timeless meaning always remains pure and untouched in its own dimension, despite all kinds of human interpolation on the level of the written words. Asking what a scripture can teach us means, above all, searching for this timeless spirit of the original revelation.

51) This point was raised by George Orwell in his famous novel *1984*. Towards the end, before the imprisoned protagonist is executed, the tormentor describes

the psychology used by the totalitarian Big Brother: 'The first thing for you to understand is that in this place there are no martyrdoms. In the Middle Ages there was the Inquisition. It was a failure. Why was that? Because the Inquisition killed its enemies in the open, and killed them while they were still unrepentant [...] We do not make mistakes of that kind. All the confessions that are uttered here are true. *We* make them true. And above all we do not allow the dead to rise up against us [...] We are not content with negative obedience, not even with the most abject submission. When finally you surrender to us, it must be of your own free will.' (Orwell, p. 212)

Another example of world literature describing a total oppression of humans is Jack London's *The Iron Heel* (1907). The protagonist of this novel, a social rebel from the lower working class, which is enslaved in industrial factories and despised by the 'arch-beasts', desperately states: 'My father was a good man. The soul of him was good, and yet it was twisted, and maimed, and blunted by the savagery of his life. He was made into a broken-down beast by his masters, the arch-beasts. [...] They looked upon themselves as wild-animal trainers, rulers of beast' (pp. 70, 190 in the Journeman-Press edition 1990).

52) These and many other names are documented, for example, by Gary Allen, Bainerman, Brüning/Graf, Cooper, Epperson, Heise, Kah, Mullins, Pfeifer.
53) quoted from: *Internationales Freimaurerlexikon,* German edition 2000, p. 337, term 'Katholizismus', t.AR
54) quoted in: Adler, p. 73, t.AR
55) Brüning/Graf, p. 399
56) Mary Bell Martinez: *Die Unterminierung der Katholischen Kirche* (German edition), Verlag Anton A. Schmid, Durach 1992, p. 119, t.AR
57) quoted from: Brüning/Graf, p. 401, t.AR
58) quoted from the German edition, published by Rex Verlag, Lucerne/Munich, Council journal vol. 13, p. 60, t.AR
59) The suspicion that Pope John Paul I was murdered was elaborated by David Yallop in his book *In God's Name?* (1984), in which he exposed many facets of Lodge and Mafia presence in the Vatican Curia and Vatican Bank. The information about O.P. and Mino Pecorelli is also taken from this book.
60) I Millenari: *Via col vento in Vaticano,* Milano 1999; title of the German edition: 'We accuse. Twenty Roman prelates talk about the dark sides of the Vatican.' The page numbers mentioned in the text refer to the German edition, t.AR.

'I Millenari' means 'The Millennialists' and is the Italian translation of the word 'Chiliasts,' followers of the theological view called Chiliasm (from Grk. *chilioi* = 1,000); it is based on the expectation of a messianic kingdom of one thousand years, also called the Millennium, as prophesied in Jewish scriptures and in the New Testament's Apocalypse (chapter 20). The 'Millenari' intended to address the topic of 'the Church in the new millennium' – thus the title of the last chapter of their book. They obviously expected something to happen in the ominous year 2000: '*This is the hour of the Lord* who tries to awaken his Church before the cock crows for the last time. [...] *This is the hour of Mary* who predicted in Fátima the victory of the Church in the year 2000 – the year in which her immaculate heart will have subdued the empire of Evil which turns the holy place of God into an unsafe place, fogging and blackening it with Satan's smoke.' (p. 340)

61) The information provided by the 'Millenari' thus complements the disclosures contained in David Yallop's book (1984); the new closing article of the 1988 edition contains the update regarding Sindona's death in 1986.

62) Buttlar, p. 53, t.AR

63) While Europe sank into an age of darkness and pseudo-religious superstition (for example, by believing that the earth was flat and that that there was hell beyond the horizon of the Atlantic Ocean), other cultures kept the former advanced knowledge and the memories of an antediluvian past. The Phoenicians, most probably, were the first ones to cross the Western Sea after the big flood (about 1000 BC). Also the controversial Book of Mormon describes two crossings of the Ocean in the centuries before Christ. The ancient Greeks, especially those in the line of Pythagoras, knew that the earth was a globe, and so did the Indians and the Chinese. In the third century BC Erathosthenes even managed to calculate its diameter with a good degree of precision.

The secret activities that led to the founding, and to the subsequent success, of the Templars must have been connected to the knowledge about the existence of rich countries on the other side of the Western Sea, obtained from Jewish scholars living in Europe, from Islamic sources accessible in Spain (since the ninth century), and then especially from the contacts made in the Middle East. Most historians refuse to draw this obvious conclusion because it is against the accepted world-view, which says, 'There were no earlier civilizations with secret knowledge, there was no cataclysm, and there are no doubts that the theories of evolution and actualism are right.' (See, for example, Gordon, Knight/Lomas, O'Brien, Holzer.)

64) Baigent, Lincoln and Leigh, *The Holy Blood and the Holy Grail*, p. 371. In the book *The Messianic Legacy*, p. 133, the same authors convey the opinion that the 'doctrine of a non-political, wholly spiritual Messiah [...] must have seemed a monstrous betrayal, or a display of contemptible cowardice' – 'must have seemed' to whom? To the alleged 'original followers' of Jesus as depicted by these authors based on their mundane theories.

65) A complete list is given in Baigent, Lincoln and Leigh, *The Holy Blood and the Holy Grail*, in chapter six and in the appendix.

66) Picknett/Prince, *The Templar Revelation*, p. 196. In the book *The Holy Blood and the Holy Grail*, the authors speculate that even the tomb of Jesus might still exist, including his bones, which would be the ultimate proof that Jesus never ascended. 'If Jesus was indeed "King of the Jews" the Temple [of Jerusalem] is almost certain to have contained copious information relating to him. It may even have contained his body – or at least his tomb, once his body was removed from the temporary tomb of the Gospels' (p. 424). Later, in AD 70, the Temple was destroyed by the Romans who took all the sacred objects they

could find, and brought them as booty to Rome. Four hundred years later, the treasure from the Temple of Jerusalem fell into the hands of the Goths when they conquered and raided Rome. Since then, it has been lost. One theory says that the Goths hid these objects in the Pyrenees in order to keep them secret – until the time of the new Messiah! '... something was concealed in the vicinity of Rennes-le-Château [...] One can only speculate about what might have been concealed there. It may have been Jesus's mummified body' (p. 425). Obviously, there are people toying with the idea of devastating Christianity by presenting the body of Jesus, or what they might propagate to be the body of Jesus.

67) *The Book of Prophecies* by John of Jerusalem was published by Prof. Galvieski in 1994 in French. The texts quoted are taken from the German edition, t.AR.

68) Baigent/Leigh, *The Temple and the Lodge: Inside Freemasonry*, p. 102. 'In Portugal, the Templars were cleared by an inquiry and simply modified their name, becoming the Knights of Christ. They survived under this title well into the sixteenth century, their maritime explorations leaving an indelible mark on history. (Vasco da Gama was a Knight of Christ; Prince Henry the Navigator was a Grand Master of the Order. Ships of the Knights of Christ sailed under the Templars' familiar red patté cross. And it was under the same cross that Columbus's three caravels crossed the Atlantic to the New World. Columbus himself was married to the daughter of a former Grand Master of the Order, and had access to his father-in-law's charts and diaries.)' (p. 88)

If it is true that some delegations of the Templar's fleet reached Central America in the twelfth or thirteenth century, then we can assume that these crews only consisted of initiated members of the Order who were sworn to absolute secrecy. A transatlantic contact could have been the source of the Templars' mysterious wealth in Europe, which otherwise remains even more mysterious. Apparently, these white 'gods' with beards made a very good impression on their native adorers, and they promised to come back. But then, they suffered the setback of 1307. When, after about two hundred years, Columbus and the following expeditions appeared on the shores of these countries, they were again welcomed like gods. Columbus and Vasco da Gama were still (secret) initiates, but they had barbarian crews. Thus, they could no longer prevent the clash of civilizations. They were soon followed by people like Cortez and Pizarro who were not initiates but unscrupulous conquerors dispatched by the European kings and popes.

69) The Battle of Bannockburn and the evidence indicating the Templars' participation are analysed, for example, by Baigent/Leigh, *The Temple and the Lodge*, pp. 42, 67 ff.

70) Knight/Lomas, pp. 375-6

71) *ibid.*, p. 457

72) Pfeifer, 'The Brothers of Shadow', p. 50

73) Knight/Lomas, *The Hiram Key*, pp. 461–3: 'The Development of Masonry in America'.

74) Throughout US history politicians of a certain background have tried to tamper with the Constitution, some even dreaming of suspending it 'when the time comes'. One example of a basic change in the Constitution was the Federal Reserve Act of 1913 that handed the State Bank over to private bankers, allowing them to print money and loan it to the government *with interest*. Today, in cases of emergency – real *and* staged – the Constitution can be suspended or even repealed. After the events of 11 September, 2001, concerned US citizens and patriots have been afraid that this might factually happen at some point. Then, the nation would be turned into a dictatorship that puts absolute power into the hands of those who proclaimed the emergency. For further information see, for example, Gary Allen, Epperson, G. Edward Griffin, Groseclose, Hufschmid (about 9/11), Josephson, McAdoo, Mullins, Quigley.
75) Thirty-six years after the Battle of Kurukshetra, Arjuna and his brothers renounced the kingdom and went to the Himalayan Mountains where they left the earth with a transfigured body, ascending into a higher-dimensional, spiritual existence due to their pure God consciousness (*Shrimad-Bhagavatam* 1.15.41–8). This is the best-known, but not the only Vedic example of a physical ascension.
76) An interesting parallel is found in the mythology of the Sioux, as reported by Joseph E. Brown in *The Sacred Pipe* (p. 9): 'According to Siouan mythology, it is believed that at the beginning of the cycle a buffalo was placed at the west in order to hold back the waters. Every year this buffalo loses one hair, and every age he loses one leg. When all his hair and all four legs are gone, then the waters rush in once again, and the cycle comes to an end./ A striking parallel to this myth is found in the Hindu tradition, where it is the Bull Dharma (the divine law) who has four legs, each of which represents an age of the total cycle. During the course of these four ages (*yugas*) true spirituality becomes increasingly obscured, until the cycle (*manvantara*) closes with catastrophe, after which the primordial spirituality is restored, and the cycle begins once again.
It is believed by both the American Indian and the Hindu that at the present time the buffalo or bull is on his last leg […]'
77) Carmin, pp. 296–7, t.AR
78) A further field of profit, one not to be underestimated, was the production of illegal drugs such as opium and cocaine. In this connection, the Far East, especially China, was the main battlefield in the nineteenth and early twentieth centuries (up to the communist 'Cultural Revolution' in 1949 by Mao, who was another agent financed by the ulterior forces). In the course of the twentieth century, the production has been drastically expanded, involving countries situated in Central and South America, in South-East Europe (the Balkans) and in the Middle and Far East (Afghanistan, Pakistan, Burma).
The huge quantities of drugs 'administered' to people world-wide are certainly not smuggled by illegal dealers in hollow heels, but are transported in airplanes and trucks from one continent to another – and hardly anything is detected. Apparently, there must be safe transporting routes tolerated or even

organized by high-ranking people who have the power to clear these ways. Some critical researchers describe a direct involvement of the secret services in these drug dealings in order to make money (billions of dollars), to make countries dependent, and to intoxicate the resisting elements of society. See, for example, Bainerman, Cooper, McCoy.
79) quoted in: Marlowe, p. 211 (emphasis by A.R.). William T. Stead was one of the prominent people who died in 1912 aboard the sinking Titanic.
80) *ibid.*, p. 211
81) Reuveni, p. 30, t.AR
82) Carmin, p. 630, t.AR. The details mentioned at the end of this quote illustrate the secret societies' ideological and supranational ties. On the levels beyond the political surface of world history it was well possible that a British imperialist like Horatio Kitchener was connected to the Austrian-German Neo-Templar Order of Lanz von Liebenfels, who had a very strong ideological influence on the young Adolf Hitler.
83) It is therefore not an exaggeration to call these executive agents 'Global Manipulators'; see Robert Eringer, *The Global Manipulators: The Bilderberg Group, the Trilateral Commission – Covert Power Groups of the West*. See also, for example, Kah, *En Route to Global Occupation,* or Perloff, *The Shadows of Power: The Council on Foreign Relations and the American Decline*.
84) Cover-text of Cuddy/Goldsborough, *The Network of Power: The New World Order II* (1993). The background of manipulated elections, especially the one in the year 2000, has been made widely public by Michael Moore in his bestselling book *Stupid White Men*.
85) Goulevitch, pp. 224, 230. These quotes also reveal the identity of the well-known 'British financier' from whom Trotsky received a 'large loan' in support of the Russian Revolution, as indicated on p. 88. This person was obviously none other than Lord Alfred Milner.
86) Bramley, p. 348
87) For a detailed explanation see, for example, Josephson, *The Federal Reserve Conspiracy* (1968), and Gary Allen, Epperson, Greider, G. Edward Griffin, Groseclose, Larson, McAdoo, Mullins.
88) quoted from Icke, *The Robot's Rebellion*, p. 157
89) In the early fifties, there was an extensive, and intrusive, anti-communist campaign in the USA, led by Senator Joseph McCarthy. According to the knowledge of Prof. Carroll Quigley this action was simply part of a propaganda campaign. In his book *Tragedy and Hope,* he reveals (on p. 931): 'Until early 1950, Communism meant little to McCarthy. He had been elected to the Senate over the incumbent, LaFollette, in 1946, as a result of Communist-controlled votes in the labor unions of Milwaukee. As a Senator he collaborated in a joint Nazi and Communist plot to injure the United States and its army by reversing the convictions of German SS troops for atrocities committed on American prisoners of war captured in the Battle of the Bulge. But, by January 1950, McCarthy was looking for an issue to be used for his reelection in 1952. At a

dinner with three men, two of them associates of mine, in the Colony Restaurant in Washington DC (January 7, 1950) he asked what issue he should use. After several suggestions, he seized upon Communism, "That's it," he said, "the government is full of Communists. We can hammer away at them."'

90) quoted from the encyclopaedia *Brockhaus* (1989), 'Harriman, Edward Henry', t.AR; for further information see Lundberg, *America's Sixty Families*.

91) All the information in these paragraphs are taken from the books mentioned in endnote 83. Additional reference is found in Abramson, *Spanning the Century: The Life of W. A. Harriman*; Chaitkin, *Treason in America: From Aaron Burr to Averell Harriman* (1985); Issacson/Thomas, *The Wise Men: Six Friends and the World They Made* (1986); and Reuveni (1994).

Regarding the financing of Germany's rearmament, official history names the German entrepreneur Fritz Thyssen, then exponent of the German 'Stahlwerke AG', as the main sponsor of Hitler. This is only a part of the truth as Thyssen was not the only sponsor and, furthermore, he became increasingly disillusioned with Hitler. In 1939 he emigrated to Switzerland. In 1940 he was arrested in France and was kept in concentration camps until 1945. That is not the typical biography of a main sponsor. So who else was?

92) reported in Chaitkin/Tarpley, 'The Hitler Project'; Maisky, *Who helped Hitler?*; Pfeifer, p. 102; and Sutton, *Wall Street and the Rise of Hitler*. See also G. E. Griffin, p. 295: 'From the beginning of Hitler's rise to power, German industry was heavily financed by American and British Bankers.'

In the sources mentioned above and in endnote 27, we find several statements by high-finance magnates and allied leaders, among them Churchill and Roosevelt, who said that they wanted to destroy the entire German nation, not only the Nazis. Already in 1954, Russell Grenfell, a former high officer of the British Army who had known Churchill closely for many years, published a book entitled *Unconditional Hatred*, referring to Churchill's attitude towards Germany. Churchill was not the only one driven by the idea that 'Germany must perish', which was a coined phrase already in the second half of the nineteenth century. (One conspiracy theory says that Hitler and the Nazis were financed from abroad to make them grow into a cancer that would ruin Germany and deliver it into the hands of the winners – those who financed both sides.) Why this irrational, and apparently ancient, mutual hatred and destruction?

At the same time, it is a divine law that in times of deepest darkness extraordinary help is offered. Thus, right in Germany, a great healer and spiritual reformer appeared, Bruno Gröning (1906–59), who became publicly active when he returned from Russian captivity. When it became known in 1949 that he could heal even blind and lame people, masses of diseased and war-disabled men and women gathered wherever he was found to be staying – up to 30,000 people (in Rosenheim near Munich), which led to miraculous mass healings. As typical for the Kali-yuga, he soon was persecuted by the lobbies and by smear campaigns in the mass media, which were intentionally staged to destroy the newly awakened public faith in spiritual healing. Bruno Gröning, who had been a simple working man, prophetically foresaw that all God-devoted people would develop their spiritual potentials in the time of greatest need, and he taught how to become connected to the universal healing stream, which causes and restores the divine harmony in all of God's creation, including our bodies.

93) in: *ZüriWoche*, 7 January 1999, p. 28, t.AR
94) *ibid.*, p. 28, t.AR
95) There is even a Bible manuscript, the *Codex Ephraemi Rescriptus*, that mentions the number 616 instead of 666. All others, however, have the number 666. Bible researchers suspect that the copier of this particular manuscript changed the number to better fit it to the name of the Roman Emperor Nero.
96) quoted from the news magazine *Der Spiegel*, 21 November 1994, p. 66, t.AR
97) quoted from the magazine *Sous la bannière* (F-18260 Vailly sur Sauldre), No. 56, Nov./Dec. 1994, p. 15. See also: Rivera.
98) Brinkley/Perry, p. 43
99) Rothkranz, a Christian author, in his book about 666, p. 81, t.AR
100) Lindsey/Carlson, p. 100
101) 'China – Woher der Wind weht', in: *Der Spiegel*, 12/1998, p. 182, t.AR
102) G. Edward Griffin, p. 306 (at the end of the chapter entitled 'The best enemy money can buy').
103) In the beginning of 1999, half a year before the Yugoslavian war began due to the crisis in Kosovo and Albania, Hollywood came out with a topical film that was to become 'the best political satire of the year', entitled *Wag the Dog*, starring Dustin Hoffman and Robert De Niro. The story went as follows: It had been exposed that the American President was involved in a sex scandal. To divert the public's attention, and to assure his re-election, the secret service NSA (National Security Agency) decided to stage a war that would exist only in the mass media. For this purpose they recruited Hollywood's best film director, and arbitrarily decided to use *Albania* as the place of the alleged war. The secret plan worked out. Using Hollywood's best tricks, they succeeded in convincing the public about the existence of this fictitious enemy and this fictitious war. Everything had to remain top-secret, of course, but Hollywood's star director (played by Dustin Hoffman) became intoxicated with the success of his ingenuity, and wanted to let the public know that it had all been orchestrated by him. When he shrugged off all warnings by the NSA he died of a 'sudden heart attack', according to the official news.

When this film came out, there was not yet a Lewinsky scandal. Soon after, however, we got the scandal and the war. Of course, the Balkan war was not fictitious, but the film indicates how public opinion can be manipulated to fit any purpose. This is also the message of the film's title. Usually, it is the dog that wags. The tail makes up only about 2 percent of the dog's body. But in global society it is the 2 percent that wags the rest of the social body. The tail is wagging the dog!

104) http://craig_pages.tripod.com/Bible_Study/Revelation/rev25.htm
105) Lawrence Wright, 'Forcing the End. Why do a Pentacostal cattle breeder from Mississippi and an Orthodox rabbi from Jerusalem believe that a red heifer can change the world?' in: *The New Yorker*, 20 July 1998.
106) As Jesus himself predicted, many have come in his name. Some tried to monopolize his teachings by declaring their interpretations to be the only proper understanding of 'the truth'. About three hundred years after the crucifixion, this process became institutionalized through the foundation of the Roman Church, which chose the Apostles Peter and Paul as its figure heads. It was especially inviting to (mis)use Paul and his missionary writings, as he was a zealous preacher of Christ's unique position as the first-born son of God.
The worldly power of this new *imperium* was based on presenting Jesus and 'his Church' as the only way to salvation. To propagate this doctrine they used Paul's statements and Paul's authority, and created (or cemented) dogmas in his name. The church leaders of this time based their institution on his epistles, changing parts of them or even adding some additional statements about 'Christian' faith and the legitimacy of the Church.
One thousand years after Christ they even used Paul to justify their dogma of celibacy although, until then, priests and even bishops had been free to marry. It is a fact that Paul had not been married, but this was a rare exception amongst Jewish men, and still is.
107) Matt. 10.22; 24.4, 13; Mark 13.5, 13; Luke 21.8, 19; John 16.1; Rev. 13.10, 14
108) Thus the wording of the subtitle of the German edition of Josef Blumrich's book *The Spaceship of Ezekiel* (1972). See also: Downing, *The Bible and Flying Saucers* (1968).
109) Blumrich, *Kásskara*, pp. 27, 29, 31, bt.AR
110) This evacuation happened about eighty years before the incident described at the beginning of Chapter Six – King Yudhisthira and his four brothers leaving their kingdom to withdraw to the Himalayan Mountains.
111) One of the most famous prophecies relating to this context ('portents in the sky and on earth') was enounced through the apparitions of Mary in Garabandal (1961–5), a small mountain village in Catholic Spain. It describes the following scenario: There will be a global 'warning' before the 'final end' of our present civilization; this warning will be visible to all people on earth in the form of a light phenomenon, confronting each and every human with the inner mirror of their lives. This global shake-up will not be physically harmful. Nevertheless, it will also affect the external levels. For example, all engines and motors will come to a standstill. Then, within one year after the 'warning', the 'Great Miracle' in Garabandal will unfold. As a supernatural monument of this miracle, a 'Great Sign' will remain there in the form of a pillar of light, which people will be able to photograph and film, but not to touch. After a certain time, the 'Punishment' will take place. Several events prophesied to happen before the 'warning' have already come to pass. The messages, in resonance to the people addressed, were very Catholic and thus pope- and liturgy-oriented.

Still, beyond the relative truths referring to the Catholic audience, the essence of the message was very universal: 'I do not demand anything extraordinary from you, but I request you, and expect from you, that you live your daily lives in a worthy way as humans and give God the All-Mighty the place worthy of HIM in your lives.' (quoted from Weber, pp. 114-5)

112) The phenomenon of trance mediums speaking in a foreign language has usually one of the following reasons: (1) They may have accessed one of their own previous lifetimes in which they spoke another language, (2) they may be channelling a discarnate source of this particular language, or (3) they may have tapped the subtle-energetic information field of the person receiving the message, thus being able to speak in his or her language. For incarnate people the latter is the most difficult ability, but for higher-dimensional beings, both good and evil, it is the natural way of communication. Therefore, we humans 'hear' our inner source of inspiration and intuition (and seductive 'inner voices' as well) in our own language and dialect. That was apparently also the case on this memorable Whitsunday morning, according to the statements of the witnesses ('each of us hears them in his own native language').

113) Again, it is important to note that the word *incarnate* literally means 'to go *in carne*, into the flesh' or 'to become flesh' in the sense of 'appearing with a physical body'. Jesus said, 'The Father and I are one', but he never said, 'I am the Father', and that is a big difference. The Vedic explanation of God and the first-born being named Brahma can perfectly reconcile the simultaneous oneness (in quality) and difference (in 'quantity', i.e. individuality) of Jesus and the Father. See also endnote 43.

114) Inspiration follows the law of resonance. If people come together with pure motives, then the highest levels of universal consciousness can be reached and transmitted, resulting in a revelation of moving, universal love. If a group is inspired by religious fanaticism and absolutism (as many of today's evangelical groups), then the field of energy invoked by them cannot be that high. When practising so-called inspired speech or speaking in tongues, they are limited to 'revelations' from sources corresponding to their collective mental framework. These congregations may be fully convinced that they are gathering in the name of Jesus and that Jesus alone is speaking to them. But if they are obsessed with the idea of 'we alone know what Jesus wanted', then it is very likely that they attract dia-bolic spirits who misuse the name of Jesus in order to build up fronts and camps between men. Like attracts like. Often, fanaticism and obsession are interdependent.

115) This aspect of reality – the omniconscious Paramatma – is an essential point of the *Bhagavad-gita*: 'Though undivided, the Paramatma is situated within every being as if divided. Know Him to be the sustainer, dissolver and the creator of all beings. [...] I am in the hearts of all living entities, and from Me come remembrance, knowledge and forgetfulness.' (13.17; 15.15)

God's aspect as Paramatma is the key to understanding karma. It takes an omniconscious presence to 'monitor' the simultaneous workings of predestination and free will. Without the presence of an all-pervading cosmic intelligence and memory, karma would be only a mechanistic and merciless law, as the atheists believe. Ignoring the absolute Individuality of God, they cannot perceive how free will is the crucial factor beyond matter and material laws. Thus, they fall into the trap of atheistic deism and monism and, as a consequence, into godless fatalism and pragmatism.

The Paramatma can be best understood in the context mentioned in this summary, namely how the spiritual individuality of each being is mirrored in the unique form of his/her/its material body. Every face, voice, fingerprint, signature etc. is absolutely unique, being an expression of one's individual consciousness and corresponding subtle (mental and ethereal) body. This 'body' is the higher-dimensional energy field, or *kshetra*, of each incarnate being. It is also appropriately called the 'form-generating (morphogenetic) field', for it is the subtle 'matrix' that creates the physical body's form. Although all predestined bodily features – down to the fingerprints – are determined by our consciousness and karma, it is not us who consciously form these features. Furthermore, the genetic information is identical in all body cells. How, then, do the cells know how to 'print out' these absolutely individual features?

This is the ancient puzzle summarized under the notion 'entelechy' by philosophers like Aristotle and Leibniz, referring to 'the metaphysical factor which causes order and unity in every organism' – which is a perfect description of the Paramatma, who monitors the bodies and destinies of all living entities according to their karma. He is the 'missing link' between the *atma*, the spiritual soul, and the material energy. The living entities, being relative individuals, cannot create matter, they can only *transform* matter, and can do so only *indirectly*. This is the deep meaning of the saying that we are all dependent on God. Our original decision to stay in unity or to go into duality is of complete consequence. In both cases we are and remain 'dependent' as parts of the Whole. In individual oneness with God we are moved by pure love. In material duality we are moved by the chain reactions of our resonance (*guna*) and corresponding actions/reactions (karma). In other words, people's free will is not as free as many think. What job we take, what tastes we have, etc., is not an expression of free will but of *guna* and karma! This concept is not pleasing to the ego because the ego is based on thinking 'I am the doer' (= *ahankara*).

116) The same date is also mentioned in the Vedic sources regarding the beginning of Kali-yuga. Tom Smith had no idea about the *yuga* cycles mentioned in the Sanskrit scriptures. He came from a catholic background and was strictly catholic for most of his life. In 1991 he felt the vocation to start writing texts which he received internally.

117) A channelled message spoken by Jeshua, the original Aramaic name of 'Jesus', which was the later (Greek) version of Jeshua and (Hebrew) Yehoshua; received by a meditation group in Germany in 1996.

118) Also in our days we hear of such incredible happenings, called shape-shifting, for example in Cathy O'Brien's book *Trance-Formation of America*; she claims

to have been used as a black-magic sex slave in blood rituals. She also names prominent people who allegedly took part in such satanic perversions (which still go on today). In orgiastic 'ecstasy' some participants even happen to shape-shift, which means that they are temporarily 'overshadowed' by their astral reptoid form, as they are incarnated Naga entities. The controversial British author David Icke mentions this witness, and many others, in his books *The Biggest Secret* (1999) and *Children of the Matrix* (2001). In this regard he is apparently confirmed by the Vedic report of the *Shrimad-Bhagavatam*.

119) When the final passages of this book were being written, the German magazine *Stern* (29/2003) published an article on Italy's Prime Minister Silvio Berlusconi, in which the same motif showed up again. On p. 55, *Stern* published an aerial photo of Berlusconi's villa Belvedere near Milan.

The picture caption described what was graphically visible: 'Depicted in the lawn of the surrounding park, the family's huge heraldic figure: a crowned dragon eating a human being' (t.AR)! This heraldic depiction is about 15 metres in length. (It is similar to the strange figure in the logo of the car-make Alfa Romeo.)

120) In his book *Middle Eastern Mythology* (1963), S. H. Hooke, Professor of Oriental Languages and of Old Testament Studies, explains (pp. 30–1): 'The central motif of the myth [of the Flood] is that the gods decide to destroy mankind [...]. It has long been known that the Biblical story of the Deluge was based on the Babylonian myth [...]. But that the Babylonian form of the myth was based on an earlier Sumerian version was not known until 1914, when the American scholar Arno Poebel published a fragment of a Sumerian tablet containing episodes of what was clearly the myth of the Flood. [...] The outlines of the Sumerian version of the Flood story are as follows. At the point where the fragment continues the story, a god appears to be declaring his intention of saving mankind from the destruction which the gods have decided to bring upon them. The reason for their decision is not given. Enki is the god who takes steps to save mankind from destruction. Apparently he instructs Ziusudra the pious king of Sippar [...] what must be done to escape the coming flood.'

In the original wording of the tablet (according to Hooke's translation), the end of the Flood is described as follows: 'Ziusudra opened a window of the huge boat, the hero Utu brought his rays into the giant boat. Ziusudra, the king, prostrated himself before Utu. The king kills an ox, slaughters a sheep.' When the cuneiform texts containing the Epic of Gilgamesh were translated, many more details and missing passages became known.

Read in comparison Gen 8.6, 18–21: 'At the end of forty days, Noah opened the window of the ark that he had made. [...] So Noah went out with his sons and his wife and his son's wives. [...] Then Noah built an altar to the Lord and, choosing from all the clean animals and all the clean birds he presented burnt offerings on the altar. The Lord smelt the pleasing smell and said to himself, 'Never again will I curse the earth because of human beings [...].'

121) For example, Bramley, Ferguson, Des Griffin, Icke; Marciniak (*Bringers of the Dawn*, chap. 9 describing the interdimensional doorway above the Middle East used by 'certain energies' to produce holographic projections) and Sitchin.

For a summary of the entire UFO phenomenon (categories, cases and chronologies) see, for example, Fowler, Hall, Good, Jacobs, Marrs, Thompson.

122) Robert Morningsky: *The Morningsky Manifesto*, § 25 and 26.

123) quoted from: Randle/Schmitt, *UFO Crash at Roswell* (1991), p. 110. In this book alone, 273 witnesses are presented!

124) The original of this and many other documents have been published by several investigators, for example by Timothy Good in the appendix of his book *Above Top Secret*, by Stanton Friedman and by Kevin Randle. See also the testimony of Air Force Colonel Philip Corso, *The Day After Roswell* (1997).

125) The amazing UFO wave of 1952 has been thoroughly reported and documented by Dr Kevin D. Randle, a captain of the US Air Force and one of the leading contemporary ufologists. For the 50th anniversary of these memorable incidents, he published a book entitled *Invasion Washington – UFOs over the Capitol*. The back cover text summarizes: 'Radar picked up what is believed to have been eight alien aircraft racing across the night sky – traveling at speeds and maneuvering in ways impossible for the era. Despite military coercion, forcing eyewitnesses to change the testimony, despite the government's suppression of films, photos and official reports, one fact remains indisputable: they were here.'

126) Described, for example, by the author-couple Bryant and Helen Reeve in their book *Flying Saucer Pilgrimage*. Bryant Reeve, an engineer and graduate of Yale University, retired in 1954 and set out with his wife to see all psychic UFO contactees of their time, which resulted in two years of constant travelling (1954–5).

127) All of this information was taken from the book *Geheimsache UFO*, chapter 26: 'Eine Herausforderung für die UNO' ['A challenge for the UN'], by Michael Hesemann (1994).

128) quoted from Beckley, p. 102. Edgar Mitchell was also one of the speakers at the World Congress 'The UFO Experience' in North Haven, Connecticut, in October 1998, where he frankly spoke about the existence of UFOs and how this issue had been covered up.

129) *ibid.* pp. 103 f.

130) quoted from Armin Risi, interview with Prof. Dino Dini, 'Die Existenz von UFOs: Ich mußte unwahre Aussagen machen' ['The existence of UFOs: I had to make untrue statements'], in: *Magazin 2000*, Nr. 119, Neuss, Sept. 1997.

131) For a documentation and discussion of the abduction phenomenon see, for example, Hopkins, Howe, Jacobs, Mack, Randles, Rimmer, Spencer.

132) The topic of animal mutilations has been extensively researched and documented by Linda Moulton Howe: *An Alien Harvest* (1989). A summary is given, for example, in Timothy Good, *Alien Liaison: The Ultimate Secret*, chapters 2–4, and Richard Thompson, *Alien Identities* (1993).
133) Cooper: *Behold a Pale Horse*, p. 196
134) Royal, *Visitors From Within*, pp. 35, 46, 70, 79
135) *ibid.* p. 110
136) Ananda, *The Alien Presence*, p. 227; this critical approach was further expanded by Prof. David Jacobs in *The Threat: Revealing the Secret Alien Agenda* (1999). A metaphysical and spiritual view of the fallen 'extraterrestrial' and the divine 'ultraterrestrial' hierarchies is given in *The Book of Knowledge: The Keys of Enoch* by Prof. James Hurtak (1973).
137) These basic descriptions found in the first chapter of the Biblical Genesis are not unique. An expanded version is given in the Sanskrit scriptures called *Puranas* ('ancient histories'), which contain many chapters about the primeval and the secondary creation, collectively labelled as 'Puranic Genesis'. Therein, it is described how God, the absolute Individuality, Vishnu (the 'omnipresent One'), enacts the creation through the cosmic creator, the first-born living entity, named Brahma (the 'expander'), who creates the different levels of the multidimensional cosmos in six major steps, manifesting the present physical earth as the seventh step. 'And on the seventh day God (*elohim*) finished the work he had done, and he rested on the seventh day' (Gen. 2.2), which means that, from then on, the created arche-typal species were able to reproduce themselves, so that there was no need of further direct creation.

At the same time, these Puranic sources emphasize that their Genesis 'only' refers to the creation of the perishable material universe and that there is a spiritual background beyond matter, namely the eternal presence of Life, the 'kingdom of God', which is all-pervading. (It is not a gnostic dualism which describes God as being opposed to matter.)

Besides these ancient sources, many contemporary revelations have contributed additional perspectives to the *mysterium* of Creation, which no one except the One can fully 'understand'. It is nothing but a concession to the dia-bolic spirit if people start fighting about the different versions of Genesis, as their common essence indicates the same absolute truth, namely that there is an omniconscious Individuality beyond material duality (with innumerable names, e.g. 'God', 'Vishnu', 'Krishna', 'Yhwh' etc.) and that we are all conscious parts of this Whole.

Those recognizing God's individuality, and their own, as the eternal reality should not be divided into antagonistic camps of 'ministries' and 'religions' on the basis of limited confessional doctrines. Theists and Creationists who fight each other due to their sectarian interpretations are making fools of themselves. The materialists laugh at them, and the dark forces are triumphant because creating this separation in the name of 'God' has been their first and foremost mission.

138) When the atom bombs were developed in the scientific camp of Los Alamos, New Mexico, several scientists feared that the nuclear explosions might trigger uncontrollable chain reactions. The following quotations are taken from a biography of the physicist leading this project: *J. Robert Oppenheimer – Shatterer of Worlds*, by Peter Goodchild, an Oppenheimer-friendly presentation.

After Germany's capitulation on 8 May 1945, an American task force commander suggested: '"If the Germans don't have the bomb then we won't need to use ours" […]. "You don't know Groves [the general behind the atom bomb project]," was the reply, "if we have such a weapon, we'll use it."' (p. 111)

By the end of May, some physicists involved in the construction of the atomic bomb calculated its vast destructive impact and raised the question whether it might not be sufficient to threaten the enemy by merely *technically demonstrating the effect of the bomb*, instead of actually dropping it on civilians. During a conference in Los Alamos on 30 May, this vital issue was discussed. 'Thus at no time during this meeting had Oppenheimer represented the scientists' moral concern over using the weapon against Japan. He dealt with it purely in terms of the political and tactical considerations involved.' (p. 139)

In June and July, some of the involved physicists were afraid of unpredictable chain reactions. 'Compton has told how the physicists in the group hummed and hawed over the problem, then on his discretion they computed a three-in-a-million chance. A three-in-a-million chance of destroying the world.' (p. 63)

The following is a description of the situation in mid July, right before the first atom-bomb test: 'Groves retired and slept soundly. Oppenheimer sat, smoking endlessly, coughing, trying to read. During that evening Bainbridge got wind of a rumour spreading like wildfire round the site. Some senior scientists had been overheard predicting that the bomb would ignite the atmosphere. They had been heard estimating how quickly the reaction would go and how far it would spread, and they had been inviting bets on the destruction first, of all human life, and second, just that of human life in New Mexico.' (p. 158)

Thank God (or: thank God's invisible helpers), there was no chain reaction, and the atmosphere was not ignited. The dropping of the bombs, however, could not be prevented, as this was an act enforced by the misused free will of those who had the power to do it. Light beings cannot go against the free will of people, nor against the free will of the dark forces. They can only act to prevent those unwanted reactions that are not within the scope of humanity's or the planet's karma.

After the dropping of the two bombs, Oppenheimer commented in an interview: 'A scientist cannot hold back progress because of fears of what the world will do with his discoveries' (p. 170). Who defines the meaning and the goal of 'progress'? Why is *this* direction of progress chosen?

139) Markides: *The Magus of Strovolos*, pp. 148–51. The chapter describing this incident is entitled 'The Guardians of Planet Earth'. Therein, the author (Markides) comments: 'I was certain that their experience was genuine and

authentic, regardless of the fact that, to us, it appeared extraordinary, to say the least. Of course I had no way of testing the "objective reality" of their experience since I could not "go up" myself.'

140) www.premierespace.com/autobooks.html about Edgar Mitchell's memories recorded in his book *The Way of the Explorer: An Apollo Astronaut's Journey through the Material and Mystical Worlds.*

141) '... more impressive than any recorded word'. Even in our days of technology, practical experience shows that it is better not to record the inner word. Recording destroys the uniqueness of the sacred moment as well as the inner reception, because one thinks, 'I can listen to it later'. Furthermore, it is an expression of weak faith. Otherwise one would trust that the connection is always there.

One might argue that recording the inner word enables us to write it down and distribute it to others. However, this is usually the first step towards dependence on some written word, sometimes even towards the foundation of a sectarian group structure.

The inner word received in a 'Light circle' is a gift for those present at the moment. Of course, other forms of revelation are meant to be recorded and written down. But even in such cases, one has to be careful of all the traps entailed with recording and propagating a certain set of written words.

The Author

Having come to the end of this book, the reader might want to know something more about the author. Who is he? Why did he write this book? What are his intentions?

My basic intention of writing it was to provide a summary of the inner contents of the Vedic and Biblical scriptures and prophecies. The Bible itself is already quite voluminous, and the 'apocryphal' texts of the Old and New Testaments are just about as long. The main Vedic scriptures comprise about five times the volume of the Bible. Not everybody has the time to read these scriptures, and that is not required either, if the essence of all these revelations is known. Personally, I had the time to read and study these scriptures as I lived in Vedic monasteries (in Europe and India) for eighteen years. One of my occupations as a monk was translating texts and commentaries of Sanskrit literature from English into German, or to check and correct the translations, respectively. Altogether I participated in the production of twenty-one books. This, however, did not turn me into a fundamentalist or an absolutizer of scriptures. I always asked myself what their real message was. What was to be learnt by reading all these books?

During my years in the monastery I began to expand my studies to biblical texts as well as to mystical and mythological sources from all cultures of the world, also including modern philosophical and esoteric works. The more I presented these complementary references and conclusions in my lectures, the more people started to express a desire of having these contents in book form. On the other hand, I was confronted by people who fanatically stood up for their absolutist religious opinions, and (unintentionally) showed me the working of the unholy spirit in the name of God. Truly absolute truths, I understood, are never dia-bolic, and to show this became my main intention, as humanity's consciousness of the coming 'new age' will be holistic and spiritual.

At the same time, as a monk I was also a kind of 'father confessor' to many people. Over the years, I got to hear the life stories of people from all walks of life; some of these people were also affiliated with the background aspects of the present society. From them I learnt a lot about secret politics and the high-finance world. These people gave or lent me many relevant books which not everybody had (some of them are mentioned in the bibliography). What I heard was not really surprising or shocking to me. First of all, I was not naive, and secondly, the prophetic sources of all cultures clearly state that humanity is presently passing through a dark age. In this way a wide spectrum of information was brought to my attention, illustrating and expanding my personal research.

Initially, considering my social background, it was not obvious that my life would take such a course. I was born on 21 February 1962 in Lucerne, Switzerland, the second son of a working-class family from the mountain regions. My father belongs to the generation born between the two world wars. Not being very 'intellectual' he attended school only sporadically for a few years, as they needed boys for certain jobs in those hard times; thus my father remained almost illiterate. My mother came from a poor mountain farmer's family.

It is said that we choose our parents ourselves. If this is true then I can say that I chose very good parents. They supported me in every way they could. They even saved money franc by franc to enable me to go to high school. In my teenage student years I became one of the best junior chess players of Switzerland, and I started to read books about the exploitation of animals and plants and of the Third World. These sobering insights prompted me to radically change my life, and I left high school right before the final exams, 'as a sign of protest against the course of the present materialistic society'.

After some time alone out in nature, I started my monastic life at the age of eighteen. When I was thirty-six, I changed into another life situation, and I married.

For the last two years I have worked almost exclusively on the manuscript of this English book. Here, I would like to thank all those who encouraged me, and helped me in this work, starting with my 'old' friend – and wife – Karuna. Then, Fabrizio, who gave me the initial impetus to write my first book in English; Debra Bacchus, who made the first English drafts; Helmut Kunkel for his patient and faithful editing work; Chris Cannizzo, who entered my life at the very right moment as an inspiring and constructive corrector of my English writing; Miro Cucuz and his wife Annik, who supported me in the final months of this book's production, and Ronald Zürrer, my publisher at Govinda Press and another 'old' friend.

Armin Risi,
30 November 2003
(in memory of my mother, who died on 30 November 1996)

List of publications:

1988: *Vegetarisch leben: Die Notwendigkeit einer fleischlosen Ernährung* ['Vegetarian life: The necessity of a meat-less diet'], 48 pages; with a total of half a million copies printed this is the most widely spread brochure on vegetarianism in the German-speaking countries.

1991: *Völkerwanderung: Epische Galerie* ['Migration of peoples: An epic gallery'], 260 pages;

1992: *Der Kampf mit dem Wertlosen: Lyrische Meditationen* ['Struggling with the worthless: Lyric meditations'; seven hundred poems and epigrams], 380 pages;

1995: *Da ich ein Dichter war: Gedanken, Gedichte und eine Begegnung mit Hölderlin* ['When I was a poet: Reflections, poems and an encounter with Hölderlin'], 164 pages;

1995: Der multidimensionale Kosmos, Band 1 – *Gott und die Götter: Das vedische Weltbild revolutioniert die moderne Wissenschaft, Esoterik und Theologie* ['The multidimensional cosmos, vol. 1 – God and the gods: The Vedic world-view revolutionizes modern science, esoterism and theology'], 432 pages, fifth edition 2002;

1998: Der multidimensionale Kosmos, Band 2 – *Unsichtbare Welten: Astrale und außerirdische Wesen im Hintergrund des Weltgeschehens* ['The multidimensional cosmos, vol. 2: Invisible worlds – Astral and extraterrestrial beings in the background of human history'], 384 pages, fourth edition 2003;

1999: Der multidimensionale Kosmos, Band 3 – *Machtwechsel auf der Erde: Die Pläne der Mächtigen, globale Entscheidungen und die Wendezeit* ['The multidimensional cosmos, vol. 3 – Changing of the guards on planet earth: The plans of the leading forces, global decisions and the transformation']; 596 pages, fourth edition 2003;

2001: *Das kosmische Erbe: Einweihung in die Geheimnisse unserer Her- und Zukunft* ['Our cosmic heritage: Initiation into the secrets of our origin and future'; channelled texts by Tom H. Smith, translation and commentaries by Armin Risi]; 376 pages, second edition 2002;

2004: *TranscEnding the Global Power Game: Hidden Agendas, Divine Intervention and the New Earth* (first edition);

as well as many articles in esoteric, philosophical and parapsychological journals.

armin-risi.ch

Bibliography

The following list is a selection of books that document and expand many of the points mentioned in *TranscEnding the Global Power Game*, and that have been used and/or quoted in it. This selection does not mean that Armin Risi agrees with all the presentations and conclusions of these authors, nor does it mean that these authors would agree with all the presentations and conclusions of Armin Risi.

About holistic science

Bohm, David. *Wholeness and the Implicate Order.* London, Boston: Routledge & Kegan Paul, 1980.
Bohm, David, and F. David Peat. *Science, Order and Creativity.* New York: Bantam Books, 1987.
Gribbin, John. *Hyperspace: Our Final Frontier.* New York: Dorling Kindersley Publishing, 2001.
Herbert, Nick. *Quantum Reality: Beyond the New Physics. An Excursion into Metaphysics and the Meaning of Reality.* New York: Anchor Books/Doubleday, 1985.
Kaku, Michio. *Hyperspace: A Scientific Odyssey through Parallel Universes, Time Warps, and the Tenth Dimension.* New York: Oxford University Press, 1994.
Mitchell, Edgar, with Dwight Williams. *The Way of the Explorer: An Apollo Astronaut's Journey through Material and Mystical Worlds.* New York: G. P. Putnam's Sons, 1996.
O'Leary, Brian [another Apollo Astronaut]. *Exploring Inner and Outer Space: A Scientist's Perspective on Personal and Planetary Transformation.* Berkeley, CA: North Atlantic Books, 1989.
—, *Miracle in the Void: Free Energy, Ufos and Other Scientific Revelations.* Kihea, HI: Kamapua's Press, 1996.
Pickover, Clifford A. *Surfing Through Hyperspace: Understanding Higher Universes in Six Easy Lessons.* New York: Oxford University Press 1999.
Sagan, Samuel. *Entities: Parasites of the Body of Energy.* Roseville, Australia: Clairvision School Foundation, 1994.
Sheldrake, Rupert. *A New Science of Life: Hypothesis of Formative Causation.* London: Blond & Briggs, 1981.
—, *The Presence of the Past: Morphic Resonance and the Habits of Nature.* New York: Vintage Books, 1989.
Talbot, Michael. *The Holographic Universe: A Remarkable New Theory of Reality That Explains the Paranormal Abilities of the Mind, the Latest Frontiers of Physics, and the Unsolved Riddles of Brain and Body.* New York: HarperCollins, 1991.
Wolf, Fred Alan. *Parallel Universes: The Search for New Worlds.* New York: Simon & Schuster, 1990.
—, *Mind Into Matter: A New Alchemy of Science and Spirit.* Needham, MA: Moment Point Press, 2001.

About alternative earth history

Allan, D. S., and J. B. Delair. *When the Earth Nearly Died: Compelling Evidence of a Catastrophic World Change 9,500 BC.* Bath, UK: Gateway Books, 1995.

Ancient American [magazine]: Archaeology of the Americas before Columbus (with many book references). ancientamerican.com

Berlitz, Charles. *Mysteries from Forgotten Worlds.* Garden City, NY: Doubleday 1972.

—, *The Mystery of Atlantis.* New York: Grosset & Dunlop, 1969.

Blumrich, Josef. *Kásskara und die sieben Welten: Die Geschichte der Menschheit in der Überlieferung der Hopi-Indianer* ['Kásskara and the seven Worlds: History of mankind according to the tradition of the Hopi Indians'], first edition 1979. München: Droemer Knaur, 1985.

Brown, Joseph Epes (editor). *The Sacred Pipe: Black Elk's Account of the Seven Rites of the Oglala Sioux,* Civilization of the American Indian Series, vol. 36. Norman, OK: University of Oklahoma Press, 1953, 1989.

Childress, David Hatcher. *Lost Cities of North & Central America / of South America / of Africa & Arabia / of Atlantis, Ancient Europe & the Mediterranean / of China, Central India & Asia / of Ancient Lemuria & the Pacific* (six volumes). *Ancient Tonga & the Lost City of Mu'a / Ancient Micronesia & the Lost City of Nan Madol.* All in: Adventure Unlimited Press (Kempton, IL).

Cremo, Michael, and Richard Thompson. *The Hidden History of the Human Race: Major Scientific Cover-up Exposed.* Badger, CA: Govardhan Hill Publishing, 1994.

Flem-Ath, Rand and Rose. *When the Sky Fell.* Toronto: Stoddart Publishing, 1995.

Frawley, David. *Gods, Sages, and Kings: Vedic Secrets of Ancient Civilization.* Salt Lake City, UT: Passage Press, 1991.

Gordon, Cyrus Herzl. *Before Columbus: Links between the Old World and Ancient America.* London: Crown Publishers, 1971.

Hancock, Graham, with Santha Faiia. *Heaven's Mirror: Quest for the Lost Civilization.* New York: Crown Publishers, 1998.

Holzer, Hans. *Long Before Columbus: How the Ancients Discovered America.* Santa Fe, NM: Bear & Co., 1992.

Rudgley, Richard, *Lost Civilisations of the Stone Age.* London: Arrow Books, 1999.

O'Brien, Terry J. *Fair Gods and Feathered Serpents: A Search for Ancient America's Bearded White God.* Bountiful, UT: Horizon Publishers, 1997.

Risi, Armin. *Gott und die Götter: Das vedische Weltbild revolutioniert die moderne Wissenschaft, Esoterik und Theologie* ['God and the gods: The Vedic worldview revolutionizes modern science, esoterism and theology']. Neuhausen, Switzerland: Govinda Press, 1995, fifth edition 2002.

Tollmann, Alexander and Edith. *Und die Sintflut gab es doch: Vom Mythos zur historischen Wirklichkeit* ['And yet, the Deluge happened: From myth to historical reality']. München: Droemer Knaur, 1993.

Velikovsky, Immanuel. *World in Collision.* New York: Macmillan, 1950.

—, *Earth in Upheaval.* Garden City, NY: Doubleday, 1955.

—, *Mankind in Amnesia.* Garden City, NY: Doubleday, 1982 (posthumously).

Zillmer, Hans-Joachim. *Darwin's Mistake: Antediluvian Discoveries ...* Kempton, IL: Adventure Unlimited Press, 2003.

About secret politics and conspiracies

Abramson, Rudy. *Spanning the Century: The Life of W. Averell Harriman.* New York: W. Morrow, 1992.
Allegro, John M. *The Dead Sea Scrolls.* Harmondsworth, UK: Penguin Books, 1956.
Allen, Gary, with Larry Abraham. *None Dare Call It Conspiracy.* Rossmor/Seal Beach, CA: Concord Press, 1971; Cutchogue, NY: Buccaneer Books, 1990 (revised and expanded edition).
Bacque, James. *Crimes and Mercies: The Fate of German Civilians under Allied Occupation 1944–1950.* Toronto: Little, Brown and Co. 1997.
—, *Other Losses: An Investigation into the Mass Deaths of German Prisoners at the Hands of the French and Americans after World War II.* Toronto: Stoddart, 1989; Toronto: Little, Brown and Co. 1999 ('Updated Edition with Shocking New Evidence'). This book also appeared under the title *Other Losses: The Shocking Truth behind the Mass Deaths of Disarmed German Soldiers and Civilians under General Eisenhower's Command,* Roseville, CA: Prima Lifestyles, 1992.
[In these books the Canadian historian James Bacque documents how about one million disarmed soldiers and 'at least' nine million German civilians were starved to death in their own country until 1950. Bacque: 'The Russians, French and Americans committed vast atrocities against surrendered German prisoners of war. They were starved in open cages without shelter or water and left to die. More than a million and a half died. Millions of German civilians also died in what Germans now remember as The Hunger Years, 1945-48. The Russians and Poles with the help of the US and Britain, seized one quarter of Germany including the best farmland and expelled some 16 million civilians.'].
Baigent, Michael, Henry Lincoln, and Richard Leigh. *The Holy Blood and the Holy Grail,* London: Jonathan Cape, 1983.
—, *The Messianic Legacy,* London: Corgi Books, Transworld Publishers Ltd, 1987.
Baigent, Michael, and Richard Leigh. *The Temple and the Lodge: Inside Freemasonry.* London: Jonathan Cape, 1989; London: Corgi Books, 1990. [From the back-cover text: '... the flight after 1309 of the Knights Templar from Europe to Scotland. There the Templar heritage was to take root, and to be perpetuated by a network of noble families. That heritage, and the Freemasonry that arose from it, became inseparable from the Stuart case. ... Even more dramatically, the influence of Freemasonry emerges as a key factor in the formation of the United States of America as an embodiment of the ideal 'Masonic Republic'.]
Bainerman, Joel. *The Crimes of a President: New Revelations on Conspiracy & Cover-Up in the Bush & Reagan Administrations.* New York: S.P.I. Books/ Shapolsky Publishers, 1992. [About Iran Contra, the first Gulf War, etc. 'Secret agendas, covert crimes, and massive media cover-ups. Why has George Bush silenced the truth about: ... Plans to arm Saddam Hussein with nuclear and chemical weapons – to orchestrate the Gulf War and create Bush's "New World Order" ... and a billion dollar secret deal with Saddam Hussein – resulting in the Justice Department's attempt to conceal the B.C.C.I scandal.']
Bell Martinez, Mary. *Die Unterminierung der Katholischen Kirche* ['The undermining of the Catholic Church']. Durach: Verlag Anton A. Schmid, 1992.

Bronder, Dietrich. *Bevor Hitler kam* ['Before Hitler came']. Hannover: Hans Pfeiffer Verlag, 1964; Geneva: Marva Verlag, 1975.
Brown, Dee. *Bury My Heart at Wounded Knee.* New York: Holt, Rinehart & Winston, 1970 [about the history of the annihilation of the Native Americans].
Brinkley, Dannion, and Paul Perry. *Saved by the Light: The true story of a man who died twice and the profound revelations he received.* New York: Villard Books, 1994.
Brüning, Erich, and Harry Graf. *Die unterschätzte Subkultur: Freimaurerei, Wolf im Schafspelz* ['The underestimated subculture: Freemasonry, wolf in sheep's clothing']. Berneck: Schwengeler Verlag, 2001.
Buttlar, Johannes von. *Auf den Spuren der Weltformel: Die Wächter von Eden* ['Tracking down the world formula: The guardians of Eden']. München: Wilhelm Heyne Verlag, 1995.
Carmin, E. R. *Das Schwarze Reich: Geheimgesellschaften und Politik im 20. Jahrhundert* ['The Black Reich: Secret societies and politics in the twentieth century']. München: Wilhelm Heyne Verlag, 1997.
Chaitkin, Anton. *Treason in America: From Aaron Burr to Averell Harriman.* New York: New Benjamin Franklin House, 1985.
Chaitkin, Anton, and Webster Tarpley. *George Bush: The Unauthorized Biography.* Washington, DC: Executive Intelligence Review, 1992 [includes the chapter 'The Hitler Project' about the secret money flow from the US to Nazi Germany].
Cooper, Milton William. *Behold a Pale Horse.* Sedona, AZ: Light Technology Publishing, 1991.
Cuddy, Dennis L., and Robert Goldsborough. *The Network of Power: The New World Order, Part II.* Baltimore, MD: The American Research Foundation, 1993.
Epperson, Ralph. *The Unseen Hand: An Introduction to the Conspirational View of History.* Tucson, AZ: Publius Press, 1985 [a well-researched exposé].
—, *The New World Order.* Tucson, AZ: Publius Press, 1992.
Erdmann, Karl-Dietrich, in: Bruno Gebhard. *Handbuch der deutschen Geschichte* ['Handbook of German history', in 22 volumes], vol. 18 (dtv-wissenschaft 4218). München: Deutscher Taschenbuch Verlag dtv, 1970ff.
Eringer, Robert. *The Global Manipulators: The Bilderberg Group, the Trilateral Commission – Covert Power Groups of the West.* Bristol, UK: Pentacle Books, 1980.
Evans, Richard J. *Lying About Hitler: History, Holocaust, and the David Irving Trial.* New York: Basic Books, 2001. [The acclaimed historian investigates the number of casualties in the destruction of Dresden, which was apparently exaggerated by revisionist authors such as David Irving. Dresden, however, was only one of more than 1000 cities destroyed in Germany, and the number of at least 35,000 killed people in Dresden alone shows that WW II was an inhuman sacrifice of humans (remember Hiroshima and Nagasaki), organized and financed by those who were not out in the battlefields.]
Farkas, Viktor. *Wer beherrscht die Welt? Die vertuschte Wahrheit über geheime Komplotte, verborgene Drahtzieher, UFO-Verschwörungen und die geplante Zukunft der Menschheit* ['Who controls the world? The covered-up truths about secret complots, hidden wirepullers, UFO conspiracies and the planned future of mankind']. Wien: Orac, 1997.
Figes, Orlando. *A People's Tragedy: The Russian Revolution 1891–1924.* London: Jonathan Cape/Pimlico, 1996.

Friedrich, Jörg. *Der Brand: Deutschland im Bombenkrieg 1940–1945* ['The Fire: Germany under aerial bombardment 1940–1945]. Berlin: Propyläen, 2002. [Both the author and the publisher are highly esteemed. Jörg Friedrich was also a co-author of the 'Encyclopedia of the Holocaust'.]

Gardner, Laurence. *Bloodline of the Holy Grail.* Shaftesbury, Dorset: Element Books Ltd., 1996.

George, Alexander and Juliette. *Woodrow Wilson and Colonel House.* New York: John Day, 1956 [shows that WW I had been planned years before its start by the 'secret government'].

Goodchild, Peter. *J. Robert Oppenheimer: Shatterer of Worlds.* London: British Broadcasting Corporation, 1980.

Goulevitch, Arsene de. *Czarism and Revolution.* Original with no date; reprint, Hawthorne, CA: Omni Publications, 1961.

Greider, William. *Secrets of the Temple: How the Federal Reserve Runs the Country.* New York: Simon & Schuster, 1987.

Grenfell, Russell. *Unconditional Hatred.* Old Greenwich, CT: Devin-Adair Company, 1954. [A former high officer of the British Army describes Churchill's 'unconditional hatred' against Germany without belittling the Nazis' war guilt; however, this hatred was already displayed during WW I and before, when there were not yet any Nazis; it was ideologically motivated, not politically.]

Griffin, Des. *Descent into Slavery / The Missing Dimension in World Affairs.* South Pasadena, CA: Emissary Publications, 1976 / 1981.

Griffin, G. Edward. *The Creature from Jekyll Island: A Second Look at the Federal Reserve.* Westlake Village, CA: American Media, 1994, fifth printing August 1996 [608 pages; a very good introduction into the hidden dimensions of history; from the backcover text: 'This book is about the most blatant scam of all history. It's all here: the cause of wars, boom-bust cycles, inflation, depression, prosperity. Your world-view will definitely change. You'll never trust a politician again – or a banker.'].

Groseclose, Elgin Earl. *Fifty Years of Managed Money: The Story of the Federal Reserve, 1913-1963.* New York: Spartan 1965.

—, *America's Money Machine.* Westport, CT: Arlington House, 1966 [how the Federal Reserve Act came about and how it influenced world economy and world politics; how war is the 'best' way to make other countries dependent].

Heise, Karl. *Entente-Freimaurerei und Weltkrieg* ['Entente Freemasonry and World War']. Zürich, 1918, third edition 1920; new facsimile printing, Struckum: Archiv-Edition, 1991 (second edition).

Hölderlin, Friedrich. 'Hyperion, or The Hermit in Greece' (translated by Willard R. Trask), in *The German Library, Volume 22: Hölderlin – Hyperion and Selected Poems.* New York: Continuum Publishing Company, 1990.

Hufschmid, Eric. *Painful Questions: An Analysis of the September 11th Attack.* Goleta, CA: Endpoint Software, 2002. [How could the two WTC towers collapse identically, and 'perfectly', although the two planes hit them in different angles (in the North Tower the kerosene exploded inside, in the South Tower *outside* the building)? Why did the firemen not expect the collapse? Why were the steel girders immediately removed in secrecy *before* the investigation? How is it that there were so obvious traces left at the airport? Who benefited? etc. etc.]

Icke, David. *The Robots' Rebellion: The Story of the Spiritual Renaissance.* Bath, UK: Gateway Books, 1994.

—, *The Biggest Secret.* Wildwood, MO: Bridge of Love Publications, 1999.

—, *Children of the Matrix: How an interdimensional race has controlled the world for thousands of years – and still does.* Wildwood: Bridge of Love Publications, 2001.

Issacson, Walter, and Evan Thomas. *The Wise Men: Six Friends and the World They Made: Acheson, Bohlen, Harriman, Kennan, Lovett, McCloy.* New York: Simon & Schuster, 1986.

John of Jerusalem:

Jean de Jérusalem. *Le Livre des Prophéties,* published by Prof. Galvieski. Editions Jean-Claude Lattès, 1994 (original edition).

Johannes von Jerusalem. *Das Buch der Prophezeiungen: Zukunftsvisionen eines großen Sehers für das dritte Jahrtausend.* München: Wilhelm Heyne Verlag, 1995.

Josephson, Emanuel. *The Federal Reserve Conspiracy and The Rockefellers: Their Gold Corner.* New York: Chedney Press, 1968.

Kah, Gary H. *En Route to Global Occupation: A High Ranking Government Liaison Exposes the Secret Agenda for World Unification.* Lafayette, La.: Huntington House, 1992. [A former high US official discovers secret plans for a global takeover by the dark forces, and converts to Jesus Christ.]

Kenworthy, Joseph M., and George Young. *The Freedom of the Seas.* New York: Ayer Company, 1929 [see endnote 30].

Knight, Christopher, and Robert Lomas. *The Hiram Key: Pharaohs, Freemasons and the Discovery of the Secret Scrolls of Jesus.* London: Century, 1996.

Knopp, Guido. *Die Gefangenen* ['The Prisoners of War']. München: C. Bertelsmann, 2003. [Describing the destiny of the 11 million captured German men during and after the war in allied and Russian imprisonment; the fate of the former aggressors. Regarding the post-war generations of Germany, the renowned German history professor Guido Knopp succinctly states that it is not a question of collective guilt but of *collective responsibility.*]

Kurowski, Franz. *Der Luftkrieg über Deutschland: Tatsachenbericht* ['Aerial warfare on Germany: Factual report.']. Düsseldorf, Wien: Econ Verlag, 1977; München: Wilhelm Heyne Verlag, 1979 [written by an official, objective historian].

Larson, Martin. *The Federal Reserve and our Manipulated Dollar.* Old Greenwich, CT: Devin-Adair Company, 1975 [about the Civil War, the conspiracy to pass the Federal Reserve Law in 1913, and manipulations that led to the First World War].

Lindsey, Hal, and Carole C. Carlson. *The Late Great Planet Earth.* Grand Rapids, MI: Zondervan Publishing Company, 1970; New York: Bantam Books, 1983.

London, Jack. *The Iron Heel,* first published in the USA in 1907. London: The Journeyman Press, 1990.

Lundberg, Ferdinand. *America's Sixty Families.* New York: The Vanguard Press, 1937.

—, *The Rich and the Superrich: A Study in the Power of Money Today.* New York: Lyle Stuart, 1968.

Marlowe, John. *Cecil Rhodes: The Anatomy of Empire.* London: Elek, 1972.

Martin, Malachi. *Windswept House.* New York: Doubleday 1996. [A novel by a Jesuit insider of the Vatican, describing the presence of the Lodge in the Vatican, and how Satan worship has been established by high Vatican members.]

Maisky, Ivan. *Who helped Hitler?* London: Hutchinson, 1964 (translated by Andrew Rothstein; original edition in Russian, 1962). [Ivan Maisky, the Soviet ambassador in London during WW II, discloses facts about the secret money flow into Nazi Germany from sources situated in England and the USA.]

McAdoo, William. *Crowded Years,* Boston and New York: Houghton Mifflin Co., 1931; New York: Kennikat Press, 1971 [describes how the Wall Street elite broke the opposition against the Federal Reserve Act].

McCoy, Alfred W. *The Politics of Heroin: CIA Complicity in the Global Drug Trade (Afghanistan, Southeast Asia, Central America, Columbia).* Chicago, IL: Lawrence Hill Books, revised edition 2003.

Millenari, The. *Shroud of Secrecy: The Story of Corruption within the Vatican.* Toronto: Key Porter Books, 2000.
Original in Italian: I Millenari, *Via col vento in Vaticano* ['Gone with the wind in the Vatican'], Milano: Kaos edizioni, 1999.
German edition: *Wir klagen an.* Berlin: Aufbau Taschenbuch Verlag, 2000.

Moore, Michael. *Stupid White Men. And Other Excuses for the State of the Nation.* Regan Books, 2001; Penguin Books, 2002.

Mullins, Eustace. *The Secrets of the Federal Reserve: The London–Jekyll Island Connections.* Staunton, VA: Bankers Research Institute, 1983.

O'Brien, Cathy, and Mark Phillips. *Trance-Formation of America: The True Life Story of a CIA Mind Control Slave.* Las Vegas: Reality Marketing, 1995, distributed by David Icke, Bridge of Love Publications, Wildwood, MO.

Orwell, George. *Nineteen Eighty-Four* (1949). New York: Harcourt, 2000.

Overmans, Rüdiger. *Soldaten hinter Stacheldraht: Deutsche Kriegsgefangene des Zweiten Weltkriegs* ['Soldiers Behind Barbed Wire: German Captives in the Second World War'], Berlin: Propyläen, 2000 [another book about the 11 million German POW; see also Bacque, Knopp].

Passos, John dos. *Mr. Wilson's War.* Garden City, NY: Doubleday, 1962 [describing how Wilson tolerated all preparations of the Bolshevik take-over].

Perloff, James. *The Shadows of Power: The Council on Foreign Relations and the American Decline.* Appleton, WI: Western Islands, 1988.

Pfeifer, Heinz. *Die Brüder des Schattens* ['The brothers of shadow']. Zürich: Übersax, 1983.

Picknett, Lynn, and Clive Prince. *The Templar Revelation: Secret Guardians of the True Identity of Christ.* London: Corgi Books, 1998.

Ponsonby, Arthur. *Falsehood in War Time.* New York: E. P. Dutton and Company, 1928 [exposing the lies and the propaganda staged for justifying the breaking of the Monroe Doctrine, which started US war participation abroad].

Price, Randall. *The Coming Last Days Temple: The Latest Developments in Bible Prophecy.* Eugene, OR: Harvest House Publishers, 1999.

Quigley, Carroll. *Tragedy and Hope: A History of the World in Our Time* (1300 pages!). New York: Macmillan, 1966. [About the secret workings of the international finance magnates; Prof. Quigley admits the existence of 'the Conspiracy' and states that he has 'no aversions to its aims', he simply wants to force it out of secrecy; overwhelming mass of details presented by an insider.]

—, *The Anglo-American Establishment: From Rhodes to Cliveden.* New York: Books on Focus, 1981.

Reuveni, Amnon. *Im Namen der „Neuen Weltordnung"* ['In the name of the "New World Order"']. Dornach: Goetheanum Verlag, 1994.

Rivera, David Allen. *Final Warning: A History of the New World Order.* Harrisburg, PA: Rivera Enterprises, 1994.

Robison, John. *Proofs of a Conspiracy,* Edinburgh, 1797. Belmont, MA: Western Islands, 1967 [about the early phase of lodge conspiracies based on the implementation of a high-finance system, and about the background and purpose of the then recent French Revolution].

Rothkranz, Johannes. *666: Die Zahl des Tieres* ['The number of the Beast']. Durach: Verlag Anton Schmid, 1998.

Scott, Ernest. *The People of the Secret.* London: Octagon Press, 1983.

Simpson, Colin. *The Lusitania.* New York: Ballantine Books, 1972; Boston: Little, Brown & Co., 1972. [Describes how the background forces of England and the USA planned and realized the sinking of this passenger ship to create a justification for USA's entrance into the European war; young Churchill, Colonel House, Franklin Roosevelt and others participated in this action.]

Sparling, Earl. *Mystery Men of Wall Street: The Power Behind the Market.* New York: Greenberg, 1930 [about the money flow in the Wilson era and WW I].

Still, William T. *New World Order: The Ancient Plan of Secret Societies,* Lafayette, La.: Huntington House Publishers, 1990.

Sutton, Anthony. *Western Technology and Soviet Economic Development, 1919 to 1930.* Stanford, CA: Hoover Institution Press, 1968 [the Hoover Institution on War, Revolution and Peace is affiliated with the Stanford University].

—, *Western Technology and Soviet Economic Development, 1945 to 1965.* Stanford, CA: Hoover Institution Press, 1973.

—, *National Suicide: Military Aid to the Soviet Union.* New Rochelle, NY: Arlington House, 1973.

—, *Wall Street and the Bolshevik Revolution.* New Rochelle, NY: Arlington House, 1974.

—, *Wall Street and the Rise of Hitler.* Seal Beach, CA: '76 Press, 1976.

—, *The War on Gold.* Seal Beach, CA: '76 Press, 1977.

—, *The Two Faces of George Bush.* Dresden, NY: Wiswell Ruffin Inc., 1978.

—, *The Best Enemy Money Can Buy.* Billings, MO: Liberty House Press, 1986 [about western financing of communism and the Soviet Union].

Tansill, Charles C. *America Goes to War.* Boston: Little, Brown & Co., 1938 [about the forces that pushed America into WW I].

Veale, Frederick J. P. *Advance to Barbarism: The Development of Total Warfare From Sarajevo to Hiroshima.* London: Mitre Press, 1968, first published in 1953. [A British author criticizes the hypocrisy and propaganda of the English, American and Russian forces that designate themselves as 'good' and those they fight as 'evil', and fears that these 'good' nations will wage many subsequent wars under the dictate of supranational interests.]

Viereck, George. *The Strangest Friendship in History: Woodrow Wilson and Colonel House.* New York: Liveright Publishers, 1932.

Waite, Arthur Edward. *A New Encyclopedia of Freemasonry (Ars Magna Latomorum), Two Volumes in One.* New York: Wing Books, a division of Random House, 1996.

Wells, Herbert George. *The Open Conspiracy: Blue Prints for a World Revolution* (1928); *The Shape of Things to Come: The Ultimate Revolution* (1933); *Experiment on Autobiography* (1934); *The New World Order* (1940).
Yallop, David. *In God's Name: An Investigation into the Murder of Pope John Paul I.* Toronto and New York: Bantam, 1984, and London: Corgi Books, Transworld Publishers Ltd, 1987 (updated edition).

Holy Scriptures of the World Religions
(in alphabetical order)

Bhagavad-gita editions:
Bhagavad-gita 'As It Is', translated and commented by A. C. Bhaktivedanta Swami Prabhupada. Los Angeles: The Bhaktivedanta Book Trust, 2001.*
Srimad Bhagavad-Gita, with commentaries by Srila Visvanatha Cakravarti Thakura and Sri Srimad Bhaktivedanta Narayana Maharaja. Mathura, India: Gaudiya Vedanta Samiti, 2000.*
The Song of God: Bhagavad-Gita, translated by Swami Prabhavananda and Christopher Isherwood. Hollywood, CA: The Marcel Rodd Co., 1944.*

Bible editions:
Das Neue Testament und frühchristliche Schriften, translated by Klaus Berger and Christine Nord. Frankfurt am Main: insel verlag, 1999.*
Die Bibel (in heutigem Deutsch). Stuttgart: Deutsche Bibelgesellschaft, 1982 (second revised edition).*
Die Heilige Schrift des Alten und Neuen Testaments, nach dem Urtext übersetzt von Franz Eugen Schlachter, Genf 1981.*
The HarperCollins Study Bible (general editor: Wayne A. Meeks). London: HarperCollins*Publishers*. New Revised Standard Version 1993.*
The Holy Bible, New King James Version. Nashville, TN: Thomas Nelson, 1982.*
The New Jerusalem Bible. London: Darton, Longman & Todd Ltd, 1985.*
The New World Translation of the Holy Scriptures. Watch Tower Bible and Tract Society of Pennsylvania, 1984.*

Etz Hayim. *Torah and Commentary,* edited by David L. Lieber. New York: The Rabbinical Assembly, 2001.*
The Koran, translated with notes by N. J. Dawood. Penguin Books, 1956; fifth, revised edition 1990.
Padma Purana, 10 volumes. Delhi: Motilal Banarsidass, 1988–92.*
Rig Veda: *Hymns from the Golden Age,* translation and commentary by David Frawley. Delhi: Motilal Banarsidass, 1986.
Shrimad Bhagavata Mahapurana, translated by C. L. Goswami. Gorakhpur, India: Gita Press, 1971, third edition 1995.*
Shrimad-Bhagavatam, *Cantos 1 to 10 (part one),* translated by A. C. Bhaktivedanta Swami Prabhupada; *Cantos 10 to 12,* translated by Gopiparanadhana Dasa. Los Angeles, CA: The Bhaktivedanta Book Trust, 1972–82.*

---

* The quotations from the Bible, the *Bhagavad-gita* and the *Puranas* are based on these respective editions, selected and combined by Armin Risi.

About religion and spirituality

Atteshlis, Stylianos (known as Daskalos). *The Esoteric Teachings: A Christian Approach to Truth*. Strovolos/Nikosia, Cyprus: Stoa Series, 1989.
Finkelstein, Israel, and Neil Silberman. *The Bible Unearthed: Archaeology's New Vision of Ancient Israel and the Origin of Its Sacred Texts*. New York: The Free Press, a division of Simon & Schuster, 2001.
Greiner, Wolfgang. *Das Antlitz des Bösen* ['The Countenance of Evil']. Dornach, Switzerland: Goetheanum Verlag, 1984.
—, *Christus und Luzifer*. Dornach, Switzerland: Goetheanum Verlag, 1987.
Hooke, Samuel Henry. *Middle Eastern Mythology*. New York: Penguin Books, 1963.
Hurtak, James J. *The Book of Knowledge: The Keys of Enoch*. Los Gatos, CA: Academy for Future Science, 1973, 1996.
Kamp, Matthias. *Bruno Gröning: Revolution in der Medizin. Eine ärztliche Dokumentation der Heilung auf geistigem Weg* ['Revolution in medicine: A documentation by physicians on healing in the spiritual way']. Mönchengladbach, Germany: Grete Häusler Verlag, 1998.
Lorber, Jakob. *Die Haushaltung Gottes: Die Urgeschichte der Menschheit* ['The household of God: The ancient history of mankind']. Original edition, Stuttgart 1852. Current edition, Bietigheim: Lorber Verlag, 1981.
Markides, Kyriacos C. *The Magus of Strovolos: The Extraordinary World of a Spiritual Healer*. First edition 1985; London, New York: Penguin Books (Arkana) 1990 [the famous biography of Daskalos].
Megre, Wladimir. *Anastasia: Tochter der Taiga* ['Anastasiya: Daughter of the Taiga', vol. 1]. Neuhausen, Switzerland: Govinda-Verlag 2003 [original in Russian, 9 volumes; about an ancient secret 'tribe' of hermits in Siberia, their wisdom and memory of ancient civilizations, their paranormal abilities and prophecies].
Michel, Peter. *Die Sternenbruderschaft* ['The stellar brotherhood']. Grafing, Germany: Aquamarin Verlag, 1995.
Weber, Albrecht. *Garabandal*. Meersburg, Germany: Weto-Verlag, 2000.

About UFOs and extraterrestrials

Ananda. *The Alien Presence: The Evidence for Government Contact with Alien Life Forms*. Svinndal, Norway: Shekinah Publishing, 1992.
Beckley, Timothy Green. *UFOs Among the Stars: Close Encounters of the Famous*. New Brunswick, NJ: Global Communications, 1992.
Berlitz, Charles, and William Moore. *The Roswell Incident*. New York: Grosset & Dunlop, 1980.
Blum, Howard. *Out There: The Government's Secret Quest for Extraterrestrials*. New York: Simon & Schuster, 1991.
Blumrich, Josef [a NASA engineer, colleage of Wernher von Braun]. *Da tat sich der Himmel auf: Die Begegnungen des Propheten Ezechiel mit außerirdischer Intelligenz* ['And then the skies opened: Prophet Ezekiel's encounter with an extraterrestrial intelligence'], 1973; Rottenburg, Germany: Kopp Verlag, 2003; English edition: *The Spaceship of Ezekiel*. New York: Bantam Books, 1974.

Bramley, William. *The Gods of Eden: The truth about extraterrestrial infiltration – and the conspiracy to keep humankind in chains.* New York: Avon Books, 1990.
Childress, David Hatcher. *Vimana Aircraft of Ancient India and Atlantis* (including the complete Vimaanika Shastra). Kempton, IL: Adventure Unlimited Press, 1995.
Corso, Philip J., with William Birnes. *The Day After Roswell: A Former Pentagon Official Reveals the U.S. Government's Shocking UFO Cover-up.* New York: Rosewood Woods Publications, 1997.
Däniken, Erich von. *Erinnerungen an die Zukunft: Ungelöste Rätsel der Vergangenheit* ['Memories of the future: Unsolved mysteries of the Past'], Düsseldorf, Wien: Econ Verlag, 1968. [Erich von Däniken's first book, which became an immediate world-bestseller; English edition: *Chariots of the Gods? Unsolved Mysteries of the Past.* New York: G.P. Putnam's Sons, 1969.]
Downing, Barry. *The Bible and Flying Saucers.* Philadelphia: J.B. Lippincott, 1968.
Fowler, Raymond. *Casebook of a UFO investigator.* Eaglewook Cliffs, NJ: Prentice Hall, 1981.
—, *The Watchers: The Secret Designs behind UFO Abductions.* New York: Bantam Books, 1990.
Friedman, Stanton. *Top Secret/Majic.* New York: Marlowe & Company, 1996 [an important book about the Roswell incident and Majestic-12].
Friedman, Stanton, and Don Berliner. *Crash at Corona.* New York: Paragon House, 1992; New York: Marlowe & Company, 1994. [This book is about the Roswell incident which actually took place near the small village Corona where the debris was found. Roswell was the nearby town with the Air Force base.]
Good, Timothy. *Above Top Secret: Worldwide UFO Cover-up.* London: Grafton, 1989.
—, *Alien Liaison: The Ultimate Secret.* London: Sidgwick & Jackson, 1991.
—, *UFO reports.* London: Sidgwick & Jackson, 1991.
—, *Beyond Top Secret: The Worldwide UFO Security Threat.* London: Sidgwick & Jackson, 1996.
—, *Alien Base: Earth's Encounters with Extraterrestrials.* London: Sidgwick & Jackson, 1998.
—, *Unearthly Disclosure: Conflicting Interests in the Control of Extraterrestrial Intelligence.* London: Arrow Books, 2001.
Hall, Richard H. *Uninvited Guests: A Documented History of UFO Sightings, Alien Encounters & Coverups.* Santa Fe, NM: Aurora Press, 1988.
Hesemann, Michael. *Geheimsache UFO: Die wahre Geschichte der unbekannten Flugobjekte* ['Secret matter UFO: The true history of the unidentified flying objects'], Neuwied, Germany: Silberschnur, 1994.
Hopkins, Budd. *Missing Time: A Documented Study of UFO Abductions.* New York: Richard Marek Publishers, 1981.
—, *Intruders: The Incredible Visitations at Copley Woods.* New York: Random House, 1987.
Horn, Arthur David. *Humanity's Extraterrestrial Origins: ET Influences on Biological and Cultural Evolution.* San Diego, CA: The Book Tree, 1996.
Howe, Linda Moulton. *An Alien Harvest: Further Evidence Linking Animal Mutilations and Human Abductions to Alien Life Forms.* Littleton, CO: Linda Moulton Howe Productions, 1989.

Jacobs, David M. *Secret Life: Firsthand Accounts of UFO Abductions.* New York: Simon & Schuster, 1992.

——, *The Threat: Revealing the Secret Alien Agenda.* New York: Fireside Books, Simon & Schuster, 1999 [original edition, New York: Simon & Schuster, 1998, entitled *The Threat: What the Aliens Really Want … And How They Plan to Get It*].

—— (editor), *UFOs and Abduction: Challenging the Borders of Knowledge.* Lawrence, KS: University Press of Kansas, 2000.

Kanjilal, Dileep Kumar. *Vimana in Ancient India,* Calcutta: Sanskrit Pustak Bhandar, 1985.

Mack, John E. *Abduction: Human Encounters with Aliens.* New York: Maxwell Macmillan International, 1994.

Marciniak, Barbara. *Bringers of the Dawn: Teachings from the Pleiadians.* Santa Fe, NM: Bear & Company, 1992.

Marrs, Jim. *Alien Agenda: Investigating the Extraterrestrial Presence Among Us.* New York: HarperCollins, 1997.

Pope, Nick. *Open Skies, Closed Minds: For the First Time a Government UFO Expert Speaks Out,* Foreword by Timothy Good. London: Simon & Schuster, 1996.

Randle, Kevin D. *The Ufo Casebook.* New York: Warner, 1989.

——, *A History of Ufo Crashes.* New York: Avon Books, 1995.

——, *Invasion Washington: UFOs over the Capitol.* New York: HarperTorch, 2001.

Randle, Kevin D., and Donald R. Schmitt. *UFO Crash at Roswell.* New York: Avon Books, 1991.

——, *The Truth about the UFO Crash at Roswell.* New York: M. Evans, 1994.

Randles, Jenny. *Alien Abductions: The Mystery Solved.* New Brunswick, NJ: Inner Light Publications, 1988.

——, *Alien Contacts and Abductions.* New York: Sterling Publishing, 1994.

Redfern, Nicholas. *A Covert Agenda: The British Government's UFO Top Secrets Exposed.* New York: Simon & Schuster, 1997.

Reeve, Bryant and Helen. *Flying Saucer Pilgrimage.* Amherst, WI: Amherst Press, 1957.

Rimmer, John. *The Evidence for Alien Abductions.* Wellingborough, Northamptonshire, UK: Aquarian Press, 1984.

Royal, Lyssa, and Keith Priest. *Visitors From Within.* Phoenix, AZ: Royal & Keith Research, 1992.

Sitchin, Zecharia. *The Twelfth Planet.* New York: Avon Books, 1978 (first published by Bear & Co. 1976).

——, *The Wars of Gods and Men.* New York: Avon Books, 1985.

Spencer, John. *Perspectives: A Radical Examination of the Alien Abduction Phenomenon,* London, Sydney: Macdonald & Co, 1989.

Steiger, Brad. *Strangers from the Skies.* New York: Award Books, 1966.

Thompson, Richard L. *Alien Identities: Ancient Insights into Modern UFO Phenomena.* San Diego, CA: Govardhan Hill Publishing, 1993.

Vallée, Jacques. *Dimensions: A Casebook of Alien Contact.* London: Souvenir Press, 1988; Chicago: Contemporary Books, 1988.

——, *Confrontations: A Scientist's Search for Alien Contact.* London: Souvenir Press, 1990/ New York: Ballantine Books, 1990.

——, *Revelations: Alien Contact and Human Deception.* London: Souvenir Press, 1992.

Index

Abraham, 168, 323, 401
Absolute, defined, 27-8, 31-2, 76, 116, 119, 300
Absolutizing, 18, 50-3, 117-19, 153, 167, 234-5, 306, 314
Adam Kadmon, 37
Adam and Eve, 147, 149, 313, 341
Adamic species, 372-3, 377
Ahankara, 413
Akarma, 134
Allegories
  cave and mercy, 143
  diver and bubbles, 60
  heat and fire, 57
  kings and queens in chess, 24
  light and darkness, 24-5, 28, 32-8, 53, 119-132, 298, 369-70
  lodges and football leagues, 110
  monsoon and end time, 387-9
  point on a wheel and ages, 371, 379
  radio and parallel dimensions, 24
  smoke and fire, 25
  staircase and way to self-realization, 116, 121, 312
  streamline and waterfall, 314
Amara, 278, 280
American Civil War, 98-9
Ancient civilisations
  abilities of, 17-18, 288-9, 372-3, 405 (63)*, ps 1-3*
  destroyed by catastrophes, 157-8
  deterioration of, 19, 165-6, 378-9
  existence of, 333
Angels
  defined, 26, 33-4, 164, 233, 293
  in the end time, 264, 272-3, 285, 301
  fallen, 26, 29, 33-4, 40, 238-9, 291, 362
  See also: Light beings
Animism, 337
Antarctica, 157, 366

---

*Numbers in parantheses refer to endnote texts, and ps to the pages in the picture section.

Anunnaki, 291, 342
Apocalypse, etym., 234
Archetype, 39, 43
Arche-types, 37, 372
Armageddon, 225, 264
Ascension, 50, 277-83, 285, 286-7, 331-2
Astral
  entities, possession by, 101, 151
  realms, 24 (6), 61-2
Asuras
  as forces opposing the light, 29, 36, 40, 50, 116
  half-truths of, 119
  live at the cost of others, 64, 69, 141, 224
  not united, 340
  See also: Dark forces
Atlantis, 157, 288, 321-2, 366, 378
Atma, 131, 315, 372
Atheism, defined, 114, 138, 183
Atom bombs, 80, 134, 225, 261, 326, 346, 360, 417, 426
Atomos, 131, 315
Augustine, 70 (25)
Aztecs, 166

Baalbek, 342, ps 2
Babylon, 247, 290-1, 342
Bar code, 242, 243-4
  for humans?, 249-50, 252, 256, ps 5
Berlusconi, 180, 414
Bhagavad-gita
  history of, 207
  quoted, 28, 59, 67, 69, 74, 116, 119-20, 141, 412, 431
Bharata, 157, 207, 334
Bhimpul (Bhima's bridge), ps 1
Biblical archaeology, 400-2
Bio-robots, 360, 363
Blavatsky, Helena, 39
Blumrich, Josef, 287-8
Body piercings, 253
Borneo, 337-9

435

Brahma
  as cosmic Christ, 307, 316, 383-4, ps 7
  as creator within the universe, 34-7, 41, 141, 280
  meaning of his name, 416 (137)
  as universal Being, 300, 303, 315
Brahmana(s), 17, 51, 166, 334-6
Branton, 360
Brinkley, Dannion, 257-8
British Empire, 105, 216-18, 237
Brotherhoods, 40, 95, 104, 291, 342
Buddha, 166, 307, 323-4
Buddhi, 67-9
Bush sen., George, 175-7, 227

Caste system, 166
Cataclysms (mega-catastrophes) in the past, 157-8, 160, 198, 373
Catholic Church
  Lodge against, 103, 171-2, 177-8
  infiltrated by lodges, 178-85
  in the Middle Ages, 310
Chakras, 299, 302, 372, 392
Chiliasm, 404
China, 49, 84, 265-7, 407 (78)
Christie, Agatha, 81-6
Churchill, 90, 174, 184, 396 (30), 409
Cistercian Order, 187-90
City of London, 81
Clinton, Bill, 228, 255, 265-7, 410 (103)
Cocteau, Jean, 184, 193
Cold war, 174, 225-9, 235
Columbus, 400, 406
Compensation, 16, 52
Condon Report, 351-2, 353-4
Consciousness
  conditioning of, 16, 43, 298
  as energy, 26, 59, 297-8
  energy as fluxes of, 300
  focus of, 15-16, 53-4, 55-6, 139, 323
  not a product of matter, 17, 23, 35, 57-9, 121, 131, 298, 315, 365, 397 (40)
Conspiracy theory, 79, 393 (9)
Consumption and destruction, 64-6
Content(edness), 53, 64, 70, 91, 233, 236-7, 394 (14)
Continental-drift theory, 288

Cooper, Gordon, 352-3, 358
Cooper, Milton William, 359, 362-3
Cosmos, etym., 120 (37)
Crash, financial, 258, 260
Creation
  causes of, 32-3
  plan/purpose of, 45, 134, 276, 315, 372, 377
  process of, 34-7, 129, 416 (137)
  in seven steps, 35-6, 37
  through a quantum leap, 35
  See also: Genesis
Crop circles, 367, ps 8
Crusades, 186-88, 270

Däniken, Erich von, 287
Dark worlds, creation of, 33-4, 36, 40
Dark forces
  deceiving the world, 92, 238-9, 264, 274, 284, 291-2, 327-8, 364, 367, 379
  incarnated, 34, 41-2, 84, 86, 92, 233, 292, 323, 324, 362, 373-4
  liberation of, 47, 120, 141, 376, 377-8
  occult aspects of, 84-6, 123-4, 223
  origin of, 34-9
  psychology of, 29, 39-41, 44
  want kingdom of God without God, 125
Daskalos, 66 (23 and 24), 375 (139)
Dawkins, Richard, 57, 135
Death, overcoming, 278, 281
Deism, 122, 134, 137, 154, 183-4
Deluge (Great Flood), 160, 321-2, 342, 373, 414-5
Demonizing, 18, 26, 50, 306
Devas, 36, 40, 164, 207-8
Devil, 27
Devolution, 36
Dharma, 208-10, 230-1, 384
Dia-bolic, 26, 29, 44, 48, 77, 113, 172, 314
Dialectic thinking, 169-70, 194
Differentiating without judging, 45, 71-5, 76, 115, 312, 314, 328, 380
Dimensions, defined, 24, 35-6, 158, 341-2
Dini, Dino, 354-6
Diversions, wanted by people, 16, 41, 55, 63, 209, 324, 362, 383

Divide and rule, 165, 170, 224-5, 229
Divine, beyond being 'good', 28, 37, 46, 115, 140
Duality
    defined, 26, 31, 35, 38, 46, 120
    earth as place of, 25, 29, 135-7
    in higher worlds, 25
    life in, at the cost of others, 141
    negating, 124-5, 133, 153
    not an illusion, 130
    reality beyond, 32, 35, 42, 129
    transcending, 27-8, 68, 72-5
Dvaraka, 289-90

Earth
    creation of, 36-7
    early phase of, 320
    light and darkness on, 25, 29, 33, 37, 114, 224, 233, 302, 370
    in the most dense dimension, 37
    quantum leaps of, 157-8, 388-9
    respiritualization/transformation of, 50, 275, 280-1, 307, 324, 376, 388-9
    symbolized as cow, 208-9
    ascension of, cannot be stopped, 327
    as battlefield of demons and gods?, 340
    as place of karma, 380
Eden, 161, 291, 342
Ego
    defined, 33, 39, 43, 45, 53, 120, 154
    destruction of, 381
Ego-justification, 44, 53-4, 141
Elementals
    defined, 61, 66
    influence of, 101, 209
Elohim, 37, 341, 372, 378, 416
Emanation, matter and energy as, 34, 38, 59, 300, 315, 392 (6)
Empowerment
    divine, 34, 77, 141, 147-8, 279, 307-8, 328
    satanic, 51, 101, 239-40, 327
'End justifies the means', 126, 133, 172
'End times', signs of, 237-8, 272-3, 302, 381
Enemy of the State, 236, 252

Energy
    defined, 23-4, 26, 59, 300
    source of, 141
    See also: Consciousness
Enki, Enlil, 40, 342, 414 (120), ps 2
Enlightenment
    false, 30, 32, 40-1, 44, 51, 124-5, 133, 138
    real, 28, 31-2, 37, 68, 72-5, 141, 300-301, 384
Entelechy, 413
Epiphany, 370
Esoteric, defined, 19, 26, 123, 302
Eternal/eternity, 28, 31-2, 35, 43, 131, 133, 300, 397 (40)
Ethics, 121
Etz hayim ('tree of life'), 159, 394 (15)
Etz Hayim (Torah), quoted, 340-1, 402-3
Evil
    allowed in duality, 45
    God not source of, 38, 42
    role of, 44-7
    source of, 26, 29, 36
    unable to match the power of love, 141
    unnecessary, 42-3, 45, 127, 137
    See also: Dark forces; Duality
Evolution(ism)
    as materialistic monism, 155
    non-proven, 288
    world-view of, 23, 121, 157, 365
    writing not a sign of, 17-18, 378
    gives wrong interpretation of early humans, 378
Exploitation
    cause of, 141, 198, 372-3
    world-wide, 92, 214-9, 337-8
Extraterrestrial(s)
    defined, 24 (7), 29
    controversy about, 365-6
    on earth, in the past, 162, 291-2, 320-3, 342, 344-5, 366-7, 372-3, 377-8
Ezekiel, ascension of, 287

False prophets, 42, 166-8, 387
Family
    destruction of, 146
    new quality of, 146, 152, 383, 385

Fear
  atmos-, 66, ps 4
  cause of, 58, 74, 135, 144, 243
  as 'food', 60, 63-4, 69, 321
  of God/gods, 102, 166, 170, 323, 373-4
  liberation from, 66-8, 71, 118, 139, 302
  being free of, 28, 57, 77, 152, 332
Federal Reserve Act, 89, 93, 218, 220, 407 (74)
First-born son of God, 34-5, 50, 278
  See also: Brahma; Jesus
'The first will be the last', 47
Ford, Gerald, 351
Forgiveness, 70-6, 135, 230, 370
Freemasonry
  condemned by the Church, 178-85
  Entente, 95-6
  etymology of, 171
  intrigues in, 100-101, 203
  mundane, 104, 173
  original, 110, 155, 163
  world-wide, 105-6, 174, 200-203
Free will
  as absolute principle, 32, 42, 53, 134-9
  loss of, 40, 43, 64-6, 137
  love as perfection of, 32, 37, 42, 71, 76, 134, 137
  in oneness with God's will, 137-9
  prophecies and, 273-4
  tested in polarity, 33, 38, 42
French Revolution, 99-100, 105, 128, 222
Friedman, Stanton, 358

Galactic beings, 299, 373
Garabandal, 411 (111)
Genesis
  biblical, 34, 37, 48, 340, 371-2, 416-17
  cosmic, 33-7, 371-3
  Puranic, 416-17
  See also: Creation; Mankind, origin of
Genetic alterations in the past, 162, 322-3, 324, 333, 342, 363-4, 368, 373, 378
Gifts of the spirit, 309-10
Gilgamesh, 342, 373, 401, 414, ps 2
Global players, invited to read this book, 121

God
  defined, 28, 116
  as absolute Individual, 31-2, 42, 45, 59, 132, 138, 300
  atheistic definition of, 124-5, 170
  as cause of all causes, 138
  as Creator, 34 (see also: Vishnu)
  does not create evil, 38, 42
  Father-Mother-, 50, 132
  intelligible and logical, 115
  kingdom of, within you, 248
  lacks our love, 144
  mathemystical analogy for, 132
  supremely merciful, 142-3, 377
  will of, 32, 45, 134-40, 155
Goethe, 106, 174
Gold, hoarding of, 209-12, 230-1
Good and evil
  beyond, 28, 37, 46, 71-5, 120, 134-5, 140, 381
  misconceptions about, 27, 28, 44-5, 57-8, 71-2, 113, 126-7, 134, 184
  as part of duality, 28, 43-4, 72-3
  purpose of, 134, 136
  See also: Duality
Gospel of Philip, 148-52, 166
Gospel of Thomas, 148, 398
Grail, 191-3
Gröning, Bruno, 409
Gunas, 394 (14), 413
Guru
  false (absolutized) form of, 51-2, 166
  incarnate or invisible, 143, 389
  as sparking factor, 143, 389
  See also: Initiation, inner; 'Two or three in my name'

Haley, Bill, 398-9
Harriman, 93, 226-9
Hierarchy
  defined, 36
  cosmic, 299-300, 315
Hiram (from Tyre), 171, 193
Hitler, 80, 118, 175, 228, 396, 410
Hölderlin, Friedrich, 5 (1), 107, 385
Holly, Buddy, 399
Holistic, 18-19, 23, 115

Holy, 19, 142, 382
Holystic, 77, 141, 145, 148, 152, 159, 299, 382
Holographic projections, 42
Hopis, 287-9, 343-4
Humanism, 114, 182-3
Hurtak, Jim, 364 (136), 403
Hussein, Saddam, 425
Hyperion, 107-9
Hyperspace, 158
Hypnosis, 298

I-AM, 42-3, 129-30, 142
Icke, David, 414
Illuminati, Order of The, 102-6, 202, 222
Illuminati
  as a mentality, 105, 153, 172
  not one particular group, 105, 124 (38)
  philosophy of, 44, 58, 101, 113, 121, 124-9
  as 'realists', 127, 133, 137, 153
  as secret elite, 85
  self-definition of, 92, 124
Illusion, 33, 35, 43, 53, 120, 130, 377
  See also: *Maya*
Independence Day, 366
Individuality, 31, 42, 53, 131-40, 154, 365
In-formation, 16
Initiation, inner, 143, 146, 150, 389
Inner word, 302, 305, 306-11, 383, 384
Inquisition, 305
Institutions, none spared of contamination, 155, 305
Intelligence, 67-8, 115
Intergalactic beings, 300
Involution, 36-7, 157
Isaiah, prophet, 167-8
Isis, 400
Islam, 185-7, 188, 269-70

Jacobs, David, 416 (136)
Jeremy, prophet, 167-8
Jesus
  ascension of, 278-9, 281, 304
  challenged 'brood of vipers', 72, 168
  differentiates, 72
  different theories about, 185-6, 191-3
  distorted by Bible fundamentalists, 248
  as the first-born of all creation, 33, 40, 278, 280, ps 7
  is forgiving, 75
  as incarnation of the highest Light being, 141 (43), 286, 303, 307, 378
  'I still have many things to say', 303-4, 316, 381
  karma of, 136
  as morning star, 39
  never said, 'I am the Father', 412
  one with and different from the Father, 132, 143-4, 412 (113)
  and Satan, 47-8, 49, 73, 137
  return of, 271-2, 276
  sudden fearlessness of his followers, 279
  talked to the woman from Samaria, 148
  wisdom of, 70, 74, 76, 286, 301
  'works greater than' his, 137
  'you are gods', 295, 382
Joel's prophecy, 147, 301-2, 304-5, 308, 328-9, 382, 385
John of Jerusalem, 187, 194-8, 311
John XXIII, 178-81, 184
John Paul I, 179
Judging, 39, 43, 46, 71-5, 115, 120

Kachinas, 164, 288
Kâlî, 48, 132
Kali, 48, 207, 208-10, 379
Kali-yuga
  began 5000 years ago, 18, 49, 165, 319
  cataclysm before, 160
  as the 'Fourth World', 163
  gold and money in, 207-23
  hypocrisy in, 210, 238, 379
  limitations through, 18, 48-9, 162, 301
  lying typical in, 230, 379-80
  religion misused in, 50-1, 165-6, 291-2, 322-3, 373-4
  reptoid influence in, 334-9
  as time of the dark forces, 92-3, 101, 370

Karma
  etymology of, 134
  directed by Paramatma, 315, 413
  misconceptions about, 122, 134, 397
  real meaning of, 134-7, 314, 380
  working of, 45, 47, 137, 362
  human, beginning of, 378
Kásskara, 157, 288
Kinesiology, 380
Knowledge, perfect but incomplete, 26, 31
Krishna, 49, 132, 207, 208, 289-90, 417
Kshetra, 297-301, 314-5, 413
Kurukshetra, 207, 297

Lear, John, 359
Lemuria, 157, 288, 321-2, 378
Lenin, 82, 87-90, 174
Life
  biggest miracle, 298, 315
  comes from life, 35, 37
  See also: Consciousness
Light, living on, 285
Light being(s)
  defined, 26
  incarnating on earth, 25, 37, 43 (13), 164, 233. 280, 293, 372
  in divine hierarchy, 36, 299-300
  do not undergo physical death, 278
  earth-mission of, 372, 376-8
  manifestation of, on earth, 371-2, 377, 378
  in polarity, 32-4
  as invisible helpers, 374-6, 417 (138)
  renewed contact with, 302-3, 383-5
  respect free will, 301, 313, 322, 362, 373, 417 (138)
Light body, 279-80, 307, 408 (75)
Light circle, 68, 307-8, 382-5, 389
Like attracts like, 62, 101, 412 (114)
Lincoln, Abraham, 97-9
Love
  defined, 32, 37, 42, 139-40, 384
  and forgiveness, 70-5, 120
  as mercy, 142-3, 377
  one heart and one soul, 154
  unconditional, 73-5, 141-2, 376, 380

'Love God ... and your neighbour as yourself', 76, 142, 147, 276, 280
Lucifer
  as archetype of duality, 38-41, 46
  as first missionary, 40, 43
  incarnation of, 49
  name of, 38-9
  self-justification of, 44, 53, 393 (11), 396 (38)
  wants to create shadows, 44
  wisdom of, 127
Lundberg, Ferdinand, 93-5
Lusitania, 96-7
Luther, Martin, 310

MacArthur, Douglas, 357-8
Mahabharata, 207, 230
Maldek, 321-2
Male-dominated lodges and churches, 155
Manipulation, 15, 52-3, 56, 63-6, 115, 224, 292, 373, 378
Mankind
  hidden history of, 316, 319, 320-8
  origin of, 18, 25, 36-7, 157-8, 371-2, 376-8
  as universal team member, 353, 357-8, 376
Man-woman relationship
  undermining of, 48, 52, 61, 119, 146-7
  as key to oneness, 32, 68, 142, 145-51, 378, 382-5
  new freedom in, 147, 385, 399 (44)
Martial arts, 298
Martin, Malachi, 184
Martyrs, 141, 164, 171, 259, 264, 284, 286, 305, 311
Mary Magdalene, 145, 148-9, 193, 279, 399 (45)
Materialism
  defined, 18, 23, 57, 122, 369
  fatal consequence of, 69, 130, 134-5, 138, 397 (40)
  as materialistic monism, 123
  introduced by dark forces, 49-50, 230, 243, 323, 365
Mathemystical, 132

Matter
  defined, 23-4, 32, 59, 120, 392 (6)
  as eternal energy, 34, 129, 314
  etymology of, 129
  function of, 133
  identification with, 243, 298, 393 (10)
  not self-organizing, 17, 34-5, 59, 298, 314, 369, 413
  transformation of, 280-1, 376-7
  See also: Consciousness; Emanation
Maya, 35, 129-30, 139, 141, 145, 398 (40)
  See also: Illusion
Mayan Calendar, 49
McCarthy, Joseph, 408 (89)
Meat-eating, 16, 41, 62, 117, 166-7, 209, 230, 388
  See also: Vegetarian(ism)
Melchizedek, 394 (15)
Mercy, 142-3, 209, 230, 264, 377, 381, 393 (9)
Millenari, 180-4
Milner, Alfred, 217-19, 408 (85)
Mind
  defined, 59, 67
  over matter, 17, 34, 36, 298
Mitchell, Edgar, 354, 376
Money
  in itself not bad, 231
  in Kali-yuga, 209-23
  paper, 87, 212, 249
  -pulation, 210, 213, 249
  abolishment of cash, 250-2, 258-9
Monism
  defined, 123
  atheistic (materialistic), 123-9, 137, 153-5
  occult, 123, 153, 155
  theistic, 123, 133
Moore, Michael, 408 (84)
Morningsky, Robert, 343-4, 364
Morphogenetic field, 413
Moses, 168, 324, 401
Musical emancipation, 146 (44)
Mutilations, animal, 361, 367, ps 4
Mystical, defined, 30, 123
Mytho-logic, 19, 158, 315
Mythos and logos, 19

Nagas, 334-6, 337-8
Nag Hammadi, 148
NASA, 287, 352, 355-6
'Necessary experience', 54, 127, 137, 153
Negative
  nothing absolutely, 27, 44-5, 73, 93, 117, 161
  two forms of, 46, 50, 113
Nephilim, 291, 340-2
Neutrality, 46, 120, 164
New age, dawning of, 147-8, 197-8, 231, 235, 261, 272-3, 293, 385
New Jerusalem, 235, 261
New World Order, 95, 114, 176, 203, 219-20, 260
Nihilism, 26, 46, 114
Noah, 313, 401, 414-15
Non-intervention, 161

Occultism
  etymology of, 123
  of asuras, 85-6, 92, 292
  as occult monism, 123-6, 155
O'Dean, Robert, 359
O'Leary, Brian, 354
One and different, 132-4, 138, 154, 392 (8), 412 (113)
Oneness
  atheistic concept of, 124, 133
  theistic concept of, 31-2, 35, 42, 72, 131-4, 139, 382-4
  in diversity, 26, 235, 237, 313
Oppenheimer, J. Robert, 417
Orwell, George, 168 (51), 184, 236
Osiris, 40

Pantheism, 122
Paradise, 48, 372, 377-8
Parallel worlds, 19, 24, 36, 158
Paramatma, 315, 412-13
Paranormal, 18-19, 286, 299, 329, 378
Pariksit, King, 207-9, 334-6
Patriarchate, 48, 51, 119, 147
Paul, apostle, 279-80, 306
Pentecost, 304
  See also: Whitsun holiday
Pharma, 69, 214, 291

442   Index

Photographic memory, 13-14, 17
Physiognomy, 315
Pillsbury, 11-14, 15, 18 (3), 56
Planetary beings, 299, 376
Polarity
  as opposed to duality, 33, 119-20
  quantum leap into, 34
  as universal principle, 137
Pope, Nick, 367
Power game, 15-17, 51-2, 73, 122-3
  transcEnding the, 16, 47, 76, 155, 203, 376, 385
Pragmatism, 46, 126, 134, 140, 183, 373
Prana, 285
Predestination, 134-7
Presley, Elvis, 399
Proto-types, 37
Psychic potentials, 17-18, 34, 35, 159, 286, 299, 320, 380
Psychosomatic, 62, 373, 400 (47)
Puma Punku, 288-9
Puranas, 166, 170, 207, 230, 289-90, 416
Pythagoras, 167, 307

Qumran 192-3

Radha-Krishna, 132
Reality
  defined, 23, 31, 35, 42, 53, 76, 300, 369
  misconceptions about, 121-30, 377
  realization of, 303, 311, 381
  two ways of approaching, 19
  See also: Absolute; God
Reign of Terror, 100, 128
Reincarnation
  defined, 398 (42)
  as natural principle, 58, 160, 199, 219, 278, 284
  Christian misunderstanding of, 136, 259, 311
Relative
  defined, 26, 31-2, 35, 115, 119
  absolutizing or negating the, 153
  'everything is', 27-8, 116, 117
  positive and negative both, 27, 43-5, 115-17
  See also: Duality; Polarity

Religion
  defined, 384
  dogmatic, 18, 26, 29, 50-2, 113, 118, 165-6, 234-5, 382
  infiltration of, 50-2, 162, 165-6, 291, 308, 316, 333, 373-4
  non-dogmatic, 19, 26-7, 38, 117-19, 168, 273, 381-4
  original form of, 17-18, 68, 70-5, 305
  scriptures and, 18, 51, 113, 166-9, 305, 310
  as 'controlled worship', 323
Rennes-le-Château, 406 (66)
Reptoids, 29, 41-2, 234, 238-9, 330, 334-40, 344, 364
Resonance, 29, 55-6, 60, 62-4, 101, 145, 313, 362, 369, 373, 412 (114)
Revelation(s)
  complementing forms of, 26, 29, 33-4, 119, 139, 233-5, 293, 301, 311, 403
  limited forms of, 30-1, 51, 312, 412(114)
  new, 48, 235, 272-3, 302-3, 306, 317-32, 333
  of St John, 55, 234-293, 329-32, 333
Rhodes, Cecil, 216-18
Rishi, 17, 336
Robison, John, 104, 202
Rockefeller, 83, 93
Roswell, 343, 346-9, 358-9
Russian Revolution, 79, 87-9, 218-19, 225

Sacred geometry, 159
Sagan, Samuel, 62 (20)
Sankirtan, 384
Satan
  as archetype of evil, 26, 29
  'Away with you', 48, 73, 145
  in disguise, 42
  as dragon, 42, 55, 234, 238-43, 263-4, 282, 291, 329-30, 333-4, 339, 379
  on earth, 238-9, 262-3
  as lord of the world, 47 (15)
  name of, 40
  has permission to tempt people, 116
  worship of, 184, 240
Satya-yuga, 208, 235, 371, 380
Schneider, Phil, 359-60

Science
  limitations of, 18, 30, 159, 311
  materialistic, 23, 26, 46, 57-8, 69, 85, 114, 397 (40)
  non-materialistic, 19, 23-4, 34-7, 59, 158-9
  origin behind materialistic, 49, 125-6
  self-justifying, 114, 374, 417 (138)
  See also: Technology
Secrecy
  as means of oppression, 103, 107
  as means to intervene secretly, 171-2
  as true responsibility, 161-3
Secret societies
  degradation/infiltration of, 101, 203
  materialistic form of, 91-2, 172
  original form of, 163
  prophecy about, 195
'Seek and you will find', 19, 260, 301, 302
Self-deception, 40, 44-6, 53, 377, 393 (11)
Self-pity, 40 (11), 47, 76
Self-realization
  as being parts of God, 31-2, 45, 132, 139, 145, 382
  sufficient knowledge for, 26, 31
  through love and forgiveness, 70-5
  in transcendence, 28, 68, 116, 162
Self-responsibility, 16, 38, 313, 383
Sentimental, 145
Seventh heaven, 36, 37
Sexuality
  materialistic, 61, 63, 209, 243
  oppressed by false religion, 52, 119
  as spiritual impulse, 142, 145-9
  See also: Man-woman relationship
Shakespeare, 25
Shambhalla, 394 (15)
Shakti, 132
Shiva, 34, 132
Shrimad-Bhagavatam, 207-9, 230, 289, 334-6, 407
Shruta-dhara, 17-18
Sin
  forgiving of, 143
  and sinner, 70, 77
  See also: Duality; Evil
Sita-Rama, 132

Six hundred and sixty-six
  as end-time code, 238-42
  original quote mentioning, 240
  represented as triple six, 240-3
  as code for humans?, 249-50, 252, 256, ps 5
  protection against, 284-5
Skull & Bones, 175, 227
Skylab, 375
Smith, Tom H., 317-18
Smoking, 41, 63
  non-, not a dogma, 117-19
Solar being (sun-god), 299, 327, 373
Solomon's temple, 171, 268-9
Soul(s)
  animating the body, 17, 58-9, 131, 298-9, 315
  as atma/atomos, 131
  each, is unique, 144
  as individual being, 31, 131-4
  fall of many but not of all, 33
Spiritual, defined, 28 (8), 31, 35, 59, 120, 129, 131, 133, 300, 311, 315, 369, 397 (40)
Spiritual healing, 17, 60, 68, 159, 233, 260, 298, 306-7, 308, 309, 394 (13 and 20), 395 (23), 409 (Gröning)
Stalin, 80, 90, 174, 229
Starvation, 113, 214, 237-8
Stevens, Wendelle, 359
Subterranean bases, 85, 86, 330, 343, 359, 360
Sumer, 291, 340-2, 357
Suras, 36
Sutton, Anthony, 88, 175, 229

Technology
  advanced through war, 99
  'imported on earth', 92, 360, 362, 373
  as means of power, 101, 249-50
  666-, 250-9, 325-6, 362, ps 5
Technomagical, 124, 247
Telepathy, 17, 159, 286, 298, 305, 320, 378
Tele-vision, 333
Templars, 171, 187-90, 194, 200-201, 211
Terror, staged and real, 64-6, 260, 340, 407 (74), 427 (Hufschmid)
'Test everything ...', 168, 306, 314, 385

Theism, defined, 114
Theosophy, 39, 217
Thoughts, as an immediate reality, 34, 38, 41, 60, 379-80
'Thy will be done', 32, 132, 140, 154, 389
Tiahuanaco, 288-9
Time
  duality of, 35, 41, 43, 145, 397
  as kâla, 48, 132
  as 'shadow' of eternity, 30-1, 35
  and space, 25, 32, 35, 120, 129, 158, 278
  in *yuga* cycles, 158, 278
Titans, 341
Tohu-wa-bohu, 34
Too little, too much, 46, 50, 113-14, 152, 234, 314, 369
Totemism, 337-9
TranscEnding, defined, 15, 28 (8), 46, 70, 74-5, 120, 141, 397 (42)
Trotsky, 82, 87-90, 174
Truth
  conclusive without being exclusive, 26, 30
  'will make you free', 139, 183, 369
Truthfulness, age of, 208, 235, 371, 380
TV, 16, 41, 56, 63-4, 146, 383
'Two or three in my name', 68, 142, 146, 152, 308, 314, 382
  as mutual initiation, 143, 384
  See also: Initiation, inner; Inner word

UFOs
  ancient reports on, 286-9, 335-6, 344-5, 366
  contemporary reports on, 345-67
  abductions by, 292, 361, 363-4, 366-7
  as 'clouds', 271, 276, 279, 281-2, 286, 287, 290, 330, 345
  contactees of, 349, 361
  UFO Cover-up Live, 359
  crashes of, 343, 346-9, 359, 360
  experiences by astronauts, 352-6, 357-8, 361, 375-6
  not all, extraterrestrial, 392 (7)
  scenario of 'unholy alliance', 326, 343, 357, 359, 360-2

  as vimanas, 290, 335-6
  See also: Extraterrestrial(s)
Ulteriors, 91-6, 115
Universe(s)
  countless, 34, 300
  as 'testing ground', 33
  as units of space and time, 34, 129
  as abstract notion for 'oneness', 127-8
  See also: Brahma; Cosmos; Creation
U Thant, 351

Vallée, Jacques, 352
Veda, Vedic, defined, 17
Vegetarian(ism), 41, 53, 167
  not a dogma, 117-19
  See also: Meat-eating
Venus, 39, 322
Vimanas, 290, 335-6, 345, 366
Vishnu, 34-5, 129, 132, 315, 416
Vishva-rupa, 159

Waldheim, Kurt, 352
Wag the Dog, 283, 410 (103)
Warwick, Kevin, 255
War, causes of, 15, 40, 63, 79, 224, 258
Washington, George, 174, 202, 222
Weishaupt, Adam, 102-6, 202, 222
Wells, H.G., 219, 220-21
Whitsun holiday, 147, 279, 304, 307
Wilson, Woodrow, 95-7, 174, 218, 220
World domination, 47-8, 52, 85, 102, 223, 236-7
World formula, philosophical, 24, 32, 59, 131-2, 138
World War
  First, 79-80, 87-90, 95-7, 220-1
  Second, 80, 90, 128, 174, 227, 395 (27), 409 (92), 425 (Bacque), 426 (Evans), 427 (Grenfell), 428 (Knopp)
World-wide grid, 259
World-wide web, 242, 247, 249, 255-6

Yoga, 384
Yuga-dharma, 384
Yugas, 158, 230, 287, 333, 371